T0336482

Government
Information
in Canada

AMANDA WAKARUK AND SAM-CHIN LI, *Editors*

Government Information in Canada

Access and Stewardship

UNIVERSITY *of* **ALBERTA** PRESS

Published by
The University of Alberta Press
Ring House 2
Edmonton, Alberta, Canada T6G 2E1
www.uap.ualberta.ca

LIBRARY AND ARCHIVES CANADA
CATALOGUING IN PUBLICATION

Title: Government information in
 Canada : access and stewardship /
 Amanda Wakaruk and Sam-chin Li,
 editors.
Other titles: Government information
 in Canada (Edmonton, Alta.)
Names: Wakaruk, Amanda, 1973–
 editor. | Li, Sam-chin, 1960– editor.
Description: Includes bibliographical
 references and index.
Identifiers:
 Canadiana (print) 20190051108 |
 Canadiana (ebook) 20190051159 |
 ISBN 9781772124064 (softcover) |
 ISBN 9781772124446 (PDF)
Subjects: LCSH: Government
 information—Canada. | LCSH:
 Government information—
 Access control—Canada. | LCSH:
 Government information agencies—
 Canada.
Classification: LCC KE5325 .G68
 2019 | LCC KF5753 .G68 2019
 kfmod | DDC 323.4450971—dc23 |
 342.7108/53—dc23

First edition, first printing, 2019.
First printed in Canada by Houghton
 Boston Printers, Saskatoon,
 Saskatchewan.
Copyediting and proofreading by
 Angela Wingfield.
Indexing by JoAnne Burek.

University of Alberta Press is
committed to protecting our natural
environment. As part of our efforts,
this book is printed on Enviro Paper: it
contains 100% post-consumer recycled
fibres and is acid- and chlorine-free.

University of Alberta Press gratefully
acknowledges the support received
for its publishing program from
the Government of Canada, the
Canada Council for the Arts, and the
Government of Alberta through the
Alberta Media Fund.

University of Alberta Press gratefully
acknowledges and thanks the
University of Alberta Libraries for its
financial support of this book, which
allows for the electronic edition to be
available as an Open Access title.

Canada Canada Council   Conseil des Arts   Alberta
        for the Arts   du Canada   Government

▶ *This collection is dedicated to government information librarians whose commitment to democratic engagement, professional values, and intellectual curiosity inspire stewardship and service for the betterment of the public good. Special thanks go to Peter Hajnal (University of Toronto), Vivienne Monty (York University), and Gay Lepkey (Government of Canada) for their leadership, passion, and years of perseverance in connecting Canadians with the works of their government.*

Contents

Abbreviations ▷ xi

INTRODUCTION:
The Evolution of Government Information Services
and Stewardship in Canada ▷ xiii
    Amanda Wakaruk and Sam-chin Li

I ▶ HISTORICAL OVERVIEWS

1   Government Publication Deposit Programs:
    The Canadian Federal, Provincial, and
    Territorial Landscapes ▷ 3
        Graeme Campbell, Michelle Lake,
        and Catherine McGoveran

2   Library and Archives Canada: Official Publications and
    Select Digital Library Collections, 1923–2017 ▷ 47
        Tom J. Smyth

3   Parliamentary Information in Canada:
    Form and Function ▷ 79
        Talia Chung and Maureen Martyn

4   Commissions and Tribunals ▷ 117
        Caron Rollins

II ▶ PROVINCIAL LANDSCAPE

5   Alberta Government Publishing ▷ 153
        Dani J. Pahulje

6   Saskatchewan Government Publications Deposit
      in the Legislative Library ▷ 189
        Gregory Salmers

7   Inside Track: Challenges of Collecting, Accessing,
      and Preserving Ontario Government Publications ▷ 211
        Sandra Craig and Martha Murphy

8   Digitization of Government Publications:
      A Review of the Ontario Digitization Initiative ▷ 227
        Carol Perry, Brian Tobin, and Sam-chin Li

III ▶ LOOKING FORWARD:
COLLABORATIVE STEWARDSHIP

9   GALLOP Portal:
     Making Government Publications in
     Legislative Libraries Findable ▷ 259
          Peter Ellinger

10   The Canadian Government Information
     Digital Preservation Network:
     A Collective Response to a National Crisis ▷ 275
          Amanda Wakaruk and Steve Marks

11   Web Harvesting and Reporting Fugitive
     Government Materials:
     Collaborative Stewardship of At-Risk Documents ▷ 295
          Susan Paterson, Nicholas Worby, and Darlene Fichter

     Contributors ▷ 325
     Index ▷ 331

Abbreviations

ABC	agency, board, and commission
ADLP	Alberta Depository Library Program
ALA	American Library Association
API	application programming interface
APLIC	Association of Parliamentary Libraries in Canada
BANQ	Bibliothèque et Archives nationales du Québec
BCLA	British Columbia Library Association
CANLII	Canadian Legal Information Institute
CARL	Canadian Association of Research Libraries
CEAA	Canadian Environmental Assessment Agency
CGI DPN	Canadian Government Information Digital Preservation Network
CLA	Canadian Library Association
COI	commission of inquiry
COPPUL	Council of Prairie and Pacific University Libraries
CPAC	Cable Public Affairs Channel
DSP	Depository Services Program
DSP-LAC	Depository Services Program Library Advisory Committee
GALLOP	Government and Legislative Libraries Online Publications
GC	Government of Canada
GCPE	Government of Canada Publications electronic collection
GCWA	Government of Canada Web Archive
HTML	hypertext markup language
IIPC	International Internet Preservation Consortium
IRSSA	*Indian Residential Schools Settlement Agreement*
ISBN	International Standard Book Number
ISSN	International Standard Serial Number
LAC	Library and Archives Canada

LACEC	Library and Archives Canada electronic collection
LOCKSS	Lots of copies keep stuff safe
LP	Library of Parliament
MARC	machine-readable cataloguing
MM	Micromedia ProQuest microform collections
NCTR	National Centre for Truth and Reconciliation
NEB	National Energy Board
OCR	optical character recognition
OCUL	Ontario Council of University Libraries
ODI	Ontario Digitization Initiative
ODW	OurDigitalWorld
OGLC	Ontario Government Libraries Council
OIC	Order-in-Council
PCO	Privy Council Office
PDF	portable document format
PDS	Publishing and Depository Services Directorate
PEILDO	Prince Edward Island Legislative Documents Online
PLN	private LOCKSS network
POR	public opinion research
PWGSC	Public Works and Government Services Canada
RCAP	Royal Commission on Aboriginal Peoples
RSS	Rich Site Summary
SI	statutory instrument
TBS	Treasury Board of Canada Secretariat
TRC	Truth and Reconciliation Commission
TSB	Transportation Safety Board
URL	uniform resource locator
UTL	University of Toronto Libraries

Introduction

THE EVOLUTION OF GOVERNMENT INFORMATION SERVICES AND STEWARDSHIP IN CANADA

▷ *Amanda Wakaruk and Sam-chin Li*

Government information is not something that most people think about until they need it or see it in a headline. Indeed, even then librarians, journalists, and intellectually curious citizens will rarely recognize or identify that the statistics needed to complete a report, or the scandal-breaking evidence behind a politician's resignation, was sourced from taxpayer-funded publications and documents. Fewer people will likely appreciate the fact that access to government information is a requirement of a democratic society.

Government Information in Canada introduces the average librarian, journalist, researcher, and intellectually curious citizen to the often complex, rarely obvious, and sometimes elusive foundational element of a liberal democracy: publicly accessible government information. While our primary goal is to provide an overview of the state of access to Canadian government information in the late-twentieth and early-twenty-first centuries, we hope that this work will also encourage its readers to become more active in the government information community by contributing to government consultations and seeking out information that is produced by their governing bodies.

Like all information, government documents and publications are a product of a socio-political environment that is informed by those in control of the mechanisms of production. For example, the political leanings of the party in power shape the policies and practices of the government that produces, disseminates, and archives the output of its agencies. In Canada, government documents and publications are produced by numerous agencies at all three levels of government: federal, provincial, and municipal. Put simply, most practitioners consider *documents* to be information objects that are produced as part of the process of governing, and *publications* to be information objects produced primarily for the purpose of communicating something to an audience external to government (e.g., members of the public).

In practice, the category of information objects labelled "government documents" normally includes output such as the verbatim record of what is said in the House of Commons (i.e., *House of Commons Debates*) and reports generated by legislative committees, because these materials are produced as part of the process of governing. However, from the perspective of those working within Canadian legislatures, this output is often referred to as "government publications" because the objects in question are disseminated outside the author agency. To complicate matters further, the colloquial phrase *government documents* also rightly refers to a wide range of records and internal reports created by government agencies. Much of this material is subject to records retention protocols, and, in jurisdictions with such protocols, a selection of these records will be deposited in the relevant archival institution. When someone submits an access-to-information request, that person is requesting a specific document or set of documents from this body of works. Published materials (i.e., publications) are excluded from the provisions of federal access-to-information legislation as they have already been or will be disseminated to the public.[1]

Inconsistent uses of these basic terms are not limited to practitioners. Official definitions of what constitutes a government publication and/ or document vary between jurisdictions, and it is not uncommon for professors of government information in graduate-level library courses to begin them with a lecture on the nature of this problem and to clarify how the terms will be used within their own classroom.

This present volume of works is primarily interested in describing the production, dissemination, and stewardship of government publications in a broad sense. When the phrase *government publication* is used here, it refers to the group of materials that has been produced for the purposes of communicating to those outside government. It includes most maps, communication products, and a wide variety of monographic and serial works, including annual and statistical reports. Although we have chosen to maintain the traditional definitional dichotomy based on production to distinguish between document and publication (i.e., the purpose for which the object was created—governance or communication), there is a strong argument for recognizing broader definitions. Given that digital production allows for a convergence of dissemination paths, publications could be defined as anything that is shared (not necessarily produced) for public consumption. This, then, would include anything placed on a government website. The potential becomes readily apparent in the chapters that refer to the current and future role of web "archiving" programs, to use another evolving and problematic term in the information professions.

One of our goals is to document the state of government information in Canada at a point of transition. To help orient readers to today's sub-discipline of librarianship, we offer four points that have been observed and learned over decades of working with government information in academic environments.[2]

1. Access to government information is the foundation of a functioning democracy and underpins informed citizen engagement. Government information allows us to assess our governing bodies—access that is required for a democracy to function.

2. Government information has enduring value. The work of countless academics and other experts is disseminated via government information. Government publications and documents are used by academics and social commentators in all areas of intellectual output, resulting in the production of books, reports, speeches, and so forth, which have shaped our society and understanding of the world. For example, the

book that introduced the public to the science of climate change, *Silent Spring*, was full of references to government information; furthermore, legal scholars, lawyers, and judges use legislative documents to interpret and apply the law; journalists use government documents to inform the electorate about its governing bodies.

3. Government information is precarious and requires stewardship. The strongest system of stewardship for government information is one that operates in partnership with, and at arm's length of, author agencies. Most content is digital, but this does not mean that it is posted and openly available online. Furthermore, content made available online does not necessarily remain accessible to the public.

4. Government publications and documents are different from most books, journals, and content born on the Internet. Government information does not fit into the traditional dissemination channels developed and simplified through customer feedback and the pursuit of higher profits. The agencies that produce government information are motivated by different factors than those of traditional publishers.

Traditionally, library collections of government information were produced in paper or micro-formats and, in Canada, organized by a provenance-based classification system called CODOC. For much of the twentieth century this system segregated the collections, and the labour that was required to process and maintain them, from main or general library systems and holdings. While this approach benefited specialized searching and expert research (and produced separate indexes and catalogues), it resulted in a secondary and unintentional barrier to access. The government information librarian served as translator, mediator, and unfortunately at times as gatekeeper.

The widespread automation of library reference tools in the 1990s (especially card catalogues) allowed for the intellectual access points to government collections to be integrated into general library systems. In many cases this required time-consuming and labour-intensive reclassification projects. These important efforts resulted in subject access to government publications, often for the first time. While the road has not always been straight or level, the integration of government print collections has largely followed. At the time of writing, only a few major academic institutions continued to maintain some type of segregated print collection of government materials.[3]

From a public service perspective, these changes often resulted in a confusing hybrid print collection, with some portion of the collection remaining in a provenance-based system of organization.[4] Many academic librarians, in particular, found themselves in the new role of peer-educator, assisting and teaching often reluctant colleagues to provide basic reference services for manifestly different collections and users.

More broadly, many of the changes in contemporary libraries were preceded by technological innovations. In some ways, government information and its related services have served as a test case for the impacts of digitization and digital publishing on general library collections and services. Government publishers were some of the first to move to digital outputs. While this allowed for vast improvements in access to new publications, these documents and publications were also the first victims of technological obsolescence associated with digital files. Publishing and access improved without suitable or stable preservation and stewardship strategies in place.[5] One long-standing case is that of *For Seven Generations* CD-ROM. This collection of research reports and transcripts submitted to the Royal Commission on Aboriginal Peoples (RCAP) was published by Libraxus in 1997 and ran on a now-obsolete software application and operating system. In addition, confusion related to the copyright status of this collected work prevented librarians from making copies for researchers, which in practice created a situation where hundreds of RCAP research papers were essentially inaccessible for well over ten years.[6]

New digital publishing policies were implemented by federal and provincial government agencies, seemingly without regard for preservation or stewardship of this new medium. As early as the mid-2000s librarians started noticing the loss of websites and web content. Today we know that much has been removed without official documentation. This is content that would have been previously produced in paper and been subject to publishing policies that required dissemination to libraries across the country. Some of these deletions are related to the Common Look and Feel and Web Renewal initiatives, and other content losses can be associated with the staggering reduction of federal departmental library budgets that has occurred in the past three decades, but especially during 2012–13.[7] While Library and Archives Canada (LAC) made repeated statements about the capture and retention of select web content between the years of 2002 and 2015, it was not until April 2016 that a publicly accessible collection of government web content was made available.[8] Previously, a limited collection of content with considerable gaps left many consumers turning to the Internet Archive (an organization based in the United States) for access to historic Canadian government web content. This is unsurprising given the massive cuts to LAC between 2010 and 2014.

The reduction in government services supporting the production and access to government information directly affected all consumers of government information and especially public and academic librarians. Government information librarians were often left scrambling to assist users who would have otherwise benefited from the defunct programs. In the course of this work many librarians also became de facto informal auditors for content availability. This role was especially challenging given that no comprehensive, systematic listing of government works was available. It could also be politically sensitive, and it is not surprising that those most active in this area hold positions in institutions that recognize the need for academic freedom protections for librarians.

The collective response of the government information community to the changes in the nature and tenor of government publishing over the past thirty years has inspired the work you are reading. This collection strives to bridge a gap in the literature by bringing together a seminal group of contributors who have lived through the noted changes. Chapter authors include librarians working in academic, parliamentary, government, and legislative libraries across Canada, and many have decades of professional experience. We are especially fortunate to have government employees contributing to this work. Restrictions on freedom of expression (and, in many cases, intellectual freedom) were severe under the Harper government's years in power and under LAC's Harper-appointed chief librarian and archivist, Daniel Caron, who attempted to implement policies that restricted the freedom of professional LAC employees.[9]

PART I: HISTORICAL OVERVIEWS

Historically, our Western democratic understanding of government information and its dissemination has been informed by the publishing of printed materials by or for author government agencies. In Canada this print-based system included federal agencies as the default publishers, the Depository Services Program (DSP) as the distributor, and depository libraries as the stewards and access points for this output. Related publishing policies were, and continue to be, established by the Treasury Board of Canada Secretariat.[10] In practice, it was the research libraries (LAC, academic, and legislative libraries) of the depository system that served as default preservationists of government information for the populace. Or, rather, these cultural-memory organizations maintained collections of what was distributed by the DSP. The DSP distributed publications that were provided to them by federal agencies, and the compliance rates for submission of print publications were variable at best.[11] Official publications not identified or distributed by the DSP are deemed "fugitive" documents or publications.

While the DSP was established in 1927, it was not until 1988 (following an extended review of the Task Group on Depository Program) that a library advisory committee was established as a vehicle for communication with government information stakeholders, a group that included practising librarians who were working with depository collections.

In the first chapter of this collection, "Government Publication Deposit Programs," academic librarians Graeme Campbell, Michelle Lake, and Catherine McGoveran introduce and compare depository systems at both the federal and the provincial or territorial level. Once referred to as our nation's information safety net, these programs are now adapting to changes in publishing formats, government policy, funding, and the progression of the open government movement. The chapter (including a DSP timeline) provides readers with a historical overview that is essential to understanding the current tensions between government publishers and consumers.

As a full depository library, LAC receives all federal DSP shipments and lists but has a mandate for acquisition that, at the policy level, grants it the potential to cast a much wider net. In chapter 2 we are fortunate to be able to offer readers a ninety-year overview of the major legislative and policy instruments that have affected LAC's work with government information. LAC manager Tom J. Smyth not only documents these governance instruments but also clarifies their influence on the stewardship role of our nation's largest and most visible cultural heritage organization. This is demonstrated, in part, through sections dedicated to programs that are currently under his purview: LAC's collection of official publications of the Government of Canada in digital format, web archiving activities, Royal Commissions and commissions of inquiry, and the federal Public Opinion Research collection.

The work of another highly visible but often misunderstood library, the Library of Parliament, is highlighted in chapter 3, "Parliamentary Information in Canada." Academic librarian Talia Chung and Library of Parliament manager Maureen Martyn introduce readers to our nation's less-than-intuitive parliamentary process, providing a clear road map for those navigating both the records and the tools that connect Canadians with their federal lawmakers. Chung and Martyn use a case-study approach, tracing the parliamentary treatment of gun control and providing readers with an accessible introduction for connecting with the federal legislative documents that ultimately define how we work and live in Canada.

Another rich source of cultural evidence in liberal democracies is the output of commissions and tribunals—initiatives by federal and provincial governments to address issues of importance to Canadians. In chapter 4, law and government publications librarian Caron Rollins defines the roles and responsibilities of these temporary but instrumental bodies, offering a clear picture of the effects of recent digital developments on the publication, dissemination, and preservation of related reports, submissions, and hearings.

PART II: PROVINCIAL LANDSCAPE

The second part of the book is dedicated to provincial practices, and reflects the regionalism that defines our nation. As noted elsewhere,[12] government publishing in the Canadian provinces has historically been decentralized, with little coordination between departmental publishing bodies. Unfortunately, such inconsistencies continue to hamper those who manage provincial government information. While we were hopeful that more jurisdictions would be covered here, we are confident that the value of the chapters in this section will motivate practitioners to continue the conversation by preparing publications that address the government publishing and dissemination situations in British Columbia, Quebec, and the Maritime provinces.

Two provinces joined Canada in 1905: Alberta and Saskatchewan. As documented in chapters 5 and 6, the similarities between government publishing in these provinces might very well have begun and ended at that time. Astute readers will see the results of two very different political histories in these chapters. In "Alberta Government Publishing," government publications librarian Dani J. Pahulje provides a historical overview of the Alberta government information landscape, including a thorough depiction of the drawbacks associated with a decentralized publishing and under-resourced distribution system and the exacerbation of these issues in a digital environment.

In the chapter that follows, a very different point of view provides an exceptional snapshot of the Saskatchewan government information experience. Gregory Salmers, a director with the Saskatchewan Legislative Library, offers a thoughtful case study of this organization's role in the province's publishing, depository, and access structure ecosystem. Salmers adeptly documents an issue of concern common to all jurisdictions: deposit compliance by author agencies. This chapter provides an examination of the Saskatchewan Legislative Library's attempt to increase awareness of its legal deposit program among author departments. A role model for other jurisdictions, this library's simultaneous efforts to increase deposit compliance and ensure the inclusion of digital government information (vis-à-vis tools like GALLOP, discussed in chapter 9) should be required reading for all library-school graduate students.

Compliance issues are also addressed in chapter 7, focusing on Canada's largest province, Ontario. Providing another unique perspective on the provincial government information system, library managers Sandra Craig and Martha Murphy, from the Legislative Assembly of Ontario and the Workplace Safety and Insurance Appeals Tribunal, respectively, expand on the challenges facing librarians in stewardship roles. Despite a deposit system operated by Publications Ontario, it is the Legislative Library's work to establish and build on partnerships with provincial government libraries and legislative libraries across Canada, which has resulted in both digitization and digital repository projects that will enable access for the next generation of government information consumers. Indeed, it is these partnerships and collaborative models that will define success for government information stewardship in the future.

The Ontario Digitization Initiative brings together partners from university libraries, the provincial legislature, and non-profit organizations. Authors Carol Perry, Brian Tobin, and Sam-chin Li provide a careful case study for practitioners, covering topics like planning, metadata creation, copyright, and the navigation inherent in sharing resources and costs across a collaborative project. Chapter 8 also presents useful overviews of nationally important government digitization projects like the Sessional Papers of Canada and communicates the results of a 2013 survey related to digitization projects more broadly. The commitment by Ontario librarians to act as stewards and provide improved access to digital government publications is commendable.

PART III: LOOKING FORWARD: COLLABORATIVE STEWARDSHIP

To many outside the small and often fervent community of government information professionals, it might seem logical that the government itself should take responsibility for the organization and stewardship of its works. Historically, however, practices based on such assumptions have been fraught with complications. Commissions dating back to the 1890s[13] called on our federal government to get its documentary house in order and to preserve the output of the state so that policy-makers and residents alike might be able to meaningfully engage in their body politic. Unfortunately, these recommendations were never fully realized. As noted earlier in this introduction, we continue to live with the complicating impacts of political decisions on the stewardship of government information in this country. Another egregious example of this insecurity was the cancellation of the long-form census of Canada in 2011, providing evidence for the need to build and maintain arm's-length systems of preservation and access for government information.[14]

Canadian librarians are responding to and leading solutions for navigating the technological and policy changes and challenges experienced in the past decade. New collaborations and initiatives were formed to address the losses of the past and to chart a new path forward. The chapters in this section discuss important digitization and web archiving projects as well as award-winning collaborative services, and highlight the one thing that made these efforts both possible and successful: a commitment to working together.

Improved accessibility is key to the genesis of the Government and Legislative Libraries Online Publications (GALLOP) portal,[15] an award-winning tool that enables users to search across the content of legislative libraries and the DSP catalogue. Contributed by Peter Ellinger, a lead on the project and manager at the Legislative Assembly of Ontario's library, chapter 9 explores both the technological and the political realities of developing a project informed by interdependent collectors with a common goal. As all librarians know, standardization and consistency are key to reliable access.

The motivation and scope of the Canadian Government Information Digital Preservation Network (CGI DPN),[16] like GALLOP, was informed by retractions in both funding and programs at LAC. Amanda Wakaruk and Steve Marks, both academic librarians, explore the context of this stressful period of government information management and stewardship in the penultimate chapter of this book. The award-winning[17] collaborative service enabled a communal approach to the digital preservation of government information in Canada and provided practitioners with a forum for interrogating and implementing secondary projects, like those covered in the final chapter of this book.

Academic librarians Susan Paterson, Nicholas Worby, and Darlene Fichter provide an introduction to the web archiving of government information by practitioners working outside of government. Projects range from a focused harvest of the City of Toronto website to the more complicated and labour-intensive identification and harvesting of federal fugitive documents. The relationships being built between government and academic libraries in the pursuit of stewardship are the types of partnerships that will reinforce and enable access to government information in the future.

MOVING FORWARD

Libraries have adapted to changing formats for millennia. The transition from print to digital resources has had an impact on the entire communication cycle of government information, from producer to consumer. Part I of this book demonstrates the current and historical role of long-standing and official organizations in the Canadian government information ecosystem. While their value in our current environment is unquestionable and continuing, expectations held by non-governmental library practitioners often exceeded the ability of these organizations, which were grossly undervalued in the final decades of the twentieth century. For many years practitioners waited expectantly for the DSP (subject to policies administered by the Treasury Board of Canada), LAC, and the Library of Parliament to step into leadership roles with the coordination of the output of federal institutions through long-promised services like the Open Government Portal and the still-to-be confirmed preservation programs. There was an assumption that these organizations would actively pursue and preserve government information on behalf of both practitioners and the general public.

The failure of the Government of Canada to deliver on open government commitments related to publications, to date, has been especially frustrating for librarians. Academic librarians patiently waited for a virtual library and/or open government portal that was first promised in 2012,[18] and for the widespread assignment of an open government licence to government publications.[19] Instead, the licence was applied to a scant couple of hundred publications, and librarians were often refused permission to capture and redistribute born-digital government publications.[20] As noted elsewhere, many of these publications were subsequently removed from government websites. More recently, references to making government publications open by default appear to have been directed to LAC and the DSP, the same organizations that were unable to prevent the previously mentioned losses of digital works.

The transition to digital government information created a gap in service at the federal level that is being filled by non-governmental actors and some provincial legislative libraries. Part II of this book highlights work undertaken by the legislative libraries of Saskatchewan and Ontario, where individuals have stepped into the breach created by LAC's removal of provincial materials from its mandate. The exemplary compliance programs undertaken by the Saskatchewan Legislative Library and the collaborative efforts of the Ontario Legislative Library (with ServiceOntario Publications and the Ontario Council of University Libraries) serve as models for other jurisdictions. We hope to see more of this work, especially from other jurisdictions, documented in the library literature in the years to come.

Collaborative digital initiatives described by pioneering practitioners in Part III of this book serve to secure access to government works in a new and changing environment. Many of these projects were only possible because librarians made unsupported interpretations of the terms of use and permissions associated with materials protected by Crown copyright.[21] A rationale for assigning economic protections like copyright to works that were created to fulfill a government mandate is unclear. We strongly believe that government information should be in the public domain instead of restricted by antiquated legislative provisions. The barriers created by section 12 of the current *Copyright Act* have delayed digitization and web archiving projects that are intended to collect, preserve, and disseminate government information in this country, and such delays have resulted in the loss of innumerable documents and publications. Furthermore, this provision is in direct conflict with successive governments' repeated commitments to the principles of open government.[22]

Government information is now solidly digital, and librarians are adapting in order to continue their role as collectors, providers, and preservationists and develop their role as observers and auditors. Like caring for the printed book, a social response is needed to make this happen. We need systems of communication and communities of practice in order to move forward. As seen in the case studies in Part III, this includes collaborative digitization and web harvesting projects, access tools, and preservation networks. It is worth noting that the results of these projects provide the only source of available federal government web content from December 2007 to September 2013,[23] filling a gap in LAC's collection. All of these resources were built on existing infrastructure, both social and technological, and informed by the socio-political environment in which we work.

Even as we move forward, unique traditional challenges remain. If the current levels of staffing and funding remain stable, it is doubtful that all government information produced in Canada will be digitized, treated for intellectual access, and preserved in a manner that will ensure its viability for the generations to come. The temptation to discard print versions upon producing a digital version is not only misguided but dangerous and offers no assurances for perpetual access.[24] Likewise, the valuable but incomplete collections accumulated by commercial vendors are also unlikely to provide reliable perpetual access to government publications.

While political and partisan challenges will likely always be a part of working with government information, the technology used today is much more precarious than what preceded it and also much more dependent on intervention by arm's-length stakeholders for its survival. It is no longer enough to catalogue and place a book in a climate-controlled environment. With paper, one could be fairly certain that a bit of light and an optical lens, bestowed on most of us by biological inheritance, would be enough to re-animate the work and to benefit from the information and knowledge contained within. Government reports produced today require intense technological intervention to ensure that multiple, stable copies are available in perpetuity and that relatively quick degradation is kept at bay. We do not know how information technologies or the governing systems that drive them will continue to evolve. In addition, it is sometimes difficult for those of us who were born into a democratic society to appreciate the fragility and importance of access to government information, especially as it relates to government policy. Programs like the DSP and provisions enshrined in the *Access to Information Act* help government librarians outside of government agencies to continue to act as stewards for these works.

With the new complexities, uncertainties, and increasing volume of digital government information, collaboration is key to future stewardship of government information. In the past ten years we have witnessed an incredible resurgence in professional interest and energy in this area, as demonstrated by the overwhelming attendance and engaged participation at both the annual Government Information Day conference based in British Columbia, established in 1998, and the annual Ontario Government Information Day conference, established in 2013.[25] In addition, it was a core group of dedicated government information librarians that reached out to managers at LAC when their web archiving activities were halted between 2008 and 2013. Working collaboratively, librarians at the University of Toronto and the University of Alberta captured content via Internet Archive's Archive-It accounts that, combined with LAC's web archive, provide Canadians with a more abundant cultural record. New leadership at LAC leaves us hopeful that this important cultural heritage institution will make space for transparent and collaborative stewardship partnerships that include academic and parliamentary libraries, and that the results of these projects will be openly accessible to everyone. We are also hopeful that the early-twenty-first century will mark the beginning of a stronger relationship between the governments of Canada, the public at large, and especially the group of librarians who chose to make enabling democracy through professional stewardship a part of, if not the driving force behind, their career contributions.

Notes

1. Canada, *Access to Information Act*, ss. 26, 68(a).
2. Adapted from Wakaruk, "Government Information Speaking Notes."
3. The University of Toronto, Queen's University, University of Ottawa, and Carleton University continue to maintain separate government print collections in addition to integrating government materials in their main print library collections.
4. CODOC is one example of a provenance-based system organized by publishing agency, not by subject.
5. Only half of the respondents to Consulting and Audit Canada's 2002 *Management of Government Publications Survey* reported that digital publications were managed to ensure long-term access (page v).
6. For more information about the RCAP case see other chapters in this volume dealing with commissions and tribunals and with the Canadian Government Information Digital Preservation Network.
7. Canadian Association of University Teachers, *Federal Library Cuts & Closures*.
8. See LAC Departmental Plans from the period as well as DSP Library Advisory Committee meeting minutes. The Government of Canada Web Archive was launched in 2016: http://webarchive.bac-lac.gc.ca/?lang=en.
9. See Groover, *Contempt for Values*; and Kandiuk, "The Rhetoric of Digitization and the Politicization of Canadian Heritage."
10. For detailed information about the history of government policy relevant to information management, see Brown, "Coming to Terms with Information and Communications Technologies."
11. Fewer than half of respondents to Consulting and Audit Canada's 2002 *Management of Government Publications Survey* reported distributing publications to the Depository Services Program (page 24).
12. Pross and Pross, *Government Publishing in the Canadian Provinces*.
13. See Canada, *Report of the Commissioners Appointed to Inquire into the State of the Public Records*, and *Report of the Royal Commission to Inquire into the State of Records of the Departments of the Public Service of the Dominion, 1912*.
14. Implications of cancelling the long-form census in 2011 were the focus of a special issue of the *Canadian Journal of Sociology*, available at https://journals.library.ualberta.ca/cjs/index.php/CJS/issue/view/1362. The long-form census was reinstated in 2015 following a change in government.
15. The Association of Parliamentary Libraries in Canada, GALLOP Portal, http://aplicportal.ola.org/aplicsearch.asp?language=eng. GALLOP received the Ontario Library Association OLITA Award for Technological Innovation in 2014. http://www.thebpc.ca/member-news/ontario-library-association-announces-2014-award-recipients/.

16. PLNWIKI, "CGI Network," http://plnwiki.lockss.org/wiki/index.php/CGI_network.

17. The Canadian Library Association honoured the CGI DPN with its 2015 CLA/OCLC Award for Innovative Technology. For more information about the award, see http://cla.ca/cla-at-work/%20awards/claoclc-award-for-innovative-technology/.

18. See section 4 of the 2012 report *Implementation of Canada's Action Plan on Open Government (Year-1): Self-Assessment Report.*

19. An open government licence for publications was listed as a foundational commitment in *Canada's Action Plan on Open Government, 2012–2014.*

20. See Wakaruk, Personal Submission, *Copyright Act* Review, to the House of Commons Standing Committee on Industry, Science and Technology; and Wakaruk, "Heavy Is the Head That Wears the Crown (Copyright)."

21. See Li, "The Vanishing Act of Government Documents—And What to Do about It."

22. See Freund and How, "Quagmire of Crown Copyright"; Wakaruk, "Canadian Crown Copyright Conundrum."

23. University of Toronto, "Canadian Government Information," Archive-It collection, https://archive-it.org/collections/3608.

24. See Jacobs, "What Are We to Keep?"

25. See https://govinfoday.ca/ and https://onesearch.library.utoronto.ca/government-information, respectively.

Recommended Reading

Kingston, Anne. "Vanishing Canada: Why We're All Losers in Ottawa's War on Data." *Maclean's Magazine*, September 18, 2015. http://www.macleans.ca/news/canada/vanishing-canada-why-were-all-losers-in-ottawas-war-on-data.

Li, Sam-chin, Nicholas Worby, and Jesse Carliner. "Page Not Found: Web Archiving Government Information and Beyond." *TALL Quarterly* 33, no.1 (Spring 2014): 10–15. https://www.talltoronto.ca.

Smugler, Sherry. *Facing Change: A Perspective on Government Publications Services in Canadian Academic Libraries in the Internet Age.* GODORT Occasional Papers, no. 9 (November 2013). http://hdl.handle.net/11213/8541.

Wakaruk, Amanda. "What the Heck Is Happening Up North? Canadian Government Information Circa 2014." *Documents to the People* (DTTP) 42, no. 1 (Spring 2014): 15–20. http://hdl.handle.net/10402/era.38740.

Whitmell, Vicki. "GALLOPING toward the Future: Building a Pan-Canadian Portal of Government & Legislative Publications." *TALL Quarterly* 33, no.1 (Spring 2014): 4–7. https://www.talltoronto.ca.

Bibliography

Brown, C.G., "Coming to Terms with Information and Communications Technologies: The Role of the Chief Information Officer of the Government of Canada." PhD diss., Carleton University, 2011. https://central.bac-lac.gc.ca/.item?id=NR83245&op=pdf&app=Library.

Canada. *Access to Information Act.* http://laws-lois.justice.gc.ca/eng/acts/A-1/.

———. *Canada's Action Plan on Open Government, 2012–2014.* https://web.archive.org/web/20180124200224/http://open.canada.ca/en/canadas-action-plan-open-government.

———. *Copyright Act.* http://laws-lois.justice.gc.ca/eng/acts/C-42/.

———. Depository Services Program. Minutes of Library Advisory Committee. https://web.archive.org/web/20181119193353/http://publications.gc.ca/site/eng/depositoryLibraries/dsp-lac/overview.html.

———. *Implementation of Canada's Action Plan on Open Government (Year-1): Self-Assessment Report.* 2012. https://web.archive.org/web/20180124202311/http://open.canada.ca/en/implementation-canadas-action-plan-open-government-year-1-self-assessment-report.

———. *Report of the Commissioners Appointed to Inquire into the State of the Public Records, 1897.* J.M. Courtney, J.L. McDougall, and Joseph Pope. Ottawa: S.E. Dawson, Queen's Printer, 1898. http://eco.canadiana.ca/view/oocihm.9_04188.

———. *Report of the Royal Commission to Inquire into the State of Records of the Departments of the Public Service of the Dominion, 1912.* Arthur Doughty, Joseph Pope, and E.F. Jarvis. Ottawa: King's Printer, 1914. http://epe.lac-bac.gc.ca/100/200/301/pco-bcp/commissions-ef/pope1914-eng/pope1914-eng.pdf.

———. Treasury Board Secretariat. Archived Departmental Plans. https://www.canada.ca/en/treasury-board-secretariat/services/planned-government-spending/reports-plans-priorities.html

Canadian Association of University Teachers. *Federal Library Cuts & Closures.* 2013. Accessed August 10, 2016. https://web.archive.org/web/20131203023120/http://www.canadaspastmatters.ca/public-libraries/federal-library-cuts-and-closures.aspx.

Consulting and Audit Canada. *Management of Government Publications Survey.* National Library of Canada. August 2002.

Freund, Luanne, and Elissa How. "Quagmire of Crown Copyright: Implications for Reuse of Government Information." *Canadian Law Library Review* 40, no. 4 (2015). https://issuu.com/callacbd/docs/cllr_40_4_final.1.

Groover, Myron. "Contempt for Values: The Controversy over Library and Archives Canada's Code of Conduct." *Academic Matters*, May 2013. https://web.archive.org/web/20151226071544/http://www.academicmatters.ca/2013/05/contempt-for-values-the-controversey-over-library-and-archives-canadas-code-of-conduct/.

Jacobs, R. James. "What Are We to Keep?" *Documents to the People (DTTP)* 43, no 1 (Spring 2015): 13–19. https://freegovinfo.info/wp-content/uploads/2015/04/jacobs-dttp-spring15-what-to-keep.pdf.

Kandiuk, Mary. "The Rhetoric of Digitization and the Politicization of Canadian Heritage." *Library Trends* 65, no. 2 (Fall 2016). https://muse.jhu.edu/article/638280.

Li, Sam-chin. "The Vanishing Act of Government Documents—And What to Do about It." Our Right to Know blog post, April 2016. https://ourrighttoknow.ca/tag/sam-chin-li/.

Pross, Paul, and Catherine Pross. *Government Publishing in the Canadian Provinces: A Prescriptive Study.* Toronto: University of Toronto Press, 1972.

Wakaruk. Amanda. "Canadian Crown Copyright Conundrum." Fair Dealing Week 2016 blog post, February 2016. https://era.library.ualberta.ca/files/b2b88qc23g#.VtYEdlsrJaQ.

———. "Government Information Speaking Notes." *Documents to the People (DTTP)* 43, no. 1 (Spring 2015): 11–12. http://hdl.handle.net/10402/era.41193.

———. "Heavy Is the Head That Wears the Crown (Copyright)." Presented at the ABC Copyright Conference on June 29, 2017. https://doi.org/10.7939/R3WH2DT50.

———. Personal Submission, *Copyright Act* Review, to the House of Commons Standing Committee on Industry, Science and Technology. June 14, 2018. http://www.ourcommons.ca/Content/Committee/421/INDU/Brief/BR9998912/br-external/WakarukAmanda-e.pdf.

I

HISTORICAL OVERVIEWS

1

GOVERNMENT PUBLICATION DEPOSIT PROGRAMS

The Canadian Federal, Provincial, and Territorial Landscapes

▷ *Graeme Campbell, Michelle Lake, and Catherine McGoveran*

What is that next to the copy of *Catcher in the Rye* on your bookshelf? Is it a Canadian government document? Probably not, but Canadian federal, provincial, and territorial governments produce abundant information, and, up until the last few decades, this took the form of printed documents and other tangible items. So, if not in your own collection, where is this published content found? The good news is that many Canadian federal, provincial, and territorial governments established policies or programs directly supporting the collection and preservation of, and public access to, government publications, though not all to the same degree. The following presents a pan-Canadian perspective on some of the ways in which governments have attempted to distribute and provide access to their own publications, both historically and with a view toward the digital era. It focuses on programs and agreements leading to the systematic deposit of the published print output of governments in one or more locations.

This chapter does not strive to provide a fully comprehensive or complete overview of deposit and distribution programs in Canada. Rather, it attempts to capture the basics of the print deposit processes that were or still are in place in each Canadian federal, provincial, and territorial jurisdiction, and the way in which these processes may have changed over time. One of the greatest challenges of this project has come from the variety of sources that exist on the topic of government publishing in Canada. In the attempt to piece together a history of the mechanics of deposit in each jurisdiction from the available literature, it became clear that some accounts differed in their interpretation of dates, their use of related vocabulary, and even their opinions concerning whether or not a program actually existed.

It also became clear that several challenges complicating the creation, maintenance, or effectiveness of deposit mechanisms were a common experience among some jurisdictions. Although financial or legislative support could directly affect a deposit program, other aspects of government operations could also have an impact on its functioning. For example, there was, and in many ways still is, a lack of consensus regarding what constitutes a government publication, as described in the introductory chapter of this volume.[1] One can see how any mechanism for the deposit of "government publications" might suffer from confusion over what that may or may not signify. Printing and distribution also vary significantly across Canadian jurisdictions, and in some cases these functions may be highly decentralized. Many challenges can emerge from decentralization, such as a lack of enforceability, an inability to determine what publications should have been received or could be acquired, a lack of clear and standard definitions, and an insufficient capacity to carry out collection and distribution on the part of government.[2]

Although other texts give fairly comprehensive overviews and histories of the federal depository library program, like Dolan's *The Depository Dilemma* and the final and commemorative issues of the *Weekly Checklist of Canadian Government Publications*, the most recent, thorough survey of provincial initiatives, known as the Pross Report,[3] was based on research conducted in the late 1960s, before many provinces had established programs of their own. In fact, one could say that many of the improvements to Canadian provincial government document access and preservation that took place in the 1970s are thanks, in part, to the dissemination of the results of the Pross Report.[4] For this reason we have chosen to provide brief overviews of each Canadian jurisdiction, federal, provincial, and territorial, with an awareness that the history of the federal depository system is thoroughly treated elsewhere.

FEDERAL DEPOSIT AND DISTRIBUTION

As might be expected, the evolution of print government publication distribution in Canada is much more thoroughly documented at the federal level when compared to the provinces and territories. Appendix 1.1, "Federal Depository Program Timeline," provides an overview of select developments that took place throughout the history of the federal Depository Services Program (DSP), which existed from 1927 to 2013.[5] As noted, resources such as the *Commemorative Weekly Checklists*, published by Government Information Services (*Weekly Checklists* 13-49, 13-50, and 13-51), and Dolan's *The Depository Dilemma* provide very detailed accounts of the changes in government publishing over time at the federal level in Canada. Many other resources provide snapshots of the government publishing landscape at specific points in time for various Canadian jurisdictions[6] and for specific issues in the publishing, distribution, collection, and preservation of publications.[7]

At the federal level, Library and Archives Canada (LAC) has had a legal deposit mandate since 1953, when the library was created, for all materials produced in Canada, according to the *Legal Deposit of Publications Regulations*, in the *Library and Archives Canada Act* (S.C. 2004, c. 11).[8] Legal deposit applies to federal government departments and agencies, producers of microforms, and electronic publications.[9] LAC was also a full depository in the DSP and received two copies of every federal government publication for legal deposit, until the DSP ended its mandate to distribute print publications in 2013.[10] In 2012, LAC, through its "modernization initiative," issued a directive for provincial and territorial governments to cease submitting their official publications to LAC,[11] and the current legal deposit mandate, on LAC's website, includes an exclusion wherein "official publications of Canadian provincial, territorial, and municipal governments" are exempted from legal deposit at LAC.[12]

PROVINCIAL AND TERRITORIAL DEPOSIT AND DISTRIBUTION

Provincially and territorially in Canada various governments have developed library deposit programs in which libraries and archives could be designated a full depository or a selective depository for publications produced in a specific jurisdiction. Jarvi describes a depository library as "one which the government has approved to receive its publications without charge, on a continuing basis. A full depository library is one which receives all available publications automatically. A selective depository is one in which the librarian may choose the publications from a checklist provided by the government."[13]

Generally, the official publishing and distribution functions of provincial governments are the responsibilities of different branches or departments. Archer notes that each province has an "office of the Queen's Printer" in the provincial capital and that the provincial Queen's Printer is responsible for publishing provincial government publications.[14] Pross and Pross add that provincial Queen's Printers do not distribute the publications they produce, unlike at the federal level.[15] For this reason, provincial library deposit programs were created to help ensure the wide and consistent distribution of publications.

There are several provincial and territorial libraries and archives that have legal or statutory mandates, requiring the automatic deposit of all provincial or territorial publications into their permanent collections. These legal deposit mandates come in many different forms, such as Orders-in-Council and statutory acts for legislatures, legislative libraries, and archives; there is no standard for legal deposit that is consistent across the country. Although not every provincial and territorial jurisdiction in Canada has legal-deposit language enshrined in statutory acts or legislation, there has been a concerted effort, both formal and informal, collaborative and independent, by libraries across Canada to collect and preserve the print publications created by provincial and territorial governments.

▶ *Newfoundland and Labrador*

In Newfoundland and Labrador there has been official support for the deposit of provincial government publications for some time. In 1960 a directive from the premier required that all departments of the provincial government deposit with the newly established Provincial Archives of Newfoundland two copies of all publications intended for use by the public.[16] There appears to have been legislative support for deposit to a few additional sites in the early 1960s as well, with statutory obligations for the Department of Provincial Affairs to acquire three copies of each government document published. These documents were then deposited to the provincial Legislative Library, the Archives, and the Gosling Memorial Library in St. John's.[17]

Although government officials had expressed an interest in the idea of the Memorial University of Newfoundland obtaining official depository status for government documents, attempts prior to the 1970s appear to have been unsuccessful.[18] Jarvi states that, as of mid-1976, Newfoundland did not have an official depository system.[19] By 1981, however, there appears to have been an informally operating depository system for the documents of the Newfoundland government. In this system the legislative librarian was responsible for distributing documents to libraries both within and outside of Newfoundland, with forty-five libraries participating in the early 1980s: thirty full depositories and fifteen selective.[20]

Even with clear legislative support for deposit to the Legislative Library and Archives, two surveys between the 1960s and 1980s reported that the largest collections of Newfoundland provincial government publications were actually in the collections of two non-government libraries: the Gosling Memorial Library (and later the A.C. Hunter Library, as described below) and the Centre for Newfoundland Studies, a division of the Memorial University of Newfoundland Libraries.[21]

The Gosling Memorial Library's collection of Newfoundland government documents benefited greatly from the deposit of many of the holdings of the original legislative library,[22] which had existed prior to the 1934 establishment in Newfoundland of the Commission of Government. For a time, the Gosling Memorial Library both served the public and acted as a central library for the province, holding many items of historical value including provincial government documents.[23] After the original library was closed, its collection was transferred to the A.C. Hunter Library.[24]

Over the last fifty years the Centre for Newfoundland Studies has grown to hold the largest provincial collection of Newfoundlandiana. Its mandate is to collect and preserve all published materials concerned with Newfoundland and Labrador, including government documents. The centre does receive certain materials automatically, some free of charge, through an arrangement with the Legislative Library. However, without official depository status, it often has to seek out and acquire much of the published output of the provincial government on its own.[25]

Current legislation names the Legislative Library of Newfoundland and Labrador as the only official depository for published information from the provincial government. The *Rooms Act* (S.N.L. 2005, c. R-15.1, s. 21) clarifies that the Archives is the official repository for government records, whereas the Legislative Library is the mandatory location of deposit for documents produced by government institutions that are intended for distribution to the public.

▶ Nova Scotia

Nova Scotia's depository program began in 1987.[26] The introduction of the program came about following a proposal for implementation of a system to ensure the deposit of Nova Scotia government publications in university and public libraries from the Steering Committee on Depository Collections, which was submitted to the Nova Scotia government in June 1985.[27] Following the government's approval of the proposal, a panel was created and met in December 1986 with the goal of establishing guidelines for the depository program. The guidelines are detailed in a 1987 memorandum to university librarians and regional chief librarians, and outlines retention requirements, the creation of a monthly checklist by the Legislative Library, and the distribution responsibilities of the Nova Scotia Government Bookstore.[28] A news release from Communications Nova Scotia[29] confirms that there were eleven full and twenty-one selective depository libraries, which are also depicted on a map in a memorandum from the co-chair of the Steering Committee on Depository Collections to the Dalhousie University Library.[30]

The program was not mandated through legislation, but guidance for the program was given in the *Manager's Manual 300*. The manual detailed the responsibility of government departments to provide twenty-five copies of various types of publications, such as pamphlets, books, and reports prepared for the public, to the government bookstore.[31] This clause was eventually removed from the *Manager's Manual*, though an exact date for this has not been verified. As evidenced in other jurisdictions, the lack of legislative authority for the program made it challenging for the Legislative Library to obtain print copies for deposit. In approximately 2011–12 the depository program was officially concluded, though the Legislative Library does continue to receive approximately two copies of each print publication.[32]

▶ Prince Edward Island

Prince Edward Island (PEI) has never developed an official depository library program. Pross and Pross note that there were earlier attempts to centralize the distribution of government publications in PEI, but they were unsuccessful.[33] Many surveys of provincial publication programs note that the Legislative Library received automatically and free of charge PEI publications and had been augmenting the availability of publications in the province by issuing lists of printed reports tabled in the legislature.[34]

The Queen's Printer publishes the statutory and legislative publications, and other publications, including documents from departments, agencies, and commissions, are published and distributed in small print runs by the Island Information Service.[35] The Island Information Service assists departments, agencies, commissions, and boards with the preparation and distribution of official provincial information, and, if the publications have not been published electronically, print versions can be requested from the service and are usually provided free of charge.[36] The service also produced the *PEI Provincial Government Publications Checklist* from 1978 to 2012.[37]

The University of PEI Library and PEI Government Services Library both have built strong collections of provincial government publications by developing good working relationships with the Island Information Service and the Clerk of the Legislative Assembly.[38] The PEI Public Archives and Records Office also acquires government records and publications, as required by the *Archives and Records Act* (A. 19.1).

▶ New Brunswick

The history of deposit for New Brunswick (NB) government publications goes back to at least the 1950s. New Brunswick Order-in-Council 52-1448 required the deposit of three copies of all documents printed, under the *Queen's Printer Act*, to the Legislative Library of New Brunswick, while Order-in-Council 56-596 extended depository status to the libraries of NB universities.[39] In 1976 the Legislative Library's status as the official site of deposit and as a mechanism of distribution to other NB depositories was strengthened through statute. The *Legislative Library Act* (R.S.N.B. 1976, c. L-3.1, s. 5 and s. 6) clearly designates the Legislative Library as both the official depository library for New Brunswick government publications and the exchange library for the Province of New Brunswick.

Drake confirms that a network of NB depository libraries was enabled in 1965 by Order-in-Council and was maintained through to at least the early 1980s with little change in the system. This Order-in-Council, having been revised as Order-in-Council 79-749, authorized the Queen's Printer to send free copies of acts, regulations, loose-leaf statutes, and the *Royal Gazette* to the Legislative Library, to members of the Legislative Assembly, to libraries having exchange agreements with the Legislative Library, and to other public and university libraries in New Brunswick. Unlike some other Canadian depository programs, the system described by Drake only had full depositories, and there were no collection maintenance obligations for depositories. In the early 1980s there were fifty-eight depository libraries participating, with five in academic institutions, two in government, and the remaining fifty-one in public libraries. Participating libraries received publications automatically each month.[40]

The Legislative Library has issued a checklist of NB provincial government documents in one form or another since the mid-1950s, with coverage beginning in 1955. Checklists from 2000 onwards are published online and comprise mostly documents received but not included in the library's catalogue.[41] Originally, however, these checklists included all items received by the library throughout the year, whether they were required to be printed by the *Queen's Printer Act* and deposited at the library or were printed by departments and acquired by other means. While the checklists undoubtedly facilitated identification of what was printed by the NB government, distribution of non-statutory documents in NB was not centralized, and ordering those documents generally had to be done through each individual authoring department or agency.[42] Perhaps this is why, in the early 1990s, New Brunswick was characterized not as having an existing depository program but as having recently submitted proposals to the provincial government calling for the establishment of such a program.[43]

At present, the NB Legislative Library is the only legislated depository for NB government publications. Although exchange agreements with other legislative and academic libraries are still active, many participating libraries have opted to rely on electronic versions of parliamentary papers rather than on their receipt in print.[44]

▶ *Quebec*

Quebec had a robust official-publications depository program between 1981 and 1997. The Ministère des Communications developed the program to ensure the "best possible access to information disseminated by the Government of Quebec."[45] The provincial Queen's Printer had been informally distributing publications to libraries, free of charge, as early as 1974.[46] The program was formalized in November 1981 with the Programme de dépôt des publications gouvernementales, wherein full depository libraries would receive "one copy each of the approximately 3000 units (books, periodical issues, bills)" that Quebec published annually.[47] These sixteen libraries included all major English and French academic libraries, Quebec public libraries, Bibliothèque nationale du Québec, and Bibliothèque de l'Assemblée nationale, as selected by Québec Official Publisher / Éditeur Officiel du Québec (former Queen's Printer), based on the libraries' level of scholarship and ability to handle a large collection.[48]

Full depository status was later extended to external legislative libraries, the Library of Parliament, the Library of Congress, the Harvard University Library, and the Quebec Delegation in Paris and could include any library willing to exchange "publications of interest" with Quebec.[49] The 180 selective depositories included both public and government libraries.[50] There were sixty participating government agencies and ministries that submitted publications to Québec Official Publisher, which ranged from statutory—such as the *Journal de debats, Statues,* and *Gazette Officielle*—to departmental annual reports.[51]

The Ministère des Communications also maintained a monthly checklist, *Liste mensuelle des publications du gouvernement du Québec,* beginning in April 1981, which contained all publications received by full depositories.[52] Selective depositories could order, without charge, any item from *Liste mensuelle,* in addition to the items that they received automatically.[53]

Not all publications of interest were distributed by the Programme de dépôt, and those publications had to be tracked down through a combination of sources, departments, and agencies.[54]

Bibliothèque et Archives nationales du Québec (BANQ; formerly BNQ) was created in 1967 with the *Act Respecting the Bibliothèque nationale du Québec* (R.S.Q., c. B-2.1). Since 1968 the BANQ has administered two key aspects of provincial publications: publishing the *Bibliographie du Québec,* a bibliography of its collections; and legal deposit. BANQ's legal deposit mandate requires the deposit of two copies of all works published by publishers, persons, and agencies in Quebec.[55] Legal deposit was partially extended to electronic publications in 1992, and as of 2007 all provincial departments were required to deposit electronic publications, except laws and statutes.[56] The Programme de dépôt was abolished in 1997 with Quebec's change in focus to the electronic dissemination of publications.[57] Quebec's system is an example of good infrastructure for provincial government information, from the Programme de dépôt through to the innovative BANQ.

Ontario has had an active depository library system since July 1971.[58] In the decade prior to the program's inception some related processes had been in place. In the early 1960s different groups of individuals and types of institutions as defined by Order-in-Council were entitled to free copies of the statutes. Copies of Government of Ontario publications were also preserved by the provincial archivist and by the Clerk of the House.[59] Also, the Ontario Legislative Assembly's *Memo re Tabling of Reports in the Legislative Library* (May 2, 1965) required that two copies of every report tabled in the legislature be deposited with the Legislative Library.[60] However, it was the Management Board Minute of August 19, 1970, that officially established Ontario's depository library system. The minute was superseded a few years later by the Management Board of Cabinet Directive 65-3-1 (July 29, 1975), which provided the authority for one complimentary copy of each available provincial government publication to be distributed to depository libraries.[61]

In May 1971 the Printing Services Branch of the Ministry of Government Services began issuing the *Ontario Government Publications Monthly Checklist*, and annual cumulations followed, the first covering 1972.[62] By 1976 the checklist had a circulation of four thousand.[63] On April 1, 1980, the Bibliographic Services Centre of the Ministry of Government Services was transferred to the Ontario Legislative Library, which had been one of the depository program's original full depositories. As a result, the library absorbed responsibility for the compilation and editing of the monthly checklists and annual catalogues.[64] Holding such a key position in the depository system work flow undoubtedly secured the library's status as a primary location of deposit for Ontario government publications, even if this status was not comprehensively supported by legislation.

In 1997 the Management Board Secretariat issued a directive obligating ministries and agencies to provide Publications Ontario with sufficient copies of their publications for distribution through the depository program. Publications Ontario was identified as responsible for the maintenance of a central public record of all government publications and for the provision of publications to the Legislative Library and to other libraries participating in the depository program. The directive also made clear what was considered a "government publication," including documents intended for distribution to the general public, whether in print or electronic, but excluding ephemera.[65]

The year 1997 also marked the end of the print run of the monthly checklists and the annual catalogues of publications, which had provided a systematic and public record of what had been historically available. By contrast, current online monthly checklists produced for the depository program remain available for only six months and are not publicly viewable.[66] In addition, while one could identify nearby depositories in the pages of the printed annual catalogues, at present there is no publicly viewable list of current depositories.[67]

Although the program originally included both full and selective depositories, today all participating libraries are selective. Feedback received by Publications Ontario over the years indicated that many libraries were no longer interested in automatically receiving all available publications. As a result, each depository library now selects the items it would like distributed to it as part of the program.[68] Retention guidelines have also evolved over time, with current depositories expected to retain most items for a minimum of five years.[69] By contrast, in the early 1980s, the Ontario program had "no rigid restrictions on the treatment, use, or retention of materials."[70]

▶ *Manitoba*

Archer proclaimed that "Manitoba has gone farther than any other province toward a centralized distributing agency."[71] Although Manitoba's official depository program began in 1991 and concluded in 2010, the mandate for departments to deposit publications with the Legislative Library existed prior to the program and remains in force. The Legislative Library was declared, through an Order-in-Council, to be a depository of provincial government publications in 1952.[72] The Order-in-Council required copies of each published document to be sent to the provincial Legislative Library, which would then maintain an accession list.[73] Following each legislative session the provincial library would distribute documents to forty-five libraries in Canada, the United States, and

Commonwealth countries.[74] Some sources indicate that this broad distribution beyond provincial boundaries was done on an exchange or reciprocal basis.[75] Both a monthly checklist of government publications and an annual cumulation were created by the Legislative Library, while the Manitoba Citizen's Inquiry Service provided information about how to obtain the publications.[76]

The formal depository distribution system was developed in 1991 and officially concluded in 2010. A letter of communication from the Legislative Library to Brandon University details the organization of provincial documents into eight categories, with retention and disposition guidelines provided for each.[77] Staff at the Legislative Library confirmed that Manitoba libraries could choose to be full depositories or to create a profile that would identify the most relevant publications based on local needs.[78] There were approximately ten libraries participating in this program, including the major universities and several colleges and public libraries in the province.[79] Both collection and distribution were handled by the Legislative Library. As publications began to be published electronically and accessible online, and as libraries began to face increasing pressure on their limited space, depository libraries started to withdraw from the program, which led to the official closure of the program in 2010. Although the print distribution program no longer exists, the Legislative Library still has the mandate to collect published government documents from departments, Crown corporations, and agencies of the Manitoba government, as outlined in the *Legislative Library Act* (S.M. 2008, c. 12).

▶ *Saskatchewan*

Saskatchewan never developed an official library depository program. Until 1982 the Legislative Library had an "informal responsibility to collect Saskatchewan government publications," and it received provincial publications free of charge for its collection.[80] In 1976 the library began publishing the *Annual Checklist of Saskatchewan Government Publications*, and in July 1982 publication of the monthly checklist began.[81] The scope of checklists was limited to publications received by the library and excluded legislative materials.[82] The development of the checklist was, in part, a response to the publication of the Pross Report in 1972, which recommended that the Saskatchewan Legislative Library "undertake the distribution of Saskatchewan documents to other libraries," and to a corresponding call to action from the Saskatchewan Library Association.[83]

The publications collected by the Legislative Library and contained in the checklist are printed by the provincial Queen's Printer and include the *Saskatchewan Gazette* and *Statutes*. Issuing the bills, orders, votes, debates, and journals, all in limited publishing runs, is the mandate of the Clerk of the Legislative Assembly.[84] Previous to online publication of official documents, the Queen's Printer would handle priced publications that individual departments were unable to distribute; however, the usual responsibility for distribution fell to individual departments.[85]

Since 1982 the Legislative Library has been receiving print, and in 2005 the Act was updated to include electronic provincial publications from all Saskatchewan government bodies, including the Legislative Assembly, through legal deposit with "statutory authority [from] section 81 of the *Legislative Assembly and Executive Council Act, 2007.*"[86] Through the years the Legislative Library had exchange agreements with the Library of Congress, the National Library of Canada, other Canadian legislative libraries (at their request), Saskatchewan Archives, and Micromedia.[87] The Micromedia exchange agreement enabled microfilming of Saskatchewan government publications, and any library could obtain a subscription, for a fee.[88] "In an effort to inform interested Saskatchewan libraries of available material, an inquiry letter was sent to all government, post-secondary, academic, special, public and regional libraries listed in the *Directory of Saskatchewan Libraries*. In 1986/87 there was an increase of 165% in surplus materials distributed in the province."[89] As noted on the website in 2016 for the monthly checklist, due to the lack of a formal distribution program, interested libraries must contact departments individually to obtain print publications.[90]

▶ Alberta

The Alberta Depository Library Program (ADLP) has been active since 1974.[91] With no legal mandate to operate, the program has relied on the goodwill of author departments to provide copies of their publications for distribution.[92] The Alberta Legislature Library's participation in the ADLP has contributed to its own comprehensive collection efforts, as there is also no legislation designating it an official depository for Alberta government publications.[93] Originally managed by the Queen's Printer and Public Affairs Bureau, the ADLP became part of the Alberta Government Library's portfolio of responsibilities in 2007, though the Queen's Printer still plays a role in the distribution of legislative materials to depositories.[94]

In the past the ADLP was "for full depositories only, not selective."[95] By the mid-1990s there were eleven selective depositories (known as "partial" depositories) and three defined types of libraries automatically receiving copies of all depository publications: full depositories, special libraries, and the Legislature Library. Special libraries differed from full depositories by receiving shipments on an infrequent basis, and the Legislature Library by receiving multiple copies of each document.[96] In current practice, participants in the ADLP are either full or partial depository libraries, though full depositories still differ in the number of copies of publications they receive.

Unlike the recently terminated federal Depository Services Program, warehousing and distribution for the ADLP are not centralized for listed publications, and partial depositories must select and order complimentary copies directly from author departments. To assist in the selection process, a catalogue of available documents has been produced in one form or another since the program started. In 1974 the Department of Government Services began issuing a quarterly catalogue of publications published by the provincial government.[97] In current practice, the Alberta Government Library prepares the quarterly list, distributes it to depository libraries, and publishes it online.[98]

In the earlier years of the ADLP there were "no specified obligations on the part of the recipient libraries."[99] Currently, however, ADLP full depositories are expected to retain depository items permanently, while partial depositories are free to retain or dispose of items as they see fit, subject only to their own internal collection management policies.[100] It is also interesting that the ADLP explicitly includes electronic documents, which can be accessed through the Queen's Printer's online

Government of Alberta Publications catalogue or by way of a quarterly listing available as an open dataset. In recent years the ADLP has been working on updating its processes to explicitly incorporate Alberta's Open Government Portal into its author-department deposit work flow for digital Government of Alberta publications.[101]

▶ *British Columbia*

An Order-in-Council (no. 497) from 1935 approved the Legislative Library and the University of British Columbia as depository libraries for British Columbia government publications. A revised Order-in-Council (no. 419) was issued in 1961 and changed the deposit requirements from two to four copies of each publication. While this Order-in-Council has never been rescinded, it has also never been updated to cover electronic publications.

Pross and Pross claim that the British Columbia provincial library was likely one of the most successful in obtaining the documents that it was mandated to collect via Order-in-Council, because they were obtained from one of the most highly centralized production systems of all Canadian provinces.[102] That said, anecdotal evidence suggests that challenges were experienced as far back as the 1930s because the Queen's Printer could not prevent ministries from using alternative printing facilities.[103] During the intervening time between the Orders-in-Council and the official deposit program that distributed publications to a network of libraries, requests for publications were made to individual departments, unless Crown Publications was listed as the official supplier.[104] Some departments would issue lists of publications, and, as there was no central office to handle acquisition requests, each department had autonomy over determining free and priced publications.[105]

It was on April 13, 1994, that the then Minister of Government Services announced the creation of a permanent provincial depository library program for British Columbia.[106] This was the culmination of lobbying from groups such as the British Columbia Library Association (BCLA), which was also successful in lobbying for the pilot program established in 1989.[107] Following a survey conducted in the winter of

1993, which yielded positive responses to the program, it was decided that the program would move from pilot to permanence.[108]

When the provincial depository library program was established, it was funded by the Ministry of Government Services and administered by the Library Services Branch of the Ministry of Municipal Affairs. An advisory committee, with representatives from a variety of types of libraries and associations, was established in 1994 to support the program. Two subcommittees of this group determined the major parameters of the program: the Core List and Retention Guidelines Sub-Committee and the Eligibility Criteria Sub-Committee.[109] The provincial depository manual contains essential information, including a contact list, detailed program eligibility criteria, the core list of publications, retention guidelines, cataloguing instructions for titles on the core list, instructions for claiming materials, a note on Legislative Library web access, as well as newsletters from February and June 1995. That said, it should be noted that the manual was continually updated, and participating libraries may have replaced pages as updated material was received.[110] This means that the contents of the binder reviewed for this publication may not be reflective of the entire history of the program.

▶ *Yukon*

The Yukon does not have a Legislative Library or a print depository distribution program. Van Haaften notes that there is no central source for information on publication issues within the Yukon.[111] Responsibility for the collection and preservation of government publications falls to the Yukon Archives, which maintains the Territorial Library. The *Archives Act* (R.S.Y. 2002, c. 9) outlines the collection mandate of the territorial archives. There is active collection in several areas beyond government publications, but in regards to territorial publications the collection focuses on current and retrospective published titles in all subject areas and media types. The Territorial Library is the only library that collects, preserves, and provides permanent access to Yukon government publications, and the library does not weed its collection.[112] The Queen's Printer is responsible for government publications, guided by the *Public Printing Act* (R.S.Y. 2002, c. 180).[113]

▶ Northwest Territories

The depository program in the Northwest Territories (NWT) initially existed in an unofficial capacity.[114] Jarvi observed in 1976 that there had been little bibliographical activity or listing of government publications published in the territory.[115] Government departments were instructed to send copies of their publications to the Government In-Service Library, established in 1973, but there was no official directive to this effect.[116] In 1983 the Government In-Service Library was renamed the Government Library of the Northwest Territories, and in April 1992 the library became the Legislative Library of the Northwest Territories.[117] The legal deposit status for government publications was made official for the Legislative Library in the *Regulations of the Archives Act* (R-056-2003, s. 1), which states that any publication or public record "produced, printed or released" by a governing body in the Government of Northwest Territories must be sent in quadruplicate to the Legislative Assembly Library, and one copy to the Archivist, within seven days of its publication or release.

Territorial publications were produced mainly by the federal Queen's Printer from 1870 to 1980, when the territories were under the jurisdictional control of the federal government.[118] The Department of Information, initially known as Information Services, was organized in Ottawa in May 1967.[119] The department was re-established in Yellowknife with the transfer of the government in September 1967.[120] In 1970 the department was organized into two divisions: Publications and Public Relations. The Publications division was responsible for meeting the graphic design and the publishing needs of the Government of the Northwest Territories.[121]

In 1979 the head of the Printing Bureau was appointed as the Territorial Printer, and the responsibility for printing all new Northwest Territories ordinances was assumed from the Queen's Printer in 1980.[122] In 1985 the responsibility for printing and production was taken on by a division in the newly formed Department of Culture and Communications. In 1992 responsibility was transferred again to the Department of Public Works and Services.[123] In 1993 the in-house printing function of government documents was privatized.[124]

In 1977 a publications catalogue was published to give residents a complete current listing of all government publications and reports and from whence the material could be acquired.[125] The last publications catalogue was printed in 1989.[126] The Legislative Library stepped in to fill the gap left by the discontinuation of the publications catalogue by providing an annual *Checklist of Northwest Territories Government Publications,* now available on the Legislative Library's website. The checklist, which begins with the year 1994, is produced as a guide to available publications, with no guarantee that it is a complete list of publications produced by departments of the Government of the Northwest Territories.[127] Tabled documents can be requested from the Legislative Library. For other publications the issuing departments and agencies must be contacted, as noted on the checklist website.[128] Requests for publications have decreased in number as born-digital electronic copies of the House documents are now available on the Legislative Assembly's website.[129]

▶ Nunavut

Nunavut does not have a territorial depository library program, and the Nunavut Legislative Library does not have legislated depository status. That said, according to the Legislative Assembly of Nunavut's website, the mandate of the Legislative Library includes the maintenance of the Legislative Assembly's public records, and the aim to build a comprehensive collection of documents published by the Government of Nunavut. Government publications tabled in the legislature do become part of the Legislative Library's collection as a matter of procedure, but, without supporting legislation, the overall comprehensiveness of the collection has been based mostly on the library's own efforts. Being responsible for the assignment of the International Standard Book Numbers (ISBNs) to Government of Nunavut publications has also contributed to the Legislative Library's success in acquiring documents, but the transition to electronic dissemination of government information has lessened its impact, as communicating ISBN requirements for digital information can be challenging.[130]

TRANSITION FROM PRINT TO DIGITAL

The amount of Canadian government information produced and distributed electronically has increased significantly over the last few decades. In the early years of this evolution there was a corresponding rise in related anxiety in the library community. In the early 1990s Nilsen stated that the "preservation of data in electronic formats is of considerable concern because of the ease with which data can be manipulated and deleted from databases."[131] Since then many authors have explored issues of permanence and preservation of digital government information. Brodie was concerned about the "fluidity" of electronic information and the ease with which that information could be divorced from its original context and creators.[132] Gnassi asserted that "the internet is transient and transparent. Websites evolve and change. They come and go. Content is updated and discarded and context is lost. Researchers who traditionally have relied on this information to build on previous knowledge increasingly find that it is not there."[133] In a report for the National Library and the DSP, Dickison observed that the estimated lifespan of electronic publications could be anywhere from forty-four days to two years, and made recommendations for the government of Canada to deploy persistent uniform resource locators (URLS) for electronic publications.[134]

A perceived lack of preparedness on the part of libraries for the shift from print to digital dissemination of government information was also an early source of concern. Vaughan and Dolan found that, although, by 1998, 89 percent of libraries participating in the DSP had Internet access, electronic government publications were still considered low use, and almost half of the libraries responding to their survey thought of print as the most common format for future government publications.[135] A few years later Moon's survey of academic depository libraries found that 65 percent of respondents printed electronic documents from the Web in order to add them to their collections, and that approximately 80 percent of responding libraries linked directly to government URLS.[136] Both of these findings illustrate an early reliance on external actors for the provision of access to and preservation of digital government information.

In a series of three reports based on a survey initiated by the Canadian Association of Research Libraries (CARL) in 2004, Hubbertz provided an important overview of how CARL member libraries, along with provincial and territorial legislative libraries, were individually approaching the collection and preservation of web-based publications from their own jurisdictions.[137] In 2005 Hubbertz found that electronic collections had already been established in six of the provinces. By 2007, electronic collections could be found in all but four jurisdictions, hosted and maintained by their respective legislative or provincial libraries. Generally, these collections were of discrete items rather than of entire websites or dynamic sources of information. As such, Hubbertz suggested that digitally published information in formats without clear print analogs were at risk of being lost to time.[138] Nevertheless, in most cases, collected publications were downloaded, catalogued, and re-hosted locally, providing a measure of stability and convenience with respect to access—so much so that most CARL libraries in Ontario and Quebec elected to link to the catalogues of the Ontario Legislative Library and BANQ, respectively, rather than downloading and re-hosting the publications themselves.[139]

In the last decade the situation has improved greatly, though, as one might expect, solutions vary significantly across jurisdictions. Following are a few examples of how different libraries and related organizations have been attempting to improve access to and preservation of electronic publications from their respective governments. The examples are not meant to provide an exhaustive list of approaches but rather to highlight the variety of initiatives found across Canada.

From the federal perspective,[140] the DSP maintains a collection of electronic Government of Canada publications. According to the DSP website, this activity began in 1995, and, although it grew slowly at first, by 2014 the collection contained over 130,000 freely downloadable items, with over 1,000 added each month. Libraries are encouraged to link directly to the DSP's re-hosted copies of publications from their own catalogues using machine-readable cataloguing (MARC) records produced in collaboration with LAC. In the last few years, preservation and access to the DSP's electronic collection have also been enhanced through collaboration with the Canadian Government Information

Digital Preservation Network (CGI DPN)[141] and through indexing by the GALLOP portal of the Association of Parliamentary Libraries in Canada (APLIC).[142]

In the east, the Centre for Newfoundland Studies at Memorial University Libraries was given dedicated space on a Memorial University Libraries web server in recent years in order to re-host government publications, and has opted to stop printing and shelving electronic documents in favour of this more flexible and space-conscious method of document storage, facilitating access to provincial government information for individuals regardless of physical location.[143] Through the Legislative Library's participation in the GALLOP portal, it is also clear that at least some of the provincial government documents in its catalogue are being re-hosted on Legislative Assembly web servers, for which one could infer that the library has strengthened its control over persistence of location and access for these documents.

The Island Information Service in PEI currently publishes many publications electronically through its publications portal. The University of Prince Edward Island Library, PEI Government Services Library, PEI Public Archives and Records Office, and the PEI Legislative Library combined their efforts and collections to co-create the PEI Legislative Documents Online (PEILDO) database in 2011, as noted on the PEILDO website, to provide public online access to PEI government publications.

In central Canada the Bibliothèque et Archives nationales du Québec (BANQ) has been acquiring digital publications, as an extension of its legal deposit mandate, since 2001. The electronic publications acquired by the BANQ include "several thousand titles from several hundred publishers in the government, parapublic and private sectors."[144] All of the digital publications collected by the BANQ are made available through various online portals, and the BANQ is contributing publications to the GALLOP portal.

In the west the Saskatchewan Legislative Library still maintains the monthly checklist of provincial government publications. Most provincial government publications in the checklist are now born digital and are available electronically through the Legislative Library catalogue. From 2002 to 2004 the University of Saskatchewan built a collection of provincial government web-based information. When that program ceased, the Saskatchewan Legislative Library took over the effort and began collecting electronic provincial publications in 2006.[145] All the publications collected digitally are available through the monthly checklist or the Legislative Library catalogue.

Moving north to Nunavut, the Legislative Library started to collect and catalogue territorial government electronic documents in 2007. Although the electronic documents used to be accessible only upon request, the library is now hosting these documents on a publicly accessible web server under its control.[146] At present, the electronic collection is not indexed by the GALLOP portal, due to the complexities of incorporating documents produced in four languages, and using two scripts, into a portal that supports primarily documents in English and French. That said, the Legislative Library has indicated a hope that this collection will be added to the portal in the future.[147]

CONCLUSION

It became clear during the preparation of this chapter that each jurisdiction had approached the deposit of tangible-format government publications with different strategies. Some governments identified one or more official locations for the deposit of their output, and others created programs to distribute systematically complete or partial sets of their published output to various institutions. The scope of the content that was deposited varied greatly across jurisdictions, as did the procedures and obligations of the depositors and the recipients of published materials. While the intent to preserve the published output of government was constant, the means to accomplish it was not. As a result, the ease and breadth of access to historical government information is not currently the same in every province and territory.

The Canadian federal, provincial, and territorial governments are also approaching the transition from print to digital publishing and distribution in very different ways, as are the libraries and archives that acquire and rely on their published output. Some governments have identified official digital locations for the deposit of electronic publications, while, in other jurisdictions, institutions within and outside of government have taken it upon themselves to collect, organize, preserve, and provide access to as much electronically published government information as possible, acting as unofficial locations of digital deposit. Many challenges and gaps still exist in this area, but it is encouraging that several collaborative efforts have developed recently in an effort to preserve and increase electronic access to government information, whether by digitizing historical printed information, by providing a single portal to digital repositories in multiple jurisdictions, by archiving digital collections in multiple locations, or by harvesting web content to save published information that can often be quite ephemeral.[148] More and more, electronic publishing is becoming the norm in government, and demand for electronic access to information the norm in libraries. As government information transitions fully into the digital age, the success of today's governments' efforts to preserve their electronic output, and of the many collaborations taking place in the greater government information community, will become even more critical to preserving our federal and regional documentary heritage for future generations.

Appendix 1.1.

FEDERAL DEPOSITORY PROGRAM TIMELINE

The following timeline provides an overview of the history of the federal Depository Services Program. Although there are many sources that detail specific aspects of the federal program, the sources referred to in the table are primarily those that provide comprehensive overviews. Not all developments that took place over the course of the DSP are detailed. Rather, a selection of key developments is provided to demonstrate the long-standing and complex nature of the program, as well as the context in which it operated for so many years.

TABLE 1.1

Federal Depository Program Timeline

YEAR	EVENT	SOURCE
1927	The Depository Services Program (DSP) created by Order-in-Council P.C. 1471.	Canada, Publishing and Depository Services Program, *Commemorative Weekly. Checklist 13-49.*
1928	The first *Catalogue of Official Publications of the Parliament and Government of Canada* was printed in April.	Canada, Publishing and Depository Services Program, *Commemorative Weekly Checklist 13-49.*

YEAR	EVENT	SOURCE
1933	The Treasury Board Minute 147371 established a committee to assess the economic efficiency of government printing.	Canada, Publishing and Depository Services Program, *Commemorative Weekly Checklist 13-49*; Dolan, *The Depository Dilemma*.
1939	The *Catalogue of Official Publications* was replaced by an annual catalogue, the title of which varied.	Canada, Publishing and Depository Services Program, *Commemorative Weekly Checklist 13-49*.
1952	The first official checklist, called the *Daily Checklist*, was published on December 1.	Canada, Publishing and Depository Services Program, *Commemorative Weekly Checklist 13-49*.
1953	The *Canadian Government Publications Annual Catalogue* supplemented a monthly catalogue and daily checklist. The catalogues and checklists had varying dates and titles and were published until approximately 1977–78.	Canada, Publishing and Depository Services Program, *Commemorative Weekly Checklist 13-49*.
1954	The minister in charge of the Department of Public Printing and Stationery sent a report to the Treasury Board recommending the review and re-enactment of Order-in-Council P.C. 1471.	Canada, Publishing and Depository Services Program, *Commemorative Weekly Checklist 13-50*.
	An ad hoc committee on publications was formed. The committee identified six publication groups and recommended distribution guidelines for each.	Canada, Publishing and Depository Services Program, *Commemorative Weekly Checklist 13-50*.

YEAR	EVENT	SOURCE
1955	Treasury Board Minute 477983 was passed on March 31, 1955. It consolidated previous policies and had the goal of reducing free distribution and increasing sales. It also named the Queen's Printer as the general distributor and seller of departmental publications.	Canada, Publishing and Depository Services Program, *Commemorative Weekly Checklist 13-49*; Canada, Publishing and Depository Services Program, *Commemorative Weekly Checklist 13-50*.
1964	The Queen's Printer was transferred to the Department of Industry and then to the Secretary of State. The Printing Bureau was moved to the Department of Defence Production.	Canada, Publishing and Depository Services Program, *Commemorative Weekly Checklist 13-50*.
1966	Resolution of the Canadian Political Science Association on the need for university depositories.	Pross and Pross, *Government Publishing in the Canadian Provinces*.
1967	The Treasury Board published *Policy and Guide on Canadian Government Publishing* (T.B. 667239).	Monty, "Due North"; Canada, Publishing and Depository Services Program, *Commemorative Weekly Checklist 13-50*.
1968	Task Force on Government Information was created to study federal information services.	Canada, Publishing and Depository Services Program, *Commemorative Weekly Checklist 13-50*.
1970	Information Canada was created.	Canada, Publishing and Depository Services Program, *Commemorative Weekly Checklist 13-50*.
1972	The Canadian Library Association (CLA) submitted a brief to Information Canada.	Canada, Publishing and Depository Services Program, *Commemorative Weekly Checklist 13-50*.

YEAR	EVENT	SOURCE
1976	Information Canada was disbanded. Publishing Division was renamed the Publishing Centre and transferred to the Department of Supply and Services.	Canada, Publishing and Depository Services Program, *Commemorative Weekly Checklist 13-50*; Dolan, *The Depository Dilemma*.
	The Canadian Library Association submitted *The Brief on Distribution of Federal Government Publications to the Standing Joint Committee of the Senate and House of Commons*.	Canada, Publishing and Depository Services Program, *Commemorative Weekly Checklist 13-50*.
1977	The Publishing Division discontinued government-run bookstores.	Morton and Zink, "We Are Here."
	A review of the DSP was undertaken in which all depositories were examined and the number of depositories was reduced.	Canada Communication Group, *Partners in Access*.
	The Treasury Board revised the *Policy and Guide on Canadian Government Publishing* (T.B. 748136).	Drake, "Federal and Provincial Depository Library System."
1978	The *Daily Checklist* was replaced by the *Weekly Checklist*.	Dolan, "The Depository Dilemma."
	The Treasury Board established a publishing directive in chapter 335 of the *Administrative Policy Manual*.	Drake, "Federal and Provincial Depository Library System"; Monty, "Due North."
1981	The Depository Services Program Library Advisory Committee (DSP-LAC) was established.	Canada, Publishing and Depository Services Program, *Commemorative Weekly Checklist 13-51*.

YEAR	EVENT	SOURCE
1981	The first guide to the federal program, titled *The Depository Services Program*, was published. It outlined objectives, definitions, eligibility for depository status, library responsibilities, mechanics of free distribution, and ordering information.	Drake, "Federal and Provincial Depository Library System."
1988	The Task Force on Depository Program Review was established to evaluate the federal depository program. Service levels, administrative structure, and machine-readable information were some of the topics examined. This task group produced the *Partners in Access Report* in 1990.	Morton and Zink, "We Are Here"; Monty, "Canadian Government Information"; Canada, Publishing and Depository Services Program, *Commemorative Weekly Checklist 13-51*.
1989	The DSP began publishing the newsletter *What's Up Doc?*, which was published irregularly until 1998.	Canada, Publishing and Depository Services Program, *Commemorative Weekly Checklist 13-51*.
1990	The Canada Communication Group– Publishing Division was given the status of a Special Operating Agency.	Morton and Zink, "We Are Here."
	Partners in Access: Report of the Task Group on Depository Program Review was published and included 35 recommendations.	Monty, "Canadian Government Information"; Canada, Publishing and Depository Services Program, *Commemorative Weekly Checklist 13-51*.

YEAR	EVENT	SOURCE
1991	A pilot project was created that made electronic publications available to a select group of depository libraries.	Canada, Publishing and Depository Services Program, *Commemorative Weekly Checklist 13-51.*
	The Task Force on Electronic Products for the DSP was established.	Canada, Publishing and Depository Services Program, *Commemorative Weekly Checklist 13-51.*
1992	The Treasury Board Secretariat agreed with the recommendation from the Task Group on Depository Review that electronic products should be included in the depository program.	Canada, Publishing and Depository Services Program, *Commemorative Weekly Checklist 13-51.*
	MINISIS was chosen as the database for cataloguing and indexing publications in the DSP.	Canada, Publishing and Depository Services Program, *Commemorative Weekly Checklist 13-51.*
1993	*Study of the Depository Services Program* by Ann Braden and Associates was published.	Monty and Depository Services Program, *Proposal for a Revised Model Depository System.*
1993 –94	The DSP implemented the first government-wide, general list of subjects to categorize and facilitate finding Canadian government publications in searchable databases.	Canada, Publishing and Depository Services Program, *Commemorative Weekly Checklist 13-51.*
1995	The DSP launched its website and the online version of the weekly checklist.	Canada, Publishing and Depository Services Program, *Commemorative Weekly Checklist 13-51.*

YEAR	EVENT	SOURCE
1995	The InfoDep listserv was created.	Canada, Publishing and Depository Services Program, *Commemorative Weekly Checklist 13-51.*
1998	*Proposal for a Revised Model Depository System* was published.	Monty and Depository Services Program, *Proposal for a Revised Model Depository System.*
2002	Groups within the library community, including CLA, CARL, and the Association pour l'avancement des sciences et techniques de la documentation (ASTED), jointly asked that the Depository Services Program be transferred to the new Library and Archives Canada.	Monty, "News from the North."
2003	A steering committee undertook a study to examine the potential transfer of the depository program from Public Works and Government Services Canada (PWGSC) to LAC. Consulting and Audit Canada was hired to study the operations and concluded that the DSP should not be moved to LAC.	Monty, "News from the North."
2013	Government of Canada announced its commitment to modernize the publishing process by focusing on electronic publication production and distribution.	Canada, Publishing and Depository Services Program, *Commemorative Weekly Checklist 13-51.*

YEAR	EVENT	SOURCE
2013	Three commemorative versions of the weekly checklist were published.	Canada, Publishing and Depository Services Program, *Commemorative Weekly Checklist 13-51.*
	The last print version of the weekly checklist was published. Only electronic versions were produced after 2013.	Canada, Publishing and Depository Services Program, *Commemorative Weekly Checklist 13-51.*
	Agreements between depository libraries and the DSP expired.	Canada, Publishing and Depository Services Program, *Commemorative Weekly Checklist 13-50.*
2014	Depositories were no longer able to order print publications from the electronic weekly checklist.	Canada, Publishing and Depository Services Program, *Commemorative Weekly Checklist 13-49.*

ACKNOWLEDGEMENTS

The authors would like to thank the following individuals and organizations whose communications cited in our chapter provided us with valuable information, without which we could not have completed this research.

- ▷ Jonathan Bowie, New Brunswick Legislative Library
- ▷ Marilyn Carr-Harris, British Columbia Legislative Library
- ▷ Peggy D'Orsay, Yukon Archives
- ▷ Yvonne Earle, Nunavut Legislative Library
- ▷ Valerie Footz, Alberta Legislature Library
- ▷ Sylvia Kalluk, Nunavut Legislative Library
- ▷ Simon Lloyd, University of Prince Edward Island Library
- ▷ David McDonald, Nova Scotia Legislative Library
- ▷ Publications Ontario
- ▷ Vera Raschke, Northwest Territories Legislative Library
- ▷ Heidi Rees, Manitoba Legislative Library
- ▷ Joan Ritcey, Centre for Newfoundland Studies at Memorial University Libraries
- ▷ Gregory Salmers, Saskatchewan Legislative Library
- ▷ Gary Weber, Government of Alberta Open Government Program

In addition to these individuals, we would like to thank sincerely the numerous others who supported this chapter by providing access to supporting documentation and answering our many inquiries along the way.

Notes

1. For discussions of the definition of *government publication*, see Archer, "Acquisition of Canadian Provincial Documents," 53; Pross and Pross, *Government Publishing in the Canadian Provinces*, 12–19; and Dolan, *The Depository Dilemma*, 15–16.
2. Pross and Pross, *Government Publishing in the Canadian Provinces*, 46–9.
3. Pross and Pross, *Government Publishing in the Canadian Provinces*.
4. Jarvi, *Access to Canadian Government Publications in Canadian Academic and Public Libraries*, 6.
5. For a pre-1927 overview of federal deposit see chapter 2.
6. Archer, "Acquisition of Canadian Provincial Documents"; Jarvi, "Tracing Canadian Provincial Government Publications"; Jarvi, *Access to Canadian Government Publications*; Drake, "Federal and Provincial Depository Library System for Government Publications in Canada"; Morton and Zink, "'We Are Here to Make Sure That Information Is Available, Accessible, and Cost-Effective'"; Canada Communication Group, *Partners in Access*; Morton and Zink, "The Dissemination and Accessibility of Canadian Government Information"; Monty, "Due North"; Johnston, "News from the North: E-Archiving in the Provinces"; Hamilton, "Democracy in an Electronic Depository World"; Johnston, "News from the North: Preservation of Born-Digital Government Publications in Canadian Jurisdictions"; and Monty, "News from the North: Canada Is a Cold Place for Government Publications."
7. Luebbe, "Recent Developments in Canadian Government Documents"; Luebbe, "Update on Canadian Government Documents in Microform"; Luebbe, "Canadian Government Documents in Microform: 1989 Update"; Luebbe, "1990 Survey of Canadian Government Documents Micropublishers"; Davies and Chalk, "Form and Function"; Vaughan and Dolan, "Electronic Dissemination of Government Information in Canada: Implications for Equitable Access"; Vaughan and Dolan, "Transition to Electronic Access of Government Information"; Brodie, "Authenticity, Preservation and Access in Digital Collections"; Gnassi, "Accessing Canadian Federal Information"; Moon, "Survey of Canadian Academic Depository Libraries Regarding Electronic Government Publications"; Boyko, "The Evolution of Census Dissemination in Canada"; and Hamilton, "Moving to Electronic in the Depository World."
8. For an in-depth discussion of the history, legislation, policy, and regulations related to federal publications, publishing and depository services, and LAC, see chapter 2.
9. National Library of Canada, *Legal Deposit = Le dépôt légal*, 4.
10. Canada, Publishing and Depository Services Program, *Quick Reference Guide for Depository Libraries*, 9.

11. Friskey, "Letter to Minister James Moore."
12. http://www.bac-lac.gc.ca/eng/services/legal-deposit/pages/legal-deposit. aspx.
13. Jarvi, *Access to Canadian Government Publications*, 2.
14. Archer, "Acquisition of Canadian Provincial Documents," 55.
15. Pross and Pross, *Government Publishing in the Canadian Provinces*, 35.
16. Pross and Pross, *Government Publishing in the Canadian Provinces*, 177.
17. Archer, "Acquisition of Canadian Provincial Documents," 58.
18. Pross and Pross, *Government Publishing in the Canadian Provinces*, 58.
19. Jarvi, *Access to Canadian Government Publications*, 12.
20. Drake, "Federal and Provincial Depository Library System," 66.
21. Pross and Pross, *Government Publishing in the Canadian Provinces*, 88; Catherine Pross, *A Guide to the Identification and Acquisition of Canadian Government Publications*, 41.
22. Pross and Pross, *Government Publishing in the Canadian Provinces*, 88.
23. "Gosling Memorial Library," *Newfoundland & Labrador Public Libraries*.
24. Pross, *A Guide to the Identification*, 42.
25. Joan Ritcey, email to Graeme Campbell, November 26, 2015.
26. Sheliah Bennett, "Depository Library System Provides Access to Information."
27. Somers, official communication, 1; Monty, "Canadian Government Information: An Update," 280.
28. Somers, official communication, 1–2.
29. Bennett, "Depository Library System Provides Access to Information."
30. Murphy, official communication, 3.
31. David McDonald, email to Catherine McGoveran, November 15, 2015, and December 1, 2015.
32. David McDonald, email to Catherine McGoveran, November 15, 2015, and December 1, 2015.
33. Pross and Pross, *Government Publishing in the Canadian Provinces*, 35.
34. Archer, "Acquisition of Canadian Provincial Documents," 58–59; Pross and Pross, *Government Publishing in the Canadian Provinces*, 89; Presser, "Canadian Provincial and Municipal Documents," 20; Drake, "Federal and Provincial Depository Library System," 65.
35. Catherine Pross, *A Guide to the Identification*, 59–61.
36. Simon Lloyd, email to Michelle Lake, November 17, 2015.
37. Catherine Pross, *A Guide to the Identification*, 59–61.
38. Simon Lloyd, email to Michelle Lake, November 17, 2015.
39. Pross and Pross, *Government Publishing in the Canadian Provinces*, 55 and 60.
40. Drake, "Federal and Provincial Depository Library System," 66.

41. Jonathan Bowie, email to Graeme Campbell, November 10, 2015.

42. Pross and Pross, *Government Publishing in the Canadian Provinces*, 37; Catherine Pross, *A Guide to the Identification*, 37–38; van Haaften, *An Index to Selected Canadian Provincial Government Publications*, 34.

43. Monty, "Canadian Government Information," 280.

44. Jonathan Bowie, email to Graeme Campbell, November 10, 2015.

45. Nielson, "How Quebec Does It Good," 28.

46. Jarvi, *Access to Canadian Government Publications*, 12.

47. Catherine Pross, *A Guide to the Identification*, 62; Nielson, "How Quebec Does It Good," 28.

48. Jarvi, "Tracing Canadian Provincial Government Publications," 12; and Nielson, "How Quebec Does It Good," 28.

49. Carpentier, "The Acquisition of the Publications of the Quebec Government," 258; Nielson, "How Quebec Does It Good," 29.

50. Nielson, "How Quebec Does It Good," 28.

51. Pross and Pross, *Government Publishing in the Canadian Provinces*, 41; Nielson, "How Quebec Does It Good," 29; Carpentier, "The Acquisition of the Publications of the Quebec Government," 258.

52. "Canadian French Language Publishing," 3; Carpentier, "The Acquisition of the Publications of the Quebec Government," 258.

53. Nielson, "How Quebec Does It Good," 28.

54. For further discussions of these sources, departments, and agencies, see Carpentier, "The Acquisition of the Publications of the Quebec Government"; Nielson, "How Quebec Does It Good"; Aiken and Barnes, "Finding and Using Canadian Government Documents," 105–30; Catherine Pross, *A Guide to the Identification;* Pross and Pross, *Government Publishing in the Canadian Provinces.*

55. Carpentier, "Quebec Government Publications in Microform," 178.

56. Hubbertz, *Update 2007*, 11–12.

57. Hubbertz, *Update 2007*, 11; Gagnon, official communication.

58. Drake, "Federal and Provincial Depository," 66.

59. Archer, "Acquisition of Canadian Provincial Documents," 58.

60. Pross and Pross, *Government Publishing in the Canadian Provinces*, 61.

61. Ontario, Publications Ontario, "Depository Libraries Online Ordering User Guide," 23.

62. Presser, "Canadian Provincial and Municipal Documents," 19.

63. Jarvi, *Access to Canadian Government Publications*, 8.

64. Ontario, Ministry of Government Services, verso of *Ontario Government Publications Annual Catalogue, 1979.*

65. Ontario, Management Board Secretariat, "Corporate Management Directives," 6–8.

66. Ontario, Publications Ontario, email to Graeme Campbell, January 9, 2015.

67. Ontario, Publications Ontario, email to Graeme Campbell, October 20, 2014.

68. Ontario, Publications Ontario, email to Graeme Campbell, December 23, 2014.

69. Ontario, Publications Ontario, "Depository Libraries Online Ordering," 24.

70. Drake, "Federal and Provincial Depository," 67. For a more thorough discussion herein of Ontario government publications, see chapter 7.

71. Archer, "Acquisition of Canadian Provincial Documents," 57.

72. Archer, "Acquisition of Canadian Provincial Documents," 57; Catherine Pross, "Bibliographies of Provincial Government Documents," 103.

73. Archer, "Acquisition of Canadian Provincial Documents," 57; Catherine Pross, "Bibliographies of Provincial Government Documents," 103.

74. Archer, "Acquisition of Canadian Provincial Documents," 55.

75. Archer, "Acquisition of Canadian Provincial Documents," 55.

76. Monty, "Canadian Government Information," 279; Catherine Pross, A Guide to the Identification, 30.

77. Smelts, official communication, 1–4.

78. Heidi Rees, email to Catherine McGoveran, December 9, 2015.

79. Rees, email to Catherine McGoveran, December 9, 2015.

80. Saskatchewan Legislative Library, Saskatchewan Legislative Library Annual Report, for the Period Ending March 31, 2011, 9.

81. Greg Salmers, email to Michelle Lake, June 23, 2016.

82. "What's New in Documents," 204.

83. Pross and Pross, Government Publishing in the Canadian Provinces, 151; Pross and Pross,"Canadian Provincial Government Publishing," 261.

84. MacDonald, "The Acquisition of Saskatchewan Government Publications," 4.

85. MacDonald, "The Acquisition of Saskatchewan Government Publications," 4.

86. Saskatchewan Legislative Library, Saskatchewan Legislative Library Annual Report, for the Period Ending March 31, 2011, 9.

87. Greg Salmers, email to Michelle Lake, June 23, 2016.

88. Salmers, email to Michelle Lake, June 23, 2016.

89. Saskatchewan Legislative Library, Saskatchewan Legislative Library Annual Report, for the Fiscal Year Ending March 31, 1987, 8.

90. For a more in-depth discussion of the Saskatchewan Legislative Library's history and development of legal deposit, library publication exchange agreements, and the transition from print to electronic publications deposit, see chapter 6.

91. For a more thorough discussion of Government of Alberta publishing, including the ADLP, see chapter 5.

92. Drake, "Federal and Provincial Depository Library System," 68; Gary Weber, email to Graeme Campbell, December 10, 2015.

93. Valerie Footz, email to Graeme Campbell, December 4, 2015.

94. Gary Weber, email to Graeme Campbell, December 3, 2015.

95. Drake, "Federal and Provincial Depository Library System," 68.

96. Alberta, Public Affairs Bureau, "Alberta Depository Library Program," 1–3.

97. Catherine Pross, *A Guide to the Identification*, 18.

98. Alberta, Service Alberta, "Depository Library Program," 2.

99. Drake, "Federal and Provincial Depository Library System," 68.

100. Alberta, Service Alberta, "Depository Library Program," 2.

101. Gary Weber, email to Graeme Campbelle, December 3, 2015.

102. Pross and Pross, *Government Publishing in the Canadian Provinces*, 54.

103. Marilyn Carr-Harris, email to Catherine McGoveran, November 12, 2015.

104. Van Haaften, *An Index to Selected Canadian Provincial Government Publications*, 18.

105. Archer, "Acquisition of Canadian Provincial Documents," 57.

106. British Columbia, Ministry of Municipal Affairs, *British Columbia Provincial Depository*.

107. Monty, "Canadian Government Information," 279; British Columbia, Ministry of Municipal Affairs, *British Columbia Provincial Depository*.

108. British Columbia, Ministry of Municipal Affairs, *British Columbia Provincial Depository*.

109. British Columbia, Ministry of Municipal Affairs, *British Columbia Provincial Depository*.

110. British Columbia, Ministry of Municipal Affairs, *British Columbia Provincial Depository*.

111. Van Haaften, *An Index to Selected Canadian Provincial Government Publications*, 78.

112. Peggy D'Orsay, email to Catherine McGoveran, November 26, 2015.

113. Aiken and Barnes, "Finding and Using Canadian Government Documents," 109.

114. Vera Raschke, email to Michelle Lake, August 22, 2016.

115. Jarvi, *Access to Canadian Government Publications*, 10.

116. Vera Raschke, email to Michelle Lake, August 22, 2016.

117. Raschke, email to Michelle Lake, August 22, 2016.

118. Catherine Pross, *A Guide to the Identification*, 43–44.

119. Raschke, email to Michelle Lake, August 22, 2016.

120. Raschke, email to Michelle Lake, August 22, 2016.

121. Raschke, email to Michelle Lake, August 22, 2016.

122. Raschke, email to Michelle Lake, August 22, 2016.

123. Northwest Territories, *Department of Information Fonds*.

124. Raschke, email to Michelle Lake, August 22, 2016.

125. Catherine Pross, *A Guide to the Identification*, 44; Aiken and Barnes, "Finding and Using Canadian Government Documents," 109; Bond and

Caron, eds., *Canadian Reference Sources / Ouvrages de référence Canadiens,* 121.

126. Raschke, email to Michelle Lake, August 22, 2016.
127. Raschke, email to Michelle Lake, August 22, 2016.
128. https://web.archive.org/web/20150416134540/http://www.assembly.gov.nt.ca/library/checklist.
129. Vera Raschke, email to Michelle Lake, August 22, 2016.
130. Yvonne Earle, email to Graeme Campbell, November 6, 2015.
131. Nilsen, "Canadian Government Electronic Information Policy," 204.
132. Brodie, "Authenticity, Preservation and Access," 229.
133. Gnassi, "Accessing Canadian Federal Information," 363.
134. Dickison, *Persistent Locators for Federal Government Publications,* 1.
135. Vaughan and Dolan, "Electronic Dissemination of Government Information"; Vaughan and Dolan, "Transition to Electronic Access."
136. Moon, "Survey of Canadian Academic Depository Libraries," 5.
137. Hubbertz, *Report on a Survey of CARL and APLIC Libraries*; Hubbertz, *An Action Plan for CARL*; Hubbertz, *Update 2007.*
138. Hubbertz, *Collection and Preservation.*
139. Hubbertz, *Collection and Preservation,* 3.
140. For more information about digital stewardship of Canadian federal government information, see chapter 2.
141. For more information about the CGI DPN, see chapter 10.
142. For a thorough overview of APLIC'S GALLOP portal, see chapter 9.
143. Joan Ritcey, email to Graeme Campbell, November 26, 2015.
144. Bibliothèques et Archives nationales du Québec, "Legal Deposit."
145. Hubbertz, *Update 2007,* 12.
146. Hubbertz, *Update 2007,* 10; Sylvia Kalluk, email to Graeme Campbell, March 7, 2016.
147. Yvonne Earle, email to Graeme Campbell, November 20, 2015.
148. See chapters 8–11.

Bibliography

Aiken, Linda, and Eleanor Barnes. "Panel—Brian Land, Lionel Levert, and John Noel: Finding and Using Canadian Government Documents; Federal and Provincial." *Canadian Association of Law Libraries Newsletter-Bulletin* 11 (1986): 105–30.

Alberta. Public Affairs Bureau. "Alberta Depository Library Program: Public Access to Government Publications through Alberta's Public Library System." Internal unpublished document, Government of Alberta, 1996.

———. Service Alberta. "Depository Library Program: Ensuring Public Access to Government Publications through Alberta's Library System." Internal unpublished document, Government of Alberta, 2014.

Archer, John H. "Acquisition of Canadian Provincial Documents." *Library Resources and Technical Services* 5, no. 1 (1961): 52–59.

Bennett, Sheliah. "Depository Library System Provides Access to Information." Last modified March 11, 1997. https://web.archive.org/web/20171008023958/ https://novascotia.ca/cmns/msrv/viewRel.asp?relID=/cmns/msrv/nr-1997/ nr97-03/97031101.htm.

Bibliothèques et Archives nationales du Québec. "Legal Deposit." Accessed March 24, 2016. https://web.archive.org/web/20180623172412/http://www.banq. qc.ca/services/depot_legal/.

Bond, Mary E., and Martine M. Caron, eds. *Canadian Reference Sources: An Annotated Bibliography / Ouvrages de référence Canadiens: Une Bibliographie annotée.* Vancouver: UBC Press, 1996.

Boyko, Ernie. "The Evolution of Census Dissemination in Canada." *DTTP* 32, no. 3 (2004): 23–28. https://journals.ala.org/index.php/dttp.

British Columbia. Ministry of Municipal Affairs. *British Columbia Provincial Depository Library Program Policy and Procedures Manual.* [Victoria]: Government of British Columbia, 2000.

Brodie, Nancy. "Authenticity, Preservation and Access in Digital Collections." *New Review of Academic Librarianship* 6 (2000): 225–38. https://doi. org/10.1080/13614530009516812.

Canada. Publishing and Depository Services Program. *Commemorative Weekly Checklist 13-49.* [Ottawa]: Public Works and Government Services Canada, 2013. http://publications.gc.ca/collections/collection_2014/tpsgc-pwgsc/P107-1-2013-49.pdf.

———. *Commemorative Weekly Checklist 13-50.* [Ottawa]: Public Works and Government Services Canada, 2013. http://publications.gc.ca/collections/ collection_2014/tpsgc-pwgsc/P107-1-2013-50.pdf.

———. *Commemorative Weekly Checklist 13-51.* [Ottawa]: Public Works and Government Services Canada, 2013. http://publications.gc.ca/collections/ collection_2014/tpsgc-pwgsc/P107-1-2013-51.pdf.

———. *Quick Reference Guide for Depository Libraries.* [Ottawa]: Public Works and Government Services Canada, 2010. http://publications.gc.ca/collections/ collection_2010/tpsgc-pwgsc/P109-6-2010-eng.pdf.

Canada Communication Group. *Partners in Access: Report of the Task Group on Depository Program Review.* [Hull, QC]: Canada Communication Group, Publishing, 1991.

"Canadian French Language Publishing." *Input* 4, no.1 (1983): 3.

Carpentier, Louise. "The Acquisition of the Publications of the Quebec Government." *Government Publications Review* 19, no. 3 (1992): 257–68. https:// doi.org/10.1016/0277-9390(92)90065-J.

———. "Quebec Government Publications in Microform and Other Non-print Formats: Past, Present and Future Years." *Microform Review* 19, no. 4 (1990): 174–80. https://doi.org/10.1515/mfir.1990.19.4.174.

Davies, Ron, and Tanis Chalk. "Form and Function: Publishing the Canadian Government 'Weekly Checklist' on the Internet." *Proceedings of the ASIS Meeting* 33 (1996): 24–29. https://web.archive.org/web/20180704104227/http://www.asis.org/annual-97/annual-96/ElectronicProceedings/DaviesChalk/davies-chalk.html.

Dickison, Meredith. *Persistent Locators for Federal Government Publications: Summary of a Study Conducted for the Depository Services Program and the National Library of Canada.* [Ottawa]: Library and Archives Canada, 2002. https://www.collectionscanada.gc.ca/obj/r4/f2/r4-500.1-e.pdf.

Dolan, Elizabeth. *The Depository Dilemma: A Study of the Free Distribution of Canadian Federal Government Publications to Depository Libraries in Canada.* Ottawa: Canadian Library Association, 1989.

Drake, Judith Anne. "Federal and Provincial Depository Library System for Government Publications in Canada." *Drexel Library Quarterly* 16, no. 4 (1980): 60–71.

Friskey, Janet. "Letter to Minister James Moore." *The Bibliographical Society of Canada: The Bulletin* 79 (2012): 10–13. https://web.archive.org/web/20180713145921/http://www.bsc-sbc.ca/wp/wp-content/uploads/2017/04/bull_12fall.pdf.

Gagnon, Jean-Pierre. Official communication. *Le Programme de Dépôt des Publications Gouvernementales.* [Quebec]: Direction des inforoutes et de l'information documentaire, 1997.

Gnassi, Bruno. "Accessing Canadian Federal Information: A Depository Program for the Twenty-First Century?" *Library Collections, Acquisitions, & Technical Services* 24, no. 3 (2000): 361–70. https://doi.org/10.1080/14649055.2000.10765687.

"Gosling Memorial Library." *Newfoundland & Labrador Public Libraries.* Accessed by the Internet Archive on June 14, 2000. https://web.archive.org/web/20000614145408/http:/www.publib.nf.ca/genealogy/50anngosling.html.

Hamilton, Elizabeth. "Democracy in an Electronic Depository World: Public Access to Government Information in a Canadian DSP Library." *DTTP* 32, no. 3 (2004): 28–31. https://journals.ala.org/index.php/dttp.

———. "Moving to Electronic in the Depository World."In *CARL Survey.* Ottawa: Canadian Association of Research Libraries, 2004.

Hubbertz, Andrew. *Collection and Preservation of Web-Based Provincial/Territorial Government Publications: An Action Plan for CARL.* Ottawa: CARL-ABRC, 2005.

———. *Collection and Preservation of Web-Based Provincial/Territorial Government Publications: Report on a Survey of CARL and APLIC Libraries.* Ottawa: CARL-ABRC, 2005.

———. *Update 2007: Collection and Preservation of Web-Based Provincial/Territorial Government Publications.* Ottawa: CARL-ABRC, 2007.

Jarvi, Edith T. *Access to Canadian Government Publications in Canadian Academic and Public Libraries*. Ottawa: Canadian Library Association, 1976.

———. "Tracing Canadian Provincial Government Publications." In *Proceedings of the Second Annual Government Documents Workshop*, edited by Michael Andrews, Elizabeth Dole, and Stephen Torok, 5–27. New York: Continuing Education Office of the State University of New York, 1975.

Johnston, Lindsay. "News from the North: E-Archiving in the Provinces; Alberta, Manitoba, and Ontario." *DTTP* 32, no. 2 (2004): 11–13. https://journals.ala.org/index.php/dttp.

———. "News from the North: Preservation of Born-Digital Government Publications in Canadian Jurisdictions." *DTTP* 33, no. 4 (2005): 13–15. https://journals.ala.org/index.php/dttp.

Luebbe, Mary. "1990 Survey of Canadian Government Documents Micropublishers." *Microform Review* 19, no. 4 (1990): 166–73.

———. "Canadian Government Documents in Microform: 1989 Update." *Microform Review* 18, no. 4 (1989): 192–98.

———. "Recent Developments in Canadian Government Documents." *Microform Review* 16, no. 4 (1987): 280–85.

———. "Update on Canadian Government Documents in Microform." *Microform Review* 17, no. 5 (1988): 254–59.

MacDonald, Christine. "The Acquisition of Saskatchewan Government Publications." *Agora* 6, no. 1 (1972): 4–6.

Monty, Vivienne. "Canadian Government Information: An Update." *Government Publications Review* 20, no. 3 (1993): 272–82. https://doi.org/10.1016/0277-9390(93)90003-8.

———. "Due North: Issues in Access to Government Information; A View from Canada." *Journal of Government Information* 23, no. 4 (1996): 491–97. https://doi.org/10.1016/1352-0237(96)00029-9.

———. "News from the North: Canada Is a Cold Place for Government Publications." *DTTP* 33, no. 2 (2005): 12–14. https://journals.ala.org/index.php/dttp.

Monty, Vivienne, and Depository Services Program (Canada). *Proposal for a Revised Model Depository System*. [Hull, QC]: Minister of Public Works and Government Services Canada, 1998.

Moon, Jeff. "Survey of Canadian Academic Depository Libraries Regarding Electronic Government Publications." Unpublished data. Queen's University, 2001.

Morton, Bruce, and Steven D. Zink. "The Dissemination and Accessibility of Canadian Government Information." *Government Publications Review* 19, no. 4 (1992): 385–96. https://doi.org/10.1016/0277-9390(92)90030-F.

———. "'We Are Here to Make Sure That Information Is Available, Accessible, and Cost-Effective': An Interview with Patricia Horner, Director of the

Canadian Government Publishing Centre." *Government Publications Review* 17, no. 5 (1990): 397–410. https://doi.org/10.1016/0277-9390(90)90049-J.

Murphy, Margaret. Official communication. *N.S. Government Publications—Depository Libraries*. [Nova Scotia]: Office of the Speaker, 1987.

National Library of Canada. *Legal Deposit: Preserving Canada's Published Heritage = Le dépôt légal: Pour conserver les publications du patrimoine canadien*. 2nd ed. Ottawa: National Library of Canada = Bibliothèque nationale du Canada, 1998.

Nielson, Paul. "How Quebec Does It Good." *Manitoba Library Association Bulletin* 13 (1983): 28–29.

Nilsen, Kirsti. "Canadian Government Electronic Information Policy." *Government Information Quarterly* 10, no. 2 (1993): 203–20.

Northwest Territories. *Department of Information Fonds*. NWT Archives. Retrieved from https://web.archive.org/web/20180713151709/http://www.nwtarchives.ca/fonds_display.asp?Fonds_Number=302.

Ontario. Management Board Secretariat. "Corporate Management Directives: Government Publications." Internal publication, Government of Ontario, 1997.

———. Ministry of Government Services. *Ontario Government Publications Annual Catalogue 1979*. [Toronto]: Queen's Printer for Ontario, 1980.

———. Publications Ontario. "Depository Libraries Online Ordering User Guide—Publications Ontario Website." Internal publication, Government of Ontario, 2015.

Presser, Carolynne. "Canadian Provincial and Municipal Documents: The Mystery Explained?" *Government Publications Review* 2, no. 1 (1975): 17–25.

Pross, A. Paul, and Catherine A. Pross. "Canadian Provincial Government Publishing: Recent Developments." *Government Publications Review* 1, no. 3 (1974): 257–68. https://doi.org/10.1016/0093-061X(74)90019-7.

———. *Government Publishing in the Canadian Provinces: A Prescriptive Study*. Toronto: University of Toronto Press, 1972.

Pross, Catherine. "Bibliographies of Provincial Government Documents." *APLA Bulletin* 32, no. 4 (1968): 100–04.

———. *A Guide to the Identification and Acquisition of Canadian Government Publications: Provinces and Territories*. Halifax, NS: Dalhousie Occasional Paper, 1983.

Saskatchewan Legislative Library. *Saskatchewan Legislative Library Annual Report, for the Fiscal Year Ending March 31, 1987*. Regina: Legislative Assembly of Saskatchewan, 1987.

———. *Saskatchewan Legislative Library Annual Report, for the Period Ending March 31, 2011*. Regina: Legislative Assembly of Saskatchewan, 2011. http://skdocs.legassembly.sk.ca/serial/69445/69445%20-%202010-2011.pdf.

Smelts, Dorryce. Official communication. Manitoba Legislative Library, 1990.

Somers, C.A. Official communication. *N.S. Government Publications—Depository Libraries*. [Nova Scotia]: Department of Education, 1987.

van Haaften, Jami. *An Index to Selected Canadian Provincial Government Publications*. 2nd ed. Roslin, ON: Jami van Haaften, 1992.

Vaughan, Liwen Qiu, and Elizabeth Dolan. "Electronic Dissemination of Government Information in Canada: Implications for Equitable Access." *Journal of Government Information* 25, no. 5 (1998): 439–52. https://doi.org/10.1016/S1352-0237(98)00031-8.

———. "Transition to Electronic Access of Government Information: Are the Depository Libraries Prepared?" *Canadian Journal of Information and Library Science* 23, no. 4 (1998): 62–88.

"What's New in Documents." *Government Publications Review* 5, no. 2 (1978): 198–206. https://doi.org/10.1016/0093-061X(78)90035-7.

2

LIBRARY AND ARCHIVES CANADA

Official Publications and Select Digital Library Collections, 1923–2017

Tom J. Smyth

On June 1, 2013, the Government of Canada (GC) transitioned to a digital-by-default model for all official publishing as required by the federal *Economic Action Plan 2013* [*Budget 2013*] and its related policy instrument, the Treasury Board of Canada Secretariat's (TBS's) *Procedures for Publishing*.[1] Considerable debate has since occurred within the media, the public, and the professional community of government documents reference librarians on the implications of this digital transition and on the state of both federal information management and the stewardship of Canadian official publications.[2] These issues, however, predate June 2013.

This chapter therefore seeks to critically examine the historical evolution and impact of the legislative, regulatory, and policy instruments that govern GC official publications, by tracking their historical development since 1923, when stewardship formally began. It will clarify the various authorities and their requirements, comment on their recent open government context, and elucidate the roles and responsibilities of the federal institutions involved in the management of GC official publications. A historical overview will be provided, with an emphasis on the stewardship of these resources in digital form since 1995.

Attention will be given to certain digital library special collections and to the acquisition and stewardship of the GC web presence under LAC's Web Archiving Program.[3]

MANDATE OF LIBRARY AND ARCHIVES CANADA

The *Library and Archives of Canada Act* (S.C. 2004, c. 11) [*LAC Act*] states that LAC functions as "the permanent repository of publications of the Government of Canada."[4] The official publications of the GC are captured in two other sections of the Act: under "Legal Deposit" (section 10, which requires all publishers to deposit copies of materials published in Canada with LAC), and under the "Powers of the Librarian and Archivist" (subsection "Sampling from Internet") (which empowers LAC to collect "a representative sample of the documentary material of interest to Canada that is accessible to the public without restriction through the Internet or any similar medium").[5]

▶ *Legal Deposit and the Legal Deposit of Publications Regulations*

The *LAC Act* provides a specific definition of what constitutes a publication for the purposes of the national library, which simultaneously defines what materials are subject to legal deposit:

> *publication* means any library matter that is made available in multiple copies or at multiple locations, whether without charge or otherwise, to the public generally or to qualifying members of the public by subscription or otherwise. Publications may be made available through any medium and may be in any form, including printed material, on-line items or recordings.[6]

The notion that all published materials documenting a society should be sent to a central government authority for the purposes of preservation and future access dates from at least the sixteenth century in Europe. As outlined in UNESCO's *Guidelines for Legal Deposit Legislation*, the statutory "development of a national deposit collection of published material" had its origins in the *Ordonnance de Montpellier* under François I of France in 1537.[7] The purpose of the *Ordonnance* was to

> mettre et assembler en notre librairie toutes les oeuvres dignes d'être vues qui ont été ou qui seront faites, compilées, amplifiées, corrigées et amendées de notre tems pour avoir recours aux dits livres, si de fortune ils étoient cy après perdus de la mémoire des hommes, ou aucunement immués, ou variés de leur vraye et première publication.[8]

> assemble and put in our library all works worthy of being seen that have been or will be made, compiled, augmented, corrected and amended in our time in order to have said books available if by chance they were lost from the memory of men, or were modified or varied from their first true publication.[9]

Since the goals and interests of future researchers can never be fully anticipated, legal deposit legislation facilitates the comprehensive collection of a nation's publications (as much as that is humanly possible) in order to respond to future demand for primary sources on potentially any subject, while supporting diverse modes of future research inquiry.

The National Library of Canada (now within the amalgamated Library and Archives Canada) was established by the *National Library Act, 1952* (R.S.C. 1985, c. N-12) and came into force on January 1, 1953.[10] This Act from its inception included the (legal) "deposit law," which also captured federal official publications.[11] The details of deposit law were originally outlined in the *National Library Book Deposit Regulations* (in force on February 1, 1953; last version SOR/95-1999)[12] and were superseded by the current *Legal Deposit of Publications Regulations* (SOR 2006-337) [*LD Regulations*] when the latter came into force on January 1, 2007.[13]

The LAC *Act* empowers the Minister of Heritage to create regulations to govern legal deposit under section 10(2); these *LD Regulations*, along with section 10 of the Act proper, define the conditions under which publications must be legally deposited with LAC. The regulations also define who constitutes a "publisher" for the purposes of the Act: "*publisher* means a person who makes a publication available in Canada that the person is authorized to reproduce or over which the person controls the content. It does not include a person who only distributes a publication."[14]

Legal deposit is the primary and legislated basis of LAC's authority to collect the official publications of the GC. Importantly, whereas LAC's archival authority applies only to those departments captured under the LAC *Act*'s definition of a "government institution,"[15] no such limitation exists for legal deposit: federal publishers are given no special distinction under the Act, and as such all federal organizations are theoretically subject to legal deposit for their publications.

▶ *Digital Publications, Editions, and File Formats*

LAC began collecting "e-publications from the Internet" on a voluntary basis when it began building a prototype system for managing digital publications in June 1994.[16] Although the *LD Regulations* did not formally capture digital publications until June 1, 2007,[17] federal resources were collected in digital format prior to 2007 where they were available (e.g., the Depository Service Program's weekly checklists of official publications,[18] and Royal Commissions and commissions of inquiry)[19] or where other, earlier policy authorities required federal publishers to submit their resources to LAC in digital form (e.g., federal Public Opinion Research as required by the *Communications Policy of the Government of Canada*).[20]

According to the LAC *Act*, 2004, "every version, edition or form of a publication shall be considered a distinct publication" and must be submitted to LAC on legal deposit.[21] Although this dimension of the legislation was closely observed for print publications in the past, in today's practice LAC collects modern digital file formats in alignment with its digital preservation and access goals and current policy instruments.[22]

The matter of the original mandate of what is now known as the Publishing and Depository Services Directorate (what many will colloquially think of as the Depository Services Program; hereinafter DSP) is an interesting one. Although an Order-in-Council in 1927 approved and established the details of the depository function,[23] discussion on the need to print, distribute, and keep "depository copies" of Canadian official publications began a little earlier.

In June 1923 the Minister of Labour submitted a report to the Committee of the Privy Council regarding a resolution of the Joint Committee of the Library of Parliament, which requested that the "Printing Bureau" deliver "not less than six copies of all official documents to the Library [of Parliament]"; the minister complained to the Privy Council that he should not have to pay the "considerable sum" for this "large number of documents" from his own budget, and so requested approval for the then King's Printer "to charge...the cost of copies...as may be delivered to the Parliamentary Library"—which was then approved.[24] In July 1927 the Secretary of State wrote to the Privy Council, outlining the "large increases in the sales of official publications" owing to the demand "beyond the confines of Canada from official and public institutions and persons entitled to consideration in such matters, for copies of such publications without charge."[25] The Order-in-Council goes on to state:

> Representations received by the Minister from heads of
> leading libraries in Canada are urgent in the view that
> present methods of contact between the Government and
> the libraries of Canada as to the matter of the distribution
> of official publications are not adequate to public necessi-
> ties and the request is made that leading libraries of Canada
> be made depositories of all official publications...Librarians
> are emphatic in the view that the adoption of such a system
> would tend to the avoidance of the delay and irritation fre-
> quently associated with the existing situation under which
> librarians are uninformed as to many official publications

and are uncertain how where and when particular publications may be procured."[26]

To address these issues, the minister drafted and submitted a regulation for approval by the Governor-in-Council, cited in full within the Order-in-Council, which defined precisely who was entitled to receive official publications of the Dominion of Canada without charge. The draft regulation section (2) also outlined the authority of the King's Printer "to print...a number of copies which shall be set aside to meet [official publication] demands...the precise number to be determined by the Minister on estimates furnished by the King's Printer."[27]

Overall, this new program had the goals of managing the budgeting, printing, and distribution of Canadian official publications in a "systematic and centralized manner...with a view to the prevention of duplication in the distribution of the documents concerned."[28] Order-in-Council P.C. 1471 in 1927 therefore established the original distributary function of the King's Printer with the legal force of a regulation under the Governor-in-Council, subsidiary to the then *Public Printing and Stationery Act*, 1906.[29] The group that was created to manage this distribution function has had several names and reporting relationships since 1927, but eventually became known as the Depository Services Program. The DSP's mandate, however, has changed several times in recent years in response to central direction and new policy instruments.

BUDGET 2013 AND THE TREASURY BOARD SECRETARIAT'S PROCEDURES FOR PUBLISHING

Within the pages of *Budget 2013* the government announced that it would transition to a digital-by-default publishing model as a cost-saving strategy:

PLAN TO RETURN TO BUDGET BALANCE AND FISCAL OUTLOOK

Economic Action Plan 2013 furthers the Government's commitment to control direct program spending with common sense proposals to make government more efficient and productive, including:...

▷ Modernizing the production and distribution of government publications by shifting to electronic publishing and making print publications the exception.[30]

To provide guidance to the GC on compliance with this direction, the Treasury Board Secretariat's procedures for publishing were developed and came into force on June 1, 2013.[31] The procedures require senior managers to ensure "that on-demand printing is carried out by default, rather than volume printing, using the most economical printing option and in black and white unless colour printing is deemed necessary."[32]

As a consequence of moving to this digital-by-default model, on March 7, 2014, the DSP ceased its operations related to the distributary activities that it had carried out since 1927; as of that date, it "no longer produces, prints, distributes or warehouses tangible publications such as printed books, DVDs or CDs, and videos, and no longer accepts tangible publications from departments and agencies for distribution to depository libraries,"[33] since, under the *Procedures for Publishing*, these should only be produced under exceptional circumstances.[34]

The *Procedures for Publishing* also introduced several new requirements, such as to inventory all departmental publications "including electronic, free and priced publications as well as co-publications"; and that this inventory should be forwarded "twice a year (November and April) to the [DSP] and the Digital Legal Deposit Unit at [LAC]";[35] it also reinforced the requirement to provide "electronic and tangible copies of all publications, in all available formats, editions and language versions to the Legal Deposit Unit" at LAC.[36]

ROLES AND RESPONSIBILITIES: LAC AND THE DEPOSITORY SERVICES PROGRAM

Modern roles and responsibilities are succinctly summarized in the TBS *Procedures for Publishing*, section 8. LAC is responsible for the following:

8.3.1. managing the Legal Deposit Program for the collection of Government of Canada publications in accordance with the Library and Archives of Canada Act;

8.3.2. acting as the permanent repository of publications of the Government of Canada and its departments;

8.3.3. ensuring a permanent record of Government of Canada publications through tools such as its national database of Canada's published heritage; and

8.3.4. issuing International Standard Serial Numbers (ISSN) to departments and issuing blocks of International Standard Book Numbers (ISBN) to the Publishing and Depository Services Directorate at Public Services and Procurement Canada.[37]

DSP's responsibilities include:

8.2.1. producing a weekly checklist of new publications in electronic or tangible format, and making it available to the depository library network and to the public until March 31, 2014;

8.2.2. producing an online report of new publications that is updated regularly, effective April 1, 2014;

8.2.3. cataloguing all submitted publications in the Government of Canada's central database;

8.2.4. issuing International Standard Book Numbers (ISBNS) and Government of Canada catalogue numbers to departments;

8.2.5. developing and maintaining an online collection of electronic publications on the Government of Canada Publications at publications.gc.ca website;

8.2.6. printing, distributing, warehousing and commercializing the Canada Gazette Part I, II, and III and print publications on behalf of departments until March 31, 2014.[38]

LAC is the International Standard Number authority for Canada.[39] As such, LAC delegates the assignment of ISBNS for official publications to the DSP; these are applied at the point of GC-publication acquisition by DSP, who simultaneously assigns GC cataloguing numbers. DSP then enters details of the publications it collects into the relevant weekly checklist and publishes the checklists via its publications.gc.ca website.[40] LAC assigns GC International Standard Serial Numbers (ISSNs) and acquires publications directly from departments on legal deposit and also via the DSP checklists; for the publications it has acquired from the checklists, LAC provides DSP with cataloguing records in MARC 21 format. All other bibliographic descriptions are created at DSP.

IMPACT OF GC COLLECTION METHODOLOGIES ON FINDING GC RESOURCES

The TBS *Procedures for Publishing* defines a "publication" as follows:

> *Publication* (publication): an information product with a long shelf-life produced by or on behalf of the Government of Canada in any medium or format, including electronic (e.g., EPUB or other portable formats), digital, print or recordings, that is made available to the public. Publications include products such as books, reports, booklets, brochures, periodicals, maps, charts, prints, audio recordings, films, videos, television programs, audiovisual and multimedia productions, guides and handbooks, online publications and serial publications. In the context of these procedures, publications do not include purely promotional or short-lived items, such as calendars, news releases, advertising, backgrounders, forms and presentation decks. Publications do not include HTML webpages.[41]

The definition of a publication within the TBS *Procedures for Publishing* differs with LAC's legislated definition under its Act;[42] the former should be understood as the scope of what is targeted and acquired at DSP.[43] The difference in roles and responsibilities between LAC and DSP is similarly elucidated by contrasting these two definitions: LAC targets and describes only official publications of the GC in accordance with its legislated definition, whereas DSP has a wider scope and collects publications in addition to GC grey literature and ephemera that may not be acquired by legal deposit at LAC (and, since description is tied to acquisition at LAC, such materials would not appear in AMICUS, LAC's online catalogue of published material).⁴⁴

Government documents reference practitioners should therefore note that these differences in collection development scope between the development policies of the two collections directly affect the resources that will be discoverable and accessible via LAC and the DSP respectively. Some materials are only discoverable via DSP (e.g., GC grey literature), and others are only discoverable at LAC (most prominently, publications in HTML and other formats for the Web, which are not collected at DSP). Moreover, because LAC continues to receive official publications from federal departments directly on legal deposit, it would be quite possible that a given publication would be discoverable and accessible at LAC but not at DSP (and vice versa, in the case that a department sent a publication to DSP and not to LAC). To complicate matters, if the publications of a department were posted on its corporate website but were never proactively transmitted to LAC or DSP, they might not be discoverable or accessible via the LAC Electronic Collection, AMICUS, or the DSP checklists. However, they may have been collected in the context of LAC's Web Archiving Program (which has collected the federal domain comprehensively but periodically since 2005); under this scenario, such publications might be discovered and accessed by consulting LAC's Government of Canada Web Archive (GCWA).⁴⁵

HISTORICAL OVERVIEW OF OFFICIAL PUBLICATIONS MANAGEMENT IN THE GC

The first *Daily Checklist of Government Publications* was published on December 1, 1952; this became the *Weekly Checklist of Canadian Government Publications* on November 17, 1978.⁴⁶ From 1953 to approximately 2012, these checklists were used as an important tool to locate and acquire GC official publications in print form, first at the National Library and then at the amalgamated Library and Archives Canada.

An examination of LAC's historical holdings in its Electronic Collection indicates that the first weekly checklist was published by DSP on the Internet on February 24, 1995 (*Weekly Checklist* 1995-08).[47] At this early period of the GC's utilization of the Web, the DSP electronic checklists were largely transcriptions of the print DSP catalogues into HTML, which outlined the official publications that were available in print; however, as early as the publication of the second weekly checklist via the Web, hyperlinks to HTML publications started to appear where they were published on the authoring department's servers—the very first being from Finance Canada (March 3, 1995, with *Weekly Checklist* 1995-09).[48]

DSP's website was launched in February 1995, and LAC started collecting the weekly checklists in this HTML format with *Weekly Checklist* 1995-30 (July 28, 1995).[49] As such, the original and earliest electronic lists (*Weekly Checklist* 1995-08 to *Weekly Checklist* 1995-29) were only available via the DSP's website of archived weekly checklists; however, each checklist from July 1995 to the present can be accessed via the LAC Electronic Collection.[50]

The chronological and historical development of official publications can be discerned by examining LAC's collection of DSP's checklists and bibliographic record structures over time.[51] A sampling of LAC's records in AMICUS from 1995 to 1997 indicates that early MARC 856 fields were populated with URLs to the HTML publications at the web domains of the federal departments that authored them; it appears that DSP then began hosting local copies of other department's HTML publications on or about the sixth checklist, in 1998 (*Weekly Checklist* 1998-06 on February 6, 1998).[52] To that point, DSP had only hosted its own HTML publications (i.e., those of the Queen's Printer).

DSP began segregating the lists into its "Full Checklist" and "an abbreviated list [that] includes only those items...which are available electronically over the Internet" from 1996.[53] GC official publications began to appear on the checklist in PDF on or about August 1997, with Finance Canada again being the early adopter (*Weekly Checklist* 1997-33 on August 15, 1997).[54] DSP began hosting PDF copies of the official publications of other departments, starting with the second checklist of

2000, the first checklist being that of Statistics Canada (*Weekly Checklist* 2000-02 on January 10, 2000).[55]

LAC began web archiving all DSP weekly checklists, on a weekly basis, with *Weekly Checklist* 2012-01, in January 2012; the transition to a web archiving work flow occurred to create efficiencies owing to the increasing scale of the checklists (in both length and data size), and to make the publications accessible at the individual title level.[56] The increasing scale of the DSP checklists could also be attributed, at least in part, to the emphasis placed on Open Government within the GC as of 2011.

OPEN GOVERNMENT

The Open Government Partnership was launched as a multilateral initiative in September 2011 and had the goal of assisting governments to become "sustainably more transparent, more accountable, and more responsive to their own citizens, with the ultimate goal of improving the quality of governance, as well as the quality of services that citizens receive."[57]

Canada officially "communicated its intent to join" with a letter from the then Minister of Foreign Affairs, the Honourable John Baird, in September 2011.[58] The then president of the Treasury Board, the Honourable Tony Clement, next presented *Canada's Action Plan on Open Government 2012–14* at the Open Government Partnership's annual meeting in April 2012.[59] This plan identified two foundational commitments: the development of an Open Government directive[60] and a related licence,[61] while grouping ten other commitments under three main categories: open dialogue, open information, and open data.[62]

Canada's Action Plan on Open Government 2014–16 was then produced, which specifically directed and required LAC to "increase Canadians' access to federal records by removing access restrictions on archived federal documents."[63] This expectation was then echoed by the *Directive on Open Government,* which came into force on October 9, 2014, and further defined LAC's early involvement in Open Government by requiring it to establish "criteria in order to make information resources transferred to its care and control available as soon as possible," and by "maximizing the removal of access restrictions on departmental information resources of enduring value [i.e., archival records] as part of planned disposition activities."[64] Put another way, LAC's involvement in Open Government, by central government direction, has primarily engaged LAC's archival responsibilities by requiring the department to expedite access to its federal archival holdings.

However, perhaps of primary interest to government information librarians is the notion of a central Government of Canada "virtual library." The need for a virtual library was identified within the "Open Information" subset of commitments as early as the *Action Plan on Open Government 2012–14*:

> *Virtual Library*: To simplify access to a range of government information available to the public in Year 1, we will begin the design of an online searchable repository of published Government of Canada documents of all kinds (e.g., publications, consultant reports, ATI summaries, government research, presentations, white papers, etc.). Moving forward in Years 2 and 3, we will launch this Virtual Library through a pilot which will provide public access to federal publications and documents via a single window. Public input will be sought throughout this pilot to make sure that the Virtual Library reflects the needs of citizens.[65]

A version of this "online searchable repository" is currently available via the Open Government website, within the "Open Information" subsection;[66] however, it appears that the Virtual Library has since been rebranded as the "Open Information Portal."[67] Descriptive text at the search page originally stated that the portal's content "consists of a consolidation of the electronic publications provided by Government of Canada Publications [i.e., DSP] and Library and Archives Canada [i.e., its Legal Deposit Electronic Collection]."[68] A visitor to the site now sees a different statement:

> As we launch this enhanced integrated Open Information Portal search, you may notice that there has been a reduction in the number of open information records. Please

note that you can still access the publications that no longer appear here by visiting: Government of Canada Publications and Library and Archives Canada.

The structure of its pages hints that the Open Information Portal may become a federated and faceted search for all the Open Government material at Canada.ca.[69]

SELECT SPECIAL DIGITAL LIBRARY COLLECTIONS AT LAC

The following section describes three special digital library collections managed at LAC that are particularly rich and could serve as versatile historical sources.

▶ *Canadian Federal Royal Commissions and Commissions of Inquiry*

Federal commissions in Canada are struck by an Order-in-Council under section I of the *Inquiries Act* (R.S.C. 1985, c. I-11) to carry out full and impartial investigations of specific national issues, or are struck under the authority of any of the approximately eighty-seven statutes that confer powers to conduct investigations into activities in federal departments, with or without reference to the *Inquiries Act*, section II.[70] As Caron Rollins' work in chapter 4 of this volume considers the commissions in detail, little will be said herein on their history.

In the words of the Privy Council Office (PCO), commissions are "led by distinguished individuals, experts or judges [and] have the power to subpoena witnesses, take evidence under oath and request documents...A Commission of Inquiry's findings and recommendations are not binding [on the government]. However, many have a significant impact on public opinion and the shape of public policy."[71] Commissions are therefore historical proceedings that capture and preserve detailed and nuanced perspectives on issues of public importance to contemporary Canadian society and government and so are an invaluable historical source for the study of Canada.[72]

The master collection of Canadian federal Royal Commissions and commissions of inquiry is managed at LAC in coordination with the Privy Council Office, the latter of which maintains an official and annotated list of historical commissions on its website.[73] Access to the published findings of historical commissions is provided via a specialized discovery portal at LAC, the *Index to Federal Royal Commissions*.[74]

At the time of writing, the collection includes 368 Canadian federal Royal Commissions or commissions of inquiry, more than 600 digitized and born-digital official publications deriving from the commissions,[75] and over 5,400 published titles dealing with the commissions and their study.[76]

▶ *Federal Public Opinion Research Collection*

The TBS *Directive on the Management of Communications* defines public opinion research (POR) in the federal government context as follows:

> The planned, one-way systematic collection, by or for the
> Government of Canada, of opinion-based information
> of any target audience using quantitative or qualitative
> methods and techniques such as surveys or focus groups...
> [POR] includes information collected from the public,
> including private individuals and representatives of busi-
> nesses or other entities. It involves activities such as the
> design and testing of collection methods and instruments,
> data collection, data entry, data coding, and primary data
> analysis.[77]

The older definition, in the *Communications Policy*, succinctly outlined the purpose of federal POR:

> Public opinion research helps the government to better
> understand Canadian society and to identify citizen needs
> and expectations. It is used to assess the public's response to
> proposals or to possible changes or initiatives; to assess the
> effectiveness of policies, programs and services; to measure

progress in service improvement; to evaluate the effectiveness of communication activities such as advertising; and to
plan and evaluate marketing initiatives, among other applications...In keeping with the principles of a non-partisan public
service, institutions may not issue contracts or expend public
funds for research on electoral voting intentions, or political
party preferences or party standings with the electorate.[78]

Federal POR can also assess public attitudes or general awareness of
Canadian historical or commemorative events (e.g., how well do Canadians know the history of the War of 1812?); it can gauge the perceived
value of federal services against the frequency with which those services
are accessed (e.g., how often do Canadians visit National Historic Sites
or Parks?), and/or determine public satisfaction with current or potential departmental directions (e.g., how should Canada Post modernize
its services?). Federal POR can be quite varied in subject matter and can
therefore serve as a robust source of primary (but anonymized) quali-
tative and quantitative research information and structured statistical
data on Canadian issues.

The key authorities for POR in the Government of Canada derive
from legislation. The *Financial Administration Act* (R.S.C. 1985, c. F-11)
requires all public opinion research[79] to be made available to the public
in the manner, and subject to the conditions, specified in the subsidiary
Public Opinion Research Contract Regulations (SOR/2007-134) [*POR Regulations*]. Following suit, the LAC *Act* requires departments, as defined
in section 2 of the *Financial Administration Act*,[80] to provide LAC with
written POR reports within six months of the completion of the POR
project's data collection.[81]

The current POR *Regulations* came into force on June 7, 2007, and
dictated what all final POR reports must contain; they also required that
the department produce, submit, and consent to the publication of narrative executive summaries describing the research via the LAC Public
Opinion Research website.[82] Under the TBS *Directive on the Management of Communications*, this now extends to publication of the full-
text of the final report in both official languages.[83] This requirement

originally derived from the since-rescinded *Communications Policy of the Government of Canada*,[84] which required LAC to establish the Public Opinion Research website in 2006—effectively converting the Public Opinion Research collection into one of LAC's oldest born-digital library special collections.[85]

At the time of writing, 1,914 born-digital final POR reports have been collected since the digital program launched in August 2006; some 5,181 final POR reports in print are also held within the national collections.[86]

▶ Web Archiving Program

Web archiving is practised internationally, largely by national and university libraries, for the purposes of capturing, preserving, and providing ongoing access to resources from the Web that constitute national documentary heritage or make important contributions to a given library's topical collections. Since access to resources via the Web is never guaranteed even day to day, planned and managed action is necessary to acquire such valuable information sources and to ensure their preservation, discovery, and accessibility for posterity and future research.

In the words of the International Internet Preservation Consortium (IIPC), web archiving is "the process of gathering up data that has been published on the World Wide Web, storing it, ensuring the data is preserved in an archive, and making the collected data available for future research."[87]

The IIPC was chartered in July 2003 with LAC as one of the twelve founding members dedicated to advancing web archiving as a discipline; providing advice to interested parties in the development of national enabling legislation or institutional policies and best practices for conducting web archiving; and addressing common technical challenges through collaborative development of web archiving standards, and open source software.[88] At the time of writing, the IIPC had fifty-two members,[89] which reflects the widespread recognition that the Web is already a primary source that must be stewarded to ensure the preservation of the "early period" of our collective digital histories.

As previously described, the LAC *Act*, 2004, empowers LAC to conduct discretionary web archiving "for the purpose of [digital] preservation";[90] the Act also indicates that Canadian web resources constitute digital publications that are also subject to legal deposit.[91] Under these authorities LAC's Web Archiving Program launched from within its Published Heritage Branch in December 2005.

The aim of LAC's Web Archiving Program is to proactively capture, preserve, and provide access to web content that constitutes documentary heritage, represents Canadian society, and reflects Canadian concerns, our history, and its evolution over time. To realize these goals and to address the challenges of preserving digital heritage from the Web, a robust methodology has been developed and refined since 2013, which currently involves domain crawls, the curation of thematic research collections, event-based harvesting, and the collection of web resources that augment other library and archival collections—and all of these activities have involved the collection of GC official publications.[92]

LAC's early operations concentrated on collecting the federal government's second-level domain (*.gc.ca, December 2005–06) and quickly expanded to include harvesting of the known federal web presence, including quasi-federal and "arms-length" organizations (2007, 2008, 2013–14,[93] and 2016–17). Thematic collection curation also began in 2006 to document, at the outset, Canadian federal elections, the Canadian experience at the Summer and Winter Olympic and Paralympic Games, and various national commemorative events. In 2013, LAC began consciously scoping and curating collections to enable their use as historical datasets for future computational and digital, humanities-oriented use.[94] The most recent thematic research collections focused on themes such as the centenary of the First World War, the Truth and Reconciliation Commission, the one hundred and fiftieth anniversary of Canadian Confederation ("Canada 150"), and collections on the PyeongChang 2018 Winter Olympic and Paralympic Games.[95]

In addition to second-level domain and large-scale thematic curation, LAC conducts "events-based" web archiving. Loosely defined, an *event* is a historical occurrence that has a direct impact on Canadians or creates intense debate among Canadians, thereby generating considerable web content that warrants collection for posterity and future research use. Examples include the Lac Mégantic rail disaster (July 6, 2013), the wildfires in Alberta and Saskatchewan with particular impact on Fort McMurray (May–July 2016), and the tragic bus accident that claimed the lives of sixteen players on the Humboldt Broncos junior hockey team.

LAC also conducts "preservation" or "rescue" archiving of Canadian resources that are at risk of immediate deletion and permanent loss. Prominent examples of preserved resources include the sites of the National Round Table on the Environment and the Economy, the Aboriginal Affairs and Northern Development Canada Aboriginal portal, and the National Council of Welfare.

In March 2016, LAC relaunched its Government of Canada Web Archive (GCWA, in the so-called blue template),[96] which contains all the data in the previous "red templated" version.[97] The new "blue" edition provides access to LAC's federal web archival holdings that were collected from December 2005 to December 2015, with newer holdings being added over time.[98]

TBS WEB RENEWAL INITIATIVE

Since 2013, LAC has worked closely with the Treasury Board of Canada Secretariat to support its Web Renewal Initiative; this initiative sought to consolidate and migrate the most critical web resources to a primary access portal, Canada.ca.[99] In accordance with its mandate, LAC conducted one second-level domain harvest of *.gc.ca in 2013–15, and collected most of the GC resources several times each in 2016–17, in order to preserve the GC web presence in its pre-migration state. LAC began this process in 2013 in order to maximize the amount of web content that it could archive in advance of the requirement to reduce "redundant, outdated, and trivial" content prior to migration.[100] LAC will eventually provide permanent access to its complete collection of federal holdings within the Government of Canada Web Archive,[101] thereby enhancing transparency and providing pre-migration (*.gc.ca) and post-migration (Canada.ca) web archival copies of the GC web for research and consultation.

LAC's plans for the near future involve deploying a robust full-text search engine for the "blue" GCWA to facilitate discovery and access to GC resources (which will enable retrieval of individual official publications), and it will also work toward arranging and providing access to its approximately 10.5 terabytes of non-federal web archival holdings. :

LOOKING AHEAD

Researchers already consider information published on the Web to be a primary source for the history of the twenty-first century, as it now records "the sorts of interactions that would rarely, if ever, have been recorded by previous generations."[102] Thus, as the Web evolves and becomes an increasingly valuable medium for expressing Canadian culture and for transparently providing federal information to Canadian citizens, LAC will evolve to capture and steward digital documentary heritage, federal and non-federal, to insure information continuity, discovery, and access for our future generations.

Notes

1. Government of Canada. *Jobs Growth and Long-Term Prosperity: Economic Action Plan 2013*; Treasury Board of Canada Secretariat, *Procedures for Publishing*.
2. See for example Kingston, "Vanishing Canada"; Creighton, "Erasing History"; and Ahmed-Ullah, "Harvesting the Government Web Space" for the experience at the University of Toronto.
3. In so doing, this chapter reflects the opinions of the author and not those of the author's employers.
4. *Library and Archives of Canada Act*, 2004, s. 7(c).
5. *Library and Archives of Canada Act*, 2004, s. 8(2).
6. *Library and Archives of Canada Act*, 2004, s. 2.
7. Larivière, UNESCO *Guidelines for Legal Deposit Legislation*, 6.
8. Larivière, UNESCO *Guidelines for Legal Deposit Legislation*, 6.
9. My translation.
10. Lunn, "The National Library of Canada, 1950–1968," 87.
11. Lunn, "The National Library of Canada, 1950–1968," 87.
12. *National Library Book Deposit Regulations*, 1953.
13. *Legal Deposit of Publications Regulations* (SOR/2006-337).
14. *Legal Deposit of Publications Regulations* (SOR/2006-337), s. 1.
15. *Library and Archives of Canada Act* (S.C. 2004, c. 11), s. 2, i.e., the same definition as the *Privacy Act* (R.S.C. 1985, c. P-21) and the *Access to Information Act* (R.S.C. 1985, c. A-1), the latter of which is clearer in referring to the schedules of the *Financial Administration Act*.
16. National Library of Canada, *Electronic Publications Pilot Project (EPPP): Final Report*, 5.
17. *Legal Deposit of Publications Regulations* (SOR/2006-337), s. 2.
18. Public Services and Procurement Canada, *Government of Canada Publications*.
19. Library and Archives Canada, *Index to Federal Royal Commissions*.
20. Treasury Board of Canada Secretariat, *Communications Policy of the Government of Canada*.
21. *Legal Deposit of Publications Regulations* (SOR/2006-337), s. 10(4).
22. That is, obsolete digital file formats are not collected if that can be avoided. See LAC's *Guidelines on File Formats for Transferring Information Resources of Enduring Value*, which encompasses publications, and amounts to a local digital-format registry in digital preservation contexts.
23. Order-in-Council P.C. 1471, 1927 (archival copy held in the Privy Council Office fonds at LAC, PCO vol. 1408).
24. Order-in-Council P.C. 1182, 1923 (archival copy held in the Privy Council Office fonds at LAC, PCO vol. 1408).

25. Order-in-Council P.C. 1471, 1927 (archival copy held in the Privy Council Office fonds at LAC, PCO vol. 1408).

26. Order-in-Council P.C. 1471, 1927 (archival copy held in the Privy Council Office fonds at LAC, PCO vol. 1408).

27. Order-in-Council P.C. 1471, 1927 (archival copy held in the Privy Council Office fonds at LAC, PCO vol. 1408). The archival copy of the Order-in-Council held at LAC has in pen on the last page: "Approved. Willingdon" (Freeman Freeman-Thomas, the 1st Marquess of Willingdon, 56th Governor General of Canada).

28. Order-in-Council P.C. 1471, 1927 (archival copy held in the Privy Council Office fonds at LAC, PCO vol. 1408). Interestingly, the "Dominion Archivist" is named in section 1 of the Order-in-Council as being a recipient of the cost-free publications, prior to the establishment of a national library or of legal deposit legislation. This was something of a precursor of Canadian legal deposit for official publications before it was enacted.

29. Repealed in 1969 by the *Government Organization Act*.

30. Government of Canada, *Jobs Growth and Long-Term Prosperity: Economic Action Plan 2013*, 257. The DSP's website points out that this transition was alluded to (but was not enacted) as early as *Budget 2012*.

31. Treasury Board of Canada Secretariat, *Procedures for Publishing*.

32. Treasury Board of Canada Secretariat, *Procedures for Publishing*, section 6.1.

33. Public Works and Government Services Canada, *Government of Canada Publications*.

34. See Treasury Board of Canada Secretariat, *Procedures for Publishing*, section 6.3.3.

35. Treasury Board of Canada Secretariat, *Procedures for Publishing*, section 6.4.

36. Treasury Board of Canada Secretariat, *Procedures for Publishing*, section 6.4, which is simply repeating the legislated requirements with respect to publications under the LAC *Act*, 2004, and the *LD Regulations*, 2006.

37. Treasury Board of Canada Secretariat, *Procedures for Publishing*, section 8.3.

38. Treasury Board of Canada Secretariat, *Procedures for Publishing*, section 8.2.

39. LAC is the Canadian authority for International Standard Book Numbers (IBSNs), the Music Numbers (ISMNs), and Serial Numbers (ISSNs). Note that Bibliothèque et Archives nationales du Québec is the Canadian authority for ISBNs in French. International ISBN Agency, April 26, 2016; International ISMN Agency, May 28, 2016; International Standard Serial Number (ISSN) International Centre, June 28, 2016.

40. Public Services and Procurement Canada, *Government of Canada Publications*.

41. Treasury Board of Canada Secretariat, *Procedures for Publishing*, appendix "Definitions." Note that some of these documents are also defined within *Procedures for Publishing* as "communications products" and are the sort

of ephemera that are collected only upon "a written request from the Librarian and Archivist" under *LD Regulations, 2006*, s. 4 (i.e., the publisher of publications falling into the genres listed in section 4 is exempt from proactively depositing them with LAC).

42. See LAC *Act*, 2004, s. 2.

43. That is, the difference between a document created within the federal government that should be made available in accordance with Open Government principles versus the legislated definition of official publications as concerns LAC.

44. Library and Archives Canada, *Web Services for AMICUS*.

45. Library and Archives Canada, *Government of Canada Web Archive* ("Blue" GCWA). In this way, web archiving helps to prevent GC official publications and documents from becoming "fugitive" (an issue in GC information management as discussed by Susan Paterson in chapter 11 on fugitive publications).

46. Canada Communications Group Publishing, "Did You Know?" *What's Up Doc?: Newsletter of the Depository Program*, 1.

47. Library and Archives Canada, *Electronic Collection*. Also Public Services and Procurement Canada, *Government of Canada Publications*, "About" section.

48. Library and Archives Canada, *Electronic Collection*.

49. Library and Archives Canada, *Electronic Collection*. Also Public Services and Procurement Canada, *Government of Canada Publications*, "About" section.

50. Library and Archives Canada, *Electronic Collection*.

51. LAC's *Electronic Collection* contains the DSP checklists in their original HTML and publication context, whereas the checklists at publications. gc.ca have all been updated and migrated to the so-called GC blue template (the template created to promote compliance with the World Wide Web Consortium's [W3C's] *Web Content Accessibility Guidelines 2.0 [WCAG]*, which ensures accessibility to web resources for persons with disabilities). See Public Services and Procurement Canada, *Government of Canada Publications*.

52. Such dates are based on database reports of the DSP checklist collection within the Electronic Collection at LAC. This is also reflected by the DSP's early URL structure: http://dsp-psd.communication.gc.ca/ Pilot/<departmental-publication-name>.

53. Public Services and Procurement Canada, *Government of Canada Publications*.

54. Library and Archives Canada, *Electronic Collection*. The portable-document format (PDF) was developed by Adobe Systems Inc. in 1993 (Adobe Systems Inc., *PDF Reference and Adobe Extensions to the PDF Specification*). Note that there are publications in the DSP checklists at publications.gc.ca that predate 1993 but are in PDF; these are therefore migrated (or digitized)

copies of historical publications. For this reason, the original details of GC publications have been discerned from the original DSP checklists as preserved in the LAC Electronic Collection.

55. Library and Archives Canada, *Electronic Collection*.
56. By the recollection of the author and even by the end of the 2011 calendar year, the DSP weekly checklists were easily surpassing about fifty printed pages and several gigabytes in data size.
57. Open Government Partnership, "Canada."
58. Open Government Partnership, "Canada."
59. Government of Canada, *Canada's Action Plan on Open Government 2012–14*.
60. Treasury Board of Canada Secretariat, *Directive on Open Government*.
61. Government of Canada, *Open Government Licence—Canada*.
62. Government of Canada, *Canada's Action Plan on Open Government 2012–14*.
63. Government of Canada, *Canada's Action Plan on Open Government 2014–16*.
64. Treasury Board of Canada Secretariat, *Directive on Open Government*, sections 9.3 and 6.5, respectively.
65. Government of Canada, *Canada's Action Plan on Open Government 2012–14*.
66. Government of Canada, *Open Information*. The top right-hand corner has a search field with the text "Search through our Open Information Portal."
67. Government of Canada, *Open Information*. Running a search in the search field used to redirect to an address that had *vl* in the URL, presumably for "virtual library," although this has since disappeared: http://open.canada.ca/vl/en/doc?q=XYZ.
68. Government of Canada, *Open Information*.
69. Open Data has by far the most hits at 7,133, but there are only twenty-five "publications" listed at the time of writing.
70. Library and Archives Canada, *Index to Federal Royal Commissions*; *The Canadian Encyclopedia*, s.v. "Royal Commissions."
71. Privy Council Office, "About Commissions of Inquiry," *Commissions of Inquiry*.
72. See also *The Canadian Encyclopedia*, s.v. "Royal Commissions" (Paul Fox), which outlines a few other opinions.
73. Privy Council Office, *Commissions of Inquiry*.
74. Library and Archives Canada, *Index to Federal Royal Commissions*. Federal commissions and commissions of inquiry could also be discovered via the LAC Electronic Collection or via AMICUS.
75. Primarily draft, interim, and final reports, findings, recommendations; consultative documents; settlements; and memoranda.
76. Database report of LAC's collections conducted by the author, which matches the count at the Privy Council Office website. As *The Canadian Encyclopedia* hints, the exact number of commissions is difficult to determine: "Since Confederation there have been close to 450 [!] federal

commissions of inquiry with and without the royal title, more than 1,500 departmental investigations, and an undetermined number of task forces" (*The Canadian Encyclopedia,* s.v. "Royal Commissions").

77. Treasury Board of Canada Secretariat, appendix A, "Definitions," in *Directive on the Management of Communications.*

78. Treasury Board of Canada Secretariat, *Communications Policy of the Government of Canada,* section 8.

79. *Financial Administration Act* (R.S.C. 1985, c. F-11) ss. 40(2) and 42(3).

80. That is, any federal organization listed in the *Financial Administration Act,* schedules I and I.1; any commission under the *Inquiries Act* that is designated by order of the Governor-in-Council as a department; the staff of the Senate, House of Commons, Library of Parliament, Office of the Senate Ethics Officer, Office of the Conflict of Interest and Ethics Commissioner, and Parliamentary Protective Service; and/or any departmental corporation, i.e., those listed in the *Financial Administration Act,* schedule II.

81. *Library and Archives Canada Act,* 2004, s. 15.1.

82. *Public Opinion Research Regulations,* ss. 2, 3, and 4(b).

83. Treasury Board of Canada Secretariat, *Directive on the Management of Communications,* section 8.3.1 and appendix C, "Mandatory Procedures for Public Opinion Research," section C.2.11.

84. The TBS *Directive on the Management of Communications,* "Appendix C, Mandatory Procedures for Public Opinion Research," took effect on May 11, 2016, and superseded the *Communications Policy of the Government of Canada* and the TBS *Procedures for the Management of Public Opinion Research,* which to that point were the two main TBS policy instruments on public opinion research in the Government of Canada.

85. Treasury Board of Canada Secretariat, *Communications Policy of the Government of Canada,* section 8(d); Library and Archives Canada, *Public Opinion Research Reports* (website).

86. Database report of LAC's collections conducted by the author; August 2006 requirement as per the *Communications Policy of the Government of Canada.* The majority of the final POR reports in print predate the 2006 requirement to produce them in digital form for publication at LAC.

87. International Internet Preservation Consortium (IIPC), "About IIPC."

88. See also the renewed charter for the most recent take on IIPC's mandate and goals. International Internet Preservation Consortium, *Consortium Agreement of the International Internet Preservation Consortium (IIPC),* 2016–2020.

89. International Internet Preservation Consortium, *Member Archives.*

90. *Library and Archives Canada Act,* 2004, s. 8(2).

91. As per the LAC *Act,* 2004, s. 2, under its definition of a *publication* that specifically captures "publications...made available through any medium

[or] any form, including...on-line items." This is also outlined in the Act, s. 10(2)(b), and the corresponding area of the *Legal Deposit of Publications Regulations* (SOR/2006-337), s. 2, "Deposit of Non-paper Publications."

92. It is well understood that even this approach is a stopgap and preserves only targeted portions of the Web that we are confident we can preserve, where the capacity does not yet exist to do what would be ideal: comprehensive country-code, top-level domain crawls (of *.ca). It is also well understood that curated collections, with all their methodological bias and sense making, could be "contaminating" the resulting digital humanities dataset by forcing future researchers to work within its production constraints. Some small attempts have been and are being made to compensate (see footnote 94).

93. Government information reference practitioners have noted the gap in LAC's Government of Canada Web Archive from 2008 to 2012. This gap can be spanned by consulting the Internet Archive and supplementing with the archives of the Canadian Government Information Digital Preservation Network (CGI DPN) and the collections of the universities of Toronto and Alberta held at the Internet Archive / Archive-It. The Web Archives for Longitudinal Knowledge (WALK) project, "spearheaded by the University of Waterloo, York University, and the University of Alberta, [plans] to bring together interested Canadian partners to provide access to their [web archival] collections" in a single location for research purposes, so it may also become an important source in the near future.

94. Textual and data mining were LAC's first perceived computational uses for web archives as data (c. 2009), leading to the expenditure of great efforts ever since to try to capture a broad spectrum of resource types, perspectives, and political opinion, and subject matter relevant to any given thematic collection. This was undertaken to ensure that the same dataset would be of interest to diverse researchers with diverse interests.

95. In July 2017 my team launched the LAC Truth and Reconciliation (TRC) web archive, which is now publicly available. LAC's collection is a part of the greater web archive curated in collaboration with our partners, the National Centre for Truth and Reconciliation (http://nctr.ca/archives-pages.php) and the libraries of the universities of Winnipeg and Manitoba. The LAC TRC web archive contains over four hundred carefully selected and described resources. For a narrative of the experience of curating the archive, please see the LAC Discover Blog article by Russell White.

96. Library and Archives Canada, *Government of Canada Web Archive* ("Blue" GCWA).

97. Library and Archives Canada, *Government of Canada Web Archive* ("Red" GCWA).

98. Library and Archives Canada, *Government of Canada Web Archive* ("Blue" GCWA).
99. Treasury Board of Canada Secretariat, *Web Renewal Initiative: Streamlining the Government of Canada Web Presence.* There appear to be no other public documents dating after 2013 on this initiative.
100. Treasury Board of Canada Secretariat, *Reduce Redundant, Outdated and Trivial Content.* The TBS *Standard on Web Accessibility* in its appendix C makes perhaps the clearest statement on the context of redundant, outdated, and trivial content; in section 3.1, it also states: "To meet the [GC] commitment to Web accessibility, the [GC] has adopted the WCAG 2.0. The WCAG 2.0 states: 'Following these guidelines will make content accessible to a wider range of people with disabilities, including blindness and low vision, deafness and hearing loss, learning disabilities, cognitive limitations, limited movement, speech disabilities, photosensitivity and combinations of these.'" See also the Jodhan decisions: *Jodhan v. Canada (Attorney General)*, 2008 FC 781; *Jodhan v. Canada (Attorney General)*, 2010 FC 1197; *Canada (Attorney General) v. Jodhan*, 2012 FCA 161.
101. Library and Archives Canada, *Government of Canada Web Archive* ("Blue" GCWA).
102. Ruest and Milligan, "An Open-Source Strategy for Documenting Events"; Milligan, Ruest, et al.; "Web Archives for Longitudinal Knowledge (WALK) Project."

Bibliography

STATUTES

Access to Information Act (R.S.C., 1985, c. A-1). http://laws-lois.justice.gc.ca/eng/acts/A-1/.

Financial Administration Act (R.S.C. 1985, c. F-11). http://laws-lois.justice.gc.ca/eng/acts/f-11/.

Inquiries Act (R.S.C. 1985, c. I-11). http://laws-lois.justice.gc.ca/eng/acts/i-11/.

Legal Deposit of Publications Regulations (SOR/2006-337). http://laws-lois.justice.gc.ca/eng/regulations/SOR-2006-337/index.html.

Library and Archives of Canada Act (S.C. 2004, c. 11). http://laws-lois.justice.gc.ca/eng/acts/l-7.7/.

National Library Book Deposit Regulations (SOR/95-1999). http://laws-lois.justice.gc.ca/eng/regulations/sor-95-199/20060322/P1TT3xt3.html.

Privacy Act (R.S.C. 1985, c. P-21). http://laws-lois.justice.gc.ca/eng/acts/P-21/.

Public Opinion Research Contract Regulations (SOR/2007-134). http://laws-lois.justice.gc.ca/eng/regulations/SOR-2007-134/.

Canada Communications Group Publishing. "Did You Know?" *What's Up Doc? Newsletter of the Depository Program*, no. 6, June (1992): 1.

Federal Court (of Canada). *Jodhan v. Canada (Attorney General)*, 2008 FC 781. June 20, 2008. http://decisions.fct-cf.gc.ca/fc-cf/decisions/en/item/55566/index.do?r=AAAAAQAGam9kaGFuAQ.

———. *Jodhan v. Canada (Attorney General)*, 2010 FC 1197. November 29, 2010. http://decisions.fct-cf.gc.ca/fc-cf/decisions/en/item/58711/index.do?r=AAAAAQAGam9kaGFuAQ.

Federal Court of Appeal. *Canada (Attorney General) v. Jodhan*, 2012 FCA 161. May 30, 2012. http://decisions.fca-caf.gc.ca/fca-caf/decisions/en/item/37507/index.do?r=AAAAAQAGam9kaGFuAQ.

Government of Canada. *Canada's Action Plan on Open Government, 2012–14*. Modified July 3, 2015. Accessed August 8, 2016. http://open.canada.ca/en/canadas-action-plan-open-government.

———. *Canada's Action Plan on Open Government, 2014–16*. Modified August 8, 2016. Accessed August 8, 2016. http://open.canada.ca/en/content/canadas-action-plan-open-government-2014-16.

———. *Jobs Growth and Long-Term Prosperity: Economic Action Plan, 2012* [*Budget 2012*]. March 28, 2012. http://www.budget.gc.ca/2012/plan/pdf/Plan2012-eng.pdf.

———. *Jobs Growth and Long-Term Prosperity: Economic Action Plan, 2013* [*Budget 2013*]. March 21, 2013. http://www.budget.gc.ca/2013/doc/plan/budget2013-eng.pdf.

———. *Open Government Licence—Canada*. Modified March 11, 2015. Accessed August 8, 2016. http://open.canada.ca/en/open-government-licence-canada.

———. *Open Information*. Modified August 8, 2016. Accessed August 8, 2016. http://open.canada.ca/en/open-information.

———. *Procedures for the Management of Public Opinion Research*. Modified September 23, 2014. Accessed August 8, 2016. https://www.tbs-sct.gc.ca/pol/doc-eng.aspx?id=28033.

Library and Archives Canada. DSP *Weekly Checklists in* HTML. Accessed August 8, 2016. http://epe.lac-bac.gc.ca/100/201/301/weekly_checklist/.

———. *Electronic Collection: A Collection of Digital Books and Journals*. Modified July 3, 2012. Accessed August 8, 2016. https://www.collectionscanada.gc.ca/electroniccollection/index-e.html.

———. *Guidelines on File Formats for Transferring Information Resources of Enduring Value*. Modified February 6, 2015. Accessed August 8, 2016. http://www.bac-lac.gc.ca/eng/services/government-information-resources/guidelines/Pages/guidelines-file-formats-transferring-information-resources-enduring-value.aspx.

———. *Government of Canada Web Archive* ("Blue" GCWA). Modified April 22, 2016. Accessed August 8, 2016. http://www.bac-lac.gc.ca/eng/discover/archives-web-government/Pages/web-archives.aspx.

———. *Government of Canada Web Archive* ("Red" GCWA). Modified October 17, 2007. Accessed August 8, 2016. http://www.collectionscanada.gc.ca/webarchives/index-e.html

———. *Index to Federal Royal Commissions.* Modified April 23, 2014. Accessed August 8, 2016. http://www.bac-lac.gc.ca/eng/discover/royal-commissions-index/pages/index-federal-royal-commissions.aspx.

———. *Legal Deposit.* Modified March 7, 2016. Accessed August 8, 2016. http://www.bac-lac.gc.ca/eng/services/legal-deposit/pages/legal-deposit.aspx.

———. *Library and Archives Canada's Truth and Reconciliation Commission Web Archive.* Posted July 20, 2017. Accessed June 15, 2018. https://www.bac-lac.gc.ca/eng/discover/aboriginal-heritage/Pages/truth-reconciliation-commission-web-archive.aspx.

———. *Public Opinion Research Reports.* Modified January 6, 2009. Accessed August 8, 2016. http://porr-rrop.gc.ca/index-e.html.

———. *Web Services for AMICUS.* Modified March 12, 2008. Accessed August 8, 2016. https://www.collectionscanada.gc.ca/amicus/index-e.html.

Library and Archives Canada Blog, and Russell White. "Web Archiving the Truth and Reconciliation Commission." Posted on September 22, 2017. Accessed June 15, 2018. https://thediscoverblog.com/2017/09/22/web-archiving-the-truth-and-reconciliation-commission/.

National Library of Canada. *Electronic Publications Pilot Project (EPPP): Final Report.* 1996.

———. *Legal Deposit: Preserving Canada's Published Heritage.* 1999.

Privy Council Office. *Commissions of Inquiry.* Modified July 30, 2015. Accessed August 8, 2016. http://www.pco-bcp.gc.ca/index.asp?lang=eng&page=information&sub=commissions.

———. *Order-in-Council P.C. 1187.* 1923. Archival copy held at LAC, PCO vol. 1408.

———. *Order-in-Council P.C. 1471.* 1927. Archival copy held at LAC, PCO vol. 1408.

Public Services and Procurement Canada. *Government of Canada Publications.* Modified August 2, 2016. Accessed August 8, 2016. http://publications.gc.ca/site/eng/home.html.

Treasury Board of Canada Secretariat. *Communications Policy of the Government of Canada.* Modified September 23, 2014. Accessed August 8, 2016. https://www.tbs-sct.gc.ca/pol/doc-eng.aspx?id=12316.

———. *Directive on Open Government.* Modified October 9, 2014. Accessed August 8, 2016. https://www.tbs-sct.gc.ca/pol/doc-eng.aspx?id=28108.

———. *Directive on the Management of Communications.* Modified May 12, 2016. Accessed August 8, 2016. https://www.tbs-sct.gc.ca/pol/doc-eng.aspx?id=30682.

———. *Procedures for Publishing*. Modified May 11, 2016. Accessed August 8, 2016. http://www.tbs-sct.gc.ca/pol/doc-eng.aspx?id=27167.

———. *Reduce Redundant, Outdated and Trivial Content*. Modified January 25, 2012. Accessed August 8, 2016. https://tbs-sct.gc.ca/ws-nw/wu-fe/rot-rid/index-eng.asp.

———. *Standard on Web Accessibility*. Modified August 1, 2011. Accessed August 8, 2016. http://www.tbs-sct.gc.ca/pol/doc-eng.aspx?id=23601.

———. *Web Renewal Initiative: Streamlining the Government of Canada Web Presence*. Modified December 13, 2013. Accessed August 8, 2016. http://tbs-sct.gc.ca/wr-rw/index-eng.asp.

OTHER WORKS

Adobe Systems Inc. PDF *Reference and Adobe Extensions to the PDF Specification*. 2016. Accessed August 8, 2016. https://www.adobe.com/devnet/pdf/pdf_reference.html.

Ahmed-Ullah, Noreen. "Harvesting the Government Web Space: U of T Librarians Step In to Preserve Electronic Information." *University of Toronto News*, March 1, 2016. Accessed August 8, 2016. https://www.utoronto.ca/news/harvesting-government-web-space.

The Canadian Encyclopedia. "Royal Commissions." Modified December 16, 2013. Accessed August 8, 2016. http://www.thecanadianencyclopedia.ca/en/article/royal-commissions/.

Canadian Government Information—Digital Preservation Network (CGI-DPN). "PLNWIKI: CGI Network." June 21, 2016. Accessed August 8, 2016. https://plnwiki.lockss.org/index.php?title=CGI_network.

Creighton, Phyllis. "Erasing History." *Our Right to Know*, October 7, 2015. Accessed August 8, 2016. http://ourrighttoknow.ca/erasing-history/.

International Internet Preservation Consortium. "About IIPC." Accessed August 8, 2016. http://netpreserve.org/about-us.

———. *Consortium Agreement of the International Internet Preservation Consortium (IIPC), 2016–2020*. Accessed August 8, 2016. http://netpreserve.org/sites/default/files/attachments/IIPC-Consortium-Agreement-2016-2020-final.pdf.

———. *Member Archives*. Accessed August 8, 2016. http://netpreserve.org/resources/member-archives.

International ISBN Agency. *International ISBN Agency*. Modified April 26, 2016. Accessed August 8, 2016. https://www.isbn-international.org/.

International ISMN Agency. *The International ISMN Agency*. Modified May 18, 2016. Accessed August 8, 2016. http://www.ismn-international.org/.

International Standard Serial Number (ISSN) International Centre. *International Standard Serial Number (ISSN) International Centre*. Modified June 28, 2016. Accessed August 8, 2016. http://www.issn.org/.

Internet Archive. "Wayback Machine." Accessed August 8, 2016. https://archive.org/.

Kingston, Anne. "Vanishing Canada: Why We're All Losers in Ottawa's War on Data." *Maclean's*, September 18, 2015. Accessed August 8, 2016. http://www.macleans.ca/news/canada/vanishing-canada-why-were-all-losers-in-ottawas-war-on-data/.

Larivière, Jules. UNESCO *Guidelines for Legal Deposit Legislation*. Paris: UNESCO, 2000. Accessed August 8, 2016. http://www.ifla.org/files/assets/national-libraries/publications/guidelines-for-legal-deposit-legislation-en.pdf.

Lunn, Jean. "The National Library of Canada, 1950–1968." *Archivaria* 15 (Winter 1982–83). Accessed August 8, 2016. http://journals.sfu.ca/archivar/index.php/archivaria/article/viewFile/10972/11905.

Milligan, Ian, Nick Ruest, et al. "Web Archives for Longitudinal Knowledge (WALK) Project." Accessed August 8, 2016. http://webarchives.ca/.

Open Government Partnership. "Canada." Accessed August 8, 2016. http://www.opengovpartnership.org/country/canada.

———. *Mission and Strategy*. Accessed August 8, 2016. http://www.opengovpartnership.org/about/mission-and-strategy.

Ruest, Nick, and Ian Milligan. "An Open-Source Strategy for Documenting Events: The Case Study of the 42nd Canadian Federal Election on Twitter." *Code4Lib* 32 (2016-04-25). Accessed August 8, 2016. http://journal.code4lib.org/articles/11358.

University of Alberta Libraries. "University of Alberta." [Institutional web archival collections available through the Internet Archive's Archive-It Service.] Accessed August 8, 2016. https://archive-it.org/organizations/401.

University of Toronto Libraries. "University of Toronto." [Institutional web archival collections available through the Internet Archive's Archive-It Service.] Accessed August 8, 2016. https://archive-it.org/organizations/75.

3

PARLIAMENTARY INFORMATION IN CANADA

Form and Function

Talia Chung and Maureen Martyn

In 1982, with the patriation of the Constitution, Canada made its last, if symbolic, step toward an independent model of governance. Although the Queen remains the head of state, the coming into force of the *Constitution Act*, 1982, gave Canada, its laws, parliament, and provincial legislatures control over important aspects of governing the nation.

With almost 150 years of parliamentary rule under a united Canada, there is a wealth of material available to Canadians who are interested in the way in which current events were treated by Parliament throughout our history; the evolution and change of the way in which the work of Parliament is recorded and accessed; and who said what in the Senate or House, when, and, in some cases, why.

Arguably, the greatest change in the parliamentary information landscape, from an access and reference perspective, was the building of the first parliamentary website (www.parl.gc.ca) in 1994–95. This established an online presence for Canada's parliamentary institutions and paved the way for the changes we witness today, including the transition to the strictly online publishing of key parliamentary publications.

The vast quantity of information related to the parliamentary record can now be found online on the parliamentary website and always in both English and French. Despite this progress, a great deal of material from 1867 to 1995 remains in analog format.

The Library of Parliament has partnered with Canadiana.org to create the Canadian Parliamentary Historical Resources portal, which provides access to digitized journals and debates from 1867 to the mid-1990s when documents began to be available regularly online.[1] The library has a "goal of providing a consolidated and growing collection of full-text searchable historical documents to the public in both official languages."[2]

As stated on the LAC website, "since 2005, Library and Archives Canada (LAC) has collected federal and non-federal web resources in the context of its Web Archiving Program. This website, the Government of Canada Web Archive (GCWA), provides access to archived federal websites."[3] The historical Parliament of Canada website (parl.gc.ca) is available via the GCWA from December 2005 to December 2007 and from February 2013 to December 2015. The content found at both Parl.gc.ca and its successor URL (parl.ca) is available via the web archiving efforts of the Internet Archive, dating from April 2001 to the present.[4]

For more than 150 years the record of Parliament continues to reflect activities with deeply rooted traditions. Parliamentary *Debates* offer a recorded account of interactions in the chamber; bills are drafted, studied, and debated, and they either pass into law or die on the Order Paper. Committees study issues, listen to testimony, ask questions, scrutinize legislation and expenditures, make recommendations, and publish reports.

Despite its deep regard for tradition and decorum, Parliament has changed, and the process by which parliamentary events are transcribed has changed enormously. The result is vastly improved methods of accessing, analyzing, consuming, and redistributing the record that reflects the working of Parliament.

This chapter will provide readers with a basic understanding of the parliamentary record and the way in which to use key parts of the record to find specific events or activities of Parliament or to research Parliament's treatment of specific topics.

A core understanding of parliamentary information requires an appreciation of (i) the foundational rules and practices governing the activities of Parliament, (ii) the parliamentary cycle, including the daily business of Parliament, and (iii), the most fundamental activity of a legislature, the making of laws.

PARLIAMENTARY RULES, PROCEDURES, AND PRACTICE

▶ *How the Chambers Govern Themselves*

Parliamentary procedures, defined through statute, written rules, and unwritten conventions and through day-to-day interpretation of the rules by the Speaker of the chamber, together constitute the ways in which politics is conducted within the parliamentary setting.[5] To understand the processes that guide parliamentary interaction, and which have an outcome on political struggles, it is important to be aware of the rules and practices that guide parliamentary interaction, both on a daily basis and in relation to other parliamentary or non-parliamentary bodies.

Decorum in the chamber, question rights, rules to limit debate, and parliamentary committee business are just a few of the processes guided by parliamentary traditions, rules, practices, and rulings. These can often shift power and influence political outcomes.[6] Both the Senate and the House of Commons have constitutional authority to regulate and establish their own rules of procedure, thereby regulating their internal proceedings.[7] Following are key sources that together provide a framework to understand better the standing rules,[8] procedures, and Speakers' rulings that form the body of practice guiding the way in which business is effectively carried out in Parliament.

▶ *Standing Rules, Procedure, and Practice*

THE SENATE OF CANADA

Guiding the deliberations of the Senate and its committees, the *Rules of the Senate of Canada* codify many of the Senate's parliamentary processes. The *Rules of the Senate* set out the responsibilities of the Speaker, the rules of debate in the Senate, and the way in which committee business is organized, among others.

With a goal of furnishing comprehensive and authoritative context to each individual rule of the Senate, the *Companion to the Rules of the Senate* (second edition, 2013) is written to reflect exactly the structure of the *Rules of the Senate*. For each rule, it provides annotated commentary and citations to relevant rules, as well as related Speakers' rulings.

Another resource that provides a larger scope of the work of the Senate is the *Senate Procedure in Practice* (2015). It affords an accessible understanding of the foundation and processes in the Senate. The *Senate Procedure in Practice* addresses subjects such as the constitutional foundations of the Senate and its functioning and deliberations in both the chamber and committee.

Comprising twelve brief documents, the *Senate Procedural Notes* outlines in clear and accessible language the key Senate procedures, such as the opening of Parliament, the process of debate, and the legislative process. In particular, it focuses on the stages that occur in the upper chamber. The *Notes* provides extensive references to the *Rules of the Senate* and can be helpful to introduce Senate parliamentary procedure to those unfamiliar with the concepts.

THE HOUSE OF COMMONS

As in the case of the *Rules of the Senate*, the *Standing Orders of the House of Commons* guides the deliberations of the lower chamber. To illustrate its importance, a review of the orders is part of the permanent mandate of the Standing Committee on Procedure and House Affairs,[9] thus ensuring their regular consideration.

Although there are many similarities in practice between the Senate and the House of Commons, there are also significant differences. These include the selection and role of the Speaker, sittings of the House, committee business, the legislative process, and private members' business.

To accompany the *Standing Orders of the House of Commons*, the *House of Commons Procedure and Practice* (second edition, 2009) provides a comprehensive explanation of rules, practices, and precedents in Canada's House of Commons. Frequently referred to as O'Brien and Bosc, this authoritative reference work is an essential guide to understanding the functioning of the House of Commons. *Procedure and Practice* includes extensive research and draws on Canadian and non-Canadian historic, legal, and procedural sources. It provides a comprehensive portrait of procedure and practice in the House of Commons and contains explanations of changes to the standing orders as a result of statutory changes. These include changes brought about by the 2004 amendment to the *Parliament of Canada Act* that created an ethics commissioner for the House of Commons, and the addition of the Conflict of Interest Code as an appendix to the *Standing Orders*. Although recognized as an authoritative reference work on parliamentary procedure in the House of Commons, *Procedure and Practice* must be used in tandem with the most current version of the *Standing Orders of the House of Commons*.

Another useful publication is the *Compendium of House of Commons Procedure*. Its structure leads readers from general to more detailed articles explaining procedure, so it can be used to understand the practical application and nuances of parliamentary procedure. The compendium is written in an accessible style and uses a broad treatment of parliamentary procedure to provide context for procedural practice in the House of Commons.

▶ Speaker's Rulings and Statements

Although parliamentary procedure is defined through statute, written rules, and unwritten conventions, the interpretations of the rules are fundamental and constitute the Speaker's rulings. Rulings can be described as Speaker-made parliamentary law, analogous to case law resulting from judge-made law in common-law practice.

It is the duty of the Speaker, in her or his impartial role in presiding over the work of the chamber, to enforce the rules of procedure. In this capacity the Speaker pronounces statements that provide clarification and information on a rule, and issues rulings that generally address procedural issues, which serve as precedents for future proceedings in the chamber. When rendering a decision, the Speaker is obligated to provide the reasons behind the decision.

All Speaker's rulings can be found in the *Debates*. However, compilations of rulings, including the Senate Speaker's rulings, from 1984 can also be found on the parliamentary website.[10]

PARLIAMENTARY CYCLE

Each parliament begins after a general election. Although legislation is currently in place to fix election dates,[11] parliaments have been as long as 2,152 days (the twelfth parliament) and as short as 66 days (the thirty-first parliament).[12]

There are many excellent resources that explain the history and tradition of the opening of a parliament. Therefore, this section will focus on finding and accessing the daily business of Parliament.

▶ *Key Events at the Beginning of Each Parliament*

Following parliamentary tradition, the House of Commons cannot convene without the election of the Speaker.[13] The Speaker and his or her deputies preside over the proceedings in the House of Commons.

Once the Speaker has been chosen by secret ballot, arrangements are made for the House of Commons to convene in the Senate chamber for the Speech from the Throne.[14] The Speech from the Throne, composed by the prime minister and Cabinet, outlines the governing party's intentions for the forthcoming legislative session. It is read by the Governor General as the Queen's representative in Canada. The Speech from the Throne is delivered in the Senate chamber and, therefore, is published in the Senate *Debates*. A copy of the speech is recorded in the *Debates* of the House of Commons. Following a long-standing parliamentary tradition, a pro forma bill[15] is introduced in each chamber asserting the right of Parliament to conduct its own business and to consider legislation without reference to the direction provided in the Speech from the Throne. Every parliament has at least one session, with at least one meeting required per year. In reality, the parliamentary calendar is planned in advance, with both the Senate and the House of Commons sitting about twenty-six weeks a year.

Prorogation effectively ends a parliamentary session. This occurs when the government has determined that it has carried out the agenda set for itself in its last Speech from the Throne. Prorogation is convened by the Governor General on the advice of the prime minister.

Dissolution is the end of a parliament's life cycle. Parliament is dissolved by order of the Governor General, on the advice of the prime minister. The new parliamentary cycle begins after the results of a federal election.

THE DAILY BUSINESS OF PARLIAMENT

▶ *The Chamber Is in Session*

ORDER AND NOTICE:
AGENDA FOR SENATE BUSINESS

The Order Paper and the Notice Paper[16] are prepared in advance of the Senate's daily session and include standard sections that follow the daily proceedings, known as routine proceedings. These sections are divided into government business and other business.

The Order Paper indicates approximately when particular debates, motions, and other routine proceedings will occur. The Notice Paper shows when particular legislation will be introduced. It also provides members with an opportunity to see written questions and motions that have not yet been debated in the chamber.

At the end of each session of Parliament, all business comes to an end. With certain exceptions, any business not yet concluded is said to have "died on the Order Paper" and must be introduced anew if further proceedings are required. The major exception to this rule pertains to private members' business. Since 2003, private members' business in the House of Commons has not died upon prorogation but has been reinstated at the beginning of the subsequent session at the same stage it was at when the last session ended.[17]

ORDER AND NOTICE:
AGENDA FOR HOUSE BUSINESS

The Order Paper is the official agenda of each sitting day in the House of Commons. The daily order of business, as listed in the Order Paper, follows a predetermined schedule. Emergency debates or other exceptional circumstances will affect the order of the proceedings.

The Notice Paper is attached to the Order Paper and indicates all bills, motions, and written questions that have been submitted to the House of Commons' Journals Branch. The Notice Paper provides members of Parliament with advance notice of items that will appear for consideration in the chamber in the next few sitting days.

The Projected Order of Business is an unofficial agenda published each evening for the following sitting day. It lists the items of business that are expected to be addressed and includes the times for debate. The Projected Order of Business is subject to change without notice.

DEBATES (HANSARD):
DAILY PROCEEDINGS IN THE SENATE

An account of routine proceedings is recorded and published on the parliamentary website on the next business day. Often referred to as *Hansard*, the *Debates* offers an edited, almost verbatim, account of every intervention in the Senate chamber.

A typical sitting of the Senate is structured in the following order:

1. *Senators' statements*: an opportunity for senators to speak briefly on a subject matter of interest.
2. *Routine proceedings*: government and individual senators may give notice of items that they are proposing for consideration. Documents and reports not requiring consideration by the Senate may be tabled for information purposes.[18]
3. *Question period*: senators may ask questions of the government members on any topic related to government responsibility.
4. *Delayed answers*: these include written responses to written

questions, as well as detailed responses to oral questions (question period).

5. *Orders of the day*: the orders include items for consideration by the Senate, as detailed in the Order Paper and the Notice Paper, related to all bills, committee reports, motions, and other inquiries.

6. *Items on the Notice Paper*: these are items called for consideration as listed on the Notice Paper.

7. *Notices of motions*: senators speak to motions for consideration.

8. *Notices of inquiries*: senators speak to inquiries listed in the Notice Paper.

Following is the fifteen-day rule:

An item under "Other Business" or on the Notice Paper under "Motions" or "Inquiries" that has not been considered during fifteen consecutive sitting days is dropped from the Order Paper and Notice Paper. This means that a senator must speak on the item during the fifteen-day period for the item to remain on the Order Paper.[19]

SEARCHING SENATE DEBATES

Senate *Debates* have been searchable by keyword since the thirty-fifth parliament, second session. Indexes from the thirty-fourth parliament, third session, to the thirty-eighth parliament, first session, are available online.

JOURNALS:
OFFICIAL RECORD OF SENATE PROCEEDINGS

The official minutes of a parliamentary daily session are published in the *Journals*. The *Journals* are useful when one is trying to determine when a particular vote was held or when a particular bill was debated. *Journals* are published the day after a Senate session. At the end of the session, they are printed and bound with an index.[20]

Senate *Journals* have been available online and searchable by keyword since the thirty-ninth parliament.

DEBATES (HANSARD): DAILY PROCEEDINGS IN THE HOUSE OF COMMONS

The *Debates* provide a transcript, after editing and translation, of what was said in the House of Commons on each sitting day and includes both the Committee of the Whole[21] and the House proceedings.

Often referred to as *Hansard*, the *Debates* offers every intervention in the chamber referenced by subject, such as oral questions, speaker, time, and duration. Since the thirty-fifth parliament, the debate proceedings have been available online. Although each day in the House of Commons is structured in a typical fashion, the business changes with the day of the week.

1. *Private members' business*: time is allotted for the presentation of private members' bills and private members' motions.[22]
2. *Government Orders*: they include the introduction of government bills, the introduction of supply and ways and means motions, and the referral of government business to committee.
3. *Statements by members*: members rise to speak about matters of interest to them and their constituents.
4. *Oral questions*: this section is commonly referred to as Question Period.
5. *Notices of Motions for the Production of Papers*: time is allotted for members to ask for written responses by the government on government business.

TABLE 3.1

Daily Order of Business: House of Commons, Canada

HOURS	MONDAY	TUESDAY	WEDNESDAY	THURSDAY	FRIDAY
10:00–11:00		ROUTINE PROCEEDINGS - - - -		ROUTINE PROCEEDINGS - - - -	Government Orders
11:00–11:15	Private Members' Business				Statements by Members
11:15–12:00					Oral Questions
12:00–1:00		Government Orders		Government Orders	ROUTINE PROCEEDINGS - - - -
1:00–1:30	Government Orders		Review of Delegated Legislation		Government Orders
1:30–2:00					
2:00–2:15	Statements by Members	Statements by Members	Statements by Members	Statements by Members	Private Members' Business
2:15–2:30	Oral Questions	Oral Questions	Oral Questions	Oral Questions	
2:30–3:00					
3:00–5:30	ROUTINE PROCEEDINGS - - - - Government Orders	Government Orders	ROUTINE PROCEEDINGS - - - - Notices of Motions for the Production of Papers - - - - Government Orders	Government Orders	
5:30–6:30		Private Members' Business	Private Members' Business	Private Members' Business	
6:30–7:00	Adjournment Proceedings	Adjournment Proceedings	Adjournment Proceedings	Adjournment Proceedings	

SOURCE: Parliament of Canada, "Daily Order of Business,"http://www.parl.gc.ca/About/House/DOB/dob-e.htm.

The official minutes of a parliamentary daily session are recorded in
the *Journals*. As each business item is listed in the *Journals*, they are
useful when one is trying to determine when a particular vote was held
or when a particular bill was debated.

Status of House Business: The House of Commons provides a summary account of the status of its daily business. This document, *Status
of House Business*, is a key resource for determining the date, time, and
content of what has transpired in the chamber with regard to bills, written questions, sessional papers, and motions. Until the forty-first parliament, a useful subject index was included. The index has been replaced
by new search tools provided by the House of Commons.

▶ Committees

The importance of committees in the parliamentary process cannot be
underestimated. Committees review legislation and budget estimates;
they examine current issues and make recommendations to Parliament
for changes to social and economic policy on wide-ranging issues. They
are composed of members of all political parties, generally in proportion to their representation in the chamber.

Committees have wide-ranging powers, including the ability to com-
pel witnesses to testify. Whereas the business of the chamber manages
how and when issues are brought forward on the agenda, committees
are the venue for parliamentarians to examine, question, investigate,
and make recommendations on the business decided by Parliament.

A substantial amount of parliamentary business occurs in committees. Each chamber has its own standing committees on broad subject
areas, including the review of proposed legislation, policy initiatives,
budget expenditures, and administrative matters. Parliamentary committees "oversee the work of government departments, to review particular areas of federal policy, to exercise procedural and administrative
responsibilities related to Parliament, to consider matters referred to

them by the House, and to report their findings and proposals to the House for its consideration."[23]

SENATE COMMITTEES

The "heart and soul"[24] of the Senate is its committee work. There are three types of Senate committees, which are governed by the *Rules of the Senate*:

1. *Standing committees*: except for the Standing Committee on Internal Economy, Budgets, and Administration, which is permanent, standing committees exist for the duration of a Parliament and cover broad subject areas, such as Aboriginal affairs and official languages.
2. *Special and legislative committees*: these committees are formed after a motion had been approved in the Senate chamber. They are struck to consider specific legislation or to investigate a particular issue.
3. *Subcommittees*: these committees have fewer members and are often administrative in nature.

As with chamber proceedings, committee meetings are transcribed and documented with minutes of proceedings. Transcriptions and minutes for all public meetings are published in conjunction with other parliamentary documents. As well, various other types of records that are not necessarily official publications are available to the public on the Senate committees' website. These include orders of reference for committee business; a searchable database of witnesses who appear before a committee; background information for potential witnesses; briefs[25] submitted to committee for consideration by third parties; administrative and substantive reports to committee; news releases that provide information about upcoming meetings; and social media content such as blogs and Twitter posts.

House of Commons committees include:

1. *Standing committees*: these committees handle broad policy areas and can include subcommittees.
2. *Legislative committees*: legislative committees study proposed bills and report back to the House.
3. *Special committees*.

Each committee website includes evidence (verbatim such as *Hansard*) and minutes (which document meetings, like the *Journals*). Also available are substantive reports; briefs; lists of witnesses; newsletters; and administrative information, such as orders of reference and administrative meeting minutes.

All House of Commons committee publications have been available online since the thirty-fifth parliament.

JOINT COMMITTEES

Joint committees have two joint chairs (one Member of Parliament and one Senator); their membership includes parliamentarians from both chambers. Two long-term joint committees are the Standing Joint Committee on the Library of Parliament and the Standing Joint Committee for the Scrutiny of Regulations. Occasionally a special joint committee will be struck to deal with matters of significant public interest.[26]

▶ *Committee Websites*

The growth of the committee presence on the Parliament of Canada website has provided both chambers with opportunities to select and categorize information outside of the procedural framework. Currently, each chamber (Senate and House) has a portal for all its committee information. As outlined earlier, it includes the official procedural documents; databases to search for witnesses and access briefs; calendars; news releases; and other ways to help users to follow committee business. This includes recorded audio and/or video of most public committee meetings on Parlvu.

Currently, there is no digital repository of Senate or House of Commons committee proceedings that occurred prior to the thirty-fifth Parliament. Historical committee proceedings are available in most depository libraries. The Library of Parliament provides a compilation of substantive reports to committees of both the Senate and the House of Commons.[27]

HARD-TO-FIND INTERVENTIONS IN THE PARLIAMENTARY RECORD

During the course of a parliamentary session there are sometimes certain procedural elements that become highly publicized or attract attention. Often these elements, as part of the parliamentary record, are not easy to find.

▶ Motions

Everything begins with a motion. Motions are requests made by members of Parliament for action, consideration, or opinion. To receive consideration from the House, the motion must be seconded by another member. Substantive motions include private members' motions, as well as both government and opposition motions, and they require some reaction from the chamber. During research, however, it can be challenging to find a motion.

As the presentation of parliamentary procedural information evolves, the retrieval of formerly obscure items, such as private members' motions in the House of Commons, is improving. As of the forty-first parliament, the work of each member is included as part of a publications search. With this feature, users can find interventions in the chamber and committees by member, including private members' motions. Prior to June 2, 2011, finding a motion included using the *Status of House Business*, especially its index, and backtracking from a date to a name in the *Hansard*.[28]

Most private members' motions made prior to the forty-first parliament can be found using the following steps:

1. Find the parliamentary session on the House of Commons Chamber Business website, Ourcommons.ca (http://www.ourcommons.ca/en#pw-in-the-house).
2. Under "Daily Publications," find *Status of House Business*.
3. Private Members' Motions, located in Part II, are listed in numerical order. Using the Find function on one's browser, one can find a keyword related to the motion. Once the date of the motion has been found, it will help with the *Hansard* search. With both the date and the number of the motion, its full text can be found in the Notice Paper, which would have been published on the next sitting day.[29]

▶ Written Questions

Written questions can be difficult to find in the parliamentary record. One requires the question number, the name of the Member of Parliament, or the subject matter. Starting with *Status of House Business* for a particular parliamentary session, one looks for Part III, "Written Questions." The text can then be searched by name, subject, or date, using the Find function of one's browser. The text of the question will be found by consulting *Hansard* for the date referred to in *Status of House Business*. If the question is not answered in the *Debates* record, a response may be seen in the Notice Paper of the next sitting day.[30]

▶ Votes

Most matters referred to Parliament are resolved with a vote. Generally, the vote is oral, and the Speaker decides whether the yeas or nays are in the majority. From time to time, votes on certain parliamentary events are recorded by name.[31] At times, the voting will conclude the debate on a proposed bill or will record the assent and dissent of members about a certain motion or order of precedence.[32] Recorded votes are documented within the text of the *Debates* and listed in the *Journals* as part of the official record. Currently, each vote is recorded as an intervention in the House of Commons *Debates* portal and can be found by selecting Votes in the portal sidebar.

▶ House of Commons Sessional Papers

Documents that are not parliamentary publications but which are tabled in the House of Commons are referred to as sessional papers. These include government responses to written questions from members of Parliament, and annual reports of government departments. The government may table documents such as green or white papers and other papers dealing with government policies or actions; Royal Commission reports; and answers to written questions.

To find references to sessional papers in the *Journals*, the following numbering sequences may be useful: for answers to written questions, 8555; for production of papers, 8550; and for miscellaneous, 8530.[33]

Adjournment tabling[34] occurs when sessional papers are deposited with the Clerk's office of the House of Commons when the House is not in session. These papers will be recorded in the *Journals* of the first occurrence of the chamber's next sitting day. Also known as "back-door" tabling, these papers are often difficult to find in the parliamentary record. As they are tabled while the House is not sitting, they are only recorded in the *Journals* for the first day of the next parliamentary session.

LEGISLATIVE PROCESS

Canada's system of governance has three branches, each of which has a defined role in the making of laws, applying laws, and interpreting laws. In broad strokes, the responsibilities are organized as follows:

▷ *Legislative branch*: composed of the Queen, the Senate, and the House of Commons, this branch is instrumental in proposing, amending, and repealing legislation.

▷ *Executive branch*: composed of the prime minister, the Cabinet, and the departments of government, it proposes and implements legislation.

▷ *Judicial branch*: this branch interprets legislation.[35]

Proposing and amending legislation are fundamental activities of Parliament; they are conducted through a structured legislative process that occurs in both the Senate and the House of Commons. Bills may be introduced in both the Senate and the House. However, the Senate may not introduce bills to spend public money or to impose taxes; these must originate in the House of Commons. No bill can become law before it has been studied and approved by both chambers. As outlined in *The Legislative Process: From Government Policy to Proclamation*,[36] the process through which a policy concept assumes the force of law involves four stages:

1. Cabinet
2. Parliament
3. Royal Assent (given by the Crown and/or the Governor General)
4. Coming into force

The progress of a bill through each of these stages is reflected in the parliamentary record. With the 2013 introduction of LEGISinfo (a research tool for finding information on legislation before Parliament), the process by which bills can be tracked through the record has been greatly simplified. Nevertheless, this section of the chapter will briefly explain the process through which a bill becomes a law. As there are many excellent descriptions of Canada's legislative process, the focus will be on the information arising from the legislative process, as reflected in the parliamentary record.

TABLE 3.2
Numbering of Bills[37]

TYPE OF BILL	INTRODUCED IN THE HOUSE OF COMMONS	INTRODUCED IN THE SENATE
Government bills	C-1 to C-200	S-1 to S-200
Private members' public bills	C-201 to C-1000	
Senate public bills		S-201 to S-1000
Senate private members' bills		S-1001 onwards

As mentioned earlier, at the beginning of each session, pro forma bills are introduced in each of the chambers with the sole purpose of asserting the right of each chamber to determine the order of their deliberations. In the House of Commons the practice is to introduce Bill C-1, *An Act Respecting the Administration of Oaths of Office*, and in the Senate, Bill S-1, *An Act Relating to Railways*. Typically, these pro forma bills receive only first reading.

Although a bill will follow similar stages in both the Senate and the House of Commons, the chamber in which it is first introduced will determine the particular process through which the bill will progress through Parliament. For our purposes, we will discuss the progress of government bills originating in the House of Commons.

▶ The Cabinet Stage

One of the means through which a government may implement its policies is to create new legislation or to amend or repeal existing legislation. Cabinet decides when a policy will be implemented through a legislative measure. On the advice of the government House Leader, it determines the timing and the chamber, either the Senate or the House of Commons, into which the proposed legislation should first be introduced.

Typically, government bills are introduced through the House of Commons. In this case, the government House Leader gives notice to the Clerk of the House of Commons of a "Notice of Introduction," as required by Standing Order 54, to table a bill. Next, the motion to introduce the bill appears on the Notice Paper. The motion is subsequently moved to the Order Paper until the bill is introduced for first reading. In contrast, when bills are introduced in the Senate, no notice is required.

▶ The Parliamentary Stage

During this stage, both chambers may pass, amend, delay, or defeat a bill.[38] Each bill follows several stages, allowing parliamentarians to debate and scrutinize the merits of the proposed legislation at each stage and before a bill can become law. Bills are introduced and given *first reading*[39] in the House of Commons. Once a bill has received its first reading, it is placed on the Order Paper for second reading. It is at this stage that the bill is printed for distribution to members and is given a bill number.[40]

The bill is then listed on the Order Paper and Notice Paper under the heading "Orders of the Day." During the *second-reading* debates, the substance of the bill is debated, and the bill is generally referred to a standing, special, or legislative parliamentary committee.[41] The substance of a bill can be better understood by reading MPs' speeches at second reading or by consulting legislative summaries prepared by the Library of Parliament; committee proceedings and reports, including testimony of witnesses; and political party papers or position statements.

COMMITTEE STAGE

At the committee stage, committee members are tasked with reviewing the bill to approve or modify it. Witnesses may be called to provide opinions on the bill, and then the committee studies it clause by clause. Members may propose changes to the bill and must vote on the bill as a whole.

If the committee has suggested numerous amendments, the bill may be reprinted before being returned to the chamber. The committee adopts a report on the bill, with or without amendments, which it then gives to the House of Commons.[42] The bill returns to the Order Paper and Notice Paper to await consideration from the House of Commons.

REPORT STAGE

The committee report is considered by the House of Commons, and the House resumes debate on the bill and can suggest other amendments. Once the debate at the report stage has concluded, the third reading of the bill is moved.

THIRD READING

Members vote to approve or reject the bill in its final form. Once a bill has passed the third reading, it is sent to the other chamber, or, if it has already received the third reading in the other chamber, it is set aside for Royal Assent.[43]

▶ The Royal Assent Stage

Before a bill can become law, it must receive Royal Assent, which is given by the Crown, represented in Canada by the Governor General. Prior to 2002, Royal Assent could only be given by means of a traditional ceremony held in the Senate in which all three bodies constituting Parliament (the Crown, the Senate, and the House of Commons) were represented. The ceremony highlights the symbolic sanctioning by the Crown of the work of Parliament. With the introduction of the *Royal Assent Act*,[44] a written declaration could be used to signify Royal Assent; however, the traditional Royal Assent ceremony must still be used twice in each calendar year.

The Royal Assent ceremony is recorded in the Senate *Debates* and takes place during the Senate's Orders of the Day segment of the day's sitting. The title of the new act, its bill number, and its chapter number in the annual statutes are recorded in the *Debates* of the specific day on which the bill received Royal Assent.

A written declaration is a less formal process during which the Clerk of the Parliaments prepares a letter indicating that a specific bill (or bills) has been passed by both chambers and that both chambers request that Royal Assent be granted to the bill(s). Once the Governor General has signed a declaration of Royal Assent, the secretary to the Governor General prepares a letter to the Speakers of the Senate and the House of Commons, formally advising them that the bills have received Royal Assent.

The Speakers inform their respective chambers that Royal Assent has been granted to the specific bill(s), and Royal Assent is only deemed to have been granted when both the Senate and the House of Commons have been appropriately notified.[45] Written declarations of Royal Assent can be found in the *Journals* and the *Debates* of both the Senate and the House of Commons.

▶ The Coming-into-Force Stage

An Act does not necessarily come into force on the day it receives Royal Assent; indeed, many bills contain provisions that allow for the entire Act, or parts of the Act, to be enacted at a later time or to be fixed by proclamation. The Act may come into force on a fixed date (for example, January 1, 2017), or on the day it receives Royal Assent, or at a later date to be determined through an order issued by the Governor-in-Council, a statutory instrument that is recorded in the *Canada Gazette*, Part II. Where an Act or any part of an Act is silent regarding its commencement, it comes into force upon Royal Assent.[46]

COMING INTO FORCE THROUGH AN ORDER-IN-COUNCIL

Orders-in-Council are a form of delegated legislation. In these cases, the authority to create subordinate legislation has been delegated by Parliament to a minister of the Crown or other public agency. This relieves Parliament of the minor law-making required to carry out the intent of the parent legislation and allows departments to respond more quickly and effectively than would Parliament to certain situations.[47]

An order issued by the Governor-in-Council is an order by and with the consent of the Queen's Privy Council for Canada. But, in reality, it is an order originating from Cabinet and approved by the Governor General. Orders can be used for purposes beyond legislative measures that include administrative matters such as civil service staffing. Legislative orders, made under the authority of an existing Act of Parliament, become part of Canada's laws and are enforceable by the courts.[48]

An Order-in-Council is assigned a consecutive number preceded by the year in which it was presented to Cabinet. For example, the first Order-in-Council presented in 2015 was numbered 2015-0001. Orders that qualify as regulations are published in the *Canada Gazette*, Part II, and are assigned a statutory instrument (SI) registration number.[49] It is worth noting that Order-in-Council numbers differ from statutory instrument numbers, although they may refer to the same legislative measure (for example: parliamentary session number 41-2, bill number

C-42, instrument number SI/2015-0080, but the Privy Council Order-in-Council number is 2015-1172).

Order-in-Council numbers are indexed and searchable using the Privy Council Office's Orders-in-Council database, which provides access to Orders-in-Council published from 1990 to the present. SI numbers are referenced in the *Canada Gazette*, Part II. Individual SIS can be found by navigating through the list of individually published issues of the *Canada Gazette*, Part II, to identify where the specific statutory instrument, organized by number, has been published.

LEGISINFO

Locating proposed legislation and its progress has been greatly simplified by the introduction of LEGISinfo in February 2003.[50] An online portal, it includes information on bills presented before Parliament from 1994 to the present. LEGISinfo brings together parliamentary documents from both the Senate and the House of Commons related to bills as they are tracked through the chambers. For the period 1994–2000, only limited bill information is available (that is, bill titles, numbers, and sometimes the text of the bills at various stages). However, as of the thirty-seventh parliament (2001), comprehensive information on bills has been available through LEGISinfo. This information includes, but is not limited to, the full text of bills in all published versions, information on the progress of bills, and links to the parliamentary record noting votes and debates. For users who require a broader understanding of the substance of a bill, LEGISinfo also assembles, where available, related non-parliamentary content, such as legislative summaries prepared by the Library of Parliament, departmental background papers, and political party press releases. LEGISinfo effectively brings together current content across the parliamentary record of both the Senate and the House of Commons and provides a comprehensive view of each bill.

FOLLOWING THE WORK OF PARLIAMENT THROUGH PARL.GC.CA

Given the volume and complexity of parliamentary business—two chambers, two languages, thousands of documents in any given parliament—the chambers are turning their attention to new ways in which to engage Canadians in parliamentary affairs as they occur.

▶ House of Commons Publications Search Tool

The House of Commons provides a powerful search tool that allows users to look through chamber and committee proceedings, linking speakers with subjects and dates across parliaments. This removes much of the guesswork from the hunt for information. However, the tool has been available only since the thirty-seventh parliament. Previously, the *Status of House Business* and *Journals* remained excellent starting points for research.

The House of Commons has recently introduced Ourcommons.ca, which allows users to interact with chamber proceedings. The site is updated continually and includes the name of the Member of Parliament speaking and the member's biographical information. Ourcommons.ca is intended as a research aid to those following the proceedings in the House.

▶ RSS Feeds

For many who follow the work of Parliament, the RSS (Rich Site Summary) feeds that are made available can help users to compile curated content based on their interests. RSS feeds are available for Parlvu, LEGISinfo, and committees in both chambers. Using the RSS functionality, one can obtain updates on new committee meetings and reports or track the progress of a bill.

▶ Webcasting

One of the best innovations in the past ten years has been Parlvu, which provides both audio and video webcasts of selected proceedings in the chambers and in committee. Those interested in watching the Senate or House proceedings can follow the Parlvu webcast.[51] The Senate's daily proceedings have been available in audio format as of the thirty-ninth parliament, first session. The House of Commons' daily proceedings are available in both video and audio format.

▶ Social Media

The Senate tweets regularly about its activities. Senate committee meetings are regularly tweeted by the @senateCA Twitter account.

THE FUTURE OF PARLIAMENTARY INFORMATION IN CANADA

Parliamentary and legislative information is evolving, yet it continues to be deeply rooted in its historic and procedural traditions. In the mid-1990s, when the parliamentary website was first created, few would have anticipated the huge growth in social media, the increased availability of media-rich parliamentary proceedings, the high levels of public pressure for transparency in reporting, and the growing levels of interest and skill in manipulating open government data.

The efforts of Parliament to make its records available to citizens in machine-readable or digital format will contribute to engaging citizens in democratic government. Open government data is leading to the development of more and more technological tools that offer opportunities to understand better the work of elected and non-elected officials.

Machine-readable, open government information allows individuals to sift through, analyze, and manipulate the parliamentary record in ways unimagined during the analog era. As an example, Openparliament.ca is a website created by an individual citizen who, using the XML format found on selected content on the parliamentary website, manipulates and presents harvested parliamentary information to create a different portrait of the work of Parliament.[52] The site itself supports the principle of openness by using open data and open source technology. It offers up much of its source code through Github for re-use and further development by like-minded individuals.

Current efforts to transform analog materials into digital format, such as the collaborative work between the Library of Parliament and Canadiana, will have a significant impact on the availability of parliamentary information. Extensive work is underway to digitize parts of the parliamentary record, which is currently available in print format only. The digitized content will be enriched with metadata to create description-rich digital records ready for innovative methods of analysis and data mining.

With the development and adoption of data standards for legislative information, such as the Akoma Ntoso metadata standard for congressional and legislative information,[53] structured information and systems will become more interoperable. This will facilitate the comparative study of legislatures across jurisdictions. With the adoption of standards will come improvements to current online platforms, such as the addition of APIS (application programming interfaces) and bulk data transfers. These will facilitate the reuse of data and digital content for mashups, visualizations, data mining, and uses not yet imagined.

In future, researchers will exploit a rich and previously unavailable visual and audio record of parliamentary proceedings. This multimedia content will offer historians an added dimension through which to understand Parliament.

Technological developments aside, Canada's Parliament has made great strides in the last decade not only to improve access to its parliamentary publications but to provide insightful, educational information about how Parliament works to support citizen engagement in democratic government. With some confidence, we can say that future generations of government document specialists will need to distinguish their *Journals* from their committee evidence and be handy with the parliamentary nomenclature. Despite dramatic changes in the ways in which the parliamentary record is made available to citizens, the language and arrangement of materials have remained essentially unchanged in the past 150 years.

TRACING AN ISSUE THROUGH
THE PARLIAMENTARY RECORD:
THE CASE OF GUN CONTROL

To illustrate how an issue of public concern is handled in Parliament, following is an example of the way in which such a question may be traced through the parliamentary record. This illustration conveniently straddles the time period preceding and succeeding the full development of the parliamentary website. It shows how searching for parliamentary information requires significantly different approaches, depending on the period in which the parliamentary event occurs.

To carry out a comprehensive search across the parliamentary-record-spanning time, one must use key resources including the search tools mentioned earlier in the chapter, such as LEGISinfo or the House of Commons search tool, and, as necessary, digitized or analog indexes to the proceedings of the Senate or the House of Commons.

With regard to gun control, for many decades, the access to, use of, and controls over firearms in Canadian society have been—and continue to be—prominent and controversial issues. Although Canada has a long history of discussing and implementing measures to control the use of firearms,[54] its society has long sought the appropriate balance of firearms control to address public safety concerns, and the protection of individuals' rights.

On December 6, 1989, a mass shooting occurred at the École Polytechnique of the University of Montreal. A heavily armed gunman entered the school, killed fourteen women, and injured fourteen others before taking his own life. This horrific event caused an eruption of emotion throughout the country and brought to the foreground the issue of gun control and violence toward women. Canada's Parliament was an important forum for discussion and action on these issues. Following the École Polytechnique shooting, the issue of gun control can be selectively traced through examples in the parliamentary record from 1989 to 2015.

STATEMENTS BY MEMBERS	DECEMBER 7, 1989 Statements by individual members, including the then Prime Minister Brian Mulroney, in reaction to the shooting at the Polytechnique were delivered on December 7, 1989, the day after the event. *Source*: House of Commons *Debates* 34-2, beginning on page 6606.
ORAL QUESTIONS / QUESTION PERIOD	DECEMBER 8, 1989 During question period Nancy Clancy, MP (Peterborough), posed a question to the government about violence against women, in light of the shooting at the Polytechnique, and Minister Barbara McDougall replied on behalf of the government. *Source*: House of Commons *Debates* 34-2, page 6662.
TABLING A PETITION	DECEMBER 13, 1990 Bill Domm, MP, tabled a petition requesting that each December 6 be a national day of remembrance for the fourteen women killed at the École Polytechnique. *Sources*: House of Commons *Debates* 34-2, page 16668. The petition can be located by first identifying a petition number, which is recorded in the House of Commons *Journals*, page 2451; petition number 342-8156.

| TABLING A SESSIONAL PAPER (GOVERNMENT RESPONSE TO PETITION) | FEBRUARY 25, 1991
The government tabled its response to the petition tabled by Mr. Domm.

Source: House of Commons *Journals*, page 2608; the government response can be located as Sessional Paper 342-9/152. |

Digitized records for the thirty-fourth parliament and earlier can be found on the Parliament of Canada Historical Resources portal (parl.canadiana.ca) in which *Debates* and *Journals* from 1867 to 1993 have been made available. Keyword searching is enabled across the *Debates* by parliamentary session, but, due to uneven retrieval, for comprehensive purposes the digitized indexes to the *Debates* must also be consulted.

Thirty-Fifth Parliament, Session 1

PROPOSING
AND PASSING
GOVERNMENT
LEGISLATION
(HOUSE OF
COMMONS)

FEBRUARY 14, 1995

Bill C-68, *An Act Respecting Firearms and Other Weapons*, was presented in the House of Commons for its first reading.

APRIL 5, 1995

The bill had its second reading and was referred to the Standing Committee on Justice and Legal Affairs.

JUNE 7, 1995

Committee members reported back to the House of Commons, having studied the bill and suggested amendments.

Source: Sessional Paper 8510-351-123.

JUNE 12, 1995

The report-stage vote was held.

JUNE 13, 1995

The bill had its third reading.

PROPOSING
AND PASSING
GOVERNMENT
LEGISLATION
(SENATE)

JUNE 14, 1995

Bill C-68 had its first reading in the Senate.

JUNE 22, 1995

The bill received its second reading and was referred to the Standing Senate Committee on Legal and Constitutional Affairs.

PROPOSING	NOVEMBER 20, 1995
AND PASSING	Committee members reported back to the Senate,
GOVERNMENT	having studied the bill and suggested amendments.
(SENATE)	NOVEMBER 22, 1995
(cont'd)	The bill had its third Senate reading and was passed
	with a recorded division/vote.

DECEMBER 5, 1995
Royal Assent was given.

Sources: first reading, Senate *Journals*, page 1022; second reading and committee referral, Senate *Journals*, page 1121; committee report, Senate *Journals*, pages 1278–83 (the substance of the report is found in the *Journals*); third reading and vote results, Senate *Journals*, pages 1306–07; Royal Assent, Senate *Journals*, page 1341.

The full text of the bill can be found on LEGISinfo; a search by bill number retrieves the text of the bill as it received Royal Assent, and its chapter number (C-68 was enacted as S.C. 1995, c. 39). Bill coverage on LEGISinfo is comprehensive from 2001 to the present and is limited for bills tabled from 1993 to 2001. Thus, there is a need for additional sources in this case.

Progress through the House of Commons can be traced through the House of Commons *Debates* and *Journals*, using indexes for the session. *Status of House Business* at prorogation of the parliamentary session (35-1) provides full reporting of the progress of the bill through the House of Commons. For committee meetings, the committee website offers verbatim reports of meetings (Evidence) as well as official records of the committee (Minutes).

Thirty-Seventh Parliament, Session 2

TABLING A
SESSIONAL PAPER

DECEMBER 3, 2002

The Auditor General tabled the *Report of the Auditor General to the House of Commons* for the year ending December 31, 2001. It contained reports relating to cost discrepancies outlined at the time the Act was introduced, compared with costs relating to the actual implementation of the gun registry program.

Source: House of Commons *Journals*, December 3, 2002. This information can be found using the House of Commons publications search tool.

Thirty-Ninth Parliament, Session 2

THE SPEECH FROM
THE THRONE

OCTOBER 16, 2007

In the opening of a new parliamentary session, the Speech from the Throne, the government stated the intent to repeal the long-gun registry.

Source: Senate *Debates*, October 16, 2007. The text of the throne speech can be found in *Debates* of the Senate; it is also recorded in the *Debates* of the House of Commons. The Library of Parliament gathers a compilation of throne speeches through its Parlinfo service.

Forty-First Parliament, Session 1

PROPOSING AND
PASSING GOVERNMENT
LEGISLATION

OCTOBER 25, 2011

To carry out its promise outlined in the Speech from the Throne, the government introduced a bill to end the long-gun *Registry Act*, entitled Bill C-19, *An Act to Amend the Criminal Code and the Firearms Act* (41-1). The bill is enacted as S.C. 2012, c. 6.

Source: For the bill's progress through both chambers, one can view the complete bill details in LEGISinfo. Additional information about the matter of the bill is found under "About This Bill," on the sidebar of LEGISinfo; it includes rich sources such as a legislative summary written by the Library of Parliament and departmental information.

Forty-First Parliament, Session 2

PROPOSING AND
PASSING GOVERNMENT
LEGISLATION

OCTOBER 7, 2014

The government introduced Bill C-42, *Common Sense Firearms Licensing Act* (41-2), with the goal of streamlining the licensing process for firearms owners. The bill is enacted as S.C. 2015, c. 27.

Source: For the bill's progress through both chambers, one can view complete bill details in LEGISinfo. Additional information about the matter of the bill is found under "About This Bill," on the sidebar of LEGISinfo; it includes rich sources such as a legislative summary written by the Library of Parliament and departmental information.

Notes

1. See http://parl.canadiana.ca/.
2. Library of Parliament Canada, *Annual Report, 2014–2015*.
3. Library and Archives Canada, *Government of Canada Web Archive*.
4. See https://web.archive.org/web/*/parl.gc.ca and https://web.archive.org/web/*/parl.ca, respectively.
5. Heard, "Constitutional Conventions and Parliament," 20.
6. Sieberer, "Reforming the Rules of the Parliamentary Game," 955.
7. Parliament's authority to regulate its own proceedings arises primarily from the *Constitution Act, 1867*, and the *Parliament of Canada Act* (R.S.C. 1985, c. P-1).
8. In the case of the standing rules or standing orders, the "standing" nature of the orders means that the rules do not lapse at the end of a parliamentary session (prorogation) or the end of a parliament (dissolution).
9. House of Commons Canada, "Order 108(3)(a)(iii)," *Standing Orders of the House of Commons*.
10. It begins in 1984 with the rulings of Speaker Guy Charbonneau.
11. *An Act to Amend the Canada Elections Act* (S.C. 2007, c. 10).
12. Library of Parliament Canada, *ParlInfo Federal Election Trivia, 2011*.
13. Election of the Speaker of the House of Commons is guided by standing orders; in the case of the Senate, "the Senate Speaker is appointed by the Governor General on the advice of the Prime Minister, usually for the life of the Parliament" (http://www.lop.parl.gc.ca/About/Parliament/Publications/speaker_senate/sen-e.asp).
14. House of Commons Canada, *Compendium, Speech from the Throne, 2015*, http://www.parl.gc.ca/About/House/compendium/web-content/c_d_speechthrone-e.htm.
15. In the Senate, Bill S-1 is *An Act Relating to Railways*, and in the House of Commons, Bill C-1 is *An Act Respecting the Administration of Oaths of Office*. These pro forma bills are traditionally given first reading but are not voted on or proceeded with any further.
16. Senate of Canada, *Order and Notice Paper*.
17. The government's obligation to provide answers to written questions, to respond to petitions, and to produce papers requested by the House also ends with dissolution. The government must wait until the new parliament is in session before tabling any document that is required pursuant to an act, resolution, or standing order. O'Brien and Bosc, *House of Commons Parliamentary Procedure* (2nd. ed.).
18. Senate of Canada, *Senate Procedural Notes*.
19. Senate of Canada, *Senate Procedural Notes*.
20. Senate of Canada, "Documents, Journals and Broadcasting," *Rules of the Senate*, chap. 14.

21. "Proceedings in a Committee of the Whole are governed by the Standing Orders as far as may be applicable, except for four major differences relating to the seconding of motions, permission to speak more than once, the length of speeches and the place from which Members may speak." House of Commons, *Standing Orders of the House of Commons*.

22. House of Commons Canada, "Private Members Business," in *Compendium*, 2015.

23. Forsey, *How Canadians Govern Themselves*, chap. 7.

24. Senate of Canada, "About Committees."

25. Witnesses may give testimony in person (oral) or in writing (brief). http:// www.parl.gc.ca/Content/SEN/Committee/421/pub/Witness_LongV2-e.pdf.

26. For example, the Special Joint Committee on Physician-Assisted Dying, 2016.

27. Library of Parliament Canada, *ParlInfo*.

28. The index to *Status of House Business* was discontinued as of the forty-first parliament and replaced with an advanced search tool.

29. All relevant dates of motions are included in the *Status of House Business* index. Dumais, "Finding Private Members' Motions."

30. Dumais, "Written Questions."

31. A recorded vote on a motion, if demanded, need not be held immediately. At the request of the chief government whip or the chief opposition whip, it may be deferred to a later time pursuant to various provisions in the standing orders or by a special order of the House. House of Commons, "Debates and Voting," in *Compendium*.

32. House of Commons, "Order of Precedence," in *Compendium*.

33. Curtin and Gagnon, "Guide to Sessional Papers."

34. House of Commons Canada, "Tabling Documents," in *Compendium*.

35. Library of Parliament Canada, *Guide to the House of Commons*.

36. Barnes and Virgint, *The Legislative Process*.

37. Bills introduced in the House of Commons are assigned a number with the prefix *C-*, while those originating in the Senate are given the prefix *S-*. Bills are categorized as government bills, private members' public bills, Senate public bills, or Senate private members' bills. Government bills are introduced by a Cabinet minister, and private members' public bills are introduced by private members, meaning those who are not a member of Cabinet. If introduced in the Senate, these private members' bills are referred to as Senate public bills. For government bills, the numbering resets and begins again from one at the start of each new parliamentary session. In contrast, House of Commons private members' public bills continue from session to session; the numbering only resets at the start of a new parliament. Senate private members' bills are generally introduced in the Senate; their main purpose is to provide a benefit or an exemption to

an individual or group from the application of a law. Parliament of Canada, "Frequently Asked Questions," LEGISinfo.

38. Senate of Canada, "The Senate Today."
39. House of Commons Canada, *Guide to the House of Commons*, 9.
40. House of Commons Canada, "Introduction and First Reading of a Bill," in *Compendium*.
41. House of Commons Canada, "Second Reading and Referral of a Bill to a Committee," in *Compendium*.
42. House of Commons Canada, "Second Reading and Referral of a Bill to a Committee," in *Compendium*.
43. Senate of Canada, "The Senate Today."
44. *Royal Assent Act* (S.C. 2002, c. 15).
45. Senate of Canada, *Senate Procedural Notes*.
46. *Interpretation Act* (R.S.C. 1985, c. I-21, s. 5(2)).
47. Levy, "Delegated Legislation and the Standing Joint Committee on Regulations and Other Statutory Instruments," 350.
48. *The Canadian Encyclopedia*, s.v. "Order-in-Council."
49. Hubley and Beaulieu, "Locating Canadian Orders in Council."
50. Niemczak and Hobbins, "LEGISinfo."
51. Not all meetings are available in both audio and video. After one has made a search by meeting, the live feed or archived feed will indicate which recordings are available.
52. Mulley, *Openparliament.ca*.
53. Africa i-Parliament Action Plan, *Akoma Ntoso*.
54. Dupuis, Kirkby, and MacKay, *Legislative Summary of Bill C-19: An Act to Amend the Criminal Code and the Firearms Act*.

Bibliography

Africa i-Parliament Action Plan. *Akoma Ntoso*. http://www.akomantoso.org/.

Barnes, André, and Erin Virgint. *The Legislative Process: From Government Policy to Proclamation*. http://www.lop.parl.gc.ca/Content/LOP/ResearchPublications/2015-52-e.htm?cat=government.

Curtin, Jennifer, and Josée Gagnon. "Guide to Sessional Papers." Unpublished paper, Ottawa, August 2015.

Dumais, Michael. "Finding Private Members' Motions: A Step-by-Step Guide." Unpublished paper. Ottawa, August 2016.

———. "Written Questions." Unpublished paper. Ottawa, August 2016.

Dupuis, Tanya, Cynthia Kirkby, and Robin MacKay. *Legislative Summary of Bill C-19: An Act to Amend the Criminal Code and the Firearms Act*. Ottawa: Library of Parliament, 2011.

Forsey, Eugene. *How Canadians Govern Themselves.* 9th ed. Ottawa: Public Works and Government Services, 2016. http://www.lop.parl.gc.ca/About/Parliament/SenatorEugeneForsey/home/index-e.html.

Heard, Andrew. "Constitutional Conventions and Parliament." *Canadian Parliamentary Review* 28, no. 2 (2005): 19–22. http://www.revparl.ca/english/issue.asp?param=168&art=1143.

Hubley, Wendy, and Micheline Beaulieu. "Locating Canadian Orders in Council." *Canadian Law Libraries* 26, no. 3 (2001): 83–84.

Levy, Gary. "Delegated Legislation and the Standing Joint Committee on Regulations and Other Statutory Instruments." *Canadian Public Administration* 22, no. 3 (1979): 349–65.

Library and Archives Canada. "Government of Canada Web Archive." http://www.bac-lac.gc.ca/eng/discover/archives-web-government/Pages/web-archives.aspx.

Library of Parliament Canada. "About Parliament—The Speaker of the Senate." http://www.lop.parl.gc.ca/About/Parliament/Publications/speaker_senate/sen-e.asp.

———. *Annual Report, 2014–15.* Ottawa: Library of Parliament, 2015. http://www.lop.parl.gc.ca/About/Library/VirtualLibrary/AnnualReport/2015/ar20142015-contents-e.html.

———. "Canadian Parliamentary Historical Resources." Accessed August 26, 2016. http://parl.canadiana.ca/.

———. *Guide to the House of Commons.* Ottawa: Public Works and Government Services Canada, 2011. http://www.lop.parl.gc.ca/About/Parliament/GuideToHoC/pdf/guide_canadian_house_of_commons-e.pdf.

———. "Legislative Summary of Bill C-42: An Act to Amend the Firearms Act and the Criminal Code and to Make a Related Amendment and a Consequential Amendment to Other Acts." Accessed August 4, 2016. http://www.lop.parl.gc.ca/About/Parliament/LegislativeSummaries/bills_ls.asp?Language=E&ls=C42&Mode=1&Parl=41&Ses=2&source=library_prb.

———. *ParlInfo Federal Election Trivia, 2011.* http://www.lop.parl.gc.ca/ParlInfo/compilations/electionsandridings/TriviaParliaments.aspx.

———. "ParlInfo Substantive Reports of Committees." http://www.lop.parl.gc.ca/ParlInfo/compilations/parliament/SubstantiveReports.aspx.

Mulley, Michael. Openparliament.ca. https://openparliament.ca/about/.

Niemczak, Peter, and Katie Hobbins. "LEGISinfo: A Single Window on Legislation before Parliament." *Parliamentary Review* 27, no. 4 (2004): 33–36. http://www.revparl.ca/english/issue.asp?art=38&param=61.

O'Brien, Audrey, and Marc Bosc, eds. *House of Commons Procedure and Practice.* 2nd ed. Ottawa: Parliament of Canada, 2009. http://www.parl.gc.ca/procedure-book-livre/Document.aspx?sbdid=7C730F1D-E10B-4DFC-863A-83E7E1A6940E&sbpid=976953D8-8385-4E09-A699-D90779B48AA0&Language=E&Mode=1.

Talia Chung and Maureen Martyn ◁ 115

Parliament of Canada. *Companion to the Rules of the Senate of Canada*. 2nd. ed. Accessed February 12, 2016. http://www.parl.gc.ca/About/Senate/Rules/pdf/Companion-Rules-Senate-2nd-Nov13-e.pdf.

———. *Compendium of House of Commons Procedure, 2015*. http://www.parl.gc.ca/About/House/Compendium/Web-Content/c_a_index-e.htm.

———. "LEGISinfo: Frequently Asked Questions." http://www.parl.gc.ca/legisinfo/Faq.aspx?Language=E#ID0EQ.

———. "Order and Notice Paper." http://www.parl.gc.ca/content/sen/chamber/411/orderpaper/ord-e.htm.

———. "Preliminary Pages." *House of Commons Procedure and Practice*. Accessed February 21, 2016. http://www.parl.gc.ca/Procedure-Book-Livre/Document.aspx?sbdid=7C730F1D-E10B-4DFC-863A-83E7E1A69040E&sbpid=CAF791AA-CC05-499A-87EC-8E4FFE38572B&Language=E&Mode=1.

———. "Publication Search." http://www.parl.gc.ca/Parliamentarians/en/PublicationSearch?PubType=203.

———. *Rules of the Senate / Règlement du Sénat*. Accessed February 12, 2016. http://www.parl.gc.ca/About/Senate/Rules/rules-senate-reglement-senat.pdf.

———. "Senate of Canada: About Committees." http://www.parl.gc.ca/SenCommitteeBusiness/AboutCommittees.aspx?parl=42&ses=1&Language=E.

———. Senate of Canada. *Companion to the Rules of the Senate*. Accessed February 20, 2016. http://sen.parl.gc.ca/portal/Companion-Rules/companion-rules-e.htm.

———. *Senate Procedural Notes*. Accessed February 12, 2016. http://www.parl.gc.ca/About/senate/proceduralNotes/procedural-notes-e.htm.

———. "Senate Procedure in Practice." Accessed February 12, 2016. http://sen.parl.gc.ca/portal/SPIP/spip-e.htm.

———. "The Senate Today." http://www.parl.gc.ca/about/senate/today/laws-e.html#aspects.

———. "Speaker's Rulings." Accessed February 12, 2016. http://sen.parl.gc.ca/portal/rulings/speaker-rulings-e.htm.

———. "Special Joint Committee on Physician-Assisted Dying." http://www.parl.gc.ca/Committees/en/PDAM?parl=42&session=1.

———. *Standing Orders of the House of Commons, April 2016*. http://www.parl.gc.ca/About/House/StandingOrders/toc-e.htm.

Privy Council Office Canada. Orders in Council database. http://www.pco-bcp.gc.ca/oic-ddc.asp?lang=eng&page=secretariats.

Sieberer, Ulrich. "Reforming the Rules of the Parliamentary Game: Measuring and Explaining Changes in Parliamentary Rules in Austria, Germany, and Switzerland, 1945–2010." *West European Politics* 34, no. 5 (2011): 948–75.

4

COMMISSIONS AND TRIBUNALS

Caron Rollins

Commissions of inquiry and administrative tribunals are agencies created and authorized by all levels of government in Canada. This chapter begins with an overview of federal Royal Commissions of Inquiry (COIs) and includes comparator information for provincial commissions of inquiry. Seven federal Royal Commissions spanning the years 1970 to 2012 are examined for their publication output and for the dissemination and stewardship practices provided for these outputs, by the commissioner(s), the Privy Council, DSP, LAC, or others. The publication output of a COI is more than just a final report. At the time of going to press, only incomplete information was available for the Truth and Reconciliation Commission, and the National Inquiry into Missing and Murdered Indigenous Women and Girls was just beginning its work. The chapter concludes with a section on tribunals—independent government agencies that may be referred to as a tribunal, an administrative board, or even a commission (in this chapter the word *tribunal* will be used). Tribunals must be created by federal or provincial legislation or municipal bylaw. Once created, tribunals deal with a particular public policy area and may move decision making out of the courts.[1] The outputs of tribunals typically consist of reports and decisions. Sources consulted to locate COI and tribunal outputs are listed in the bibliography at the end of the chapter.

COMMISSIONS OF INQUIRY

All of the outputs produced by COIs, particularly Royal Commissions, inform citizens, have enduring value, are precarious, and, because of their "difference," require attention to their dissemination and stewardship. These four points are explained in full in the introductory chapter to this book. Attention to dissemination and stewardship must be more focused in the digital era, where changing digital formats pose challenges, analog formats (print and microform) play a lesser role, and the dissemination practices of traditional publishers, including the Government of Canada and commercial publishers, have changed (e.g., open government) or ceased, and where documents have become subject to access-to-information laws. *Budget 2012* required Publications Canada to transition to exclusively electronic publication by 2014.[2] These changes require that a variety of sources and approaches be employed to find all the output of COIs. Attention should focus on government websites; web archives; electronic collections including text and video; libraries; archives; public legal information institutes like CANLII (a website project of the Federation of Law Societies of Canada); and open government initiatives. It is important to consider the possibility that donations of COI material may be found in local archives or libraries.

It is through the Privy Council Office (PCO) of Canada, the Prime Minister's Office, and the federal Cabinet that federal COIs come into being. The Privy Council website states that "although Canadians are perhaps most familiar with 'royal commissions,' there are several different kinds of Commissions of Inquiry. These can be established under either Part I or Part II of the *Inquiries Act*, or any one of 87 or more federal statutes."[3]

A federal COI is officially established when the Privy Council of Canada issues an Order-in-Council (OIC), designated by the abbreviation "P.C." plus a numeric identifier consisting of a number and the year. Federal COIs may or may not be designated *Royal Commissions*, and it was recommended by the Law Reform Commission of Canada in its 1997 report that "technically a royal commission is a commission issued under the great Seal of Canada, which in practice generally means a commission established under Part I of the *Inquiries Act*. But the adjective 'royal' is much abused with some commissions technically entitled to its use not employing it, and others appropriating it when they have no business doing so. In our view the term is best ignored."[4]

Federally, in Canada, departmental inquires also exist; these are created under Part II of the *Inquiries Act*.[5] As well, a federal statute may allow a federal minister to create a COI. Two notable examples of federal inquiries created under statutes other than the *Inquiries Act* are the Mackenzie Valley Pipeline Inquiry (Berger, 1974),[6] established on March 21, 1974, by Order-in-Council P.C. 1974-641 under s. 19(f) and (h) *Territorial Lands Act*; and the Truth and Reconciliation Commission, established by schedule N of the *Indian Residential Schools Settlement Agreement*.[7]

Provinces may also create COIS under their respective inquiry statutes. For a list of these statutes see the "Table of Authorizing Statutes" in *The Conduct of Public Inquiries: Law, Policy, and Practice*.[8] Current versions of these provincial inquiry statutes (as well as the federal *Inquiries Act*) are available on CANLII.[9] Every province has a bibliography covering its inquiries. See, for example, *Royal Commission and Commissions of Inquiry under the "Public Inquiries Act" in British Columbia*, a 1945 publication updated twice (1946–80 and 1981–2009),[10] and *Royal Commissions and Commissions of Inquiry in the Province of Alberta, 1905–1976*.[11] There is an older bibliography that covers all provinces, *Provincial Royal Commissions and Commissions of Inquiry, 1867–1982: A Selective Bibliography*.[12]

Digitized collections of provincial COIS are available for some provinces. Four examples are *British Columbia Royal and Special Commissions: 1872–1980*, *Alberta Digital Royal Commissions*, *New Brunswick Digital Commissions of Inquiry: The Early Years*, and *Royal Commissions of Ontario*. The Registry of Canadian Government Information Digitization Projects (see chapter 9 herein) lists these four.

For a fuller discussion of the distinction between a commission of inquiry and a Royal Commission, see *Canadian Official Publications*[13] and

Records of Federal Royal Commissions (RG 33).[14] For greater detail about the historical, legal, and political aspects of cois, consult *Administrative Law: Commissions of Inquiry;*[15] *Commissions of Inquiry: Praise or Reappraise;*[16] and *The Conduct of Public Inquiries: Law, Policy, and Practice*.[17] The first two titles discuss in detail policy and advisory cois and investigative cois. *Commissions of Inquiry and Policy Change: A Comparative Analysis,*[18] in its case studies of ten cois, includes both types.

▶ Output and Checklists

The output of a coi includes interim reports, the required final reports,[19] research studies, briefs, submissions, and evidence presented at hearings, as well as minutes or transcripts. Final reports should provide listings of these documents, as well as the names of the commissioners and other members of the commission's staff, secretariat, researchers, and consultants hired. The Order-in-Council should include section(s) detailing disposition of the outputs of the coi. The oic should be included in the final report; when it is not included, the oic may be difficult to obtain. Although federal oics are a type of statutory instrument, oics that establish a coi and appoint its commissioner(s) are not of the type whereby the full text is required to be published in the *Canada Gazette*, Part I.[20] The Privy Council database only includes the full text of oics approved "after November 1, 2002," and older oics must be requested from lac; those published between 1867 and 1924 can be searched online.[21] Provincial oic lists are maintained either by the Queen's Printer for the province or by the office of the Executive Council (the provincial equivalent of the Privy Council).

Final reports of federal cois are tabled in the House of Commons, recorded in the *Debates (Hansard)* and *Journals*, and assigned a sessional paper number. Prior to *Budget 2012*, final reports were available in print from Publications Canada and at federal depository libraries (see chapter 1) and have been available online from lac for a number of years (see chapter 2). A comparison of the names of the commissioners submitting the final report, and those originally appointed, may reveal changes over the course of a commission's inquiry. The names of participating individuals have research value because these individuals may write about a COI afterwards or donate their documents to an archive or library.

Print, microfilm, and online bibliographies and checklists exist for federal COIs. George Fletcher Henderson's *Federal Royal Commissions in Canada, 1867–1968: A Checklist* [Henderson],[22] is a listing of 396 federal COI entries; in 1977 Micromedia issued a complete microfiche edition of the reports listed.[23] Additionally, with permissions from COI staff, official reporters, and Public Archives of Canada (now Library and Archives Canada), Micromedia had worked with official reporters and commission office staff to create microform collections of final reports and transcripts of public hearings. Content guides were created by Micromedia for these COI collections. Micromedia's last production of COI transcripts of proceedings was in 1984.[24] Final reports and select documents other than proceedings continue to be added to the Microlog microfiche collection and the Canadian Public Policy e-book collection. Canadian Public Policy is a commercial product produced by the Canadian publisher Des Libris. Henderson has been updated by the Library of Parliament a total of four times,[25] which has continued the numbering system established by Henderson and included federal COIs regardless of the use of the word *Royal* in the title of the COI. "Each entry contains the title of the commission, date of appointment, Order in Council, P.C. number, the Minister recommending the commission, commissioner(s), report title, when tabled in the House, sessional paper number, whether or not public meetings were held and whether there are any supplementary reports, or studies commissioned."[26] The group of federal COIs now numbers 436: 433 listed in the 2009 Library of Parliament update plus three listings (Air India, Indian Claims, Cohen) retrieved from the PCO Commissions of Inquiry website.

According to OCLC WorldCat, digitized versions of *Federal Royal Commissions in Canada, 1867–1968: A Checklist* exist at Google Books, Hathi Trust, and the Library of Parliament, sources not publicly accessible in Canada.

Two important online sources for listings of COIs are the *Index to Federal Royal Commissions* from Library and Archives Canada (LAC)[27] and the Commissions of Inquiry website from the PCO.[28] Both list COIs established under the *Inquiries Act*. The *Index to Federal Royal*

Commissions includes bibliographic records for all documents held at LAC including print, microformat, and online holdings. The Commissions of Inquiry website is organized by name of commissioner chair and includes the title of the final report, date of final report, and a link to the LAC Electronic Collection where a PDF copy of the final report resides. LAC also maintains the Government of Canada Web Archive (see chapter 2). OCLC WorldCat is a source for bibliographic information with holdings from academic and public libraries, and from the Library of Parliament. AMICUS is also a source for bibliographic information and Canadian library holdings.[29]

Whalen's *Records of Federal Royal Commissions (RG 33)* provides details about COIs, from Order-in-Council to transfer of records at the end of a commission.[30] According to Whalen, between 1960 and 1985, records were transferred directly to the Dominion Archivist (now Library and Archives Canada); by 1985 and with the coming into force of the *Access to Information Act*,[31] they were transferred directly to the Clerk of the Privy Council. The PCO website states that "Commissions of Inquiry created under Part I of the *Inquiries Act* file their records with the Clerk of the Privy Council at the end of their work. The Privy Council Office then arranges for the safe transfer of the records to Library and Archives Canada."[32] Once transferred, COI records may be subject to review under the *Access to Information Act*[33] and by restrictions on Cabinet records.[34] Records not available to the public are subject to review prior to release. Records of COIs can be difficult to access (i.e., only upon request) if held only at the PCO or the LAC or by the Library of Parliament. However, the PCO has underway a project to digitize documents that are supplementary to the final reports of federal COIs. Supplementary documents, referred to as *outputs* in this chapter, include research studies, briefs, submissions, and minutes or transcripts of hearings. The digitized documents will initially be available only by request, but plans are in place to add them to the Publications Canada electronic collection.

► Current Scholarship

Commissions of Inquiry and Policy Change: A Comparative Analysis, the most recent (2014) study of Canadian COIs, includes studies of eight federal and two provincial commissions. A "theoretical framework of ideas, institutions, actors and relations"[35] was employed to study the selected COIs; each COI was studied by a separate researcher, with a separate chapter devoted to it. Inwood and Johns state that "where COIs are concerned, key actors include the commissioners, COI staff, researchers, the public and the media."[36] In the examination of the actors in each of the COIs, the researchers did not restrict themselves to just the commissioner's final reports but also cited documents relating to public hearings (transcripts, submissions, exhibits) and research reports. The importance of long-term access to COI documents is underscored by research of this type. One argument refuted in *Commissions of Inquiry and Policy Change* , and by other scholars, is that unless a COI results in legislative change, it is a failure.[37] Current scholarship on COIs in Canada and Britain points to the complexity of policy change and that all "COIs have some potential to be the source of, or stimulus for, policy change."[38] The importance is in the doing: "the value of a royal commission may arise from its report, the data compiled, and the analysis made, indeed, in the process itself...one can easily be misled by making assumptions based only [on] a commission's report."[39]

► Stewardship and Dissemination

Of the ten COIs studied in *Commissions of Inquiry and Policy Change,* six and the Cohen Commission were examined for this chapter's review of dissemination and stewardship practices. The tables show the results particularly for the dissemination and stewardship of the reports, submissions, hearings, and exhibits of each COI. It cannot be emphasized enough the importance of examining the complete table of contents and appendices of a COI, as well as any web archive, to ascertain all of the outputs. The chief commissioner is responsible for dissemination of material during the inquiry and for the contents of the final report. It is often assumed that a final report contains just the report; other outputs of the COI are likely included.

Following are the seven Canadian federal COIs examined (with the chair and the year of final report following the name):

▷ Royal Commission on the Status of Women (Bird; 1970). See table 4.1.
▷ Mackenzie Valley Pipeline Inquiry (Berger; 1988). See table 4.2.
▷ Royal Commission on New Reproductive Technologies (Baird; 1993). See table 4.3.
▷ Royal Commission on Aboriginal Peoples (Erasmus and Dussault; 1996). See table 4.4.
▷ Commission of Inquiry on the Blood System in Canada (Krever; 1997). See table 4.5.
▷ Commission on the Future of Health Care in Canada (Romanow; 2002). See table 4.6.
▷ Commission of Inquiry into the Decline of Sockeye Salmon in the Fraser River (Cohen; 2012). See table 4.7.

Once the outputs of the seven COIs were determined by examining the reports of each, information about dissemination and stewardship of the outputs was obtained from bibliographic verification of reports, submissions, hearings, and exhibits; location of Canadian holdings and public accessibility for these holdings; examination of the final reports of each COI for information about the disposition of final reports and papers; and contact with official agencies such as the PCO, Library of Parliament, LAC, federal departments, plus court reporters and the Cable Public Affairs Channel (CPAC).

ACCESS TO COMMISSION OF INQUIRY MATERIALS

The specific sources consulted for the seven COIs, and which should be consulted when looking for documents from any particular COI, are listed as follows; all sources are freely available on websites (as shown in this chapter's bibliography).

▷ Privy Council Office, *Commissions of Inquiry*, for commission name, name of chair, OIC number, and link to final report in LAC Electronic Collection
▷ Library and Archives Canada
  » *Index to Federal Royal Commissions* [LAC *Index*], for bibliographic information on materials associated with 200 federal COIS
  » AMICUS search, for holdings in various libraries and at LAC
  » Archives search, for archival holdings at LAC
  » LAC Electronic Collection website, for locating e-books and MARC records
  » Government of Canada Web Archive
▷ Government of Canada Publications Catalogue, for bibliographic information, particularly final reports and links to Government of Canada publications electronic collection
▷ OCLC WorldCat website, for holdings at research libraries and other contributing member libraries, in particular Canadian academic libraries and the Library of Parliament
▷ Archive-It website, for web archives created by member institutions that may include COIS
▷ The Cable Public Affairs Channel (CPAC), for video archives of select COI hearings

For provincial COIS, additionally consult:

▷ Government and Legislative Libraries Online Publications (GALLOP) portal, for locating "full-text and bibliographic content from the electronic government documents collections of 10 Canadian jurisdictions"[40]
▷ Legislative Library websites, for library catalogues and digital collections
▷ Provincial archives websites, for online catalogues and finding lists
▷ Provincial Queen's Printer and Executive Council websites, for OIC listings

The Commission of Inquiry into the Wrongful Conviction of David Milgaard is a good example of a provincial inquiry in which careful checking of alternate sources can unearth previously inaccessible material. The final report was published in print in two volumes with an accompanying CD-ROM that contained nineteen appendices; one appendix includes the complete transcript of the trial by jury. The report and appendices have been digitized by the Saskatchewan Legislative Library, and the website of the inquiry is in the Internet Archive.

The precarious nature of commissions is illustrated by the access issues that the CD-ROM *For Seven Generations* presents.[41] It contains everything collected and published by the Royal Commission on Aboriginal Peoples. See figure 4.1 for the six sections of *For Seven Generations*.

For over a decade there have been problems in accessing the content of the CD-ROM. The operating system on which it was based is obsolete. The CD-ROM was created in 1996 for use with a microprocessor 386; it was originally distributed by the DSP and was available for purchase until 2010. With a patch, the compact disc could be used with Windows 2000, Vista, and XP. Now only older machines can access the content. The CD-ROM continues to be sought by researchers, for it is the only source for two hundred research reports[42] and, until a University of Saskatchewan digital archives project in 2012, for the transcripts of public hearings.[43] The digitization project of the Privy Council Office offers hope for access to the research reports through Publications Canada. The reasoning behind the creation of the CD-ROM is documented in the final report.[44] References to the intended content of the disc are found in the opening pages of volume 1, page xiii, of the final report and in the appendices to volume 5 (appendix C, page 303, and appendix G, page 332).

> At the close of our work, a CD-ROM containing a large part of the evidence we considered will be available: the public hearing transcripts, this report and other special reports, discussion papers and much of the research conducted for us. The CD-ROM will include a guide for use by teachers in secondary schools and adult learning programs.

FIGURE 4.1

Title screen, Canada, *Royal Commission on Aboriginal Peoples,* For Seven
Generations: An Information Legacy of the Royal Commission on
Aboriginal Peoples *(Ottawa: Libraxus, 1997).* CD-ROM.

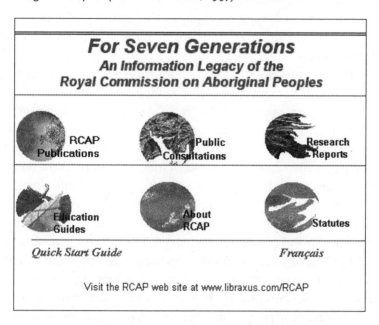

The University of Victoria Archives holds manuscripts from commission staff who worked on the commission's CD-ROM project. The University of Saskatchewan Archives holds the transcripts of hearings and round-table discussions, donated by Commissioner Alan Blakeney.

In contrast to the inaccessible outputs stored on the Royal Commission's CD-ROM are the very accessible outputs of the Mackenzie Valley Pipeline Inquiry. Most outputs of this COI are available in a Micromedia collection and a (still usable) CD-ROM issued in 2004. On November 2016, LAC released on its website a database of the Royal Commission on Aboriginal Peoples; the database contains the previously inaccessible outputs.[45]

Will researchers working on other commissions of inquiry encounter similar technical problems in accessing research reports and transcripts of public hearings? The spring 2016 addition of more years of content to the Government of Canada Web Archive has improved access to the outputs of cois; the latest version of the archive, released in 2016, includes the web archives of four recent cois (Cohen, Major, Iacobucci, and Oliphant). Commissioners of cois choose the material that is to be placed for public dissemination on a coi website. Websites do provide improved access (over physical format) to coi outputs. Web archives, properly preserved, can provide for long-term dissemination and stewardship.

For the seven federal cois chosen for this chapter, tables 4.1 to 4.7 show the results of examining each coi for dissemination and stewardship of its outputs, in particular the reports, submissions, hearings, and exhibits. It can be assumed that final reports are all listed in the Government of Canada Publications Catalogue, in all formats available at the time of publication and as added afterwards, for example, PDF versions. As previously noted, the Privy Council Office transfers all records of a coi (outputs) to LAC. When the oic establishing a commission has included a section on disposition of documents, this has been noted in the table for the coi. Questions about federal cois may be sent to the Privy Council Office. Abbreviations used in the tables an be found in the Abbreviations section at the start of this book. As with the Royal Commission on Aboriginal Peoples, commercial publication of outputs and donations of papers to libraries and archives are not unusual for federal cois.

Access to the documents of the Truth and Reconciliation Commission (TRC) and the *Indian Residential Schools Settlement Agreement* [IRSSA] is still evolving. The work of the TRC ended in December 2015. As of August 2016, the TRC website was live. It has been web archived and is available in two Internet archive collections: Canadian Government[46] and Columbia University.[47] The National Centre for Truth and Reconciliation (NCTR) at the University of Manitoba will continue the work of the TRC, including the responsibility for the core of material gathered by the commission, described as "7,000 video statements of Survivors and intergenerational Survivors of the schools, and in the millions of documents from government and churches that attest to their experience."[48] The NCTR has underway a project, "Websites of Reconciliation," that will include the websites of the TRC and IRSSA.[49] The final report of the TRC was published on the TRC website and is included in the Publications Canada electronic collection; the print version was published for the TRC by McGill-Queen's University Press.

The National Inquiry into Missing and Murdered Indigenous Women and Girls was established on August 3, 2016, by Order-in-Council P.C. 2016-0742 (website http://www.mmiwg-ffada.ca/).[50] The OIC details the requirements for interim and final reports, the availability of transcripts of public hearings, and the deposit of records with the Clerk of the Privy Council. The Government of Canada held a "pre-inquiry design process" that lasted from December 2015 to January 2016.[51] Overviews of the pre-inquiry design meetings and a final report are available on the Pre-Inquiry Design Process website. This COI is also referred to as the Joint National Commission into Murdered and Missing Indigenous Women and Girls; to date, OICs from Saskatchewan and Alberta have been issued. A previous example of provinces joining a federal COI was during the Commission of Inquiry on the Blood System in Canada.

TABLE 4.1.

Royal Commission on the Status of Women, 1970 (Chair: Florence Bird)

OUTPUT	DISSEMINATION	STEWARDSHIP
OIC P.C. 1967/312, section 9(d), "file with the Dominion Archivist the papers and records of the Commission"	Privy Council, Final report included	Privy Council, LAC
Final report	Print; Publications Canada	DSP, LAC, LACEC
Commissioners	Listed in OIC, Final report	
COI staff/secretariat	Final report, listed in appendix	
Studies prepared	Final report, listed in appendix. Print, Publications Canada	DSP, LAC, LACEC
Consultants	Final report, listed in appendix	
Submissions (briefs)	Final report, listed in appendix	LAC
Briefs and transcripts	Final report, listed in appendix. Micromedia 1972 briefs drawn from *RG 33/89*, vols. 11–18, National Archives of Canada	LAC, MM
Information kit	Print, Publications Canada	LAC, DSP

TABLE 4.2.

Mackenzie Valley Pipeline Inquiry, 1977 (Chair: Thomas Berger)

OUTPUT	DISSEMINATION	STEWARDSHIP
OIC P.C. 1974/641 pursuant to s. 19(f) and (h) *Territorial Lands Act*; now 23(h), "report to the Minister of Indian Affairs and Northern Development...dispatch and file with the Minister the papers and records of the inquiry"	Privy Council, Final report included	LAC
Final report	Print, Publications Canada 1977; republished 1988. CD-ROM INAC, published 2004	INAC, LAC, LACEC, DSP, GCWA
Transcripts of community hearings	INAC CD-ROM	INAC, LAC, DSP
Transcripts of public hearings, briefs, exhibits, submissions, and index	Print; Micromedia film of verbatim transcripts of public hearings and most textual exhibits (briefs, submissions)	INAC, LAC, MM

TABLE 4.3.

*Royal Commission on New Reproductive Technologies, 1993
(Chair: Patricia Baird)*

OUTPUT	DISSEMINATION	STEWARDSHIP
OIC P.C. 1989-2150	Privy Council, Final report (excerpt included)	Privy Council, LAC
Final report	Print, Publications Canada	Privy Council, LAC, LACEC, DSP
Commissioners	Final report, listed in vol. 1	Privy Council, LAC, LACEC, DSP
COI staff/secretariat/ contractors	Final report, listed in vol. 2, appendix F	Privy Council, LAC, LACEC, DSP
Participants in public hearings	Final report, listed in vol. 2, appendix B	Privy Council, LAC, LACEC, DSP
Participants in symposia colloquia, and other commission activities	Final report, listed in vol. 2, appendix C	Privy Council, LAC, LACEC, DSP
Written submissions and opinions	Final report, listed in vol. 2, appendix D, plus a report of 500 personal submissions in research report volumes	LAC
Briefs submitted at public hearings with lists of intervenors	30 print volumes of transcripts of hearings, submissions, and related material	LAC, LP
Research studies	15 print volumes, listed in vol. 2, appendix E; Print, Publications Canada	LAC, DSP
Background papers, other contributors	Final report, listed in vol. 2, appendix E	LAC
Information kit	Print, Publications Canada	LAC, DSP

TABLE 4.4.

Royal Commission on Aboriginal Peoples, 1996
(Chairs: George Erasmus and René Dussault)

OUTPUT	DISSEMINATION	STEWARDSHIP
OIC P.C. 1991/1597, section 11, states "the Commissioners be directed to file papers and records and papers of the inquiry as soon as reasonably may be after the conclusion of the inquiry with the Clerk of the Privy Council"	Privy Council, Final report (only schedule 1 to the OIC included)	Privy Council, LAC
	The Mandate Royal Commission on Aboriginal Peoples: Background Documents[52]	DSP
Final report	Print, Publications Canada; Libraxus CD-ROM; INAC html, Queen's IR[53]	Privy Council, LAC, LACEC, DSP, GCWA
Commissioners	Final report, listed in appendices	
Staff and advisors	Final report, listed in vol. 5	
Commission consultations and research	Final report, listed in vol. 5, appendix C, providing an overview of the public hearings	
Commission publications	Final report, vol. 5	LAC, LACEC, DSP
Research studies, special studies	Libraxus CD-ROM	LAC, LACEC, DSP
Round-table reports	Print, Publications Canada; Libraxus CD-ROM	LAC, DSP, LACEC
Transcripts of hearings and round tables	Libraxus CD-ROM; University of Saskatchewan Archives (Smith 2009); StenoTran Services Ltd.	LAC, University of Saskatchewan Archives[54]

TABLE 4.4. *(cont'd)*

OUTPUT	DISSEMINATION	STEWARDSHIP
Briefs and submissions, and research studies not published in book or CD-ROM	Final report, vol. 1, page ii	LAC
Education guide	Libraxus CD-ROM; University of Victoria Archives holds manuscripts	University of Victoria Archives
Videos (VHS)	Final report, listed in VHS format, vol. 5, appendix C, p. 303; streaming digital, University of Victoria Libraries	Privy Council, LAC, University of Victoria Libraries

TABLE 4.5.

*Commission of Inquiry on the Blood System in Canada, 1997
(Chair: Horace Krever)*

OUTPUT	DISSEMINATION	STEWARDSHIP
OIC (1 federal, 3 provincial) P.C. 1993-1879, section J, states that the Commissioner "is directed to file papers and records of the inquiry with the Clerk of the Privy Council"	Privy Council, Final report includes Saskatchewan, Ontario, and Prince Edward Island	Privy Council, LAC
Final report	Print, Publications Canada	Privy Council, LAC, LACEC, DSP
Commissioner	Listed in OIC	
Persons appearing before the inquiry	Final report, listed in vol. 3, appendix F	
Public submissions	Final report, listed in vol. 3, appendix G	
Exhibits of hearings and supplementary documents	Print	LAC, Dalhousie Law School Library
Transcripts	Computer disc by International Rose Reporting	LAC, computer disc by international Rose reporting, held at Health Canada, Saskatchewan Legislative Library, LP

TABLE 4.6.

Commission on the Future of Health Care in Canada, 2002
(Chair: Roy Romanow)

OUTPUT	DISSEMINATION	STEWARDSHIP
OIC P.C. 2001/569, section d(vii) states: "the Commissioner is to file papers and records of the inquiry with the Clerk of the Privy Council."	Privy Council, Final report included	Privy Council, LAC
Final report	Print; Publications Canada	Privy Council, LAC, LACEC, DSP, GCPE
Website	Health Canada	GCWA
Staff	Final report, listed in appendix D	
Submissions	Final report, listed in appendix A; Gc.ca web archive	GCWA
Consultations including open public hearings	Final report, listed in appendix B; CPAC video archive (partial); website includes summaries of open public hearings	LAC, GCWA
Research	Final report, listed in appendix C; website, discussion papers; research projects summarized on others by request to LAC or by request to principal researchers. Expert research round tables by request to host. Selected papers republished in *Romanow Papers*, 3 vols. (Marchildon, McIntosh, and Forest 2003)[55]	LAC, GCWA
Transcripts	Website	GCWA

TABLE 4.7.

Commission of Inquiry into the Decline of Sockeye Salmon
in the Fraser River, 2012 (Chair: Bruce Cohen)

OUTPUT	DISSEMINATION	STEWARDSHIP
OIC P.C. 2009/1860, directs the commissioner to use an automated document management system specified by the Attorney General of Canada and the Privy Council; directs the commissioner to ensure that members of the public can obtain transcripts of public proceedings; all records to Privy Council for transmittal to LAC; Ringtail Legal database to remain confidential	Privy Council, Final report included	Privy Council, LAC
Final report	Print, Publications Canada; DVD, Publications Canada; website	Privy Council, LAC, LACEC, DSP, GCPE, SFU
Interim report	Print, Publications Canada; CD-ROM, Publications Canada; website	LAC, LACEC, DSP, GCPE, SFU
Commissioner and staff, public forum presenters, submitters, witnesses, hearings, participants	Final report, listed in appendices	
Commission process	Final report: see its vol. 3, ch. 5, "Commission Process," which outlines use of Ringtail Legal database for document management	

TABLE 4.7. *(cont'd)*

OUTPUT	DISSEMINATION	STEWARDSHIP
Exhibits	Website; Ringtail Legal	LAC, SFU, GCWA, DSP
Research reports	Website; DVD; Ringtail Legal	LAC, SFU, GCWA, DSP
Technical reports	Website; DVD; Ringtail Legal	LAC, SFU, GCWA, DSP
Policy and practice reports	Website; DVD; Ringtail Legal	
Transcripts	Website; DVD; Ringtail Legal	
DVD: terms of reference, final report, interim reports, statutes, transcripts, cited exhibits, 15 technical reports, 21 policy and practice reports	CD-ROM, Publications Canada	LAC, DSP
Website: introductory videos, calendar, transcripts, exhibits, policy and practice reports, submissions, witness and participant lists, reports and publications. The website will continue to be available through LAC.	Fisheries and Oceans Canada	LAC, GCWA, SFU

TRIBUNALS

Tribunals are created by federal, provincial, or municipal legislation. They fall under the area of administrative law. There are many legal and scholarly works available that discuss Canadian boards and administrative tribunals, such as *Administrative Law in Canada*,[56] which opens with this quotation: "in Canada, boards are a way of life. Boards and the functions they fulfil are legion."[57] Tribunals issue decisions on applications, conduct investigations, and issue reports, guidelines, and standards. These outputs have the same characteristics as other government documents; they inform citizens, have enduring value, are precarious, and, because of their "difference," require attention to their dissemination and stewardship.

Tribunal decisions may involve citizens as individuals or affect all citizens collectively. Tribunals are created by government and can be dissolved by government. A recent example is the establishment of British Columbia's Civil Resolution Tribunal in July 2016 to focus on strata title and small claims disputes. The Canadian Wheat Board was established by the Government of Canada in 1935 and dissolved in 2012. The National Energy Board regulates pipelines and energy in Canada, and its recent panels and decisions (regarding Trans Mountain pipeline, Kinder Morgan Canada, Energy East pipeline) affect all Canadians. The decision of a provincial workers' compensation board can have grave consequences for workers and their families—as may the decision of a veterans tribunal.

The "Federal Organizations by Category" section of the Government of Canada website lists 27 "administrative tribunals" and 110 "agency/boards"; a description of the difference between the two categories is not provided.[58] A 1970s study examining the print publication practices of administrative boards in Canada surveyed 145 Canadian boards, of which 35 were federal boards, agencies, or tribunals.[59] Recently, Wakaruk examined losses in access to the content of federal government databases, comparing the *Weekly Checklist of Canadian Government Publications* and *InfoSource: Directory of Federal Government Databases*.[60] She found that tracking changes and migrations of databases was "difficult and convoluted" and that publication of some board decisions on government websites ceased in favour of publishing on CANLII. For example, the Immigration and Refugee Board states on its website: "A selection of decisions rendered by the IRB are available on the Canadian Legal Information Institute's (CANLII) website."[61]

ACCESS TO TRIBUNAL MATERIALS

Tribunal websites may publish their decisions as browsable or searchable lists or may embed them in a database. Some federal tribunals, such as the National Energy Board, had reports and decisions disseminated by the DSP. Prior to the Internet, requesting to be added to a tribunal's "mailing list" for receipt of print reports and decisions was routine work for government documents librarians. Final reports and other documents of tribunals may also be found in the Microlog microfiche collection and the Canadian Public Policy e-book collection.

Tribunal decisions may also be republished by commercial legal publishers, as stand-alone print (or electronic) subject reporters (lists of these can be found in legal research handbooks and citation manuals)— for example, the *Canada Energy Law Service*, in which are published select National Energy Board decisions. Tribunal publications, including decisions, may be found in commercial online legal databases, such as LexisNexis Quicklaw, particularly true prior to the advent of the Internet. Commercial online legal databases would provide access to many individual databases on their mainframe computers, and the databases were accessible, pre-Internet, via "terminal access to mainframe computers via a telecommunications network."[62] As far back as the 1990s, Quicklaw (which merged with LexisNexis in 2002) had a practice of actively seeking board decisions for inclusion in its online service. Since the advent of the Internet and the creation of government websites and websites like CANLII, more decisions are easily and freely accessible. CANLII includes federal and provincial board decisions on its site; in 2008 alone, twenty-five databases of labour board and tribunal decisions were added. To date, nineteen federal boards have been included. The interest of CANLII and legal publishers in tribunal decisions likely arises from the right of appeal to the courts that is provided for by some tribunals.

A comparison of three important federal tribunals—the National Energy Board (NEB), the Canadian Environmental Assessment Agency (CEAA), and the Transportation Safety Board (TSB)—shows completely different approaches to online access to outputs. NEB uses a document management system (OpenText Content Service) for its *Decisions & Filings* and its *Regulatory Document Index*. The CEAA *Registries* and the TSB *Reports* use website search and browse functions for document retrieval.

When locating information from a particular board, agency, or tribunal, the following open sources should be checked:

▷ The website of the board, agency, or tribunal. Determine the kind of publications that the board releases—annual reports, reports of investigations, decisions on applications—and whether these are available on the website. If there is no website, check the website of the government ministry or department responsible for the enabling statute that created the tribunal.

▷ The enabling statute of the board, agency, or tribunal. Use the Government of Canada's Justice Laws Website, CANLII, or a provincial laws website.

▷ Print publications. Determine whether publications have been or continue to be released in print, and where they might have been deposited, i.e., federally, in a provincial legislative library, a local university library, or a courthouse library.

▷ OCLC WorldCat (for holdings at research libraries and other contributing member libraries, in particular Canadian academic libraries and the Library of Parliament).

▷ Government of Canada Publications Catalogue website. Decisions by the federal board, agency, and tribunals listed in schedules I, I.1, and II of the *Financial Administration Act*[63] are required to be sent to the catalogue (see Canada Treasury Board Secretariat, *Procedures for Publishing*).[64]

▷ Government and Legislative Libraries Online Publications (GALLOP) portal website for provincial boards.

▷ Government of Canada website. Search for "decisions."

- ▷ The Open Government Portal's search function does not provide useful results, i.e., links to the decisions of a specific federal board, agency, or tribunal.
- ▷ Municipal websites.
- ▷ Web archives.

CONCLUSION

The starting point for locating all outputs, documents, and activities of a commission of inquiry should be the enabling Order-in-Council, followed by the final report itself. Next, examine each for information relating to the documents that have been made publicly available and those that are subject to restrictions. Look for digital collections, websites, web archives, videos (including streaming), CD-ROMS, DVDS, and databases. Look for donated collections. Search for secondary works.

The starting point for locating all outputs, documents, and activities of a tribunal is its website or the website of the government ministry or department responsible for the enabling statute that created the tribunal. Then, look for collections of decisions published in print reporters and in online commercial and free databases. Determine if the publication of decisions is required and where deposit is mandated. Contact your local law library.

Commissions of inquiry are established by our governments to examine issues, events, or institutions within Canadian society. Tribunals are established to deal with specific interactions between government agencies and particular individuals or groups. During and at the conclusion of their inquiries, COIs and tribunals produce government publications that "underpin informed citizen engagement."[65] Identifying the dissemination and stewardship practices for this category of government publications is complex and challenging. Complete, full-text collections of all the outputs of COIs and tribunals should be freely accessible with discovery technologies linking the activities of the producers of the outputs, the disseminators of the outputs, and the stewards of the outputs.

Notes

1. Maczko, "The Trend towards Administrative Tribunals," 146.
2. Government of Canada Publications, "The 2012 Budget and Publishing and Depository Services."
3. Canada, Privy Council Office, "About Commissions of Inquiry." See also chapter 2.
4. Law Reform Commission of Canada, *Administrative Law*, 5.
5. *Inquiries Act* (R.S.C. 1985, c. I-11).
6. Canada, Mackenzie Valley Pipeline Inquiry and Thomas R. Berger, *Northern Frontier, Northern Homeland*.
7. Residential Schools Settlement, "Official Court Notice: Settlement Agreement."
8. Ratushny, *The Conduct of Public Inquiries*, xix.
9. Canadian Legal Information Institute, CANLII.org.
10. Holmes, *Royal Commissions and Commissions of Inquiry*.
11. Backhaus and Alberta Legislature Library, *Royal Commissions of Inquiry in Alberta*.
12. Maillet, *Provincial Royal Commissions*.
13. Bishop, *Canadian Official Publications*, 130.
14. Whalen and Government Archives Division, *Records of Federal Royal Commissions (RG 33)*, ix.
15. Law Reform Commission of Canada, *Administrative Law*.
16. Manson and Mullan, *Commissions of Inquiry*.
17. Ratushny, *The Conduct of Public Inquiries*.
18. Inwood and Johns, *Commissions of Inquiry and Policy Change*.
19. Ratushny, *The Conduct of Public Inquiries*, chap. 9.
20. Hubley and Beaulieu, "Locating Canadian Orders in Council," 85.
21. http://www.bac-lac.gc.ca/eng/discover/politics-government/orders-council/Pages/orders-in-council.aspx.
22. Henderson, *Federal Royal Commissions in Canada, 1867–1966*.
23. Micromedia Limited and Henderson, *Guide to Microform Edition*.
24. Micromedia ProQuest, *Canadian Government Information on Microform*, 10–14.
25. Ledoux, *Commissions of Inquiry*. Updated in 1991, 1994, and 2009.
26. Bishop, *Canadian Official Publications*, 132.
27. Library and Archives Canada, *Index to Federal Royal Commissions*.
28. Privy Council Office, "Commissions of Inquiry."
29. Library and Archives Canada, AMICUS *Canadian National Catalogue*, accessed September 21, 2016, https://www.collectionscanada.gc.ca/amicus/index-e.html.
30. Whalen and Government Archives Division, *Records of Federal Royal Commissions*, xvii.

31. *Access to Information Act* (R.S.C. 1985, c. A-1), accessed July 27, 2016, http://laws-lois.justice.gc.ca/eng/acts/a-1/index.html.
32. Privy Council Office, "About Commissions of Inquiry," https://www.canada.ca/en/privy-council/services/commissions-inquiry/about.html.
33. Library and Archives Canada, *Legislative Restrictions: Records of the Government of Canada*, http://www.bac-lac.gc.ca/eng/services-public/access-documents/Pages/access-documents.aspx#a.
34. http://www.bac-lac.gc.ca/eng/discover/politics-government/cabinet-conclusions/pages/cabinet-conclusions.aspx.
35. Inwood and Johns, *Commissions of Inquiry and Policy Change*, 19.
36. Inwood and Johns, *Commissions of Inquiry and Policy Change*, 35.
37. Lauriat, "'The Examination of Everything,'" 45.
38. Inwood and Johns, *Commissions of Inquiry and Policy Change*, 24.
39. Lauriat, "'The Examination of Everything,'" 45. Michael Orsini, "Manufacturing Civil Society? How the Krever Inquiry on the Blood System in Canada Shaped Collective Action and Policy Change," ch. 9.
40. "GALLOPP—Portal Search Help," accessed July 27, 2016, http://aplicportal.ola.org/aplichelp-eng.asp?language=eng.
41. Canada, Royal Commission on Aboriginal Peoples, *For Seven Generations*.
42. Castellano and Hawkes, "Research Reports Prepared for the Royal Commission on Aboriginal Peoples."
43. Smith, "The Royal Commission on Aboriginal Peoples Transcripts Online," 135–40, accessed July 27, 2016.
44. Canada, Royal Commission on Aboriginal Peoples, Dussault, and Erasmus, *Report of the Royal Commission on Aboriginal Peoples*.
45. https://www.bac-lac.gc.ca/eng/discover/aboriginal-heritage/royal-commission-aboriginal-peoples/Pages/introduction.aspx.
46. Canadian Government Information Web Archive (University of Toronto), accessed September 27, 2016. Searched for http://www.trc.ca and found fourteen captures between May 14, 2011, and June 11, 2013. https://wayback.archive-it.org/3608/*/http://www.trc.ca.
47. "You are viewing an archived web page, collected at the request of Columbia University Libraries using Archive-It. This page was captured on 21:22:27 Mar 06, 2013, and is part of the Human Rights collection" (Truth and Reconciliation Commission of Canada), accessed September 27, 2016, https://wayback.archive-it.org/1068/20130306212227/http://www.trc.ca/websites/trcinstitution/index.php?p=3.
48. National Centre for Truth and Reconciliation website, http://umanitoba.ca/centres/nctr/commisioners.html, accessed August 3, 2016.
49. Email communication with the National Centre for Truth and Reconciliation, July 2016.

50. Order-in-Council P.C. 2016-0736, Privy Council of Canada Orders in Council Database, accessed August 3, 2016, http://www.pco-bcp.gc.ca/oic-ddc.asp.

51. Government of Canada, "Pre-inquiry Design Process," accessed September 21, 2016, https://www.aadnc-aandc.gc.ca/eng/1449240082445/144924010 6460.

52. Canada, Royal Commission on Aboriginal Peoples, and Dickson, *The Mandate Royal Commission on Aboriginal Peoples*. Section A, Press release by Prime Minister Brian Mulroney re the Royal Commission on Aboriginal Peoples; section B, Federal order in council dated 26 August, 1991, reference P.C. 1991–1597; section C, Report of the special representative respecting the Royal Commission on Aboriginal Peoples.

53. *Report of the Royal Commission on Aboriginal Peoples*, accessed September 27, 2016, http://hdl.handle.net/1974/6874.

54. University of Saskatchewan Archives, "Our Legacy," Government Commissions: Royal Commission on Aboriginal Peoples, accessed September 27, 2016, http://scaa.usask.ca/ourlegacy/.

55. Marchildon, McIntosh, and Forest, *Romanow Papers*.

56. Blake, *Administrative Law in Canada*, 3.

57. *Newfoundland Telephone Co. v. Newfoundland (Board of Commissioners of Public Utilities)*, [1992] 1 SCR 623.

58. "Federal Organizations by Category," accessed October 3, 2016, https://www.appointments-nominations.gc.ca/lstOrgs.asp?type-typ=3&lang=eng.

59. Janisch and Canadian Association of Law Libraries, *Publication of Administrative Board Decisions in Canada*.

60. Wakaruk, "What Do You Mean You Don't Have a Copy?"

61. Immigration and Refugee Board of Canada, "Decisions."

62. John N. Davis, "The Digital Storage, Retrieval, and Transmission of Case Reports in Canada: A Brief History," in *Law Reporting and Legal Publishing in Canada: A History*, ed. Martha L. Foote (Kingston, ON: Canadian Association of Law Libraries, 1997).

63. *Financial Administration Act* (R.S.C. 1986, c. F-11).

64. Treasury Board Secretariat, *Procedures for Publishing*, accessed October 3, 2016, http://www.tbs-sct.gc.ca/pol/doc-eng.aspx?id=27167.

65. Wakaruk and Li, "Introduction," herein.

Bibliography

Access to Information Act, R.S.C. 1985, c. A-1. Accessed July 27, 2016. http://laws-lois.justice.gc.ca/eng/acts/a-1/index.html.

Alberta Digital Royal Commissions. Accessed August 3, 2016. http://royal.library.ualberta.ca/royal.cfm.

Backhaus, Christine E., and Alberta Legislature Library. *Royal Commissions of Inquiry in Alberta, 1905–1976*. Edmonton, AB: Legislature Library, 1977.

Bishop, Olga B. *Canadian Official Publications*. 1st ed. Guides to Official Publications, vol. 9. Oxford and New York: Pergamon Press, 1981.

Blake, Sara. *Administrative Law in Canada*. 5th ed. Markham, ON: LexisNexis Canada, 2011.

British Columbia Royal and Special Commissions: 1872–1980. Accessed August 3, 2016. https://www.llbc.leg.bc.ca/commissions/.

Cable Public Affairs Channel. "CPAC Digital Archive." Accessed September 13, 2016. http://www.cpac.ca/en/digital-archives/.

Canada. Commission of Inquiry into the Decline of Sockeye Salmon in the Fraser River, and Bruce I. Cohen. *The Uncertain Future of Fraser River Sockeye*. Ottawa: Commission of Inquiry into the Decline of Sockeye Salmon in the Fraser River, 2012.

———. Commission of Inquiry on the Blood System in Canada, and Horace Krever. *Final Report*. Ottawa: Commission of Inquiry on the Blood System in Canada, 1997.

———. Commission on the Future of Health Care in Canada, and Roy J. Romanow. *Building on Values: the Future of Health Care in Canada: Final Report*. Saskatoon, SK: Commission on the Future of Health Care in Canada, 2002.

———. Government of Canada Publications Catalogue. Accessed July 27, 2016. http://publications.gc.ca/site/eng/ourCatalogue.html.

———. Immigration and Refugee Board of Canada. "Decisions." Accessed August 4, 2016, http://www.irb-cisr.gc.ca/Eng/BoaCom/decisions/Pages/index.aspx.

———. Justice Laws Website. Accessed July 27, 2016. http://laws-lois.justice.gc.ca/.

———. Mackenzie Valley Pipeline Inquiry, and Thomas R. Berger. *Northern Frontier, Northern Homeland: The Report of the Mackenzie Valley Pipeline Inquiry*. Ottawa: Supply and Services Canada, 1977.

———. Mackenzie Valley Pipeline Inquiry (Canada), and Thomas R. Berger. *Northern Frontier, Northern Homeland: The Report of the Mackenzie Valley Pipeline Inquiry*. Rev. ed. Vancouver, BC: Douglas & McIntyre, 1988.

———. Mackenzie Valley Pipeline Inquiry (Canada), Thomas R. Berger, and Indian and Northern Affairs Canada. *Northern Frontier, Northern Homeland: Mackenzie Valley Pipeline Inquiry, 1974–1977; Berger Commission Reports & Community Transcripts*. Yellowknife, NWT: Indian and Northern Affairs Canada, 2004.

———. Privy Council Office. "About Commissions of Inquiry." Accessed July 27, 2016. http://www.pco-bcp.gc.ca/index.asp?lang=eng&page=information&sub=commissions&doc=about-sujet-eng.htm.

———. Privy Council Office. "Commissions of Inquiry / Commissions d'enquete." Accessed July 27, 2016. http://www.pco-bcp.gc.ca/index.asp?lang=eng&page=information&sub=commissions.

———. Privy Council Office. "Info Source: Sources of Federal Government and Employee Information—Privy Council Office." Accessed July 27, 2016. http://www.pco-bcp.gc.ca/index.asp?lang=eng&page=information&sub=publications&doc=info-source/index-eng.htm.

———. Royal Commission on Aboriginal Peoples, and Libraxus Inc. *For Seven Generations: An Information Legacy of the Royal Commission on Aboriginal Peoples.* CD-ROM. Ottawa: Libraxus, 1997.

———. Royal Commission on Aboriginal Peoples, and R.G. Brian Dickson. *The Mandate Royal Commission on Aboriginal Peoples: Background Documents.* Ottawa: The Commission, 1991.

———. Royal Commission on Aboriginal Peoples, René Dussault, and Georges Erasmus. *Report of the Royal Commission on Aboriginal Peoples.* Ottawa: The Commission, 1996.

———. Royal Commission on New Reproductive Technologies, and Patricia Baird. *Proceed with Care: Final Report of the Royal Commission on New Reproductive Technologies.* Ottawa: Minister of Government Services Canada, 1993.

———. Royal Commission on the Status of Women in Canada, and Florence Bird. *Report of the Royal Commission on the Status of Women in Canada.* Ottawa: Information Canada, 1970.

———. Treasury Board. *Info Source: Directory of Federal Government Databases.* Ottawa: Treasury Board Secretariat, 1996.

Canadian Legal Information Institute. "CanLII." Accessed July 27, 2016. https://www.canlii.org.

Castellano, Marlene Brant, and David C. Hawkes. "Research Reports Prepared for the Royal Commission on Aboriginal Peoples: Introduction." In Canada, Royal Commission on Aboriginal Peoples, and Libraxus Inc., *For Seven Generations: An Information Legacy of the Royal Commission on Aboriginal Peoples.* Ottawa: Libraxus, 1997.

Financial Administration Act (R.S.C. 1985, c. F-11). Accessed August 3, 2016. http://laws-lois.justice.gc.ca/eng/acts/f-11/.

Government and Legislative Libraries Online Publications (GALLOP) Portal. Accessed July 27, 2016. http://aplicportal.ola.org/.

Government of Canada. "Federal Organizations by Category." Accessed October 3, 2016. https://www.appointments-nominations.gc.ca/lstOrgs.asp?type-typ=3&lang=eng.

———. "Pre-inquiry Design process." Accessed September 21, 2016. https://www.aadnc-aandc.gc.ca/eng/1449240082445/1449240106460.

Government of Canada Publications. "The 2012 Budget and Publishing and Depository Services." Accessed July 27, 2016. http://wayback.archive.it.org/5060/20150611005749/http://www.publications.gc.ca/site/eng/news/2012/2012-006-eng.html.

Henderson, George F. *Federal Royal Commissions in Canada, 1867–1966: A Checklist*. Toronto: University of Toronto Press, 1967.

Holmes, Marjorie C. *Royal Commissions and Commissions of Inquiry under the "Public Inquiries Act" in British Columbia, 1872–1942: A Checklist*. Victoria, BC: King's Printer, 1945. Updated by Judith Antonik Bennett and Legislative Library of British Columbia, 1943–80 and 1981–2009.

Hubley, Wendy, and Micheline Beaulieu. "Locating Canadian Orders in Council." *Canadian Law Libraries* 26, no. 3 (2001): 83–86. Accessed September 27, 2016. http://heinonline.org/HOL/Page?handle=hein.journals/callb26&start_page=83&collection=journals&id=95.

Inquiries Act (R.S.C. 1985, c. I-11). Accessed July 27, 2016. http://laws-lois.justice.gc.ca/eng/acts/i-11/page-1.html.

Inwood, Gregory J., and Carolyn Johns. *Commissions of Inquiry and Policy Change: A Comparative Analysis*. Toronto: University of Toronto Press, 2014.

Janisch, Alice H., and Canadian Association of Law Libraries. *Publication of Administrative Board Decisions in Canada*. London, ON: Canadian Association of Law Libraries, 1972.

Lauriat, Barbara. "'The Examination of Everything': Royal Commissions in British Legal History." *Statute Law Review* 31, no. 1 (2010): 24–46. https://doi.org/10.1093/slr/hmq001.

Law Reform Commission of Canada. *Administrative Law: Commissions of Inquiry*. Ottawa: The Commission, 1977.

Ledoux, Denise. *Commissions of Inquiry under the "Inquiries Act," Part I, 1967 to Date*. Ottawa: Information and Reference Branch Library of Parliament, 1980.

———. *Commissions of Inquiry under the "Inquiries Act," Part I, 1967 to Date*. Ottawa: Library of Parliament, Information and Technical Services Branch, 1991.

———. *Commissions of Inquiry under the "Inquiries Act," Part I, 1967 to Date*. Ottawa: Library of Parliament, Information and Technical Services Branch, 1994.

———. *Commissions of Inquiry under the "Inquiries Act," Part I, 1967 to October 2009*. Library of Parliament, 2009.

Library and Archives Canada. *Index to Federal Royal Commissions / Index des commissions royales federals*. Accessed July 27, 2016. http://www.bac-lac.gc.ca/eng/discover/royal-commissions-index/pages/index-federal-royal-commissions.aspx.

Library and Archives Canada Electronic Collection. Accessed July 2016, not available September 2016. http://www.collectionscanada.gc.ca/electroniccollection.index-e.html.

Maczko, Frank. "The Trend towards Administrative Tribunals." *The Advocate* 32 (1974): 146. http://heinonline.org/HOL/Page?handle=hein.barjournals/advvba0032&collection=journals&id=146.

Maillet, Lise. *Provincial Royal Commissions and Commissions of Inquiry, 1867–1982: A Selective Bibliography*. Ottawa: National Library of Canada, 1986.

Manson, Allan, and David J. Mullan. *Commissions of Inquiry: Praise or Reappraise.* Toronto: Irwin Law, 2003.

Marchildon, Gregory P., Thomas A. McIntosh, and Pierre-Gerlier Forest. *Romanow Papers.* 3 vols. Toronto: University of Toronto Press, 2003.

Micromedia Limited, and George F. Henderson. *Guide to Microform Edition of the Reports of the Royal Commissions of Canada, 1867–1966: A Supplement to Henderson, "Federal Royal Commissions in Canada, 1867–1966: A Checklist."* Toronto: Micromedia, 1977.

Micromedia ProQuest. *Canadian Government Information on Microform.* Ann Arbor, MI: Micromedia ProQuest, 2010.

National Centre for Truth and Reconciliation. Accessed July 27, 2016. http://umanitoba.ca/nctr/.

New Brunswick Commissions of Inquiry: The Early Years. Accessed October 6, 2016. http://www.lib.unb.ca/texts/nbhistory/commissions/about_it1.htm.

Newfoundland Telephone Co. v. Newfoundland (Board of Commissioners of Public Utilities), [1992] 1 SCR 623. CANLII 84 (SCC). Accessed October 3, 2016. http://canlii.ca/t/1fsfo.

Ratushny, Ed. *The Conduct of Public Inquiries: Law, Policy, and Practice.* Toronto: Irwin Law, 2009.

Residential Schools Settlement. "Official Court Notice: Settlement Agreement." Accessed July 27, 2016. http://www.residentialschoolsettlement.ca/settlement.html.

Royal Commissions of Ontario. Accessed October 6, 2016. https://archive.org/details/royalcommissions&tab=collection.

Saskatchewan. Commission of Inquiry into the Wrongful Conviction of David Milgaard, and Edward P. MacCallum. *Report of the Commission of Inquiry into the Wrongful Conviction of David Milgaard.* Saskatoon, SK: Commission of Inquiry into the Wrongful Conviction of David Milgaard, 2008.

Smith, David A. "The Royal Commission on Aboriginal Peoples Transcripts Online." *Native Studies Review* 18 no. 2 (2009): 135–40. https://ecommons.usask.ca/handle/10388/302.

University of Saskatchewan Archives. "Government Commissions—Royal Commission on Aboriginal Peoples." Our Legacy. Accessed September 27, 2016. http://scaa.usask.ca/ourlegacy/.

Wakaruk, Amanda. "What Do You Mean You Don't Have a Copy? An Attempt to Document Government of Canada Web Content Removed from Open Access." Paper presented on Government Information Day 2015 in Vancouver, BC, hosted by Simon Fraser University Libraries. https://doi.org/10.7939/R3H12VB2D.

Whalen, James Murray, and Government Archives Division, National Archives of Canada. *Records of Federal Royal Commissions (RG 33).* Ottawa: National Archives of Canada, 1990.

II

PROVINCIAL LANDSCAPE

5

ALBERTA GOVERNMENT PUBLISHING

Dani J. Pahulje

Alberta has a parliamentary system of government that is divided into three branches: legislative, judicial, and executive. The legislative branch is represented by the Legislative Assembly, and the documents produced by this branch are statutory or official. The courts represent the judicial branch and are independent from government in the carrying out of their functions; however, they have the responsibility of interpreting the laws created by the Legislative Assembly. The executive branch is represented by the Lieutenant-Governor, the premier, and Cabinet. Members of Cabinet are assigned responsibility for specific departments or ministries. The executive branch makes and implements the decisions that are required to maintain the rule of law and the well-being of Albertans. Documents produced by this branch are non-statutory and often referred to as departmental or administrative publications.

This chapter focuses on the Alberta government's publishing activities at the executive branch and, in particular, on publications that are made publicly available rather than on information within the internal government environment. Any publishing done by the judicial or legislative branches of government will not be covered but may be mentioned for clarification. The terms *department* and *ministry* will be used interchangeably. The chapter attempts to expand and build on the work done by A. Paul Pross and Catherine A. Pross in their book *Government Publishing in the Canadian Provinces: A Prescriptive Study*.

CREATION AND PRODUCTION

Paul and Catherine Pross defined government publications as those that are created by or for a department or agency of the government and "circulated to individuals and groups other than those advising or negotiating with the government concerning the subject matter of the document."[1] The decision to create and produce publications for public use rests with individual government departments. The only exceptions are publications that are mandated by legislation to be made available to the public—for example, *The Alberta Gazette,* the *Statutes of Alberta,* and ministry business plans.[2] This decision may be based on public demand for information or anticipation of a public need for information or may be the result of research that has been conducted by the government using government funds and then reported and made available to the public.

The creation of government publications is the responsibility of individual government departments and is, therefore, a decentralized activity. In the past, there was no co-operation or coordination among departments as to what was going to be published, and even within departments there was often little knowledge of what was being created and published by different units of the department. As a result, anyone looking for government information ran into difficulties because it was hard to determine whether or not the information they were looking for existed.

▶ Printing

Once a publication was created, it was printed or produced in a tangible (physical) format, often using paper as a medium. In 1906 Alberta's official government printer was established by *An Act Respecting Public Printing.* It was given responsibility for the printing and publishing of "the Acts of the Province, *The Alberta Gazette*, and such documents and announcements as may from time to time be required."[3] Its other responsibilities included the purchase of stationery and supplies for departments; the printing of blank forms of receipts and licences that were used in the collecting or accounting of revenue; and the printing of forms needed by the deputy provincial treasurer.[4] In 1911–12 its responsibilities were expanded to include the printing and binding of publications needed by the Legislative Assembly and government departments, as well as the procurement of all stationery and office supplies.[5]

Jurisdiction over the government printer, later known as the King's Printer[6] and then in 1954 as the Queen's Printer,[7] changed with time. This responsibility initially lay with Executive Council and then moved to the Public Affairs Bureau,[8] where it has remained since 1973.[9] In 2006 the Public Affairs Bureau moved under the jurisdiction of the Service Alberta ministry.

For the most part, with the exception of some additions, the mandate of the Queen's Printer has remained almost the same as when it was established in 1906. Significant changes, however, were made in 1976 when several sections of the *Queen's Printer Act* were struck from the legislation. This removed the responsibility for blank forms of receipts and licences, procurement of stationery and office supplies, and printing and bindery work required by the Legislative Assembly and government departments. The sections were replaced by a general statement indicating that responsibility for the Act would lie with the Minister of Government Services, which included the Public Affairs Bureau.[10]

Despite the changes, the printing of Alberta government publications remained with the Queen's Printer. Unlike its federal counterpart, the Queen's Printer did not do all the printing for the government. Although printing requests were supposed to go through the Queen's Printer, this did not always happen. Costs also continued to rise. At one time, in the early 1920s, the University of Alberta's printing plant did quite a bit of government printing and even suggested that with an additional outlay of money it "could do all of the government printing at a saving of 15 per cent or more over prices for printing at present."[11]

In 1956 the Alberta government hired a Vancouver consulting firm to conduct an efficiency survey report, specifically looking at the operations of the Queen's Printer that were proving to be very costly. The report, which was completed in 1957, found that much of the government's printing and duplicating was being done by individual government departments "without reference to the Queen's Printer."[12] It suggested that "all printing should be brought under the control of the printer"[13] and be done in the central printing plant or in proposed "duplicating pools" or "with equipment assigned to departments by the Queen's Printer." This suggestion was largely ignored, and government departments continued to choose how their printing was going to be done. The options available included the department's own reproduction and printing facilities and the use of centralized government facilities like those at the Queen's Printer Plant, Central Duplicating Plant, and three Quick Print Centres. Central Duplicating Plant specialized in long-run duplicating. Photocopy services were also available. All of the centralized government facilities were the responsibility of Duplicating and Copying Services in the Print Procurement and Distribution Branch of the Public Affairs Division of Alberta Government Services. In addition to these government facilities, departments could use designated commercial printers. Interestingly, responsibility for the acquisition of printing production, which included pricing, scheduling, and tendering from the private sector, also lay with the Print Procurement and Distribution Branch.

Whenever it was feasible, the Alberta government used the private sector rather than in-house resources for its printing. The work was distributed among several printers in Edmonton, Calgary, Medicine Hat, and other cities in the province.[14] In 1975–76 there were 256 registered printers producing work for the Alberta government. Approximately 82 percent of the printing was done by the private sector, the rest taking place in house.[15] Government printing resources were only used if significant economic benefits could be achieved.

Throughout the 1980s and well into the 1990s the government continued to use the private sector for printing as well as the government's Central Duplicating and Quick Print centres. In August 1991 the two remaining Quick Print Centres were amalgamated with Central Duplicating to create a consolidated in-house printing service.[16] In the early 1990s there was also an increase in the use of automation and the use of computers for printing. This, combined with the privatization and outsourcing of printing, and the government's desire to be more "green," resulted in the elimination of two ammonia-based printers.[17] Over time, even centralized computer print services were outsourced. As more publications are produced in digital rather than in print, the need for government printing has diminished.

The Alberta Queen's Printer is now one of the branches in the Open Government Program within Service Alberta. It is the official publisher of Alberta's laws and the *Alberta Gazette*. It partners with Alberta government ministries to produce and distribute various government publications.[18]

DISTRIBUTION

Once a publication has been created, published, and printed and a decision made to have it publicly available, the next step is to distribute the information. A consequence of decentralized printing is decentralized distribution. Unlike the federal government, where printing and distribution was done by the Queen's Printer, in Alberta the role of the Queen's Printer was focused on statutory publications (i.e., Acts and both parts of the *Alberta Gazette* only). Other government bodies distributed their own publications. For example, the Legislative Assembly Office had responsibility for distributing legislative publications like the *Order Paper, Votes and Proceedings, Journals, Alberta Hansard,* and the first-reading copies of bills. Also, individual government departments distributed their own publications using a variety of methods.

▶ Mailing Lists

Factors like the size of the department, its ability to set up its own sophisticated distribution mechanism, and the volume of information produced determined the distribution method. Some departments were equipped to deal with mass mailing lists or created checklists of their publications that were widely distributed, while others created publication blurbs, letters, or postcards announcing new publications. Unfortunately, those in receipt of such materials often treated them like junk mail and discarded them. Library acquisition procedures rely on some evidence showing that the library has consciously decided to acquire an item. If an item arrived that did not have an order or request attached to it, it was treated as junk mail and discarded. Only examination of the document by a subject or government information specialist ensured the addition of an item to the library's collection.

Some departments published very little and therefore did not keep mailing lists. If lists had been established, they would be for individual publications and not for everything produced by the department. Few departments had the capability of setting up standing orders for serial publications, and so they could not distribute these on a consistent schedule. This was a problem for the organizations that needed a reliable system that would allow for the automatic receipt of any new issues of ongoing publications like annual reports, journals, magazines, and newsletters.

Creating and maintaining mailing lists was time and labour intensive. Many departments did not have adequate staffing to monitor and maintain these lists. Often libraries were dropped from distribution lists without any notice. The haphazard nature of this distribution method led library staff to establish and maintain personal relationships with individuals in government departments to ensure the receipt of publications and to prevent the removal from mailing lists.

▶ *Alberta Depository Library Program*

Although the decentralized system of distribution had its drawbacks, it did provide government departments direct contact with requesters. It also provided the government control over who received its publications and over the information being provided. Centralized distribution systems were seen to be expensive and required huge warehouse facilities to store the publications, as well as sophisticated methods of inventory control.

In 1974 a depository system for distribution of Alberta government publications was set up by the government. This initiative created a partnership between the Government of Alberta, represented by Queen's Printer Bookstore, and Alberta libraries, especially public libraries. The purpose of the partnership was "to provide free public access to government publications through a network of public libraries in Alberta."[19] It expanded the mandate of the Queen's Printer to include items published by the Alberta Public Affairs Bureau—*Government of Alberta Publications (GAP) Catalogue, Queen's Printer Bookstore Catalogue,* and RITE *(Regional Information Telephone Enquiries) Directory*—as well as various publications from government departments that were listed in the GAP *Catalogue.* These included books, handbooks, research reports, and other publications that contained information for the public; publications that were produced with government funds; and promotional materials for ongoing government programs and services.

The Alberta Depository Library Program (ADLP) distributed publications not only to public libraries but also to academic and government libraries, including the Alberta Legislature Library. Participating libraries were designated as either full depositories receiving all publications, or partial or select depositories receiving all legislative materials and publications from Alberta Public Affairs but not items listed in the GAP *Catalogue.* Items in the catalogue were to be selected by individual libraries and requested from individual government departments.

Although libraries welcomed the receipt of Alberta government publications via the ADLP, inconsistencies in the full depository shipments created frustration. The program could not be relied on for the continued receipt of publications, especially serials. Also, there was always the question as to whether or not everything had been included in the shipments. In the 1990s the Government Information Committee of the Library Association of Alberta, with members representing public, special, and academic libraries, conducted an informal comparison of the libraries, considering what was being received by each library participating in the program as well as what was listed in the quarterly GAP *Catalogue.* Several inconsistencies were found, such as different libraries, sometimes in the same city, receiving different publications, and the exclusion of some items from the listings. As no checklist of shipped items was provided, it was difficult for libraries to determine whether or not an item was missing from their shipment. As a result, claiming for missing materials was very difficult. This uncertainty and unreliability meant that libraries had to continue requesting publications directly from government departments or learn to live with gaps in their collections of Alberta government publications.

In spring 1996 the government budget discussions and departmental business plans provided an opportunity for a review of ADLP with streamlining as its goal. Streamlining efforts included the renewal of commitments from government departments to provide materials to the depository program for distribution. It appeared that many government departments were not aware of their responsibilities regarding this centralized method of distribution, and some were not even aware of the program. The manager of the Queen's Printer received support from the information and privacy commissioner, who wrote letters to departmental deputy ministers strongly encouraging their departments to participate in ADLP. His letter stated that "this program has a lot to do with the concepts of routine disclosure and active dissemination of government information."[20] He indicated that the processing of Freedom of Information and Protection of Privacy requests and reviews was more time consuming and expensive than providing "predictable access" to government information. Libraries saw an improvement in the ADLP shipments, with more publications coming from government departments; there were still inconsistencies but not as many as before.

Other efforts in streamlining included the cessation of the paper version of the GAP *Catalogue* in February 1996. The Queen's Printer began to use the Internet for the posting of this quarterly listing of publications. More departments were producing their publications in digital format, so it made sense to have an online listing that would include links to these born-digital items. However, since not all publications were being created in digital format, the Queen's Printer continued to send out shipments of non-digital publications to full depository libraries.

In October 1996 the Alberta Public Affairs Bureau drafted new guidelines for ADLP.[21] Partial depositories were to continue to use the quarterly list of publications to make selections suitable for their libraries, and to use the list of government department contacts to request items from each department. Although retention guidelines were not provided in detail, libraries, especially those with full depository status, were expected to keep permanent collections of the publications and have them catalogued and made available for public access.

The increasing use of technological advancements for creating and distributing government publications created challenges for libraries. Some government departments experimented with technology to deliver their publications. Some used online applications to launch them. For example, Alberta Innovation and Advanced Education decided to cease the paper production and distribution of the *Monthly Economic Review Report*; this would now be available through the Alberta Economic Dashboard, an online application. In another example, the Alberta Energy Regulator decided to provide its information in CD-ROM format as well as online; some of the online documents were distributed via an FTP (file transfer protocol) server.

Retrieving these items and making them publicly accessible via library catalogues was often difficult. These challenges continued when, in 2011, depository libraries were asked if they would like to receive, via email, links to online publications. Concerns were expressed about the stability of these links, which often resulted in dead URLs and lost publications. Libraries asked that links point to a stable online archive rather than to a department's website.

In 2006 the ADLP became the responsibility of the Alberta Government Library, which is part of the Library and Open Government unit within Services Alberta. It continues to be responsible for "ensuring free public access to Alberta government publications through the Alberta Depository Library Program which facilitates the distribution of government information through the province's library system."[22] Print-based publications are still being distributed, as well as publications in other formats like CD, DVD, and online (HTML, PDF, etc.).

In 2013–14 the Alberta Government Library, as part of the Library Transformation Project, which consolidated several government department libraries into one, made several changes. The quarterly listings of departmental publications are no longer being distributed to depository libraries but are being posted regularly in the government's Open Government Portal and are also added to the "Government of Alberta Publication (GAP) Search" on the Queen's Printer website.

In April 2016 an email was sent to all libraries participating in the ADLP, announcing the resumption of distribution of the quarterly listings, this time in Excel format.[23] These are currently being sent to any library wishing to receive them. New depository guidelines were also distributed.

ACQUISITION

The first step in acquisition is identification, finding out if the publication exists. The next step is determining where to go to obtain the item. Decentralized creation, production, and distribution mean that documents are scattered among several departments, and identification and sourcing become a challenge. This was especially true when government information was only being produced in tangible formats. Libraries used several acquisition strategies to meet this challenge, including private booksellers, who sometimes stocked Alberta government publications.

As mentioned before, library staff members have had to be proactive in establishing and nurturing personal relationships with staff in government departments so that they could find out about any newly released publications. Some libraries created tracking systems for requests made directly to a government department. Tracking provided a record of the request so that, if a publication was sent to the library, it would be treated as something that should be added to the collection and not as junk mail, as was often the case with, what some libraries labelled as, "unsolicited" publications. Many large libraries asked government departments to send items to specific individuals like a government information specialist. This ensured that the items would be added to the collection.

▶ *Selection Tools*

Selection tools that can be used to acquire new publications have always been difficult to find. Often libraries had to determine whether or not a tool existed and, if it did, then to request it from the government department or ask to be placed on a mailing list to receive future issues. To make up for the lack of selection tools, libraries often resorted to careful scrutiny of newspapers, legislative documents (e.g., the *Journals of the Legislative Assembly*, which list sessional papers), and departmental annual reports and budget documents to see if there was any mention of new government publications.

Very few traditional selection tools like bibliographies and publication listings have been available in Alberta. The most comprehensive tool was the bibliography compiled by Joseph Forsyth, published in 1972. The eight-volume set, titled *Government Publications Relating to Alberta: A Bibliography of Publications of the Government of Alberta from 1905 to 1968, and of Publications of the Government of Canada Relating to the Province of Alberta from 1867 to 1968*, lists Alberta official publications by government body and provides author, title, and subject indexes as well as Alberta statutes from 1905 to 1968, and Northwest Territories ordinances relating to Alberta that were still in force at the time of the publication. A supplement, *Western Canadiana Collection: Supplementary Bibliography*, was compiled by the Edmonton Public Library in fall 1986. It includes listings of monographs, serials, and official publications relating to Alberta, and any other items that were not listed in the Forsyth bibliography.

GOVERNMENT DEPARTMENT SELECTION TOOLS

Some government departments, especially those who were prolific in their publishing, compiled their own bibliographies, publication catalogues, checklists, and listings (e.g., *Alberta Environment Publications List*) and distributed them to libraries. Some departments also distributed announcements about newly released publications with pricing and ordering information and order forms. Other departments that had their own libraries published library acquisitions lists providing information about new items that had been added to the departmental library's collection (e.g., *Library Recent Additions* from Alberta Agriculture Library).

Success in obtaining publications depended on their availability from the department and whether or not they were generally distributed. Some public items had limited supply because not enough copies were created; others had limited distribution because they were prepared for a specific audience and not distributed widely. Individuals wishing to see these documents had to make arrangements to examine them in the publisher's (department's) offices or the departmental library, if one existed.

Librarians could also use selection tools that listed publications from all government departments. The first listing of this kind was published in 1973 by the Alberta Public Affairs Bureau in co-operation with the Queen's Printer. The *Publications Catalogue* listed free and priced publications as well as legislative documents like bills and statutes. It was distributed to all public, school, university, and community college libraries, members of the Alberta Legislature, heads of all departments and agencies within the Government of Alberta, legislative libraries of the other nine provinces, the National Library, and any interested individuals.[24] The title listings also included addresses of the issuing agencies so that anyone who wanted to acquire an item could do so by going directly to that government department.

The format and content of this catalogue changed over time. Once, it had a KWIC (keyword-in-context) format.[25] Later, a catalogue was published that included MARC catalogue records. In 1978, legislative items (bills, statutes, and regulations) were removed, and, in 1979, public documents compiled by the Bibliography Section of the Alberta Public Affairs Bureau were added and could be obtained from the Queen's Printer or directly from the government department. Microfiche copies of "Alberta publications possessing lasting reference value"[26] could also be purchased from Micromedia Limited. In August 1977, another catalogue, the *Periodical Publishing Record* (PPR), was published as a companion to the *Publications Catalogue*. It provided details on all Government of Alberta public periodicals except annual reports, which were already listed in the *Publications Catalogue*.

Both the *Publications Catalogue* and the PPR were printed from the SPIRES (Stanford Public Information Retrieval System) database, which consisted of two public sub-files. The Government of Alberta Publications (GAP) sub-file included bibliographic records and library locations of publications dating back to 1905. The other sub-file was the PPR. The SPIRES online database was maintained by the Alberta Public

Affairs Bureau working with the Information Systems Group of the Alberta Research Council. It initially included items dating back to 1905, but when the online portion of the database was completely rebuilt, it only included items that had been published since 1980.[27]

The content of the two catalogues produced from the SPIRES database continued to change. In 1988 the catalogues were combined into one, with a new title, *Alberta Government Publications*. It consisted of two separate sections: the "List of Publications," which included those items received in a specific year by the Publication Services Branch of the Alberta Public Affairs Bureau; and the "Periodicals Publishing Record," which contained periodicals published in a specific year. In 1989–90 these two separate listings were combined into one.

For a short period of time, from 1990 to 1993, the catalogue included publications labelled "Internal Document" that were accessible only to government employees, departments, and agencies, but not the public. A minor change to the title was made in 1994, renaming it *Government of Alberta Publications (GAP) Catalogue*. The public could obtain publications from the issuing department or source, or from Micromedia, or via interlibrary loan from the departmental library or the library in which the item had been deposited. The source and library locations were listed in the catalogue to help anyone determine how to obtain the publication or where to go to get it. In 1995 the print GAP *Catalogue* ceased publication, although, "at a future date, information regarding Government of Alberta publications will be found on the Government of Alberta world-wide web Internet home page...or by contacting individual government departments."[28]

Another Alberta departmental listing of publications was also available via the *Alberta Queen's Printer Bookstore Catalogue*, first published in March 1987 and later known as the *Alberta Queen's Printer Catalogue (QP Catalogue)*. This catalogue "lists Alberta legislation (Statutes and Regulations), publications and specialty items available for purchase from Alberta Queen's Printer."[29] Most of the catalogue is focused on the availability of statutes and regulations, with a small section listing titles available from individual government departments and including a list of department contacts that can be called to obtain specific publications. The print version of the catalogue ceased publication in 2004.

The Alberta Queen's Printer also published a newsletter titled *Alberta Bookmark* in 2002. It is now called the *e-Bookmark*, a free electronic, monthly newsletter to which the public can subscribe. It provides information on both new and updated publications. Previous editions dating back to October 2008 have been archived and can be viewed at the Alberta Queen's Printer Archives on the Internet.[30]

As can be seen, there is no single source listing all of Alberta government publications. Libraries need to gather together the various catalogues available. Some attempts have been made to provide guides on the selection tools that are available for acquiring Alberta government publications. These include *Canadian Provincial Government Publications: Bibliography of Bibliographies* by Mohan Bhatia, first published in 1970 as *Bibliographies, Catalogues, Checklists and Indexes of Canadian Provincial Government Publications*, and revised and enlarged in 1971; and *A Guide to the Identification and Acquisition of Canadian Provincial Government Publications* by Catherine Pross and Paul Pross, published in 1977; a second edition, *A Guide to the Identification and Acquisition of Canadian Government Publications: Provinces and Territories* by Catherine Pross, was published in 1983. All these guides have small sections on Alberta. To date, no other guides have been published.

DISCOVERABILITY

The ability to find government information is dependent on a complete and current record of what has been published. Several methods may be used. One is direct contact with the government department, by mail (post or email), by telephone, or in person. To help with determining which department to contact, the Alberta Public Affairs Bureau created the *Government Services Guide*, which was published between 1955 and 1972 and later replaced by the *Telephone Directory: Government of Alberta and the Legislative Assembly of Alberta*, often referred to as the RITE *(Regional Information Telephone Enquiries) Directory*. This directory was published by Alberta's Department of Government Services (1975–82) and the Alberta Public Affairs Bureau (1983–2005). The RITE Network system was created to help "minimize long distance toll charges within government, to facilitate faster and more direct communications among public service employees, and to provide Albertans with convenient free-of-charge access to government departments."[31]

The SPIRES online database that was used in the production of the GAP *Catalogue* and PPR was also used for discovery, although its availability for public use was limited. Initially available for online searching through the Alberta Information Retrieval Association,[32] it was later made freely available to anyone who had a user account at the University of Alberta Computing Centre. Those who did not have an account were able to conduct searches through information systems at the Alberta Research Council and were charged for these searches on a cost-recovery basis.[33]

OPEN GOVERNMENT

New technologies, new formats, and the Internet have changed the ways in which government publications are created and produced. Today the Government of Alberta produces information in many formats, both tangible (e.g., printed works, CD-ROMS) and intangible (e.g., files accessible online via government web servers). Unlike the federal government, which had decided in 2014 to create and produce federal government information in digital format only, the Alberta government "has a strong preference for digital-by-default publishing of publicly-released information, but there is no requirement that it be produced *only* in digital format."[34] The decision about which format to use rests with the individual government department. If it sees a value in releasing information in a tangible format, it may do so.

Alberta government executive branch publishing has been a decentralized activity, often lacking in coordination or co-operation within and among government departments. A major cultural change in government publishing began to take place in the 2000s with open government. Underlying this major change was the government's desire to transform the government into becoming more open, transparent, participative, and collaborative as well as more accountable to its citizens.

The idea of open government is not new for Alberta. It was first mentioned in the Alberta Legislative Assembly in the Throne Speech of March 2, 1972. The government stated its commitment to "the principle of open government; providing citizens with easier access to their Legislature and its deliberations."[35] It promised to provide a written record of Legislative Assembly proceedings and to open the business of the Legislature to the media (radio and television).[36] Open government also meant that the Legislative Assembly would sit twice per year, and assured elected Members of the Legislative Assembly that there would be opportunities to debate all public bills and that further discussions would take place by expanding the use of special legislative committees.[37]

Open government today is much broader in scope than it was in 1972. It represents a significant change in how the government, not just the Legislative Assembly, interacts with its citizens. Rather than an environment of "them" (the government) versus "us" (the citizens), it hopes to foster an environment of "we," in which government and citizens work together. One way of accomplishing this is by "releasing more of the information it creates, collects and manages; improving the daily interactions it has with Albertans; and encouraging and facilitating greater engagement of Albertans with their government."[38]

▶ Underlying Policies

Two key government policies provide the foundation for open government: *Government of Alberta Communications Policy* and the *Government of Alberta Open Information and Open Data Policy*.[39] Alberta's *Communications Policy* was approved by Cabinet on May 15, 2007. Its purpose is to "ensure that communications across the Government of Alberta are well coordinated, effectively managed and responsive to the information needs of Albertans."[40] The policy focuses on what the government can do and how it can enhance communication not only with Albertans but within the government itself. The government's plans are outlined in the "Communications Policy Statement," which states the policy of the Government of Alberta as follows:

▷ Providing the public with timely, clear and accurate information about government's priorities, policies, programs and services.
▷ Consideration of Albertans' interests and concerns when

establishing priorities, developing policies, and planning and delivering programs and services.

▷ Ensuring that the Government of Alberta is identified in a clear and consistent way—in communications ranging from signage to the telephone, mail, print and multimedia materials, advertising and the Internet.

▷ Employing a variety of ways and means to communicate, and provide information in the most appropriate formats to accommodate diverse needs.

▷ Delivering prompt, courteous and responsive communications that are sensitive to the needs and concerns of the public, and respect privacy and individual rights.

▷ Using public funds responsibly to obtain maximum value for taxpayer investments in all communication activities.

▷ Keeping government employees informed about Government of Alberta priorities, policies, programs and services.

▷ Respecting the integrity and impartiality of the Alberta Public Service in keeping with the *Alberta Code of Conduct and Ethics*.

▷ Ensuring all ministries of the Government of Alberta work collaboratively to achieve clear and effective communications with the public.

▷ Coordinating communications activities with other governments, industry and other partners, where possible, in an effort to communicate more effectively and efficiently with the public.[41]

The policy provides guidance to the government in the following areas:

1. Informing and serving Albertans
2. Listening to Albertans
3. Communicating clearly
4. Meeting diverse audience needs
5. Clearly identifying programs of the government
6. Delivering coordinated communications
7. Communicating with government employees
8. Making information available electronically
9. Communicating through the media (government spokespeople)

10. Advertising government policies, programs and services
11. Entering partnerships and sponsorships
12. Communicating in emergencies
13. Retaining copyright[42]

The *Open Information and Open Data Policy* was introduced in 2015. It provides a framework to support "a single approach to providing Government of Alberta information and data for public use, adaptation and distribution under the Open Government Licence."[43] This policy is a reflection of the Alberta government's move toward greater proactive disclosure of both information and data. "Proactive disclosure refers to steps public bodies take to provide information to the public on their own accord, as opposed to providing information only when responding to a freedom of information request."[44] The aim is to be open by default and to provide quality information that empowers citizens to fully participate in the development of government programs, services, and policies. The hope is to create an informed citizenry that is fully engaged with its government.

The Government of Alberta developed its *Open Government Action Plan* in September 2013, with a revision and expansion on June 23, 2015;[45] a strategic plan in August 2015;[46] and the *Open Government Program Plan* in June 2016.[47] The action plan outlines the government's commitment to transparency and accountability to Alberta citizens. This will be done by "releasing more of the information it creates, collects and manages; improving the daily interactions it has with Albertans; and encouraging and facilitating greater engagement of Albertans with their government."[48]

When it comes to information, the plan is to develop publication standards that harmonize the structure and content of documents across government and harmonize metadata initiatives within Service Alberta and across ministries.[49] Internal collaboration would encourage the "vision of a single government coming together to create a citizen-focused structure that best serves the needs of Albertans."[50] Another component of the plan is to expand and modernize the Alberta Queen's Printer so that it will implement an "enterprise publishing and distribution plan and work toward making digital versions of laws the official ones."[51] Information would also be made available and easier to find. Users would be educated on the meaning and use of the information.

The strategic plan identifies three streams of activity:

1. Open Data: releasing the raw data the government has in order to increase transparency and encourage innovative uses of data.
2. Open Information: a focus on making information routinely available and easy to find in order to encourage informed discussion.
3. Open Engagement: the process of bringing more, and better informed voices into the discussions necessary to improve outcomes for Albertans.[52]

Plans are underway to develop a virtual library that is integrated with the Open Data portal. The Alberta government is committed to the development of standards and processes that will support the collection and publication of information in conjunction with national and international initiatives. The publishing paradigm will shift to one of centralization. Governance structures will be created to foster a sustainable program.[53]

Open Information, that is the releasing of more government information to the public, is a result of several developments, including

1. the increasing amount of information made available in a wide variety of tangible and digital formats and the use of the Internet to produce, publish, distribute, retrieve, store and preserve government information, and,
2. the government's desire to become more open and to inform Alberta citizens in a way that is understandable, accessible, reliable, consistent, sustainable and barrier-free.[54]

▶ *Publishing Guidelines*

A more open and transparent relationship between the government and its citizens depends on the availability of publications that are reliable, trustworthy, and of high quality. The Open Government Program within Service Alberta has developed publications guidelines to help those involved in the production of publications for the Government of Alberta. These guidelines align and support the *Government of Alberta Communications Policy* and the *Government of Alberta Open Information and Open Data Policy*. Several drafts of the *Publishing Guide for the Government of Alberta* have been released, with the current one published in May 2018. According to Gary Weber, head of Library and Open Information for the Open Government Program, "the value of having guidelines for publishing was put forward by the Library and Open Government unit, which is part of the Open Government Program, and stems in large part from our work managing the Alberta Depository Library Program."[55]

The new digital publishing environment had put strains on ADLP, including

- ▷ fewer and fewer print publications being released by the government, and, when publications are released in a print format, they very often have very small print runs.
- ▷ lack of persistent access to government documents on GoA [Government of Alberta] websites.
- ▷ URLS of ministries change, thus breaking links to publications at their previous locations.
- ▷ different ministries have different policies around retention of publications on websites.
- ▷ lack of consistent publishing practices within the GoA.[56]

Online publishing has led to some issues with access to government information but, at the same time, has provided "an enormous opportunity to *improve* access to government information...a 'depository library on every desktop.'"[57]

The *Government of Alberta Publications Guideline (Draft)* provides a new definition for government publication, and the requirements for all publications, and outlines the steps that need to be taken in the publishing process to ensure consistent and trustworthy publications. A publication is any item that is

▷ created to inform the public,

▷ of more than temporary interest,

▷ not released in an open data format,

▷ not continually or dynamically updated (e.g., web pages), and

▷ complete (does not require additional information to be understood).[58]

All text-based publications are required to have an ISBN, ISSN, or stable URL; clear identification of the creator or owner of the publication; use of an Alberta government signature; and easily found title, date, or other identifiers like contact information (website, email, telephone number, or mailing address). A copyright statement showing the copyright holder and the terms specifying reuse of the publication's content are also required.[59]

The *Guideline* also describes the publishing process within a government department. This process has always been a mystery to those working outside government, but today the process is more transparent. Several steps need to be taken before a government publication is finally released:

1. A publication creator prepares the publication and submits an "Intent to Publish" form to the Open Government Program.

2. The Open Government Program creates a draft private-catalogue record in the Open Government portal. This catalogue record is not visible to the public. An ISBN, ISSN, and/or URL are provided to the creator, who ensures that the publication has all the requirements that have been outlined in the publishing guidelines.

3. A departmental publication approver does the final review and gives permission for the publication to occur, including the posting in the Open Government portal.

4. The publication creator gives the final version of the publication to the publication custodian. At the moment, the custodian is the Open Government Program; however, in the future, those departments with high volumes of production will appoint their own custodians.

5. The publication custodian finalizes the catalogue record, making it publicly available, and posts the publication for public viewing.[60]

The draft form of the *Guideline* is in the process of being communicated throughout government. Adoption is "on an ad hoc basis for now, with the intent of implementing it government-wide as a guideline sometime in the future."[61]

Both the Alberta government's *Communications Policy* and the *Open Information* and *Open Data Policy* have contributed to the changes in the way that publications are published and made available to the public. Creation is still a decentralized activity among departments and will likely always be this way. Departments are assigned mandates describing their areas of responsibility and have developed expertise in determining the information that is needed by the public, which could be arguable. The *Communications Policy*, by helping to alleviate the lack of collaboration and coordination among government departments, and the *Open Information and Open Data Policy*, by aiming to alleviate the haphazard production of information and focusing on a single approach for all government departments, will hopefully diminish the challenges that the public has faced in finding Alberta government documents. By setting standards for the creation and production of uniform publications, the publishing guidelines will help in the identification of Alberta's government documents, something that was difficult to do in the past.

The Open Government Program uses advancements in technology, especially the Internet, to create, produce, distribute, and preserve government information. The process of acquisition has almost become obsolete as distribution and acquisition are blending into a single function. However, the *Alberta Government Publishing Guideline (Draft)* states that content creators and managers will still have the responsibility of "providing tangible copies of all publications produced in physical format to the Alberta Government Library, in sufficient quantities to enable their distribution in the Alberta Depository Library Program."[62] As noted before, government departments have the discretion to decide how their information will be created, whether it be tangible or digital. There is no requirement to produce information in a tangible format.

The Alberta government has not yet adopted a digital format only for its publications and continues to create and produce information in tangible formats. As a result, acquisition and distribution processes are essentially the same as they were in the past, that is, separate processes and not yet blended into one. In terms of tangible publications distributed through the ADLP, each full depository library (currently University of Alberta, University of Calgary, Calgary Public Library, Library of Congress, and Provincial Archives of Alberta) will receive one copy. Three copies will be deposited in the Alberta Legislature Library, and two copies will be retained in the Alberta Government Library. Partial depository libraries will be able to request free copies of both priced and free publications from individual government departments. This means that, upon request, departments will need to be prepared to make copies and to supply them in the format in which they were originally published.[63]

In the Open Government environment there are two main selection tools available for libraries to search, both available online. One is the Government of Alberta Publication (GAP) Search,[64] searchable back to 1996. This is a continuation of the print GAP *Catalogue* that ceased publication in paper in 1995. The GAP Search is designed to help in the location of specific government publications. Listings of current publications are updated quarterly, and an archive of older items of historical value is available for searching. Links to online items are provided. Many of these are in PDF, but other formats like XLSX, JPEG, and MP3 will be available in the future.

The other selection tool is found in Alberta's Open Government Portal, part of Alberta's Open Government Program. It includes two information resources, Open Data and Publications. Both are defined as government-owned information resources that are "not subject to privacy, security or legislative restrictions"[65] and are made available to the public. Data is available in machine-readable format; publications may include reports, studies, maps, and legislation. The government's Open Government Licence[66] allows users "to copy, modify, publish, translate, adapt, distribute or otherwise use the information within the Open Government Portal in any medium, mode or format for any lawful purpose with only a few conditions."[67] Also, whenever possible, data and publications are released proactively.

Dani J. Pahulje ◁ 175

The GAP Search available via the Alberta Queen's Printer website and searchable back to 1996, the Government of Alberta Publications listings within the Open Government Portal, and the listings of publications in Excel format provided to depository libraries are several selection tools available today. These also serve as tools for discovery.

THE ROLE OF LIBRARIES

Members of the public have relied on libraries (academic, public, and governmental) to have the information they need. Librarians have tried to develop collections of Alberta government publications that are as complete as reasonably possible given the decentralized environment in which they were created, produced, and distributed. Descriptions or catalogue records are created and entered into library catalogues. The publications are either coded by government author or classified by subject, and placed in separate or integrated collections. Some libraries have kept the selection tools used in the process of acquisitions and have added them to their collections. These can be used to aid in discovery by verifying the existence of a publication.

The increasing production of born-digital publications has led libraries to question the role of the library catalogue as a discovery tool. Although many digital sources also include MARC records, some libraries do not have the staff resources to do this and have not included current born-digital sources in their catalogues.

▶ *Alberta Legislature Library*

Initially known as the Provincial Library from its inception in 1906 until 1974, the Alberta Legislature Library "served as a parliamentary library, a general reference library for the entire provincial government and the Provincial Archives."[68] Several changes, notably the establishment of a separate Archives Branch in 1963, and the development of separate government department libraries in the late 1960s and early 1970s, led to greater emphasis on the collecting of Alberta government documents, on the provision of parliamentary library services for the Province of Alberta, and on the provision of technical advice concerning the development of provincial government department libraries and co-ordination of several co-operative programs that have been established among these libraries.

The type of information collected by the Legislature Library varied with its changing role. At the beginning, the library collected government publications, broad subject reference works and even literature, including fiction. Now its focus is on the collection of Alberta government documents. Items are received via the ADLP as well as other sources.

In 1981 the Legislature Library received its first computer-output-microfiche (COM) version of its CODOC indexes. In 1985 the library began to automate its card catalogue. Using the SPIRES database at the University of Alberta, a COM version of the catalogue was produced and made available to other libraries that could use this discovery tool to supplement their own library catalogues. Production of the microfiche catalogue ceased in 1993.

The Alberta Legislature Library started collecting born-digital publications in 2012. This has become an electronic archive with PDFS available through the library catalogue. According to Val Footz, Legislature Librarian, the library has "over 13,000 digital Alberta government documents."[69] Records are contributed to the Government and Legislative Libraries Online Publications (GALLOP) portal, sometimes called the APLIC portal.[70] This is a pilot project through the Association of Parliamentary Libraries in Canada that aims to develop a single access point to electronic resources from the provinces, the territories, and the federal government.

In terms of services, the parliamentary library services of the Alberta Legislature Library are available to the Members of the Legislative Assembly, their staff, the staff of the Legislative Assembly Office, and the public service.[71] The Members of the Legislative Assembly are the top priority, however. Questions from the public are answered by the library staff.[72] In 2012 the Legislature Library took over the staffing of the Legislature information line. The Legislature Library is a member of The Alberta Library (TAL). Those living in Edmonton who have a TAL card may borrow materials. Those living outside of Edmonton may borrow materials using interlibrary loan services.[73]

▶ *Government of Alberta Libraries*

Several government departments and agencies had their own libraries, which included their own departmental publications as well as other publications that could be used by the staff and researchers in that department. Many of the government publications could also be requested via interlibrary loan or, in some cases, could be viewed by the public in the library, if it was open to the public.

The Alberta Legislature Library provided technical advice on the development of departmental libraries through the Consulting and Bibliographic Services Section, later known as the Cooperative Government Library Services Section and then the Legislature Library Support Section, which was established in 1970. There was significant growth in the number of government department libraries during the 1970s. They were separate entities and were administered and financially supported by their respective government departments. Although it had no authority over provincial government libraries,[74] the Alberta Legislature Library provided expertise in their development, and coordinated programs among them. Some of the co-operative programs included the *Alberta Government Libraries' Union Catalogue*, providing an index to the collections across departmental libraries; a *Union List of Serials in Alberta Government Libraries*; and the Alberta Government Libraries' interlibrary loan service to help facilitate loans between department libraries and the University of Alberta Libraries. There was co-operative acquisition and the sharing of indexing guides, duplication of catalogue cards, and binding.

The growth in the number of government department libraries began to diminish in the mid-1980s. Some libraries were downsized or closed. In the early 1990s Alberta was faced with difficult economic challenges and, under the leadership of Premier Ralph Klein, developed a new economic strategy, described in the publication *Seizing Opportunity: Alberta's New Economic Development Strategy*.[75] The new strategy included a four-year plan to balance the budget by reducing government spending. Every department was instructed to find new ways to cut costs and to consolidate and improve efficiencies in the delivery of government services. Many departments and agencies consolidated, and merged their libraries. The Alberta Legislature Library was the recipient of many collections from these libraries.

By 2000 the Legislature Library's role in supporting government libraries had been reduced by the establishment of the centralized Alberta Government Library (AGL).[76] AGL provides library services to the Government of Alberta, and it is also open to the public. Its collection includes both current and historic Government of Alberta publications. The library is a member of NEOS, a consortium of eighteen government, health, college, and university libraries in central and northern Alberta.[77] AGL's collection is searchable using the *NEOS Library Consortium Catalogue*, a shared online catalogue. The AGL is one of three branches in the Open Government Program within Service Alberta. It is responsible for the maintenance of the publications section of the Open Government Portal.

ROLE OF THE PRIVATE SECTOR IN DISCOVERABILITY

The private sector has developed discovery tools that not only help in the location of government publications but also provide copies of the publications in either microfiche or electronic formats. In 1972 Micromedia Limited, a Canadian company formed by Gary and Bob Gibson, began to explore microfilm as a publishing medium. After confirming that there was a growing need to microfilm government documents, it created the *ProFile Index: Canadian Provincial and Municipal Publications*, a microfiche monthly subscription service with accompanying printed indexes. Several provinces, including Alberta, agreed to participate in this endeavour, and filming began in 1973.[78] The coverage of the microfiche service was very dependent on the efforts of government staff who forwarded new publications to the publisher for microfilming and indexing.[79] The Alberta Legislature Library performed the clearing-house function for the Government of Alberta and provided copies of "significant government publications to Micromedia."[80] Although the first *ProFile Index* was published in 1973, it did not include Alberta government publications, because Micromedia had not yet received copyright clearance from the government to include them.[81] Only publications that were of "general, lasting reference value"[82] were selected. The service includes serials and monographs but not legislative publications, ephemera, or maps. Several subscription plans are available, including the complete collection, all provinces and municipalities, and regional or subject collections.[83] Any item that was listed was also available in microfiche from the publisher and later as priced paper reprints.

In 1979 Micromedia merged its services. The *ProFile Index*, the *Urban Canada* index, and the *Publicat Index*, and their microfiche collections covering Canadian provincial, municipal, and federal government documents respectively, were combined. The merger resulted in a more comprehensive microfiche service called Microlog and the accompanying paper index titled the *Microlog Index*. In 1995 the *Microlog Index* was renamed the *Canadian Research Index*, which is currently available from ProQuest. It includes both the microfiche subscription service called Microlog as well as a searchable database that is used to locate provincial, municipal, and federal government publications in the microfiche collection. If a publication is available online, links are provided.

In 2005 Gibson Library Connections, founded by Gary Gibson, launched the Canadian Electronic Library, which includes the Canadian Public Policy Collection and the Canadian Health Research Collection. Both of these are searchable, full-text databases that include a selection of government publications, including those from Alberta. Libraries that subscribe to these resources have used them to find Alberta government publications, especially those that have been born digital.

PRESERVATION

The availability of Alberta government information for future generations has become a growing concern as more publications are created in born-digital formats. Even when information was created and produced in tangible formats, there was concern about future availability. Items could be lost, borrowed and not returned, or become irreparable. Software and equipment have become obsolete, and, as a consequence, the information produced in tangible electronic formats (e.g. CD-ROM) is unusable. There have never been any assurances that publications will be infinitely available, but steps are being taken to preserve what Alberta has and what will be produced in the future.

These steps are being taken by several organizations, many of them libraries, either on their own or in partnership with other libraries and organizations that have expertise in preservation. The Alberta Legislature Library has increased its emphasis on the preservation of important historical collections.[84] It is participating in a number of joint projects with the library community. One of these is the digitized Alberta Royal Commissions, a joint project with the University of Alberta Libraries that digitized the reports and Orders-in-Council that established the commissions as well as a selection of briefs, exhibits, and testimonies. Another project, with the University of Calgary, was the digitization of the historical collection that included *Bills, Statutes of Alberta, Debates* and *Journals,* the *Alberta Gazette,* and the *Ordinances of the Northwest Territories* before 1905, resulting in the Alberta Law Collection.

In 2002 the Alberta Legislature Library "began the creation of an Alberta Electronic Government Documents Archive, making electronic versions of government documents available through its catalogue, thus ensuring improved accessibility and availability of these documents."[85] The library has also "recently embarked on a digitization project with the University of Alberta."[86] Library staff members have met with the University of Alberta Libraries and the AGL (Open Government Program) to discuss the digitization of Alberta government publications. Progress has been slow due to lack of time. Also, concerns around the interpretation of copyright and terms of use are a challenge, and obtaining permission from the Government of Alberta has been difficult for all three organizations.

The University of Alberta Libraries has made significant contributions to the preservation of Government of Alberta publications. Some of the preservation initiatives include *University of Alberta Libraries Education Curriculum Guides,* digitized Alberta Education curriculum guides dating back to the early 1900s; and Government of Alberta Publications Collection, digitized Alberta government publications dating back to the mid-1980s. As well, when a change in government was being anticipated in 2012, the university took a proactive approach by crawling all the Government of Alberta web domains and partnering with the Internet Archive to ensure future access.

CONCLUSION

From creation and publication to distribution and acquisition, the Alberta government publishing environment has been one based on a decentralized model in which individual government departments decided what was to be published and how it was to be distributed. Attempts at centralization (e.g., having all publications printed by the Alberta Queen's Printer) have proven futile. Libraries have played a significant role in assisting the public by being innovative and diligent in their acquisition activities and by creating centralized discovery tools like library catalogues to find the information requested by the public. Today's open government environment has created a major paradigm shift toward centralization. The increased use of new technologies has removed the need for distribution and acquisition processes. The Internet is now being used for distribution, acquisitions, and discovery, and these activities have increasingly blended into one. The challenge for libraries in the future will be how to alert the public to the traditional discovery tools as well as those tools that are now available online like Alberta's Open Information Portal. Improvements have been made in the availability of several discovery tools, but this has proven to be both a blessing and a curse. While having several discovery tools at one's disposal appears to be ideal, it is often difficult to identify what these tools are. Discovering the discovery tools and alerting the public to their availability is the new challenge.

ACKNOWLEDGEMENTS

Many thanks go to Gary Weber, Head of Library and Open Information, Open Government Program, Service Alberta, and Val Footz, Alberta Legislature Librarian, for their generosity in responding to numerous questions. Also, thanks go to my colleagues Nadine Hoffman, for taking the time to read this chapter and providing thoughtful comments, and Kim Clarke, for her advice.

Notes

1. Pross and Pross, *Government Publishing in the Canadian Provinces,* 17.
2. *Government Accountability Act* (R.S.A. 2000, c. G-7, s. 13).
3. *An Act Respecting Public Printing* (S.A. 1906, c. 9, s. 3).
4. *An Act Respecting Public Printing* (S.A. 1906, c. 9, s. 7).
5. *An Act to Amend the Act Respecting Public Printing* (S.A. 1911–12, c. 12).
6. *An Act to Amend the Statute Law* (S.A. 1916, c. 3, s. 41).
7. *An Act to Amend the King's Printer Act* (S.A. 1954, c. 50).
8. Alberta Public Affairs Bureau was established in 1972 by Order-in-Council 191/72.
9. "The Public Affairs Bureau began reporting to the Executive Council in 1972. Although the Bureau was established as a separate entity in 1973, it continued to report to the Executive Council. In 1975 the responsibility for the Public Affairs Bureau was transferred to the Department of Government Services. The Public Affairs Bureau became a division of the Department of Government Services until dissolution of the Department in 1982. In 1983, an Order in Council 0503/83 under the *Public Service Act* (R.S.A. 1980, c. P-32) designated the Public Affairs Bureau as a department for purposes of the *Public Service Act.* In 1984 the Public Affairs Bureau was once again established as a separate entity reporting to the Minister without a Portfolio, Bill Payne. In 1986, the responsibility for the Public Affairs Bureau was transferred to the Minister of Advanced Education (O.C. 0341/86). In 1989, the responsibility for the Public Affairs Bureau was transferred once again to the jurisdiction of the Executive Council (O.C. 0194/89)." https://hermis. alberta.ca/paa/Details.aspx?ObjectID=GR0048.001SF&dv=True&deptID=1.
10. *The Department of Government Services Amendment Act* (S.A. 1976, c. 15, s. 1).
11. *The Department of Government Services Amendment Act* (S.A. 1976, c. 15, s. 1), last paragraph.
12. *Edmonton Journal,* "$89,000 Saving Seen in Printing Proposals."
13. *Edmonton Journal,* "$89,000 Saving Seen in Printing Proposals," para. 10.
14. *Edmonton Bulletin,* "Printing Costs Are Discussed."
15. Alberta, Government Services, *Annual Report, 1976–77,* 32.
16. Alberta, Public Works, Supply and Services, *Annual Report, 1990–91,* 11.
17. Alberta, Public Works, Supply and Services, *Annual Report, 1993–94,* 44.
18. Service Alberta, *Open Government Program Plan, 2016,* 4.
19. Alberta, Public Affairs Bureau, "Depository Library Program," November 1995.
20. Robert C. Clark, Commissioner, Office of the Information and Privacy Commissioner, to Deputy Ministers, July 9, 1996 (sample letter) re Alberta's Depository Library Program, in the author's possession.
21. Alberta, Public Affairs Bureau, "Alberta Depository Library Program Guidelines (Draft)," October 1996.

22. Service Alberta, "Appendix D: The Alberta Library Depository Program," in *Government of Alberta Publications Guideline (Draft)*, *January 2016*, 16.

23. Jadwiga Windyga, email message to author, April 19, 2016.

24. Alberta Public Affairs Bureau, preface to *Publications Catalogue, 1976*.

25. Alberta Public Affairs Bureau, *Publications Catalogue, No. 3, April–September 1974*.

26. Alberta Public Affairs Bureau, *Publications Catalogue, No. 4, October–December 1974*, vii.

27. Alberta Public Affairs Bureau, *Publications Catalogue, No. 4*, iii.

28. Alberta Public Affairs Bureau, *Government of Alberta Publications (GAP) Catalogue, 1995*, i.

29. Alberta Queen's Printer, *Catalogue, Fall 2004*, 1.

30. *Alberta Queen's Printer Archives.*

31. Alberta Government Services, *Annual Report, 1976–77*, 31.

32. Alberta Public Affairs Bureau, preface to *Periodical Publishing Record, 1976*.

33. Alberta Public Affairs Bureau, *Publications Catalogue, 1979 Cumulation*, iv.

34. Gary Weber, email message to author, June 27, 2016.

35. Alberta, Legislative Assembly, *Alberta Hansard*, 17th Leg, 1st Sess (March 2, 1972), at 3.

36. Alberta, Legislative Assembly, *Alberta Hansard*, 17th Leg, 1st Sess (March 2, 1972), at 4.

37. Alberta, Legislative Assembly, *Alberta Hansard*, 17th Leg, 1st Sess (March 2, 1972), at 4.

38. Alberta, Service Alberta, *Open Government Action Plan, March 2015*, 4.

39. Government of Alberta, *Government of Alberta Open Information and Open Data Policy* (Edmonton: Government of Alberta, 2015), http://open.alberta.ca/policy.

40. Government of Alberta, *Government of Alberta Communications Policy*, 1.

41. Government of Alberta, *Government of Alberta Communications Policy*, 2.

42. Government of Alberta, *Government of Alberta Communications Policy*, 3.

43. Government of Alberta, *Government of Alberta Open Information and Open Data Policy*, 1.

44. Alberta, Office of the Information and Privacy Commissioner, *Review of the Government of Alberta's Public Disclosure of Travel and Expenses Policy, June 2015*, 1.

45. Government of Alberta, *Open Government Action Plan, September 2013*.

46. Government of Alberta, *Open Government Strategy*.

47. Alberta, Service Alberta, *Open Government Program Plan, 2016*.

48. Government of Alberta, *Open Government Strategy*, 4.

49. Government of Alberta, *Open Government Strategy*, 7.

50. Government of Alberta, *Open Government Strategy*, 8.

51. Government of Alberta, *Open Government Strategy*, 8.

52. Government of Alberta, *Open Government Strategy*, 5.
53. Government of Alberta, *Open Government Strategy*, 15.
54. Alberta, Service Alberta, *Publishing Guide for the Government of Alberta (Draft)*, August 2015, 2.
55. Gary Weber, email message to author, March 22, 2016.
56. Gary Weber, email message to author, March 22, 2016.
57. Gary Weber, email message to author, March 22, 2016.
58. Alberta, Service Alberta, *Government of Alberta Publications Guideline (Draft)*, January 2016, 3.
59. Alberta, Service Alberta, *Government of Alberta Publications Guideline (Draft)*, January 2016, 4.
60. Alberta, Service Alberta, *Government of Alberta Publications Guideline (Draft)*, January 2016, 7.
61. Gary Weber, email message to author, March 22, 2016.
62. Alberta, Service Alberta, *Government of Alberta Publications Guideline (Draft)*, January 2016, 5.
63. Alberta, Service Alberta, "Appendix D: The Alberta Library Depository Program," in *Government of Alberta Publications Guideline (Draft)*, January 2016, 16.
64. Government of Alberta Publication (GAP) Search, http://www.qp.alberta.ca/511.cfm.
65. Alberta, Service Alberta, *GoA Staff User Guide*, September 2015, 4.
66. Government of Alberta, "Open Government Licence—Alberta," http://open.alberta.ca/licence.
67. Alberta, Service Alberta, *GoA Staff User Guide*, September 2015, 4.
68. Alberta, Legislature Library, introduction to *Annual Report, 1978*.
69. Val Footz, email message to author, July 4, 2016.
70. For a thorough overview of APLIC'S GALLOP portal, see chapter 9.
71. Alberta, Legislative Assembly, "Library Services."
72. Val Footz, email message to author, July 4, 2016.
73. Val Footz, email message to author, July 4, 2016.
74. Alberta, Legislature Library, *Annual Report, 1978*, 8.
75. Klein, *Seizing Opportunity*.
76. Alberta Legislative Assembly Office, *Annual Report, 2000*, 28.
77. Historically, NEOS was an acronym for Networking Edmonton's Online Systems.
78. Varma, "An Interview with Robert Gibson," 41.
79. Micromedia, introduction to *ProFile Index, 1978*, vol. 6.
80. Alberta Legislature Library, *Annual Report, 1979*, 5.
81. Micromedia, *ProFile Index, 1973*, v.
82. Micromedia, *ProFile Index, 1973*, iii.
83. Micromedia, *ProFile Index, 1973*, n.p.

84. Alberta Legislature Library, *Annual Report, 2000*, 28.
85. Alberta Legislature Library, *Annual Report, 2002*, 19.
86. Val Footz, email message to author, July 4, 2016.

Bibliography

An Act Respecting Public Printing (S.A. 1906, c. 9).

An Act to Amend the Act Respecting Public Printing (S.A. 1911–12, c. 12).

An Act to Amend the King's Printer Act (S.A. 1954, c. 50).

An Act to Amend the Statute Law (S.A. 1916, c. 3).

Alberta. Government Services. *Annual Report, 1976–77*. Edmonton: Government of Alberta, 1977.

Alberta. Legislative Assembly. *Alberta Hansard*, 17th Leg, 1st Sess (March 2, 1972).

Alberta. Legislative Assembly Office. *Annual Report, 2000*. Edmonton: Alberta Legislative Assembly Office, 2001. http://www.assembly.ab.ca/lao/library/egovdocs/2000/alla/76198_00_LAO.pdf.

———. "Library Services." N.d. Accessed September 10, 2016. http://www.assembly.ab.ca/lao/library/services.htm.

Alberta. Legislature Library. *Annual Report, 1978*. Edmonton: Alberta Legislature Library, 1979.

———. *Annual Report, 1979*. Edmonton: Alberta Legislature Library, 1980.

———. *Annual Report, 2000*. Edmonton: Alberta Legislature Library, 2001.

———. *Annual Report, 2002*. Edmonton: Alberta Legislature Library, 2002.

Alberta. Office of the Information and Privacy Commissioner. *Review of the Government of Alberta's Public Disclosure of Travel and Expenses Policy, June 2015*. Edmonton: Government of Alberta, 2015. http://www.oipc.ab.ca/media/387034/report_review_goa_travel_expenses_policy_june2015.pdf.

Alberta. Public Affairs Bureau. "Alberta Depository Library Program Guidelines (Draft)." October 1996.

———. *Alberta Government Publications, 1988 Cumulation*. Edmonton: Government of Alberta, 1989.

———. *Depository Library Program*. November 1995.

———. *Government of Alberta Publications (GAP) Catalogue, 1995*. Edmonton: Queen's Printer Bookstore, 1995.

———. *Periodical Publishing Record, 1976*. Edmonton: Government of Alberta, 1977.

———. *Publications Catalogue, No. 3, April–September 1974*. Edmonton: Government of Alberta, 1975.

———. *Publications Catalogue, No. 4, October–December 1974*. Edmonton: Government of Alberta, 1976.

———. *Publications Catalogue, 1976 Cumulation*. Edmonton: Government of Alberta, 1977.

———. *Publications Catalogue, 1979 Cumulation*. Edmonton: Government of Alberta, 1980.

Alberta. Public Works, Supply and Services. *Annual Report, 1990–91*. Edmonton: Government of Alberta, 1991.

———. *Annual Report, 1993–94*. Edmonton: Government of Alberta, 1994.

Alberta. Queen's Printer. *Catalogue, Fall 2004*. Edmonton: Alberta Queen's Printer, 2004.

———. *e-Bookmark: Alberta Queen's Printer Archives*. Edmonton: Alberta Queen's Printer, n.d. Accessed September 11, 2016. http://www.mailoutinteractive.com/ Industry/Archives.aspx?m=4685&qz=5e8fdd7f

———. Government of Alberta Publication (GAP) Search. N.d. Accessed July 12, 2016. http://www.qp.alberta.ca/511.cfm.

Alberta. Service Alberta. *Government of Alberta Publications Guideline (Draft), January 2016*. Edmonton: Government of Alberta, 2016. http://open.alberta. ca/dataset/3e4bccf4-6758-4e4a-bfb9-f7f063b83962/resource/a51090fc-2a94-4b42-91f1-d6aa330ce249/download/Publications-Guideline-DRAFT-V.4.docx.

———. *Open Government Licence—Adoption Guidelines*. Edmonton: Government of Alberta, 2015. http://open.alberta.ca/dataset/f833dd5d-ecb4-4f15-832a-60f1aaf7b99d/resource/55caa06d-e738-4c31-8ec8-98e99bbd2b15/download/ LicenseAdoptionGuidelinesv50.pdf.

———. *Open Government Portal: GoA Staff User Guide, September 2015*. Edmonton: Government of Alberta, 2015. http://open.alberta.ca/dataset/009c2954-e5c0-46e6-a613-30ab8d0dd31c/resource/f97640f3-d74e-4d66-8067-854e16857ed0/ download/OGP-User-Guide-2015.pdf.

———. *Open Government Program Plan, 2016*. Edmonton: Government of Alberta, 2016. http://open.alberta.ca/dataset/40a07487-3984-4184-9216-d2c635402964/resource/094256e1-1ce7-481d-a138-85ae11708727/download/ Open-Government-Program-Plan-2016.

———. *Open Government Strategy*. Edmonton: Government of Alberta, 2015. http://open.alberta.ca/dataset/3beca82e-c14a-41d0-b6a3-33dd20b80256/ resource/b4661609-03a2-4917-84f8-41d0fe4d7834/download/Open-Government-Strategy.pdf/.

———. *Publishing Guide for the Government of Alberta (Draft), August 2015*. Edmonton: Government of Alberta, 2015. https://open.alberta.ca/dataset/ pubguidedraft/resource/3ec9aefd-7049-457d-94a2-dcfa8b8fa9bd (site discontinued).

Bhatia, Mohan. *Canadian Provincial Government Publications: Bibliography of Bibliographies*. Rev. ed. Saskatoon: University of Saskatchewan Library, 1971.

The Department of Government Services Amendment Act, 1976 (S.A. 1976, c. 15).

Edmonton Bulletin. "Printing Costs Are Discussed." April 4, 1925. Alberta Legislature Library Scrapbook Hansard Collection. http://scrapbook.assembly. ab.ca/cdm/singleitem/collection/scrapbook2/id/6796/rec/3.

Edmonton Journal. "$89,000 Saving Seen in Printing Proposals." March 21, 1957. Alberta Legislature Library Scrapbook Hansard Collection. http://scrapbook. assembly.ab.ca/cdm/singleitem/collection/scrapbook2/id/22946/rec/1.

Freedom of Information and Protection of Privacy Act (R.S.A. 2000, c. F-25).

Government Accountability Act (R.S.A. 2000, c. G-7).

Government of Alberta. *Government of Alberta Communications Policy*. Edmonton: Government of Alberta, 2007. http://open.alberta.ca/dataset/61edaa20-a93b-4d8c-80d4-fb42c27d5274/resource/0ba86ad9-d3cc-4bba-99bc-e8dc6641f2cc/download/2007-Communications-Policy-May-15-07.pdf.

———. *Government of Alberta Open Information and Open Data Policy*. Edmonton: Government of Alberta, 2015. http://open.alberta.ca/policy.

Jarvi, Edith T. *Access to Canadian Government Publications in Canadian Academic and Public Libraries*. Ottawa: Canadian Library Association, 1976.

Klein, Ralph. *Seizing Opportunity: Alberta's New Economic Development Strategy*. Edmonton: Government of Alberta, 1993. https://archive.org/details/seizingopportunio0klei.

Micromedia Limited. *Microlog Index, 1979: Canadian Government Publications and Reports*. Toronto: Micromedia, 1980.

———. *ProFile Index, 1973: Canadian Provincial and Municipal Publications*. Toronto: Micromedia, 1974.

———. *ProFile Index, 1978: Canadian Provincial Publications*. Toronto: Micromedia, 1978.

Pross, A. Paul, and Catherine A. Pross. *Government Publishing in the Canadian Provinces: A Prescriptive Study*. Toronto: University of Toronto Press, 1972.

Pross, Catherine A. *A Guide to the Identification and Acquisition of Canadian Government Publications: Provinces and Territories*. 2nd ed. Dalhousie University Library, Occasional Paper 16. Halifax, NS: Dalhousie University Libraries and Dalhousie University School of Library Service, 1983.

Pross, Catherine A., and A. Paul Pross. *A Guide to the Identification and Acquisition of Canadian Provincial Government Publications*. Dalhousie University Libraries, Occasional Paper 16. Halifax, NS: School of Public Administration, Dalhousie University, 1977.

Varma, Divakara K. "An Interview with Robert Gibson, Founder of Micromedia, a Major Business Information Provider in Canada." *Journal of Business & Finance Librarianship* 3, no. 2 (1998): 39–46.

6

SASKATCHEWAN GOVERNMENT PUBLICATIONS DEPOSIT IN THE LEGISLATIVE LIBRARY

Gregory Salmers

This chapter will look at the history of the acquisition of provincial government publications in Saskatchewan at the Legislative Library, an organization that serves as an official publication depository for the province. The findings of a recent assessment of the function of Saskatchewan's legal deposit and related processes will be given, and details concerning the challenges of new formats will be discussed.

GENESIS OF LEGAL DEPOSIT IN SASKATCHEWAN

From its beginning the Saskatchewan Legislative Library had a strong sense of responsibility and ambition to collect, preserve, and make accessible the government publications produced in its jurisdiction. It evolved a variety of activities and programs over time to achieve this ambition. Legislation affirming a legal-deposit role for the library was part of this evolution. Not all jurisdictions in Canada have legislation requiring the deposition of government publications to their legislative library. Saskatchewan is one jurisdiction that does have legislation.

The legislation was passed into law in 1982 as an amendment to *The Legislative Assembly and Executive Council Act* of 1979. Passage of the legislation was a critical step in the efforts of the province to preserve its government publications, in that it acknowledged the importance of preserving government publications and designated the Legislative Library as the official repository and as the agent for carrying out this work. While there was no opposition to the amendment expressed during the debate, Mr. Blakeney, former Saskatchewan premier and then leader of the official opposition, made a comment that foresaw the challenges that the library would encounter in effectively implementing this important stewardship role, in particular the management of the volume and the definition of the publications.

HON. MR. BLAKENEY: —Mr. Chairman and Mr. Minister, I don't want to belabor this point, but it seems to me that we should understand what we're doing here, in making the Legislative Library a repository of a very, very large amount of written material. If they have to deposit six copies of every government publication, and there are a very large number of them—I don't know whether it includes leaflets put in power bills and these sorts of things or not, that are published—but there's going to be a lot of them over a period of ten years. We are probably going to have to have a look at this and exclude some of it because there's no earthly reason for keeping some of it. I don't have any answer as to which and which, but I make that point and doubtless the board of internal economy will grapple with that years hence.[1]

The drive to make the Legislative Library a repository for every Saskatchewan government publication grew out of several factors. One of these was the experience over many decades at the Legislative Library of attempting to identify, gather, and make available to clients suitable content in general and government publications in particular. The attempt to collect government publications was met with partial success. According to Christine MacDonald, legislative librarian from 1973 to 1982 and author of *The Legislative Library of Saskatchewan: A History*, "although this function was supported by memoranda circularized by Premiers Douglas, Thatcher and Blakeney these communications provided insufficient authority and, not surprisingly, all departmental publications did not arrive automatically."[2]

Another factor was the Legislative Library's desire to establish government publication exchange agreements with other libraries including legislative libraries in other provinces or countries. An example of this is the exchange arrangement for federal publications. In 1927 the library became a full depository for Canadian federal publications. By 1953, in exchange for these publications, the library provided Saskatchewan government publications to the federal government.[3] In order to perform the exchange function with other institutions and other jurisdictions, the Legislative Library needed a list of its own jurisdiction's publications.[4] Without a complete submission of Saskatchewan government publications each year, it was impossible to produce a comprehensive list.

Finally, the library held the enduring, deeper philosophy that a legislative library should have a complete collection of government publications from its jurisdiction. As the authors of the 1981 *Report of the Special Committee on the Review of the Legislative Library* indicated, there is a direct connection between the aspirations of a democracy, the function of the Legislative Assembly and its members, and access to the public record:

> In democratic societies Legislative Assemblies are the centre of the democratic process...For a Legislative Assembly to perform this distinguished role with any reasonable degree of success presumes that informed debate and wise judgement will take place amongst the Members of the House... An Assembly requires a number of supports to assist the Members to perform their responsibilities. One such support is the collection, organization and communication of all information relevant to the processes and issues before the Assembly.[5]

In 1889, in his report on the North-West Government Library (predecessor of the Legislative Library), J.W. Powers, the clerk in charge of the library at the time, commented on the composition of the collection in general, with a view to improving its quality.[6] By 1896 a library committee of the Legislative Assembly had stated in its report that an emphasis should be placed on items relating to "political, historic, and economic" fields.[7] After Saskatchewan became a province in 1905, more focus on government publications in particular occurred, with consideration of exchange agreements with other libraries.

The Legislative Library is the oldest library in Saskatchewan and predated the existence of other institutions such as the provincial archives and individual government department libraries that could assist in the collection and preservation of government publications and records. Early in Saskatchewan's history the Legislative Library had both an archival and a library function, and as a result it collected internal government records as well as government publications intended for public consumption.

In 1947, with the establishment of the Division of Archives and Government Publications within the library, the role of being a repository for Saskatchewan publications was embraced more vividly. Although the Legislative Library had accepted this role philosophically from the start, now this philosophy was becoming articulated in the way the library was structured. However, at this time it was up to the library to identify, locate, and acquire Saskatchewan government publications. The library was not always successful in these efforts, even though three premiers issued memoranda endorsing the collection of publications by the Legislative Library. This lack of success became more evident and unsatisfactory as the Division of Archives and Government Publications attempted to produce a checklist of Saskatchewan government publications.[8]

During the 1960s, 1970s, and 1980s the library had selective and/or full depository status for Quebec and Ontario government publications.[9] These relationships made it even more compelling to be able to produce a checklist of Saskatchewan publications, as was mentioned in the 1981 report of the special committee:

> Clearly the Legislative Library is the only agency in Saskatchewan which will have knowledge of all the official

publications of the Saskatchewan government. The Library, therefore, has a major obligation to communicate this information very widely to Members, libraries across the Province, the Saskatchewan public at large, and to national and international agencies who have an interest in our Province.[10]

In 1972 an arrangement began with Micromedia in which the library provided Saskatchewan government publications to Micromedia for it to microfilm. In exchange Micromedia provided copies of this microfiche to the Legislative Library.[11] This development improved access to, and preservation of, Saskatchewan government publications. The library acquired subscriptions to the other jurisdictions' government publications that were available through Micromedia, underscoring the general value of the access provided by microfiche at that time.

In 1972 a first attempt was made to formalize the deposit of Saskatchewan government publications. The librarian asked the premier for an Order-in-Council to strengthen and formalize the deposit function, but this was not possible owing to the lack of a legislative framework for the library.[12]

Nevertheless, the Legislative Library was able to arrange the acquisition of many publications. It received publications such as legislative papers including standing orders, debates, votes, proceedings, bills, journals, and reports; statutes; regulations; gazettes; loose-leaf items; annual reports of departments; financial statements; monographs on a wide range of topics; news releases; serials, such as crop reports and drilling reports; environmental impact statements; brochures, flyers, posters; and electoral and other maps.

These publications formed a collection that was important because it contained information about, and debate on, current and previous legislation. It also documented both the activities of provincial government departments and the state and development of the province over time, politically, economically, and culturally.

In October 1972 the Saskatchewan Library Association presented a submission to the Queen's Printer about improving access to Saskatchewan government publications. It recommended that the Saskatchewan

Legislative Library "be a full depository library and receive all publications which are made available by the government, and that the status of the existing depository arrangement be examined with a view to making it a matter of permanent record by such means as the government deems appropriate."[13] The submission also recommended that the term *government publications* be defined to include "any printed or processed material prepared by or for an agency of the government and made available to the public." The association cited *Government Publishing in the Canadian Provinces* by A. Paul Pross and Catherine Pross relative to the wording of this definition.[14] The Pross Report, as it is known, examined government publishing in the Canadian provinces and made specific recommendations for improved preservation and access including through legislative libraries as official deposit libraries.[15] The Saskatchewan Library Association referenced the Pross Report as a key stimulus for its submission to the Queen's Printer about improvement of access to Saskatchewan government publications. The Saskatchewan Library Association's Committee on Government Publications was formed to study the report.

On August 8, 1973, the committee presented a brief to the Saskatchewan Cabinet, recommending that there be both a central distribution agency for government publications, and a monthly listing of publications; the Saskatchewan Legislative Library be a full depository, receiving six copies of publications; the Legislative Library distribute copies to the Saskatchewan Archives, the National Library of Canada, and the Library of Congress; and ten other libraries be designated full depositories.[16] A successful attempt to formalize deposit of government publications began in the late 1970s. The library's desire for a provincial checklist of Saskatchewan government publications and a legislated deposit function was closely examined during a review of the Legislative Library that was conducted by a special committee of the Legislative Assembly in 1979–81. The *Report of the Special Committee on the Review of the Legislative Library*, of May 7, 1981, recommended "that the library, as a high priority, investigate procedures which would provide for a regular *Monthly Checklist of Saskatchewan Government Publications* as well as an annual cumulation." In addition, the committee asked that the deposit role be formalized:

In connection with the depository function, the Committee
has observed that if there was a Legislative Library Act, one
would expect to find the depository function mandated in
the Act. To confirm the Assembly's wish that the Legislative
Library should possess this depository function in perpetuity, the Committee further recommends...[t]hat a resolution
of the Assembly be passed at the earliest convenient time to
assign to the Legislative Library the depository function for
all Saskatchewan government publications.[17]

The committee also recommended improved organization of and access to the library's government publications through implementation
of an online library catalogue and the CODOC classification system.

EVOLUTION OF LEGAL DEPOSIT LEGISLATION IN SASKATCHEWAN

In 1982 the Legislative Assembly made amendments to *The Legislative
Assembly and Executive Council Act* that provided legislative authority
for the Library as the official repository for Saskatchewan government
publications and as the official exchange library for the Province of Saskatchewan. The legislation required government agencies to deposit six
copies of every publication within twenty days of release to the public:

(5) The Legislative Library is designated as the official library
for the deposit of Saskatchewan government publications,
and all departments, boards, commissions and agencies
of the Government of Saskatchewan shall deposit with the
Legislative Library six copies of every government publication,
pamphlet, or circular issued or released for general or limited
public distribution and printed by them or under their authority within 20 days after the item is released to the public.

(6) The Legislative Library is designated as the official exchange library for the province of Saskatchewan and is responsible for collecting government publications, for depositing

government publications with the National Library, the Library of Congress and any other library with which exchange agreements are made.[18]

This legislation remained in force, unchanged, for over twenty years.

During this period, legal deposit had a strong impact on the collection and services of the Legislative Library, as detailed in its annual reports during the 1980s and 1990s. For example, in concert with the new legislation requiring deposit of provincial publications, in 1982 the library staff contacted all government departments, boards, and agencies in order to facilitate deposit. Twenty-one deposit contacts were designated, and 1,192 Saskatchewan government publications were received and listed in the monthly *Checklist of Saskatchewan Government Publications*, a Legislative Library publication.[19] In 1987 the annual report stated that 90–95 percent of all acquisitions of library material occurred through exchange agreements with other jurisdictions. These agreements were facilitated by the availability of the Saskatchewan government publications to be exchanged.

The agreement with Micromedia, starting in 1972, produced a noticeably positive result in service. For example, the 1985 annual report indicated that 4,955 copies were produced from microfilm for clients, some of which copies involved government publications—an increase of 545 percent over the prior period.[20] The same annual report indicated that 4,281 Saskatchewan government publications were received in the reporting period and listed in the monthly checklist, a dramatic increase from 1982.[21] At this time, six copies of each title were received under the deposit legislation. In 1986, 352 serial and 266 monograph titles were deposited and listed. During the same period Micromedia was provided with 516 titles for microfilming.

In 1987 an agreement was struck with the provincial purchasing agency wherein the Legislative Library received notification of new publications.[22] Of the six copies of each Saskatchewan government publication received since the 1982 Act, two copies were retained by the library, two went to the Saskatchewan Archives, and two fulfilled exchange agreements with the Library of Congress and the National Library of Canada.[23]

The effectiveness of the 1982 legislation began to suffer somewhat with the rise of the Internet. In the library's 1996 annual report it was noted that production of Saskatchewan government publications was decentralized, and it was challenging to identify and receive all publications. In the four years covered by the same report, only 4,251 Saskatchewan government publications had been received. A further decline occurred later in the 1990s. In the two-year period of the 1998 annual report, 1,899 monographs and serials were deposited. The rise of the Internet and born-digital publications was creating problems in the deposit program in that some Saskatchewan government agencies were not depositing these publications, in spite of the Act of 1982 requiring them to do so. This experience was added to the concern that electronic publications might have uncertain accessibility and durability over time.

For the eight fiscal years between 1998 and 2005 the number of Saskatchewan government publications received through the deposit program varied: 911; 1,185; 1,354; 1,072; 976; 1,012; 1,170; and 1,527—with 736, 973, 750, 727, 914, 705, 840, and 654 sent to Micromedia. The numbers of publications received on deposit and sent to Micromedia varied due to the criteria for microfilming, which excluded publications below a certain size, and some by type. The concern over the refusal of some agencies to deposit electronic publications continued.

On May 27, 2005, legislation came into force that expanded the details about the deposit function. The development and widespread use of the Internet meant that provisions were needed to include electronic publications, and this in turn brokered a change in the speed of deposit required. The quantities in which publications were expected were also adjusted at that time. Crown corporations were now included in the scope of the Act, and this was an important clarification. Eight copies of paper publications were to be deposited within ten days of release, and one copy of every electronic publication within twenty-four hours of its being posted on the Internet. *The Legislative Assembly and Executive Council Act*, 2005, read as follows:

LEGISLATIVE LIBRARY AS OFFICIAL DEPOSITORY
81(1) In this section, "government publication" means a publication, pamphlet or circular that:

(a) is issued for general or limited public distribution by a ministry, board, commission or agency of the Government of Saskatchewan or a Crown corporation; and

(b) is published by or pursuant to the authority of a department, board, commission or agency of the Government of Saskatchewan or a Crown corporation.

(2) The Legislative Library is the official library for the deposit of government publications.

(3) Every ministry, board, commission and agency of the Government of Saskatchewan and every Crown corporation shall deposit with the Legislative Library eight complimentary copies of every government publication that:

(a) is released in any form, including print and electronic, for general or limited public distribution either for free or for sale; and

(b) is issued by them or pursuant to their authority in collaboration with a commercial publisher.

(4) The copies mentioned in subsection (3) must be deposited within 10 days after the government publication is released to the public.

(5) If a government publication mentioned in subsection (3) is made available to the public in both print and electronic form, the department, board, commission or agency of the Government of Saskatchewan or Crown corporation shall provide eight copies and one electronic copy to the Legislative Library.

(6) If a government publication mentioned in subsection (3) is made available only in electronic form on the Internet, the department, board, commission or agency of the Government of Saskatchewan or Crown corporation shall provide one electronic copy to the Legislative Library within 24 hours after it is posted on the Internet.

(7) The Legislative Library is designated as the official exchange library for Saskatchewan and is responsible for:

(a) collecting government publications; and

(b) depositing government publications with the National
Library, the Library of Congress and any other library
with which exchange agreements are made by the
Legislative Library.[24]

In 2007 a minor change was made to the legislation on legal deposit to reflect the Government of Saskatchewan's decision to rename provincial government departments *ministries*.

In 2015 the legislation was more substantially amended. The number of copies of government publications to be deposited was changed from the fixed eight copies to "the number of complimentary copies required by the Legislative Librarian."[25] This was done to allow more flexibility as circumstances changed and to reduce waste. For example, the number of exchange agreements and the number of copies required for these were reduced over the years because a number of exchange libraries no longer wished to receive publications. At the same time, the Legislative Library indicated on its website and in a brochure the number of copies required, depending on the type of publication: serial publications, four; monographs, four; environmental impact statements, one; and annual reports and financial statements, five. The Act continued to require one copy of the electronic versions of these items or of items born digital. The scope of the Act was amended to add "the Legislative Assembly or an Officer of the Legislative Assembly" as sources of publications to be deposited, in addition to "every ministry, board, commission and agency of the Government of Saskatchewan and every Crown corporation."[26]

Examples of officers of the Legislative Assembly include the Clerk of the Legislative Assembly, the advocate for children and youth, the chief electoral officer, the conflict of interest commissioner, the ombudsman for Saskatchewan, the provincial auditor, and the public interest disclosure commissioner.

2014 LEGAL DEPOSIT ASSESSMENT: INTENT AND METHODOLOGY

In 2014 the Legislative Library conducted an assessment of legal deposit to gather facts about its current state. The assessment was also designed to increase understanding among Saskatchewan government bodies about the *Legislative Assembly Act* and their duties under it; to increase Legislative Library knowledge of the conditions in which government publications are produced and distributed; to improve compliance with the Act; and to increase interaction between the Legislative Library and the ministries, boards, commissions, agencies, and Crown corporations as named in the Act. The initiative was also an opportunity to highlight the Legislative Library services available to government bodies. As a result, another main effort was to promote the services of the Legislative Library and their potential benefits for public sector clients. Finally, the assessment was to produce a set of recommendations for improving the legal deposit function.

The methodology involved the library making telephone, email, and site-visit contact with every Saskatchewan government ministry, board, commission, agency, and Crown corporation listed on the Saskatchewan government's website. The library's intended tone of interaction was one of awareness building and encouragement rather than enforcement.

The Legislative Library used a first interaction with government agencies to determine an appropriate contact. Often this was a communications person in the particular government body. The library's ensuing site visits focused on sharing a brochure about legal deposit, along with an extract of section 81, the part of the Act that involved legal deposit. The library supplemented the legal-deposit information with a brochure about the Legislative Library services, collections, and mandate, as well as a brochure about the Government and Legislative Libraries Online Publications (GALLOP) portal—a portal through which legislative libraries in Canada make available online their digital repositories of jurisdictional government publications.[27]

The immediate outcome of each visit was an updated contact listing; points learned about the location's publications, publishing patterns, and challenges in publishing; and a sense of how much the contact had known about legal deposit prior to being visited. The Legislative Library also learned whether or not government agencies were complying with the Act, partially or completely. In total, twenty-one metrics were gathered from each location. These included whether the agency had heard of legal deposit, and, if so, from what source; how long they had been aware of it and/or were complying; what the obstacles were to compliance; how many locations were involved in producing publications for the agency; whether the agency maintained a list of its own publications and, if so, would share that list with the library; whether the agency found the visit helpful in facilitating compliance and would like ensuing visits annually or at some other frequency; the name of the staff member responding and how long the member had been in that role; whether the respondent felt that staff turnover was an obstacle to awareness and compliance, and how frequently staff turnover occurred in the office; and if there were specific questions for the Legislative Library about legal deposit. Notes were also taken about unique suggestions, topics, and follow-up actions.

At first the library's goal was to visit about 25 percent of government bodies. In the end, library representatives visited sixty-two of the sixty-three identified ministries, boards, commissions, agencies, and Crown corporations. Some offices located outside Regina were contacted by telephone and email only. Visits required between thirty-eight and fifty-five minutes to complete. They were conducted by the Legislative Library's support services director (manager of the legal-deposit program) as part of the normal work cycle over a period of several weeks between October 2014 and January 2015.

During 2015 and 2016, second and third rounds of visits were made. The second round of visits imparted the news about the 2015 changes to the Act, including expansion of the scope to the Legislative Assembly and officers of the Legislative Assembly, and changes in the required number of copies of publications. The third round of visits was made as a result of a recommendation arising from the initial findings, that site visits should occur every two years. This round involved about a third of the offices, with the intent of visiting the rest within two years.

▶ Findings of the Assessment

Site visits to the government agencies produced valuable information regarding awareness of legal deposit, and valuable insights into compliance challenges and issues. Only 39 percent of government bodies were sufficiently aware of legal deposit to comply with the Act. Of the contacts consulted, 86 percent thought that staff turnover was likely a factor in the reduced awareness. Of the government bodies, 23 percent produced publications in more than one location in the province. The number of publications produced annually by each office varied from a minimum of one to over a thousand. Of those contacted, 100 percent found the visit helpful. About a third of the contacts said that they would like a site visit once a year, and most of the remaining contacts thought that every two years would suffice.

The assessment also found that the definition of *publication* might require further refinement and policy definition by the Legislative Library. Remembering the quotation from Mr. Blakeney at the start of this chapter, exactly what constitutes a publication can become unclear. During site visits the government agencies raised a number of ambiguities regarding the definition. The library made an effort during the assessment to explore and document the "edges" of legal deposit, that is, those aspects of legal deposit that were unclear due to a need for interpretation or adjudication, especially in cases of new technology and formats.

The Act has always worded its definition of a government publication as "a publication, pamphlet, or circular."[28] The wording "released in any form, including print and electronic" was added in 2005,[29] but it is challenging to apply in the context of continually evolving electronic formats. Examples of government publications with evolving formats include tourism content on a website with a simulated page-turning feature; and oilfield drilling reports that used to appear as recognizable paper publications and, after 2007, appeared online, which then morphed into a comma-separated stream of data. Certain electronic formats such as web pages and database-driven output strain the Act's definition beyond its original intent, and challenge the Legislative Library and government agencies when it comes to depositing, receiving, and managing such material. Some print formats also strain the definition. Again, it is good to remember the comment made during the legislation's initial debate: "I don't know whether it includes leaflets put in power bills and these sorts of things or not."[30]

The assessment process also identified that government agencies often need assistance in understanding the distinction between government documents and government publications. A government publication is created with the intent of releasing it for distribution to the public. Internal office forms, emails, reports, memoranda, and drafts of items intended for internal use are not publications and in Saskatchewan are handled under records management by the Provincial Archives of Saskatchewan.

Since the beginning of the outreach visits and the awareness campaign there has been an increase in the deposit of publications. During the twelve months commencing April 1, 2015, for example, 5,046 monographs and serials in paper and digital formats were received and retained in the Legislative Library's collection. This was an increase of 43 percent over the prior fiscal year. During the same period 1,738 monographs and serials were sent to Micromedia.

▶ *Web and Other Electronic Content*

New digital formats, especially those on the Internet, pose particular problems for legal deposit in terms of determining whether such formats meet the definition of a publication and whether it is feasible for the library to accession publications in these formats. Many releases of government information take the form of a web page (not in a Word document format or a P D F), and these web pages are changed often, sometimes daily. The Legislative Library does not currently accession web pages under its legal-deposit function, and significant resources would be required if the library pursued doing so. If the library does not assume this role, who will archive and make available this enormous content?

Interactive maps online, social-media content embedded in tweets and Facebook pages, or other complex electronic formats are not being captured through legal deposit, yet they sometimes contain content that may be defined as a publication under the Act. Other grey areas raised by government agencies include government presentations using a PowerPoint format in a speech for a select audience; Highway Hotline reports that automatically feed Twitter; organizational newsletters distributed broadly to the homes of current and former employees; and publications released via third-party commercial websites.

▶ *Recommendations of the Assessment*

In March 2015 the Legislative Library compiled an internal report on its legal-deposit assessment. It summarized the findings and recommendations for the library's consideration. Most important, the assessment found a strong need for the library to maintain routine site visits to government agencies in order to increase understanding and compliance. The library has proceeded to operationalize site visits so that each government agency will be visited every two years. A variety of strategies for supporting communication of legal deposit is under consideration by the library as a result of feedback from the assessment, including a suggestion to give the program a more meaningful and easily understandable name (other than "Legal Deposit"). The report also recommended that the Legislative Library consider further policy development regarding the definition of *government publication* in order to manage better the ambiguities associated with new formats and technologies. The library is undertaking this work.

IMPLICATIONS OF LEGAL DEPOSIT FOR COLLECTIONS, CATALOGUING, AND FACILITIES

The implications of legal deposit for library collections are significant. As many publications become electronic only, or a hybrid, a challenging time for all libraries exists. Libraries must retain their excellence with traditional, paper-based library services and collections management. They must also develop policy, technology, and staff expertise to manage complex electronic formats. This reality creates pressure on library staff expertise, budgetary resources, and information-technology infrastructure. The long-term preservation and accessibility of print and electronic government publications require substantial resources.

▶ *Digital-Repository Development*

An interesting connection to the legal-deposit function, in the context of the overall picture of access to Saskatchewan government publications, and those of other jurisdictions, for clients of the Saskatchewan Legislative Library, is digital-repository development for government publication collections. Library employees add electronic government publications daily on a server in the Legislative building. We know from evidence given earlier in this chapter that varied formats create problems, and obtaining publications generally is an age-old issue. Nevertheless, the number of electronic Saskatchewan government publications on this server has grown from 6,172 items in 2009 to 33,676 items in 2016. Each item is a file in PDF. Of these, 7,799 files are monographs, and 25,877 are serials. During the 2014–15 fiscal year 3,529 Saskatchewan government publications were added to the collection. Of these, 28 percent were acquired in print on paper only, 38 percent were digital only, and 34 percent were in both formats.

The Legislative Library's repository is structured by locating deposited publications in PDF on a server and assigning a name and a URL to that publication. Then a bibliographic record is created in the library's catalogue in which there is a link to the electronic resource. This method works well for the library's clients. It is a manual process, however, which is labour intensive, does not process the desired content as systematically or as automatically as is possible, and offers limited processes for long-term preservation. The library seeks to acquire a content-management product at a suitable scale to handle the number of resources in a more automatic fashion.

Meanwhile, in the selection of "next-generation" library systems, it is necessary to weave concerns about government publications—their acquisition, cataloguing, preservation, and access—into the selection process. The Saskatchewan Legislative Library is currently implementing a new system. The hope is that its primary clients (Members of the Legislative Assembly and their staff), secondary clients, government employees, and the general public will be presented with a coordinated, searchable display of all its physical holdings, commercial electronic databases, and the electronic items in the Legislative Library's repository.

The repository is a resource that improves and centralizes access to digital provincial-government publications. In addition, the repository feeds a national portal to digital government publications called GALLOP.

SASKATCHEWAN GOVERNMENT PUBLICATIONS IN GALLOP

The Government and Legislative Libraries Online Publications (GALLOP) portal provides one-stop access to electronic provincial, territorial, and federal government publications and legislative materials dating back to 1995. Members of the public who search GALLOP find digital Saskatchewan government publications and can access the Saskatchewan repository in order to retrieve them on their screen. As part of its commitment to store and make available government publications, the Legislative Library of Saskatchewan has partnered with other legislative libraries in Canada to sustain the GALLOP portal. The portal is a creation of the Association of Parliamentary Libraries in Canada (APLIC) and provides a public access point to the electronic publications of all jurisdictions except Nunavut, Prince Edward Island, and Yukon Territory. This fact was offered as a motivator to government employees during site visits. The more thoroughly they comply with the Act and deposit their electronic publications, the better the GALLOP portal will be for everyone, including researchers in government offices in Saskatchewan. This is especially noteworthy when researchers desire multiple jurisdiction comparisons on certain topics of interest to them. At present there are 10,533 Saskatchewan government publication titles available through the portal. GALLOP is a national hope among librarians for a means to address the concerns about preservation of, and access to, digital government publications in Canada. Provincial questions of format, scope, and function all have an impact on GALLOP.

SUMMARY

This chapter has covered one interesting part of the story of how a legislative library is using new systems, collaborative efforts, outreach and promotion, and detailed assessments of current services and function in order to ensure a comprehensive access to the government publications of its jurisdiction. It is a story about meeting the challenge of sustaining collections and access during a time of extremely rapid change in technology, formats, and service expectations, while mandates remain constant. Over time, the focus of the Saskatchewan Legislative Library has remained on a few key objectives. One of these is the acquisition and preservation in perpetuity of all Saskatchewan government publications. The current realities of electronic formats create the latest impetus for a change in the legislation defining legal deposit. New library systems offer hope for coping effectively with these challenges.

Notes

1. Saskatchewan, Legislative Assembly, *Debates and Proceedings*, 20th Leg, 1st Sess, No 40A (17 December 1982) at 1916 (Hon. Mr. Blakeney).
2. MacDonald, *Legislative Library of Saskatchewan*, 53.
3. MacDonald. *Legislative Library of Saskatchewan*, 48.
4. MacDonald. *Legislative Library of Saskatchewan*, 53.
5. Legislative Assembly of Saskatchewan, *Report of the Special Committee*, 2.
6. Power, *Report on the Territorial Library*.
7. MacDonald. *Legislative Library of Saskatchewan*, 43.
8. MacDonald, *Legislative Library of Saskatchewan*, 53.
9. MacDonald, *Legislative Library of Saskatchewan*, 51.
10. Legislative Assembly of Saskatchewan, *Report of the Special Committee*, 28.
11. MacDonald, *Legislative Library of Saskatchewan*, 51.
12. MacDonald, *Legislative Library of Saskatchewan*, 53.
13. Saskatchewan Library Association, "Submission to Mr. Reid," 3.
14. Saskatchewan Library Association, "Submission to Mr. Reid," 1.
15. Pross and Pross, *Government Publishing in the Canadian Provinces*, 17, 158–59.
16. Saskatchewan Provincial Library, *Focus on Saskatchewan Libraries* 20, no. 7 (July–August, 1973).
17. Legislative Assembly of Saskatchewan, *Report of the Special Committee*, 28.
18. *An Act to Amend the Legislative Assembly and Executive Council Act* (S.S. 1982–83, no. 2, c. 38).
19. Saskatchewan Legislative Library, *Annual Report, 1982–1983*, 7.
20. Saskatchewan Legislative Library, *Annual Report, 1985*, 9.
21. Saskatchewan Legislative Library, *Annual Report, 1985*, 12.
22. Saskatchewan Legislative Library, *Annual Report, 1986–1987*, 8.
23. Saskatchewan Legislative Library, *Annual Report, 1996*, 17.
24. *The Legislative Assembly and Executive Council Act* (S.S. 2005, c. L-11.2).
25. *The Legislative Assembly Act* (S.S. 2015, c. 14), 11(3).
26. *The Legislative Assembly Act* (S.S. 2015, c. 14), 11(1)(c).
27. For a thorough overview of APLIC'S GALLOP portal, see chapter 9.
28. *The Legislative Assembly and Executive Council Amendment Act* (S.S. 1982–83, no. 2, c. 38).
29. *The Legislative Assembly and Executive Council Act* (S.S. 2005, c. L-11.2).
30. Saskatchewan, Legislative Assembly, *Debates and Proceedings*, 20th Leg, 1st Sess, No 40A (17 December 1982) at 1916 (Hon. Mr. Blakeney).

Bibliography

The Legislative Assembly Act (S.S. 2007, c. L-11.3).
The Legislative Assembly Amendment Act (S.S. 2015, c. 14).
The Legislative Assembly and Executive Council Act (S.S. 2005, c. L-11.2).

The Legislative Assembly and Executive Council Amendment Act (S.S. 1982–83, no. 2, c. 38).

MacDonald, Christine. *The Legislative Library of Saskatchewan: A History*. Regina: Saskatchewan Legislative Library, 1986.

Pross, A. Paul, and Catherine Pross. *Government Publishing in the Canadian Provinces*. University of Toronto Press, 1972.

Saskatchewan. Legislative Assembly. *Report of the Special Committee on the Review of the Legislative Library*. May 7, 1981.

———. Legislative Assembly. *Report on the Territorial Library, 1889*. Sessional Papers 1889, no. 1. Regina, SK: J.W. Power, 1889.

———. Legislative Library. *Annual Report*. Various years. 1982 forward, published; 1889–1981, unpublished.

Saskatchewan Library Association. "Submission to Mr. Reid, Queen's Printer, by the Committee on Government Publications." Unpublished internal document, Saskatchewan Legislative Library, October 1972.

Saskatchewan Provincial Library. "Saskatchewan Library Association News." *Focus on Saskatchewan Libraries* 20, no. 7 (July–August, 1973): 1–2.

7

INSIDE TRACK

Challenges of Collecting, Accessing, and Preserving Ontario Government Publications

Sandra Craig and Martha Murphy

This chapter will discuss the current state of government publications in Ontario and reflect on their history. There is no provincial library or trusted digital repository system with a mandate to preserve and collect Ontario's government documents. An overview of government publications, print and electronic, will be given with respect to the creation, capturing, managing, and retaining of documents. Publications Ontario, the Legislative Library, the Archives of Ontario, and government libraries are facing many challenges in collecting, accessing, and preserving publications, especially in the born-digital era. Overall, there is a lack of stewardship, which has an impact on government transparency and accountability. This chapter aims to highlight the urgency of developing options for the centralized collection, preservation, and access to Ontario's print and digital publications.

PUBLICATIONS ONTARIO

Ontario government publications can be accessed through Publications Ontario and the depository network. The depository libraries system provides Ontarians with access to information through a network of public, educational, and government libraries. Publications Ontario manages the official distribution of print publications, and publications can be ordered directly through its website or consulted in depository libraries. Depository status is given to libraries that are governed by the *Public Libraries Act*, to educational or institution libraries, and to the libraries of Ontario government ministries. The *Guidelines for Depository Libraries* states that libraries must retain a title for a minimum of five years unless it is superseded by a revised edition or replaced by a new publication, or Publications Ontario has approved the termination or discontinuation of the title.[1]

Government publications are also available at the Ontario Legislative Library and the Archives of Ontario Library, along with the libraries of twenty-two dedicated ministries and agencies, boards, and commissions (ABCS). They provide publications, information, and research services to their own clients, and a few of these libraries are open to the public. Many of the ministries and ABCS do not have a library and are particularly at risk for loss of access to government publications. Ministries and ABCS are responsible for their own publications and their distribution whether it be through Publications Ontario or directly from their websites. Under the *Archives and Recordkeeping Act* and the *Corporate Policy on Recordkeeping*, publications are explicitly excluded from the responsibilities of the Archives of Ontario. This means that while libraries are collecting government publications, and while there is a depository system through Publications Ontario, there is no mechanism in place to capture all of Ontario publications both print and electronic.

At the general meeting of the Ontario Government Libraries Council (OGLC) in December 2011, Vicki Whitmell, Legislative Librarian of Ontario, stated:

> [With] LAC's decision and no provincial library with a
> mandate to preserve and collect Ontario's government doc-
> uments there are concerns that many of these documents
> will either be lost or inaccessible over time. While individ-
> ual ministry libraries along with the Ontario Legislative
> Library may continue to collect and maintain government

documents based on their collection development policies and criteria, a cohesive, centralized approach to collecting and providing access to Ontario's documents does not exist.[2]

In 2012 the Government of Canada's budget announced a series of cuts to Library and Archives Canada (LAC) services. Of primary importance, collecting, maintaining, and providing access to provincial government publications would no longer form part of LAC's mandate. The Ontario government libraries took the opportunity to retrieve holdings of interest from LAC and to backfill their collections. An informal survey of Ontario documents held by LAC showed that the majority could also be found at the Legislative Library. While the Legislative Library is not mandated to collect all Ontario government publications, it strives to collect the majority of published materials in order to serve its clients.

ONTARIO LEGISLATIVE LIBRARY

The Ontario Legislative Library staff members provide research and analysis, reference, news, and access services to the Members of Provincial Parliament and their staff, the legislative committees, and the staff of the Legislative Assembly. The Legislative Library is the descendant of the parliamentary libraries of the Province of Upper Canada (1792–1841) and of the united Province of Canada (1841–67) and, as a result, has an extensive collection of Ontario government documents.[3] Ontario government documents form the core of the library's collection. The collection is extensive, but not meant to be comprehensive, and reflects the needs of its primary clientele. It also serves to preserve the publishing output of the Ontario government. Resources collected include policy and program documents, financial reports, consultation documents, research reports, commissions of inquiry and task force reports, annual and quarterly reports, and sessional papers. Items that are not collected include consumer-directed publications; forms; tax bulletins; highly technical, scientific, or medical publications; and government datasets. Traditionally the Legislative Library has collected multiple copies (at least two) of print publications in both English and French.

Beginning in the late 1990s government ministries began to also publish their documents in electronic format and post them on their websites. Initially, only a link to the Internet version was provided in the Legislative Library's catalogue records. However, with the continually changing nature of government websites, documents were moved or deleted after a short period of time. If the document was born digital, access to the resource was permanently lost. A solution was needed to ensure that persistent access to electronic Ontario government documents was maintained.

In 1999 the library began a pilot project to build a document repository of born-digital Ontario government publications. Beginning with monographs, simple and streamlined procedures were developed that integrated with acquisition and cataloguing work flows. In July 2000 the Legislative Library began to formally build an archive of Ontario government publications. A few years later the scope of the archive was expanded to include news releases and all of the Ontario serials that the library collected in electronic format. To date there are over 100,000 Ontario government files (monographs, serials, and press releases) in the repository.

Four metadata services technicians monitor Ontario government websites on a daily basis for new publications. They monitor the websites of all the ministries and of over sixty selected ABCS. They use monitoring software called Website Watcher that alerts them when new content has been added to the pages they monitor. This software is less effective on the government's new website, Ontario.ca, because content is often added as a new page instead of being added to an existing publications page. The technicians also review news releases, newspapers, and government Twitter and Facebook accounts for notification of new publications. The ISN program also alerts staff to new publications; however, not all ministries request ISBNS or ISSNS for their publications. When new publications are found, they are archived to the local server and catalogued to provide permanent access to them through the Legislative Library's publicly available online catalogue.[4]

The majority of files in the repository are in PDF. Initially staff captured the files in the formats in which they were posted. However, HTML files were difficult and time consuming to archive. The decision was made to have PDF as the consistent file format in the repository. PDF is widely used, and it was felt that migration and emulation methods of preservation would be supported into the future. Also, the majority of documents posted on the ministries' websites were already in PDF. In 2015, however, HTML became the official format for posting content on Ontario.ca. This decision was made in order to support responsive design and accessibility issues. The Legislative Library continues to harvest content from the ministries' websites and convert it from HTML to PDF, ensuring that the files comply with the accessibility standards of the *Accessibility for Ontarians with Disabilities Act* [AOD Act].

The Legislative Library has entered into partnerships with other library communities to provide broader public access to the repository and to ensure that this valuable resource is preserved for the long term. In 2007 a formal agreement was signed between the Legislative Library and the Ontario Council of University Libraries (OCUL), a consortium of twenty-one public university libraries in the province. Scholars Portal is OCUL's shared technology infrastructure, which, at the time, used the open institutional repository platform DSpace. An important function of DSpace is the preservation of digital files. It uses checksums to ensure file authenticity, assigns persistent identifiers using the Handle System, and ensures preservation support by file type. Monograph files from the repository were loaded into DSpace on a regular basis. Serials proved to be more complicated, and, despite carefully examination, it was concluded that DSpace was not appropriate for the library's archived serials.[5] The monograph files have since been migrated to the e-book platform of Scholars Portal, and Scholars Portal is preparing for trusted-digital-repository status for this platform and related content. The Legislative Library is now looking into using the e-book platform for its serials too and is working through the challenges of serial records.

The Legislative Library also has an agreement with OurDigitalWorld (ODW). Catalogue records for Ontario government publications are sent to ODW regularly (see chapter 8 for more details). The metadata from the MARC record is indexed into the Gov. Docs portal (http://govdocs. ourdigitalworld.org), and points back to the repository. Gov. Docs portal provides full text access to the library's resources, both monographs and serials. Additional access to government documents is provided through the GALLOP portal,[6] which was recently developed by the Association of Parliamentary Libraries in Canada to improve access and availability to each library's electronic resources.

ONTARIO GOVERNMENT LIBRARIES COUNCIL'S WORKING GROUP ON GOVERNMENT PUBLICATIONS

The OGLC includes librarians and information professionals working in ministries, ABCS, the Archives of Ontario, and the Ontario Legislative Library. Its members have an active interest in collecting, providing access to, and preserving Ontario government publications. In response to the LAC service cuts, in May 2012 a committee was formed within OGLC called Working Group on Ontario Government Publications. The main concern of the group's members is the fact that, the majority of new publications being born digital, there are great challenges in ensuring that they are collected and preserved.

A series of Ontario Government Publications round tables was initiated in 2012 for the purpose of bringing together stakeholders with a professional interest in Ontario government publications. As of the spring of 2018, representatives from libraries—government, university, and public—as well as from not-for-profit government document repositories, had attended nine round tables. The meetings indicated that no one was collecting everything, and there was no plan for long-term access or preservation. The Legislative Library collects Ontario publications extensively but not comprehensively. The University of Toronto is archiving websites in an attempt to capture government documents and information, such as annual report and statistics, from selected federal and Ontario government websites.[7] Publications Ontario and Ontario. ca provide access to current publications only if they follow the requirements of the AOD *Act*. The result of the AOD *Act* and mobile technology is the shifting of content from PDF files to HTML web pages.[8]

The Working Group on Ontario Government Publications spent considerable time defining the scope of publications to be included by the libraries in preserving the published history of the Ontario government.

Publications are defined as "information, regardless of its format, that is made available to the general public, or to an identified public, either free of charge or for a fee"[9] by Ontario ministries and ABCS and intended for public distribution. Generally this includes any publication with or eligible for an ISBN or ISSN or a Queen's Printer copyright in print, digital, audio, and video formats, such as the following:[10]

▷ annual reports
▷ backgrounders
▷ brochures/pamphlets
▷ bulletins
▷ committee / task force reports
▷ conference proceedings (where copyright allows)
▷ databases
▷ datasets (no functionality)
▷ fact sheets
▷ forms
▷ green papers (discussion papers)
▷ guides and pointers, tip sheets
▷ information notices
▷ interpretation letters (tax)
▷ journals and serials (TBD)
▷ manuals
▷ maps/photographs/video and audio files
▷ newsletters
▷ plans (accessibility plans, results-based plans)
▷ press/news/media releases
▷ public consultation documents (including environmental impact statements)
▷ research reports
▷ scientific reports
▷ speeches (substantial ministerial, departmental)
▷ technical reports
▷ web pages (internet)
▷ white papers (proposals)

Out of scope are internal-facing publications. Generally covered by records schedules and/or not primarily intended for public distribution, these documents are sometimes referred to as grey literature.[11]

DEPOSITORY LIBRARY SYSTEM

Publications Ontario manages the depository library system in Ontario. The system includes academic, government, and some public libraries that receive selected items based on their government information requirements.

Depository libraries access Publications Ontario's monthly checklist through a password-protected website, which alerts them to new print publications available from Publications Ontario. The checklist also catalogues electronic publications and provides links to the publications on ministry websites. From the checklist the libraries choose the publications they would like for their collection. Some libraries have entitlements for a certain number of copies. The number of print publications is decreasing in favour of electronic publications. No depository library collects everything.

Under the *Government Publications* directive, ministries are to send copies of their print publications and to provide links to electronic documents. The definition of *government publications* under the directive is "Ontario Government documents in any form, including print and electronic, intended to be distributed to the general public. They include, for example, statutes, regulations, annual reports of ministries and agencies and statutory reports."[12]

The Notice of Intent to Publish form has been replaced by the Initiation form, which is to be completed for each print or electronic publication and submitted to Publications Ontario. This directive is not always followed by the ministries and agencies and results in gaps in the government documents being available through Publications Ontario.

Since 2015, Publications Ontario has, on a regular basis, compiled lists of active Ontario government publications, both print and digital, that are available to the public. The lists, in the form of csv files, are hosted on the Open Data catalogue (https://www.ontario.ca/data/

print-and-digital-publications). If the links to a ministry's electronic documents are broken, the onus is on the ministry to supply a compliant document as per the *AOD Act*. Often the ministry will choose to remove the file rather than update it to the Act's standards. Publications Ontario is working toward a pricing model for digital publications that will also include digital rights management. It is currently reviewing its 1997 *Publications* directive, and stakeholders will be consulted.

▶ ISN and Checklist Programs

In 1972 the Ontario government created Publications Service under the Ministry of Government Services to centralize publishing activity and to make provincial publications and information more readily available to libraries and the public.

One of its units was the Bibliographic Services Centre, which had the function of cataloguing new government publications and keeping the MacTaggart bibliographies up to date. Hazel MacTaggart had compiled two bibliographies for Ontario government publications, one covering the years 1901–55, and the other, 1956–71. The new unit began to prepare the monthly checklist (an ordering tool) and the annual catalogue (a bibliography).

The Bibliographic Services Centre was given the responsibility of maintaining the log of ISBNs and assigning them to new titles. It also acted as the Ontario government liaison with the National Library in the assignment of ISSNs for serial publications.

In 1979 the Ministry of Government Services reorganized Publications Service, resulting in the elimination of the Bibliographic Services Centre. The ministry approached the Speaker of the Legislative Assembly, in his role as chair of the Board of Internal Economy, to request that the Legislative Library carry on the functions of the centre. The library supported this request because the checklist and the annual catalogue were invaluable tools for staff. Under the terms of the agreement, effective April 1, 1980, the Legislative Library assumed the responsibility of the editorial role, and the Ministry of Government Services continued to pay the cost of printing and distributing the checklist. The staff of the

Bibliographic Services Centre transferred to the Legislative Library, and the unit was renamed the Checklist and Catalogue Service.

In April 1996 the Checklist and Catalogue Service was disbanded, and its functions were integrated into Technical Services and Systems. The annual catalogue was also discontinued in 1996 on the condition that the Legislative Library's online catalogue be made available to the library community and function as a bibliography of Ontario government publishing. Later that year the monthly checklists became electronic only.

The Legislative Library continues its role of producing the monthly checklist. Government documents are coded for the checklist at the time they are catalogued. Shipments of print publications distributed by Publications Ontario are also coded for the checklist. There is a smaller stock of print publications because ministries are producing fewer titles in print; therefore, the majority of titles listed in the checklists are Internet-only titles.

The library also continues to assign ISBNS and ISSNS to forthcoming Ontario government publications. Although it is stated in the *Publications* directive that all publications must have an ISBN or an ISSN,[13] not all ministries comply with this request. Also, with the increasing amount of electronic-only content being added to government websites, the definition of a publication has become less clear.

▶ Ontario.ca

Ontario.ca is the official website of the Ontario government. In 2015 the website was launched as a redesign from the former government-ministries-centric format in favour of a portal that enables users to access information quickly and efficiently without having to search individual ministry websites. The new portal is created using a visual design that is open, accessible, accurate, and informal and has broad subject headings.

The site is created to be accessible, which means that almost all PDFS have been removed unless they comply with the AOD *Act*. A small portion of documents that were formerly available in PDF have been converted to HTML. A few of these HTML documents can be read as e-books. The challenge for Publications Ontario, Ontario Legislative Library, and government libraries is to locate legitimate publications, or identify new content, that formerly were PDFS and are now HTML documents. For example, brochures, policy papers, annual reports, information notices, and tip sheets are now in HTML format. However, some publications, like the *Ontario Gazette*, are available in both HTML and PDF. Many ministries do not adhere to the *Publications* directive regarding the use of an ISBN, an ISSN, or the Queen's Printer copyright symbol, which creates further barriers for proper distribution of government documents.

The webmasters rely on the content producers to apply proper tagging of documents, which provide effective access to documents. Staff members at Ontario.ca are aware that it is critical to have a digital archiving mandate to identify the historical reports. There are a large number of historical PDFS that are not being migrated to Ontario.ca from individual ministry websites. The historical PDFS are requested by public servants, researchers, scholars, and the business and legal communities who require open and available access to ten-plus years of government information. Ontario.ca recognizes the need for ongoing public access to historical documents and is looking at developing an archiving strategy. This will be an ongoing process as there are greater policy issues with regard to the preservation of government information.

PRINT VERSUS BORN-DIGITAL PUBLICATIONS

Ontario government libraries are facing many challenges in collecting and preserving their own ministry publications, especially in this born-digital era. Government libraries at one time received all print documents produced by their ministry, agency, board, or commission. As more publications, policy papers, brochures, and documents are produced electronically and posted to government websites, the library is often at a disadvantage when trying to collect and preserve this digital-born content. The decisions to keep publications available online are often at the discretion of the ministries' webmasters and the communications department.

All too frequently, digital publications are not collected because library staff members are not made aware of their existence, or an initiation form is not submitted to Publications Ontario. The majority of electronic publications on websites come from various branches of the government and are posted directly to their ministry or agency websites. Often library staff members do not begin their search until someone requests a publication that has already been removed from the website. Ministries and ABCs without library staff to actively collect publications are at risk of permanently losing their digital-born documents.

Government libraries are actively scanning and digitizing older paper publications through OCUL grants and by sending them to the Internet Archive. The costs for these projects are not within the government departmental budgets.[14]

▶ Open Data

In 2012 the Ontario government initiated an open data plan and asked each of the twenty-seven ministries to contribute their datasets to an open data portal. In 2016 the government published an inventory of over four hundred datasets, which are available to the general public, researchers, public servants, academics, and the legal and business communities to use for personal or commercial purposes. Users of the data can copy, modify, publish, translate, adapt, distribute, or otherwise use the information in any medium, mode, or format for any lawful purpose. *Open data* refers to raw datasets from databases and metrics to be released in the *Ontario Data Catalogue*. It is worth noting that these open datasets are used within government publications. For example, dataset results of water-quality tests, freedom-of-information access requests, Ontario camp permits, conditions of bridges, and salary disclosures would be included in government documents.[15]

Data is defined as "facts, figures and statistics objectively measured according to a standard or scale, such as frequency, volumes or occurrences, but does not include Information (as defined by this directive)."[16] The Treasury Board Secretariat's *Sharing of Government Data: Ontario's Open Data Directive*

▷ instructs ministries and Provincial Agencies to release Government Data that they create, collect, and/or manage as Open Data, unless the Data is exempt from release as Open Data, pursuant to this directive;
▷ defines principles and requirements for publishing Government Data as Open Data; and
▷ promotes a culture of openness and collaboration—both within the public service and externally with the people of Ontario.[17]

CONCLUSION

Over fifty years ago the president of the Ontario Library Association, Hilda M. Brooke, wrote in the preface to MacTaggart's *Publications of the Government of Ontario, 1901–1955*, that "government documents form one of the most extensive and valuable sources of information available to us. Much important reference material is to be found in the reports, surveys, bulletins, and other publications issued by the various departments of our Provincial Government."[18] This statement holds true today. The library community in Ontario has been active in its efforts to collect, provide access to, and preserve government documents, but challenges remain especially as governments publish more documents electronically and fewer in print. Key to overcoming these challenges will be the continuation of our efforts, by working together, sharing our problems and concerns, and finding solutions to ensure that these valuable resources will "furnish an important historical record of the activities of the Government of Ontario."[19]

Notes

1. Publications Ontario, *Guidelines for Depository Libraries.*
2. Whitmell, "Preserving and Making Accessible Ontario's Government Documents."
3. Devakos and Toth-Waddell, "Ontario Government Documents Repository D-Space Pilot Project," 41.
4. Legislative Library of Ontario, Online Catalogue.
5. Devakos and Toth-Waddell, "Ontario Government Documents Repository D-Space Pilot Project," 43.
6. Association of Parliamentary Libraries in Canada, Government and Legislative Libraries Online Publications Portal (GALLOP Portal), http://aplicportal.ola.org/. See chapter 9 herein for details of the GALLOP portal.
7. Ahmed-Ullah, "Harvesting the Government Web Space."
8. Ontario Government Libraries Council, *Terms of Reference*, 3.
9. National Archives of Australia, *Keeping Government Publications Online: A Guide for Commonwealth Agencies*, 4.
10. Ontario Government Libraries Council, *Terms of Reference*, 4.
11. Ontario Government Libraries Council, *Terms of Reference*, 4.
12. Ontario, Management Board Secretariat, *Government Publications.*
13. Ontario, Management Board of Cabinet, *Government Publications Directive.*
14. For details about the OCUL-UTL and OCUL Government Information Community Digitization Project, see chapter 8.
15. Ontario, Treasury Board Secretariat, *Sharing of Government Data.*
16. Ontario, Treasury Board Secretariat, *Sharing of Government Data.*
17. Ontario, Treasury Board Secretariat, *Sharing of Government Data.*
18. MacTaggart, *Publications of the Government of Ontario*, vi.
19. MacTaggart, *Publications of the Government of Ontario*, vi.

Bibliography

Ahmed-Ullah, Noreen. "Harvesting the Government Web Space." *U of T News*, March 1, 2016. Accessed June 30, 2016. https://www.utoronto.ca/news/harvesting-government-web-space.

Association of Parliamentary Libraries in Canada. Government and Legislative Libraries Online Publications Portal (GALLOP Portal). Accessed March 31, 2016. http://aplicportal.ola.org/.

Devakos, Rea, and Annemarie Toth-Waddell. "Ontario Government Documents Repository D-Space Pilot Project." *OCLC Systems & Services: International Digital Library Perspectives* 24, no. 1 (2008): 40–47. https://doi.org/10.1108/10650750810847233.

Legislative Library of Ontario. *Online Catalogue*. Accessed July 12, 2018. https://www.ola.org/en/offices-divisions-branches/library-catalogue.

MacTaggart, Hazel I. *Publications of the Government of Ontario, 1901–1955*. Toronto: University of Toronto Press, 1964.

National Library of Australia, National Archives of Australia, and Australia National Office for the Information Economy. *Keeping Government Publications Online: A Guide for Commonwealth Agencies*. [Canberra: National Library], 2002. Accessed March 31, 2016. http://pandora.nla.gov.au/pan/49643/20050513-0000/www.nla.gov.au/guidelines/govpubs.pdf.

Ontario. Management Board of Cabinet. *Ontario's Open Data Directive, 2016*. Accessed March 31, 2016. https://www.ontario.ca/page/ontarios-open-data-directive.

———. Management Board Secretariat. *Government Publications* . Toronto: Queen's Printer, 1997.

———. Ontario Government Libraries Council. *Terms of Reference: Working Group on Ontario Government Publications*. Toronto: Ontario Government Libraries Council, 2015.

———. Treasury Board Secretariat. *Sharing of Government Data: Ontario's Open Data Directive*. Accessed March 31, 2016. https://www.ontario.ca/page/sharing-government-data#section-4.

Publications Ontario. *Guidelines for Depository Libraries*. Toronto: Publications Ontario, April 1993.

Whitmell, Vicki. "Preserving and Making Accessible Ontario's Government Documents." Document prepared for Ontario Government Libraries Council general meeting, December 15, 2011.

8

DIGITIZATION OF GOVERNMENT PUBLICATIONS

A Review of the Ontario Digitization Initiative

Carol Perry, Brian Tobin, and Sam-chin Li

Managing published government information in an era of rapidly changing technology and shifting dissemination methods can be challenging at best and even overwhelming. These challenges are further compounded by dwindling resources and changing priorities. Those tasked with managing the information must be resourceful in utilizing current technological advances to preserve, and provide access to, both born-digital and print collections.

One of the great difficulties in recent years in the provision of services surrounding the collection and dissemination of government publications lies in the instability of access to and preservation of the materials created and published by governments. In the Canadian context this has been particularly concerning in the absence of well-defined policies on access and retention at all levels of government, as outlined in the introductory chapter of this book.

This chapter will focus on strategies and initiatives designed specifically by a number of concerned groups to mitigate the uncertain future of print-based publications. Working singly or through consortia arrangements, these service providers have made concerted efforts to digitize historically significant government publications while there are still opportunities to save materials from risk of further loss due to a wide array of factors including fragility, scarcity, and collection downsizing or closure.

An environmental scan of major initiatives was carried out to provide insight into the types of projects undertaken, the partnerships formed, and the methods utilized to digitize and host Canadian government publications online. This was followed by a brief survey. The results may not have captured all Canadian projects. A review of several selected initiatives is presented, primarily in chronological order, to provide context and to establish a clearer picture of how these initiatives developed and continue to flourish. Specific projects based in Ontario will be highlighted, including a case study of the Ontario Digitization Initiative, to illustrate some key factors involved in initiating large-scale digitization projects. These factors range from establishing the project scope and identifying funding sources to developing project plans, setting criteria for material selection, developing quality-control methods, and establishing work flows.

DEFINING DIGITIZATION

Digitization has been defined as the reformatting of analog materials to a digital format that can be accessible electronically. Through the process of digitization, scanned content can be accessed around the clock anywhere via the Internet. With the enhancement of technology tools such as optical character recognition (OCR), additional functionalities such as faceted searching, full-text searching, and text mining can greatly increase the use of the materials. It also captures the content of the fragile materials and helps to preserve them by providing alternative forms of at-risk holdings.

EARLY INITIATIVES

Many efforts in digitizing government publications in Canada have been made over the past several decades. Among them, Early Canadiana

Online (ECO), Library and Archives Canada (LAC), Library of Parliament, and Law Library Microform Consortium are the key players. Many government departments, including Statistics Canada and the Depository Services Program (DSP), as well as institutions such as the University of Toronto Libraries and Ontario Legislative Library, have undertaken individual digitization projects. A few key initiatives will be described to illustrate the early endeavours in digitizing Canadian government publications. No attempt has been made to compile a comprehensive list of all digitization projects.

ECO developed an Early Official Publications collection,[1] which includes more than 1.5 million pages of historical pre-1901 colonial and federal government documents. This collection encompasses government acts, bills, committee reports, court rules, debates, journals, ordinances, a selection of official publications from France and Great Britain, sessional papers (1867–1900), regulations, Royal Commission reports, and treaties.

LAC has digitized many government publications and built databases to enhance access to the digital contents such as Orders-in-Council (1867–1924), Cabinet Conclusions (1944–79), *Canada Gazette* (1841–1998), Indian Affairs annual reports (1864–1990), and Canadian Patents (1869–1919).[2]

The Statistics Canada Library built a historical collection of the *Canada Year Book* from 1867 to 1967,[3] digitized publications of the Census of Canada (1851–1996) and the Census of Agriculture, and hosted the volumes at Internet Archive.[4] There are approximately 120,000 official publications of Statistics Canada and Dominion Bureau Statistics available as full-text PDFs through the Government of Canada Publications Catalogue.[5] Publications and Depository Services began making this historical collection, scanned by Statistics Canada, available on the Services' website in November 2015. The Statistics Canada Library will begin adding links to its catalogue once coverage is more complete.[6]

The Parliament of Canada has scanned many government materials including the Speech from the Throne[7] and the Budget Speech[8] back to Confederation.

Budget documents including the Budget Plan, Budget Speech, and Budget in Brief (1968–94)[9] were scanned by the Library of Finance

Canada, and complement the existing HTML collections, which cover 1995 onward.

As government agencies look for methods to build and preserve their collections, they frequently turn to collaborative efforts as both a cost-saving means and a method for building larger collections and increasing exposure. Examples such as the Canadian Parliamentary Historical Resources,[10] Canada Treaty Series,[11] Statements and Speeches (1948–95),[12] and the Documents on Canadian External Relations[13] are the results of partnerships with Canadiana.org.

The University of Alberta Libraries has been actively engaged in digitization projects over the years. One such project—in partnership with Canadiana.org, Canadian Research Knowledge Network, and Internet Archive Canada—digitized the microfilmed collection produced by the Canadian Institute for Historical Microreproductions. The institute's digital archive,[14] which contains many government documents, begins with pre-1900 non-serial materials and continues forward to 1920.[15]

▶ Digitization at the University of Toronto Libraries

The University of Toronto Libraries (UTL) began digitizing government publications through the Internet Archive Canada's centre in 2007.[16] The Canada Sessional Papers (1901–25) were scanned in 2008.[17] A pathfinder[18] was created to facilitate the access to this collection with links to scanned indexes and previous scanned volumes in ECO.

Digitizing these federal papers was a particular challenge. Sessional papers are a collected series of reports, documents, and papers tabled in the House of Commons or the Senate. They contain the important government documents of the times, with the exception of the bills, *Journals*, and *Debates*. The large size and huge volume of the fold-outs and maps of this collection posed many challenges to digitization. In-house facilities had to be used to capture the large images; these images were then linked back to volumes hosted on the Internet Archive website.

As a number of loose maps within the collection have been integrated into the Map collection, and many volumes of the sessional papers are either damaged or not suitable for scanning, extensive loans from the Ontario Legislative Library were arranged to fill the gaps. After the scanning, quality checking was performed by library-student helpers to make sure the images, especially numbers within tables are complete and visible. In order to enhance discovery, metadata was created for each of the scanned sessional papers to build a Sessional Papers of Canada by Title collection.[19]

UTL has also been involved in many collaborative digitization projects such as Internet Archive Canada's strategy meetings, Ontario Digitization Initiative's projects, the joint Ontario Council of University Libraries and University of Toronto Libraries (OCUL/UTL) Digitization Project, and the Ontario Council of University Libraries' Government Information Community (OCUL GIC) digitization projects to scan thousands of federal and Ontario government publications. As Internet Archive Canada is located in the Robarts Library of UTL, UTL has been automatically involved with the identification of scanning materials; material shipping; metadata creating; and arranging interlibary loans to fill the gaps for all the titles digitized for the OCUL/UTL and OCUL GIC projects.

In response to curriculum changes and user requests, UTL has digitized a few Ministry of Education publications, including the *Circular 14* (1887–1996) and *Curriculum I-29* (1963–78). Working together with the Toronto Reference Library, UTL has developed a wish list for digitizing municipal government publications and in 2015 scanned the first municipal publication—*Municipal Handbook: City of Toronto (1905–1922)*.

SESSIONAL PAPERS OF CANADA BY TITLE (1901–1925)

Digitization will not stop at just making the materials available online; if the digitized content is not discoverable, curation works still need to be done.

A collection of reports, documents, and papers tabled in the House of Commons or the Senate, sessional papers include annual reports of departments, boards, and Crown corporations; government estimates and public accounts; Royal Commission and task force reports; election returns, census, and statistics; government responses to committee reports; papers dealing with government policies; and written responses to questions asked in the House and the Senate. They comprise an important primary source for the study of the political, social, and economic life of Canada.

Before the launch of the Sessional Papers of Canada by Title collection, this wealth of documentary sources was buried in a large paper collection with very limited keyword indexing. Even after the 594 volumes had been digitized and made available via the Internet Archive site in 2008, researchers were still required to locate the sessional paper numbers across multiple years and multiple volumes in order to access individual documents.

In 2013, UTL created metadata for more than 1,700 sessional papers. Internet Archive Canada, with the assistance of UTL, completed the transclusion by manually splitting the scanned content into individual files. A great deal of time was spent researching and grouping serial titles together to enhance discovery. Higgins's *Canadian Government Publications* was used to follow the ever-changing names of serial titles, departments, and portfolios within departments.[20] In 2016, UTL collaborated with Internet Archive Canada to have the Sessional Papers of Canada by Title collection launched and hosted by Internet Archive.

Large fold-out maps were scanned by UTL and are hosted at the Map Library of UTL with detailed metadata, including some geographic information system (GIS) data, along with two file formats to suit the different needs of researchers.[21]

This collection brings a twenty-five-year run of Canadian government documents to light by making them not only digitally accessible to the public but also discoverable at the individual sessional paper and map levels.

▶ Digitization at the Ontario Legislative Library

Like many parliaments and legislatures around the world, the Ontario Legislature began making its documents available electronically in the 1990s, improving access to bills, *Debates*, and *Journals* (see chapter 7 for details). While an important first step, it did not tell the whole story: print versions of Legislative Assembly publications going back to

Confederation and earlier were only available in print. In early 2007 the Ontario Legislative Library drafted a digitization program plan that would partially address the situation with the scanning of key documents and making them available electronically. The plan had four goals, in particular the improvement of access to Assembly resources and the preservation of the integral nature of the information.

The plan proposed digitizing the first *Journal of Upper Canada, Debates,* and *Journals of the Legislative Assembly of Ontario* as well as other government documents. The first *Journal* was a primary and important item for digitizing. A scarce item, it covers the activities of the Legislative Assembly of Upper Canada in September and October 1792. Scanning reduced the use and handling of the original handwritten document, thus contributing to its preservation. Making it available electronically gave access for many more researchers, students, and other users than would be possible otherwise. Its forty-eight pages were still legible, making it suitable for image capture and rendering a legible digital copy. The Legislative Library entered into a contractual agreement with a local institution to conduct the scan, and the contract included a physical description of the work (number of leaves, total number of pages, dimensions of the work, and technical specifications such as resolution, bit depth, file types, file size, equipment, and software). This project was one of the first undertaken by the library working with another institution, and its success laid the groundwork for the library to pursue similar collaborative projects.

The *Journals of the Legislative Assembly* were also part of the original project plan. They contain the list of bills, motions, and petitions introduced in the House, as well as the Orders of the Day. The years covered by the scanning project were 1867 to 1968–69, 1975, and 1979. The Legislative Library entered into an agreement with Internet Archive Canada for the scanning of the entire series: 101 volumes plus five general index volumes, or approximately 50,450 pages. Internet Archive Canada offered several benefits: low cost, a variety of file formats and file types, optical character recognition, and a reasonable turnaround time. The digitized product is accessible online through the Internet Archive's website. Scanning on a fairly large scale is labour intensive, both in the preparation for the scanning and in the post-scan follow-up.

As Internet Archive Canada charges by the page, a page count had to be estimated in the preparation phase, and volumes had to be checked to ensure that bindings were secure, there were no loose pages, and the pages were clean, free of marks and notations. Internet Archive Canada scans from bound volumes, which is another advantage because volumes do not need to be de-bound and then re-bound, thus saving costs.

Post-scanning quality assurance had to be conducted. The Legislative Library solicited staff from several Legislative Assembly offices to check each scanned page, ensuring that each page and text were captured. The digitized versions were made accessible through the library's government documents repository. As a result of the digitization of the collection there is now an extensive collection of the Ontario *Journals* dating back to 1867, preserved and permanently accessible for the benefit of parliamentarians, researchers, and historians.

The *Official Report of Debates (Hansard) of the Legislative Assembly of Ontario* is the verbatim account of the debates and procedures of the Legislature. Before its beginning in 1944, the media was the main source for proceedings of the Assembly. The digitization project was similar to that of the *Journals*, but on a larger scale: 175 volumes, or roughly 185,000 pages. The Legislative Library contracted with Internet Archive Canada for scanning, following the same steps and procedures as with the *Journals*: checking volumes for secure binding, and clean pages, for example, and then checking extensively the quality of the scanned images—enlisting the help of several Assembly offices and staff. The date range scanned was 1945–81; the 1944 volume could not be scanned owing to poor paper quality. As with the *Journals*, the benefits of long-term access for a broad range of researchers, historians, and parliamentarians were sufficient reason to pursue the project, which was well worth the investment in staff time and resources.

THE ONTARIO DIGITIZATION INITIATIVE

The Ontario Digitization Initiative (ODI) had its inception in the fall of 2008 when a number of interested, concerned, and devoted librarians met to discuss and prepare a plan to digitize Ontario government publications. The initial group included representatives from the Ontario Council of University Libraries, as well as from York University, University of Toronto, OCAD University, Knowledge Ontario, and the Legislative Library of Ontario.

▶ *Internet Archive Strategy Meeting, 2008*

As in any collaboration, the partners recognized that no one library had the resources, staffing, or funding to reach the end goal of making government publications more accessible and available on a permanent basis. Each party recognized the benefits gained by working together to achieve a common goal. Although the Legislative Library had successfully completed its initial digitization project, funding for additional digitization projects was problematic. For its part, OCUL was able to secure funding to begin creating a digitized government document collection to meet the needs of its users.

The group identified several selling points for the project: access opportunities, space savings, cost efficiencies, engaged citizens, and competitive advantage. In order to maintain momentum the project needed a long-range plan for a sustainable digital library. Toward that end, OCUL provided a project manager to coordinate the strategy and prepare a project plan.

By late fall 2008 two project managers had been appointed. The group met with the senior copyright adviser for the Government of Ontario to formulate a strategy and address issues related to the digitization of Ontario government publications. The development of a strong infrastructure for the project was required to support decisions related to drafting a clearly defined purpose, identifying sustainable funding, reviewing existing collaborative projects, establishing scanning priorities, developing project work flows, meeting staffing needs, controlling the quality of scanned documents, and providing indexing capabilities.

In early 2009, OCUL formed a working group, the ODI, whose membership comprised OCUL institutions including McMaster University, Queen's University, York University, University of Guelph, Wilfrid Laurier University, University of Toronto, and Carleton University. The mandate focused on the digitization of Ontario government publications only. Fifteen OCUL libraries collaborated to provide an initial commitment of $100,000 toward the digitization of Ontario government documents.

The ODI group was tasked with setting up a pilot project having two objectives. The first was to carry out a pilot project focusing on the processes involved in implementing a digitization project. The second objective was to apply the processes and develop a five-year digitization plan. The plan included an environmental scan of digitization projects already in progress, and consultations with stakeholders. Potential funding sources and partners were identified. A project selection document was created to establish the criteria for evaluating and prioritizing the materials to be digitized. Work flows and timelines were established for selected projects, as well as the identification of elements such as copyright-clearance procedures and metadata requirements.

▶ Pilot Project

The initial pilot project was established with ODI members and colleagues at the Ontario Legislative Library, the Ministry of the Environment, Osgoode Hall Law School Library, Bora Laskin Law Library, and the Department of Justice. Senior administration from all partners supported and approved the projects, and the partners contributed their collections and expertise. ServiceOntario provided copyright support throughout the project.

The deliverables for the pilot project involved the scanning of over 900,000 pages of documents. Collections selected for the project primarily focused on Ontario legislative papers, including the following:

▷ Bills, 1867–1998
▷ Signed bills, 1975–2007
▷ Ministry of the Environment reports, 1975–2007
▷ Regulations of Ontario, 1944–2007
▷ Revised Regulations of Ontario, 1960–90
▷ Statutes of Ontario, 1867–1999
▷ Revised Statutes of Ontario, 1914–90

Bills, statutes, regulations, and commissions were the top publica-tions selected. The rationale for this selection was primarily pragmatic: copyright clearance was easily obtained, the documents were fragile and of prime historical importance, and timelines were tight. Funds had to be spent by the end of the fiscal year (April 2009). It was recognized that not all priority items could be scanned within that time frame.

The logistics of preparing for a scanning project are complex. Each library must consider how long the materials can be removed from the collection; assess the quality of the items, including fragility, margin widths, the condition of the binding, and the number of pullout pages; and plan the transfer of materials using established practices.

Finally, conducting quality assurance on the scanned images is crit-ical for ensuring that the images were scanned appropriately, that all pages were scanned, that all text on the page was captured, and that OCR was satisfactory. Coordinating the collaboration between the part-ners added to the logistical planning.

The first two scanning projects focused on the Ontario bills and the Ontario Ministry of the Environment publications. The Bills project (as it came to be known) included a collection from Confederation to 1998 of over 300,000 pages, as well as the 31,000 signed-bills collection. The volumes were provided by the Legislative Library, which was consid-ered to have the most complete collection, and funding was supplied by OCUL.

The Ministry of the Environment collection consisted of 500,000 pages of environment reports, many kept off site. Scanning these re-ports would improve access for the ministry and others who needed them. Internet Archive Canada was contracted to conduct the scans be-cause it already had a proven track record in scanning operations and was known to the group's participants. The location of Internet Archive Canada—within the University of Toronto and central to the Legislative Library and the Ministry of the Environment—was another factor that contributed to the success of the project.

Quality-assurance checking of the scanned documents was an inte-gral part of the process. It speaks to the very purpose of scanning: acces-sibility. If pages are not scanned properly (and there are many reasons a page does not scan—torn or loose pages, faded type, or poor page quality, among others), they will not be rendered accessible. Checking the project files was very labour intensive and took many months to complete; it involved staff from the Legislative Library, the Department of Justice, and the university libraries of Guelph and Queen's. The result is an extensive collection of public information that is available online to legislators, researchers, and the public.

To initiate a project related to the digitization of statutes, a document trade was established between OCUL and ECO. ECO agreed to provide digital copies of pre-Confederation statutes. Law Library Microform Consortium (LLMC) offered OCUL digital images of post-Confederation statutes. Due to a variety of issues, these documents from ECO and LLMC were never loaded onto OCUL's Scholars Portal platform. In subsequent years, in a joint project OCUL and UTL re-scanned the Ontario statutes.

As the pilot project began to wind down, the economic downturn drastically affected all the ODI's projects. OCUL was unable to sustain funding at its original level, and the council's goal of digitizing more than fifty million pages was no longer possible. Individual institutions were encouraged to prioritize documents for digitization and to provide funding in order to complete their selected projects. The University of Guelph and York University agreed to jointly fund and manage another Ontario government documents digitization project: the Ontario sessional papers comprising 558 volumes dated from 1869 to 1948. These papers include the annual reports of provincial departments, institutes, and associations to the Legislative Assembly. Detailed reviews of activities by county include reports on agriculture, land use, education, health, crime and punishment, and services for the poor and destitute, to name a few. The wealth of information contained within these volumes makes them a vital resource for researchers of provincial history in all areas of society.

As with the initial pilot project, Internet Archive Canada was selected as the scanning facility for the Ontario Sessional Papers project. The ODI adapted protocols developed during the pilot project to be used for this and any future project. The University of Toronto provided its volumes for scanning, thereby ensuring that digitization was completed within a nine-month period. The quality-assurance work that followed the scanning took considerably longer than anticipated due to the sheer quantity of material.

Digitized material from both the pilot project and subsequent projects was housed on the platform of Scholars Portal's e-book Public collection as well as on the Internet Archive website. It became apparent that the limited metadata associated with the records for government series such as the Sessional Papers would hinder discoverability. OCUL provided Scholars Portal with staff to enhance records over an extended period of time in order to increase accessibility.

▶ Law Foundation of Ontario

In order to pursue its goal of digitizing all Ontario-based government publications, the ODI group investigated the solicitation of funds from external sources. In March 2009 the OCUL executive submitted a successful application to the Law Foundation of Ontario for funds to digitize the Ontario Royal Commissions and commissions of inquiry, 1792–1996, with the project slated to begin in early 2010.

The project provided new challenges for the group. This series of reports had been identified as fragile and scarce, but the true nature of the fragility only became apparent once the project was underway. The ODI working group engaged with five institutions in an attempt to provide a complete collection for scanning: Archives of Ontario, Ontario Legislative Library, Toronto Public Library, University of Toronto, and York University. In the case of materials held at the Archives of Ontario, a loan agreement was negotiated to ensure the safe transfer of documents. Specific criteria had to be met related to environmental conditions and care and handling of materials during transfer and scanning, as well as documenting assigned credit. These negotiations delayed the project well beyond the original six-month timeline. Obtaining copyright clearance for volumes where necessary, and performing quality-assurance checks, extended the project further to a final completion date of January 2012.

This project resulted in the scanning and archiving of 286 volumes of Ontario Royal Commissions and commissions of inquiry reports. The volumes are available through the Internet Archive website.[22]

Approximately twenty-four volumes of commission reports within the specified project framework were not scanned owing to the inability either to locate good-quality print copies for loan or to, in several cases, receive copyright permission.

A final report was prepared for the Law Foundation of Ontario. Other project deliverables included a recording of all procedures undertaken to complete the project, which resulted in the establishment of protocols and procedures to be followed in all future projects. This documentation of procedures provided a unique learning opportunity for a University of Western Ontario graduate student. Once again, the establishment of partnerships with other institutions and organizations made this project possible.

▶ Bulletins from the Ontario Agricultural College of the University of Guelph

In late 2010 the University of Guelph provided funds for a digitization project from its own priority list: the bulletins from the Ontario Agricultural College and Department of Agriculture. Internet Archive Canada was once again selected to digitize and provide access to the documents. This series of publications was chosen due to the fragile state of the print collection and the small number of institutions holding this title. It was not possible to locate print copies of *Bulletins* 1–57 for digitization within the parameters of the project. The Ontario Legislative Library provided its volumes for scanning. Internet Archive Canada agreed to add individual bulletin titles to the metadata in order to facilitate better access. In all, *Bulletins* 58–527 (1891–1958) were scanned and made available through the Internet Archive, for a total of approximately 13,000 scanned pages.

All Ontario Digitization Initiative projects followed the same work flow and set of procedures developed during the initial phase of the working group.

BEYOND THE ONTARIO DIGITIZATION INITIATIVE

▶ *OCUL-UTL Digitization Project (2012–14)*

The ODI working group was disbanded in August 2013 during a reorganization of OCUL committees and working groups. A new OCUL community was formed through the merge of the ODI group and the OCUL: Information Resources (IR) Government Information group, called the OCUL Government Information Community (OCUL GIC).

During this transition period to the newly formed OCUL GIC, a grant-funded project was initiated in 2012 among a few OCUL universities,[23] with UTL matching the contributed funds, to digitize government publications. More than two thousand government volumes were scanned through this project with the partnership of Internet Archive Canada. UTL managed the project in its entirety.

ODI advised on title selections, and most of the materials have been provided by UTL, with backup from the Ontario Legislative Library, the Manitoba Library, and government department libraries for scanning.

Among the materials scanned in this project, the more than seven hundred cases of Human Rights Tribunal of Ontario Board of Inquiry Decisions (1963–2002) are unique as they only existed in paper copy within binders at the Ontario Workplace Tribunals Library. This collection provides a unique look into human rights case law in Ontario regarding discrimination. A spreadsheet was used to create metadata for each case in order to enhance access. Following are a few important titles being digitized through this joint project:

▷ *Statutes of Canada* (1901–2000)
▷ *The Labour Gazette* (1900–75)
▷ *Canada Expenditure Estimates* (1873–1980)
▷ *Bank of Canada Statistical Summary* (1937–70)
▷ *Report of the Auditor General to the House of Commons* (1879–1960)
▷ *Canadian Statistical Review* (1927–87)
▷ *Statutes of Ontario* (1868–2012)

- ▷ *Vital Statistics* (Ontario, 1877–1989)
- ▷ Ontario Budgets (1868–1995)
- ▷ Ontario Expenditure Estimates (1871–2001)
- ▷ Public Accounts of Ontario (1868–1998)
- ▷ Annual reports of the Ontario Municipal Board (1933–71)
- ▷ *Ontario Gazette* (1868–1966)

▶ OCUL Government Information Community Digitization Projects

A working group from the OCUL GIC secured OCUL funding to continue the digitization of government publications in 2016. Three Ontario government publications were selected:

- ▷ Ontario government publications checklists and annual catalogues (1972–96)
- ▷ Annual reports of the Ontario Ombudsman (1975–2009/10)
- ▷ Annual reports of the Ontario Department of Reform Institutions (1946/47–91)

▶ Historical Note on the Internet Archive

Digital-collection building is an expensive undertaking, requiring a large investment for scanning and computer equipment as well as staff hiring, training, and expertise. The advantages of partnership and outsourcing are many.

In 2004, when Carol Moore, the chief librarian of UTL, met with Brewster Kahle, founder of the Internet Archive, a pilot Internet Archive Canada project was established at Gerstein Science Information Centre, with an eventual move to the John M. Kelly Library of UTL in 2005.

In 2006 Microsoft entered into an agreement with the Internet Archive for the digitization of public domain books. Internet Archive Canada received not-for-profit status and augmented its equipment with additional machines and moved the Internet Archive Canada centre to the Robarts Library of UTL.[24] As a non-profit organization, Internet Archive

FIGURE 8.1

Process Flow Chart: Ontario Government Publication Digitization Project.

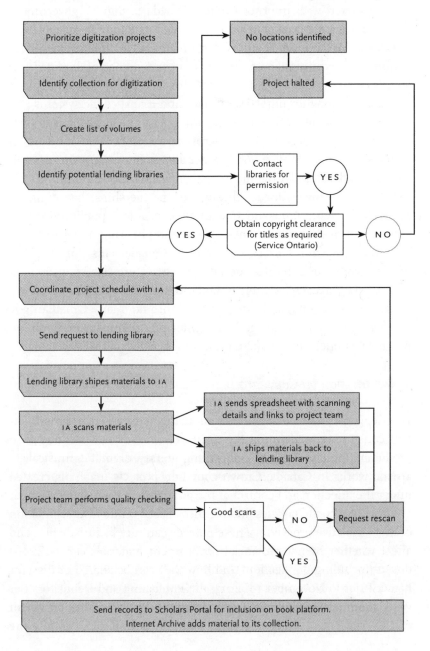

Canada is financially supported by libraries and foundations. The Ontario Legislative Library and the UTL were among the early supporters who partnered with Internet Archive Canada to digitize government publications.

Internet Archive Canada provides a ready-made digitization service that includes scanning, OCR, and hosting and storage of digitized content. It creates and uploads JPEG 2000 images, adds persistent identifiers, provides long-term hosting of files, and manages file systems and file access. A variety of formats including PDF are available for downloading from its site. OCR is run across text to allow "search inside" of all books. An open-source book reader allows content display, unlimited downloads, and lifetime file management.

Internet Archive Canada, through its partnerships, has digitized more than twenty thousand Canadian government publications and made them freely available online. Beginning in 2004, it began to digitize materials from Library and Archives Canada. This work has continued steadily over the last decade as part of projects sponsored by the ODI, Legislative Assembly of Ontario, OCUL, University of Ottawa, University of Alberta, and University of Toronto. Many Canadian government documents archived by the Internet Archive can be found on its website under the Canadian Government Publications Portal.[25]

▶ *Information on Copyright*

The *Copyright Act* mediates the relationship between creators and content consumers by defining the rights associated with producing, reproducing, publishing, and performing literary, dramatic, musical, or artistic works in Canada. Crown copyright protects materials created under the direction and control of the government. In practice, Canadian provinces create policies and practices based on their interpretation of this legislative provision. These policies can vary by jurisdiction and affect whether or not provincial government materials can be reproduced (including digitization) and how they can be shared or disseminated. Prior to November 18, 2013, the Publishing and Depository Services administered federal Crown copyrights and licensing on behalf of Government of Canada departments and agencies. Currently the individual departments or agencies creating information are responsible for granting copyright related to their material.

In Ontario the term of Crown copyright is the same as Canadian federal copyright—the remainder of the year of publication plus fifty years. The Queen's Printer currently claims copyright for Ontario statutes, regulations, and judicial decisions. However, it allows the reproduction of the text and images contained in them without permission or charge. The materials must be reproduced accurately, and the reproductions must not be represented as an official version. The scanned copies of Ontario statutes should contain a notice stating "This is an unofficial version of Government of Ontario legal materials." No distinction is made between non-commercial and commercial use.

A licence is not required to reproduce materials posted on Government of Ontario websites for non-commercial purposes (distributed either free or on a cost-recovery basis) if they do not contain third-party materials and are not altered or edited. The source of the material must be fully credited, and Crown copyright acknowledged. Formal permission is required if the material is being revised or altered in any shape or form, to ensure that there is no misrepresentation.

Published documents other than those just mentioned are protected by copyright and may only be reproduced under a licence from the Queen's Printer. The Ministry of Government Services is a cost-recovery agency that is concerned about being undercut by third-party sales for current materials. A notice indicating that they cannot be used for commercial purposes must accompany scanned items.

Publications Ontario administers Crown copyright on behalf of the Queen's Printer for Ontario, which holds copyright over all Government of Ontario works. Copyright requests are submitted to Publications Ontario, which then reviews the requests before forwarding them to the responsible ministry or agency for approval. If the request is approved, Publications Ontario issues a licence authorizing reproduction.

▶ *Information on Metadata*

Digitized content should be described so that it can be discovered. The description of the characteristics of a collection include scope, format, restrictions on access, ownership, and any information significant for determining the collection's authenticity, integrity, and interoperation. Metadata provides information about one or more characteristics of the digitized content.

Internet Archive uses MARC records as the primary source of metadata. All the materials contributed to Internet Archive have to be accompanied by a MARC record to link the documents with library collections. A Z39.50 search parameter with the Internet Archive has to be set up for the MARC records being transferred. Metadata can also be provided by a .csv file if the material is catalogued using a metadata scheme other than MARC or if only basic metadata is available. This allows fields to be crosswalked to other schemes once they are online.

In addition to the MARC records, Dublin Core and XML are used by Internet Archive for each scanned item to satisfy the archival aspect; provide information that is relevant for presentation, and supplemental information added by the library partner that is not necessarily in the catalogue record (such as serial items that have generic catalogue records); and provide details of the scanning process. Metadata resides in the meta.xml file and may include the following:

- ▷ Identifier: a unique identifier for the item
- ▷ Media type: texts, audio, movies, software, data
- ▷ Scanning centre: location where the item was scanned
- ▷ PPI: pixels per inch
- ▷ Camera: type of camera used to photograph the item
- ▷ Operator: operator who digitized the item
- ▷ Scanner: scanner used for scanning the item
- ▷ Scan date: date the item was archived
- ▷ Image count
- ▷ Identifier, access: the URL where it can be found on Internet Archive
- ▷ Identifier, ARK: archival resource key; another identifier to provide persistence
- ▷ Sponsor date, related to billing and invoicing cycle; not necessarily relevant externally

Also available are administrative information about the digital objects (such as who sponsored and deposited the content) and the intellectual property rights.

▶ Scholars Portal: Sustainable Access Model

Scholars Portal is a service of the Ontario Council of University Libraries. It provides a shared technology infrastructure and shared collections for twenty-one university libraries in Ontario. The e-book platform of Scholars Portal provides an additional access point for the scanned materials. A procedure has been developed to upload JPEG 2000 documents to the platform once they have been scanned at the Internet Archive Canada site. To access the scanned title, one can select the Internet Archive Canada Canadian Libraries collection or the Public collection from the platform for browsing and searching.

FURTHER EFFORTS, PARTNERSHIPS, AND COLLABORATION

▶ Ontario Government Publications Round Table

As noted in chapter 7, the Ontario Government Libraries Council (OGLC) created a working group to make recommendations to the OGLC executive on issues related to access to and preservation of electronic government publications. (See chapter 7 for an overview of the purpose and scope of the OGLC and its working group.) To address the issues the working group established a series of round tables. The round tables bring together academic, government, and public libraries, along with institutions devoted to the issue of preserving and sharing government and non-government documents and information. Round tables have included presentations by Canadiana.org, OurDigitalWorld, Scholars Portal, Internet Archive Canada, Toronto Public Libraries, Publications Ontario, academic libraries in Ontario, and Ontario ministry libraries.

Through knowledge sharing, participants in the round tables have heard about the digitization projects of various libraries and institutions, shared the lessons learned, developed key contacts, and become aware of programs and services offered by institutions dedicated to the preservation of digital information. The OGLC, its working group, round tables, and participants have helped to create an awareness of the need for digitized publications. Several digitization projects have been completed because of participants' efforts. For example, with the support of OCUL and the coordination of UTL, the following Ontario government publications have been digitized:

▷ Ontario Human Rights decisions, 1961–2000
▷ Hydro Electric Power Commission of Ontario's annual reports, 1908/09–70
▷ *Ontario Hydro Statistical Yearbook*, 1971–92
▷ Annual reports of the Ontario Energy Board, 1960–2000
▷ Fish and Wildlife Management reports, 1951–60
▷ *Ontario Fish and Wildlife Review*, 1961–81

The ministries were responsible for providing the materials and copyright clearance and sometimes for creating the metadata. With continued support from OCUL more material is expected from the Ontario Ministry of the Attorney General and the Ministry of Finance.

Lacking still is a mandate for a comprehensive collection, but the identification of the issues and challenges has opened the sharing of information, and some headway has been made by several libraries and institutions to preserve government information; the progress is encouraging. The fact that the round table exists and continues to draw a dedicated number of participants from various libraries and institutions to a twice-yearly forum is indicative of the concern to deal with the issues and work on solutions. The spirit of collaboration is a positive step toward developing partnerships, encouraging co-operation, and identifying workable solutions.

▶ *OurDigitalWorld*

OurDigitalWorld (ODW; http://ourdigitalworld.org/) is a not-for-profit organization (originally OurOntario, formed in 2006). Its goal is to make information in digital format, including newly digitized collections, discoverable. It supports digital stewardship by providing the technology and expertise for creating sustainable digital collections and enhancing the online discovery of community cultural collections. Working with government ministries, community groups, universities, publishers, and libraries, ODW provides solutions for the creation, delivery, and discovery of digital content, to organizations looking to make their content accessible to a wide audience. One collaboration includes ODW, Scholars Portal, Project Conifer, Ontario ministries, and the Ontario Legislative Library. Through ODW's Gov. Docs portal (http:// govdocs.ourdigitalworld.org/), users can access more than thirty thousand Ontario government documents and more than two million pages of full text.

SURVEYS

One of the outcomes of the biannual Ontario Government Publications round table was a collaboration between the ODI, OGLC, and ODW to conduct a survey of libraries in 2013.[26] This unpublished survey was intended to reveal the scope of government publication digitization projects undertaken throughout the country. Of the twenty-two respondents, 63.6 percent were currently undertaking a digitization project. Respondents came primarily from government departments or post-secondary institutions, with special libraries and archives rounding out the group. A full 91.0 percent of respondents cited the enhancement of access as the primary reason for digitizing documents; 75.0 percent also listed preservation as an important consideration. The output format for 81.8 percent of the projects was PDF. Staffing shortfalls was the most prevalent reason (90.9 percent) for not pursuing digitization projects. Of the projects undertaken, 63.6 percent were collaborative in nature. The collections chosen for digitization ranged widely from annual reports to policy papers, scientific reports, serials, and monographs.

In preparation for writing this chapter, the authors conducted a follow-up survey to identify any subsequent changes in initiatives for the digitization of Canadian government publications. Although the survey resulted in too few responses (thirteen) to make definitive statements on projects across Canada, a few notes can be taken from the results.

Responses were received from British Columbia, Alberta, Manitoba, Ontario, and Newfoundland and Labrador. Of these respondents, 46 percent were post-secondary institutions. Of the ten respondents who indicated that they had completed government publications digitization initiatives, four had undertaken more than one project.

All projects had employed some measure of quality control to ensure that high-quality versions of the documents were being produced. They all used OCR processing to facilitate an enhanced search-and-access capability. Dublin Core and MARC were the two metadata standards used to describe the material. All the digitized materials from these projects are openly available, indicating a shared goal to provide continued public access to government information. The Internet Archive was the most frequently used platform for sharing the materials.

REGISTRY OF PROJECTS TO DIGITIZE CANADIAN GOVERNMENT INFORMATION

A working paper called the *Digitization of Publications Relating to the Parliament of Canada* was released in 2009 in an attempt to identify all digitization projects related to the parliamentary materials of Canada.[27] Members of the team that drafted the working paper included Canadiana.org, Library and Archives Canada, Library of Parliament, Department of Justice, and University of Toronto. The purpose of the working paper was to provide an overview of the documents relating to the operations of Parliament that had been digitized, and to include information about the organization that had conducted the digitization, the location of the digitized works, who was permitted access, and plans for future digitization. However, it was outdated as soon as it was released because there was no way to update this document with new digitization projects. A more robust system has to be established to keep track of the projects in order to avoid duplication and ensure resource discovery. The U.S. Federal Depository Library Program maintains a listing of efforts to digitize U.S. government publications in its Digitization Projects Registry. As a by-product of the 2013 Government Information Day[28] at UTL, a digitization projects registry was identified as a centralized access point for Canadian digitized government documents and publications.

Launched in September 2016, the Registry of Canadian Government Information Digitization Projects, which is hosted at UTL, is "an index of digitized government documents held by Canadian libraries and information centres. It functions as a centralized access point for digitized government documents and publications in Canada and a resource for the library and archives community to find partners for digitization projects. The Registry aims to streamline the discovery process for researchers by collecting, in one place, an index of government documents which have been digitized in Canada."[29] The registry is full-text searchable and can be browsed by project title, digitizing institution, corporate author (government agency or department), and jurisdiction. Canadian libraries and archives will continue to add records as materials are digitized.

CONCLUSION

There are many lessons to be learned from the initiatives to digitize Canadian government publications. The proposition to embark on digitization programs began with an understanding of the technological capabilities available and the desire of librarians and others to preserve government information and make it discoverable. At the initial meeting of representatives from OCUL, the Ontario Legislative Library, OurDigitalWorld (then called Knowledge Ontario) the group discussed the appetite for digitizing Ontario government documents and preserving the vast amount of information contained in *Debates*, reports, commissions of inquiry, and sessional papers, among many other documents. Once the need had been established, the Ontario Digitization Initiative followed, giving organizational structure to the endeavour.

The effort to digitize was not without its challenges. For many of the individuals and institutions involved, scanning and digitization were new endeavours. Individuals still needed to build expertise. Fortunately the community invested in the interests of digitization: librarians, systems applicators, organizations such as ODW and the Internet Archive, and project managers, among others, worked together to share knowledge and expertise. Through sharing and collaboration, the knowledge and expertise developed.

The reasons to digitize were typical: improve access to government information, making it available to more people, more readily, and more conveniently; and preserve the information. Preservation was acknowledged as a prime motivator; not all government ministries or libraries retain government documents permanently, and the quality of early documents has deteriorated. Digitization helps to preserve the published record.

Once the projects had been selected, and the scanning had begun, a number of issues arose that became typical: funding and staffing resources were in short supply. The whole process of digitization from identification to final scanning is labour intensive. Staff members are required to check the condition of the items: if the items are bound, they have to ensure that the pages and signatures are intact (loose pages can fall out and be missed in the scanning process), and they have to make sure that the items are clean so that the images are also clear. This is also critical for the OCR to capture the text. If one institution does not have a complete set, or if the set is not appropriate for scanning, a search must be undertaken to locate the materials, evaluate their condition, and negotiate with the host institution to borrow them. Unless the scanning is done in house, loan agreements need to be made with the scanning institution, and arrangements made for the pick-up and return delivery. Following the scanning, quality assurance has to be conducted to ensure that the criteria have been met. If acceptable conditions have not been met, it means negotiating to have pages or whole volumes re-scanned.

These processes are now considered routine, but initially it took time to understand and establish them. Good project-management skills are paramount for a successful digitization project.

There was and continues to be much enthusiasm for digitization. However, the staffing and funding of the projects continue to be a challenge to the digitization effort. With the launch of the Registry of Canadian Government Information Digitization Projects, which aims for collaboration and the avoidance of duplication of effort, it is hoped that the staffing and funding issues will lessen.

The Sessional Papers of Canada by Title (1901–25) project

demonstrated how to actively curate digital content in order to add value to digital research data; this was accomplished by adding metadata, GIS applications, and finding aids.

Nevertheless, through the efforts of the ODI, individuals, and groups, many projects initiated by the ODI have proven fruitful. There are many more government documents available electronically now than ever before, and procedures that can be shared are in place for digitization projects including quality assurance. The various projects involving the ODI created new efforts among libraries to collaborate, share resources, and work toward a common goal. It also spawned discussion groups and conferences concerned with the need to preserve and make accessible government documents and to continue the work already started. More work needs to be done. There are few libraries and institutions with trusted digital repositories. Canadiana.org is one example; however, most libraries are still saving their digital collections on local servers. Despite the growing pains, libraries and institutions across Canada continue to work on digitization projects, collaborating across institutions and clearly seeing the benefits of moving forward and expanding the volumes of printed documents in electronic format for a wider audience now and in the future.

Notes

1. Canadiana.org, "Early Official Publications."
2. Library and Archives Canada, "Politics and Government."
3. Statistics Canada, "Canada Year Book Historical Collection."
4. Statistics Canada, "Census Publications." *Internet Archive* refers to the U.S.-based, non-profit digital library that hosts and provides access to collections of digitized materials including the scanned publications mentioned in this chapter. *Internet Archive Canada* is a Canadian non-profit entity that provided the scanning services for the projects cited in this chapter.
5. Public Works and Government Services Canada, "Our Catalogue."
6. Statistics Canada, "Catalogue."
7. Parliament of Canada, "Speeches from the Throne."
8. Parliament of Canada, "Budgets."
9. Government of Canada, "Archived Budget Documents."
10. Library of Parliament, "Canadian Parliamentary Historical Resources."
11. CommonLII, "Canadian Treaty Series."
12. Global Affairs Canada, "DFATD Library."
13. Global Affairs Canada, "Documents on Canadian External Relations."
14. University of Alberta Libraries, "Canadiana Collection."
15. Other digitization projects by the University of Alberta are discussed in chapter 5.
16. Internet Archive Canada, "Canadian Government Publications Portal."
17. Internet Archive Canada, "Sessional Papers of Canada Collection."
18. University of Toronto Libraries, "Sessional Papers of the Dominion of Canada."
19. Internet Archive Canada, "Sessional Papers of Canada by Title."
20. Higgins, *Canadian Government Publications.*
21. University of Toronto Map and Data Library, "Canadian Sessional Papers Maps (1901–1925)," accessed August 17, 2016, http://maps.library.utoronto.ca/datapub/digital/scss_papers/maps3.html.
22. Internet Archive, "Royal Commissions of Ontario."
23. In 2012 the University of Guelph, University of Windsor, and York University agreed to contribute $90,000 in total to digitize government publications and agricultural and social sciences materials. UTL matched this funding from 2012 to 2014, and York University discontinued this funding in 2013.
24. Calamai, "Archivists Embrace Digital Page."
25. Internet Archive, "Canadian Government Publications Portal."
26. O'Byrne, Duerr, and Fantin, "Digitization Survey of Government Documents."

27. Canada, Parliament, "Working Paper: Digitization of Publications Relating to the Parliament of Canada."
28. University of Toronto, "Government Information Day."
29. University of Toronto, "Registry of Canadian Government Information Digitization Projects."

Bibliography

Calamai, Peter. "Archivists Embrace Digital Page." *Toronto Star*, April 16, 2007. Accessed August 17, 2016. http://www.thestar.com/news/2007/04/16/archivists_embrace_digital_page.html.

Canada. Parliament. "Working Paper: Digitization of Publications Relating to the Parliament of Canada." Ottawa: Parliament, 2009.

Canadiana.org. "Early Official Publications." Accessed August 17, 2016. http://eco.canadiana.ca/?usrlang=en.

CommonLII. "Canadian Treaty Series." Accessed August 17, 2016. http://www.commonlii.org/ca/other/treaties/CATSer/.

Global Affairs Canada. "DFATD Library." Accessed August 17, 2016. http://dfait-aeci.canadiana.ca/.

———. "Documents on Canadian External Relations." Accessed August 17, 2016. http://dfait-aeci.canadiana.ca/view/ooe.b1603413E.

Government of Canada. "Archived Budget Documents." Accessed August 17, 2016. http://www.budget.gc.ca/pdfarch/index-eng.html.

Higgins, Marion Villiers. *Canadian Government Publications: A Manual for Librarians*. With an introduction by Gerhard R. Lomer. Chicago: American Library Association, 1935.

Internet Archive Canada. "Canadian Government Publications Portal." Accessed August 17, 2016. https://archive.org/details/governmentpublications&tab=about.

———. "Royal Commissions of Ontario." Accessed August 17, 2016. https://archive.org/details/royalcommissions.

———. "Sessional Papers of Canada by Title." Accessed August 17, 2016. https://archive.org/details/sessionalpaperscanada_title.

———. "Sessional Papers of Canada Collection." Accessed August 17, 2016. https://archive.org/details/sessionalpaperscanada&tab=collection.

Library and Archives Canada. "Politics and Government." Accessed August 17, 2016. http://www.bac-lac.gc.ca/eng/discover/politics-government/Pages/politics-government.aspx.

Library of Parliament. "Canadian Parliamentary Historical Resources." Accessed August 17, 2016. http://parl.canadiana.ca/.

O'Byrne, Simone, Peter Duerr, and Loren Fantin. "Digitization Survey of Government Documents." Unpublished survey, 2013.

Parliament of Canada. "Budgets." Accessed August 17, 2016. http://www.bdp.parl.
    gc.ca/parlinfo/compilations/parliament/budget.aspx?Language=E.

———. "Speeches from the Throne." Accessed August 17, 2016. http://www.lop.
    parl.gc.ca/ParlInfo/compilations/parliament/ThroneSpeech.aspx?Language=E.

Public Works and Government Services Canada. "Our Catalogue." Accessed
    August 17, 2016. http://publications.gc.ca/site/eng/ourCatalogue.html.

Statistics Canada. "Canada Year Book Historical Collection." Accessed August 17,
    2016. http://www65.statcan.gc.ca/acyb_r000-eng.htm.

———. "Catalogue." Accessed August 17, 2016. http://statcan.egcatalogue.ca/eg/
    opac/home?set_eg_locale=en_ca.

———. "Census Publications." Accessed August 17, 2016. https://archive.org/
    details/statisticscanada.

University of Alberta Libraries. "Canadiana Collection." Accessed August 17, 2016.
    http://canadiana.library.ualberta.ca/index.html.

University of Toronto. "Canadian Sessional Papers Maps." Accessed August 17,
    2016. http://maps.library.utoronto.ca/datapub/digital/sess_papers/maps3.html.

———. "Government Information Day." Accessed August 17, 2016. https://
    onesearch.library.utoronto.ca/government-information-day.

———. "Registry of Canadian Government Information Digitization Projects."
    Accessed August 17, 2016. https://govreg.library.utoronto.ca.

University of Toronto Libraries. "Sessional Papers of the Dominion of Canada."
    Accessed August 17, 2016. http://prod.library.utoronto.ca/maplib/dmgis/
    ca1_ys_s27.htm.

III

LOOKING FORWARD: COLLABORATIVE STEWARDSHIP

9

GALLOP PORTAL

Making Government Publications in Legislative Libraries Findable

Peter Ellinger

This chapter describes the development of the Government and Legislative Library Online Publications (GALLOP) portal. An initiative of the Association of Parliamentary Libraries in Canada (APLIC), the portal is intended as a one-stop access point for Canadian government documents. APLIC libraries have much in common in terms of their collections and collection policies, and discussions began in 2004 regarding how those collections might be made more accessible to member libraries. The initiative was successful, not only because it was a good idea but also because an effective collaboration developed between libraries with a common interest.

The goals of APLIC, which was founded in 1975, are to "improve parliamentary library service in Canada, foster communication among members concerning matters of mutual interest, identify issues requiring research, and encourage cooperation with related parliamentary officials and organizations."[1] For a significant portion of its existence, APLIC was concerned with information sharing, communication regarding best practices, and describing and publishing the collection patterns of its members.

Early in the 2000s a recognition developed among APLIC members that, in the face of static or reduced budgets, existing collection practices needed to change. The association increased its focus on finding more effective ways of leveraging each province's unique collection. As a result, an early initiative involved the increased sharing of reference services among member libraries through the development of a listserv in which libraries could ask their peers in other jurisdictions for assistance in answering reference requests. This and other collaborative and communication initiatives led to the exploration of other means for libraries to extend the use of their specialized collections. It was this exploration, and readiness for increased collaboration, that eventually led to the development of the GALLOP portal.

APLIC understood that its collection practices, developed to meet the demands of paper-based libraries, could be open for review in the face of the changing user demands and expectations. A common practice among member libraries was to collect material of significance (annual reports, major issue papers, etc.) from other jurisdictions on a "just-in-case" basis. Periodic reviews of member collections revealed that there was an overlap of varying degrees in those collections. Where once this had been considered a necessary expense in order to meet their user service requirements, libraries now felt that this represented an opportunity to find efficiencies and reduce costs.[2]

A concern, which in some cases inhibited the reorientation of collection policies, was that an increased reliance on other jurisdictions to maintain and make available material no longer held locally might reduce the quality of service that the member libraries could deliver. While the increased collaboration among member libraries in the area of reference support mitigated this risk, some libraries felt that a more formal, robust means of sharing access to collections was in order.

Member libraries felt that there was a need to have a commitment to participate in any sharing endeavour before they curtailed their own collection activities of material outside their own jurisdiction; that is, the material they had been collecting for their own purposes would continue to be collected and made available to APLIC by the library in the originating jurisdiction.

Shortly before the GALLOP initiative began, the Ontario Legislative

Library had concluded a memorandum of understanding with the Ontario Council of University Libraries (OCUL).[3] The Legislative Library had begun identifying and capturing electronic government documents in the late 1990s and by this time has built a significant collection. Academic libraries had approached the Ontario Legislative Library regarding their concerns relating to long-term preservation and access to government documents. By the spring of 2004, OCUL and the Legislative Library had embarked on a pilot project aimed at developing a shared Ontario government documents repository. The collaboration between the library and OCUL made the library's electronic government document collection more widely available, while ensuring that material's long-term preservation. The agreement with OCUL meant that the Ontario government documents collection would be copied to the University of Toronto's TSpace institutional repository.[4] The model of sharing collections to improve access and also enhance preservation was one that the Legislative Library was keen to promote more broadly. The OCUL collaboration demonstrated some of the benefits and also the shortcomings of this type of initiative. The preservation goal of both groups was met but only in part. While the monograph collection continues to be sent from the Legislative Library to OCUL for safekeeping, the library's serials collection is not. This is due in part to shortcomings in how the available DSpace implementation deals with serials and in part to the different expectations of how that material should be managed and made available.

Beginning in 2007, Vicki Whitmell, director of the Ontario Legislative Library, promoted the notions of leveraging technology to allow sharing of collections and of identifying "last copies" of material of common interest among APLIC libraries. At that time there had been some hope that a national strategy for the preservation of and access to Canadian documents would emerge. The expectation had been that Libraries and Archives Canada could take a leadership role in this initiative and that a central, managed repository (which would include government documents) could be developed. LAC underwent a strategic review at that time, and, as an unfortunate result, the comprehensive collection and preservation of government documents was no longer part of its mandate. For members of APLIC, this provided added impetus for developing a solution that met their own needs.

Further inspiration came from work in other jurisdictions, in particular Australia. In 2007 the National and State Libraries Australasia (NSLA) released its strategic plan. Known as "the Big Bang,"[5] the plan suggested making the NSLA's government documents collections more accessible through focusing on digitization, shared access, and collaboration. These values were adopted by APLIC in its investigation and became a part of the "shared" principle focusing on collaboration and resource sharing. APLIC took the shift toward managing electronic information seriously, observing emerging usage trends and trying to ascertain the role of legislative libraries in providing access to government documents.[6] Developing agreement on moving ahead with such an endeavour was not always straightforward. The concerns over issues regarding potential loss of control of material under jurisdictions' stewardship, implications on staffing and maintenance workload, and governance, to name a few, all required negotiation and deliberation by APLIC and the GALLOP portal working group in order to achieve the consensus required to move forward.

SOLUTION APPROACH

Over the course of several months APLIC members considered various approaches to dealing with the issue at hand. They discussed a shared catalogue, a shared digital repository, and a shared discovery tool as potential solutions. To further the goal of developing a resource-sharing initiative, a working group made up of APLIC members was struck in 2007. That group outlined some basic requirements of any initiative going forward. Key among those was that any development of a finding tool would be limited by the initial and ongoing costs of ownership (APLIC is not a particularly well-funded organization). APLIC also determined that any solution should have little impact on existing work flows and have minimal cost.

The notion of a shared or union-type catalogue gained support in the discussions, but, at Vicki Whitmell's urging, the group looked for a more ambitious goal. Two issues helped that argument. Federated search, the most easily achievable means of sharing cataloguing by a group such as APLIC, had not met its initial promise. While the cost of entry and ongoing maintenance tended to be low, issues of latency and incompatible record formats had meant that the user experience did not meet expectations. The second argument related to the nature of government documents and the use to which they were commonly put. Researchers often look for material within volumes that may not have been identified in the cataloguing record, either in the main record or in analytics. The ability to search within documents and the availability of technology to allow this encouraged the group to look beyond the federated-search model.

A shared digital repository was contemplated briefly but was soon dismissed on the grounds of high initial and ongoing costs of maintenance and infrastructure resources. In addition, Ontario's experience with OCUL notwithstanding, there was reluctance on the part of some APLIC members to have content for which they were responsible held in a repository outside their provincial jurisdiction and over which they might have no control.

The idea of developing a shared index soon took hold among the APLIC working-group members. This approach had the advantage of having a relatively low initial cost and a low impact on existing work flows. In addition, the target documents could continue to reside with, and be under the control of, contributing libraries. While a shared index might not directly meet any goals related to the preservation of materials, it was felt that the goals of collaboration and resource sharing would be achieved.

The fact that the GALLOP portal is an indexing and finding tool, rather than a repository of publications, reflects a pragmatic decision made by APLIC. While the issue of preservation of material was and continues to be a concern of its members, APLIC felt that a centrally managed repository was beyond the reach of the resources available to the group. A fully functional, fully supported repository of Canadian government documents remains a necessary and as yet unfulfilled goal.

THE SOFTWARE: SELECTING SOLR

At the time, no APLIC member owned a full-text indexing software application. The choice of software therefore became part of the development project and, for budgetary reasons, was restricted to open source.[7] A number of open-source packages were considered, including Swish-e, Zebra, and Solr.

The selection of Solr for the indexing application was not controversial.[8] Based on Apache Lucene, Solr is a full-featured, purpose-built, full-text indexing software. Unlike some other applications (e.g., Swish-e), it is capable of handling and processing large volumes of documents and data. In addition, and unlike for example Zebra, it is able to handle both structured and unstructured content. Perhaps, however, the strongest argument in favour of using Solr for APLIC was the availability of staff with the skills to develop the platform.

Shortly before the APLIC initiative began, the Ontario Legislative Library had been closely involved in the development of OurOntario, a portal that aggregates and facilitates access to Ontario's cultural and historic collections.[9] The development of the open-source, Solr-based tool kit used for the OurOntario portal demonstrated the possibility of a low-cost, relatively low-maintenance application that would suit APLIC's needs.[10]

The Solr tool kit seemed to be well suited to meet the GALLOP portal requirement of indexing large amounts of textual data without inordinate resource usage. One of the main attractions of the Solr software is its efficiency in the indexing process. The size of the index, relative to the corpus of information being indexed, is small compared to that required by many other enterprise indexing systems.[11] The compact index comes with no loss of efficiency in search-and-retrieval operations. Solr compares favourably on most other aspects of functionality, such as search-and-retrieval speed and search-and-retrieval accuracy. Additionally, features such as the relatively easy management and merging of indexes, its scalability, and its broad adoption by a variety of user communities confirmed the software choice.

INDEXING WORK FLOW

As mentioned, a requirement by the group for the portal was that it not significantly change or increase the work effort in the participants' routine collection processes. To meet this goal it was agreed that libraries should be able to simply supply cataloguing records to initiate the processing and indexing of content. Given that there was some variation in cataloguing practices and standards used by APLIC libraries, the ingest process converted the native cataloguing record to a format with elements common to all collections.

Solr uses an XML schema to identify and mark up the content to be indexed. Content must therefore be converted from its native record standard to XML prior to being indexed. Based on the work of Our-Ontario, a modified Dublin Core schema was developed to support the portal's functions. A schema that would accommodate the fields common to all contributors and deemed necessary for accurate retrieval was created.[12]

The conversion of the original MARC record to its Dublin Core analog allowed the developers to remove MARC record fields that were not required for functionality in the portal. It also allowed the conversion process to normalize data in some of the fields, in particular the date field. Figure 9.1 is an example of a MARC record prior to conversion, and figure 9.2 is a rendering of that record after it has been converted to the modified Dublin Core format. A brief comparison reveals that the number of fields required for the portal is considerably smaller than that of the MARC record.

The portal record contains some fields that are not found in the MARC record, including those related to date-range searching ("<datestart>" and "<dateend>"). Also, the record has had a French-language subject heading introduced to it.

FIGURE 9.1.
Original MARC Record Example

```
=001  ocm26618263
=008  920917c19879999nscar\\\\\\\\\000\\oeng\d
=040  \\$aNSHL$beng
=092  \\$aNOVA SCOTIA ANNUAL REPORTS
=110  1\$aNova Scotia.$bHouse of Assembly.$bStanding Committee on
      Veterans Affairs.
=245  10$aAnnual report of the Standing Committee on Veterans Affairs
      /$cStanding Committee on Veterans Affairs.
```

=246 10$aAnnual report to the House of Assembly of the Standing
Committee on Veterans Affairs
=260 \\$a[Halifax, N.S.] :$bStanding Committee on Veterans Affairs,
$c1987-
=300 \\$av. ;$c28 cm.
=310 \\$aIrregular.
=362 0\$a1986/1987, 2000/2001-2001/2002, 2003/2004-2004/2005,
2006/2007, 2009/2010-
=501 \\$a1987 issue is bound with minutes and submissions.
=530 \\$aAlso available on the Internet.
=650 \0$aVeterans$zNova Scotia.
=856 4\$uhttp://nslegislature.ca/index.php/committees/reports/veterans_
affairs$zStanding Committee on Veterans Affairs publications website
=856 4\$uhttp://o-fso1.cito.gov.ns.ca.legcat.gov.ns.ca/deposit/
b10036106.pdf$zElectronically deposited January 5, 2015
=907 \\$a.b10036106$b15-01-15$c06-05-24
=998 \\$als$b06-05-24$csdae-$feng$gnschoi11
=910 \\$aLegislative Assembly$bStanding Committee on Veterans Affairs
=930 \\$a2011/12$b1 $cAdded to GALLOP on October 3, 2013
=930 \\$a2014/15$b1
=930 \\$a2012/13$b1 $cAdded to GALLOP on October 3, 2013
=998 \\$a36401
=945 \\$c2013/2014$g1$i33283001232175jollsan $o-$p{dollar}
0.00$q-$r-sot10uovowoxo$y.i10956529$z15-01-05
=945 \\$c2011/2012$g1$i33283001311466jollsan $o-$p{dollar}
0.00$q-$r-sot10uovowoxo$y.i10917299$z12-11-27
=945 \\$c2010/2011$g1$i33283001271249jollsan $o-$p{dollar}
0.00$q-$r-sot10uovowoxo$y.i10894780$z11-11-09
=945 \\$c2009/2010$g1$i33283001229668jollsan $o-$p{dollar}
0.00$q-$r-sot10uovowoxo$y.i10860241$z10-11-10
=945 \\$c2007/2008$g1$i33283001179129jollsan onp{dollar}
0.00$q-$r-sot10uovowoxo$y.i10793501$z09-01-07
=945 \\$c1999/2000-2001/2002, 2003/2004-2004/2005,
2006/2007$g1$i33283001151490jollsan $o-$p{dollar}
0.00$q-$r-sot10uovowoxo$y.i10057742$z06-05-24
=945 \\$c1986/1987$g1$i33283000992647jollsan onp{dollar}
0.00$q-$r-sot10uovowoxo$y.i10057729$z06-05-24
=945 \\$c1987 c. 2$g2$jo$lo $nBox 9$on$p{dollar}
0.00$q-$r-sot1uovowoxo$y.i10958162$z15-01-15

Converting the MARC records to their modified Dublin Core analogs
allowed APLIC considerable flexibility in capturing and making accessible metadata associated with the indexed documents. Metadata elements that were considered critical to search-and-retrieval functionality
were retained.

FIGURE 9.2.
Modified Dublin Core Conversion

```
<doc><field name="source">NS</field>
<field name="dc-title">Annual report of the Standing Committee on
    Veterans Affairs / Standing Committee on Veterans Affairs.</field>
<field name="titleSort">Annual report of the Standing Committee on
    Veterans Affairs /</field>
<field name="dc-creator">Nova Scotia.House of Assembly.Standing
    Committee on Veterans Affairs.</field>
<field name="bibtype">m</field>
<field name="id">NS4471</field>
<field name="dc-type">text</field>
<field name="dc-publisher">[Halifax, N.S.] : Standing Committee on
    Veterans Affairs,</field>
<field name="dc-date">1987-</field>
<field name="datestart">1987</field>
<field name="dateend">9999</field>
<field name="dc-language">eng</field>
<field name="dc-description">1987 issue is bound with minutes and
    submissions.</field>
<field name="dc-subject">Veterans Nova Scotia.</field>
<field name="dc-subject">Anciens combattants Nouvelle-Écosse</field>
<field name="dc-identifier">
http://nslegislature.ca/index.php/committees/reports/veterans_affairs
    </field>
<field name="dc-identifier">http://o-fs01.cito.gov.ns.ca.legcat.gov.ns.ca/
    deposit/b10036106.pdf</field>
 </doc>
```

The processing work flow involves several steps (see fig. 9.3). Contributing libraries first identify and select records that are to be included in the portal according to their own work flows. These record collections are then uploaded via FTP to the GALLOP processing site. The catalogue records are run through an application that identifies subject headings and attempts to match these to the French analog. This utility, developed and contributed by the Library of Parliament, uses the Répertoire de vedettes-matière subject-heading database as the source for translation.[13]

Using MarcEdit[14] and appropriate style sheets, the resulting records are then converted from the native (generally MARC format) to the modified Dublin Core XML format developed for the portal. Part of

FIGURE 9.3
Bibliographic Record Conversion Work Flow

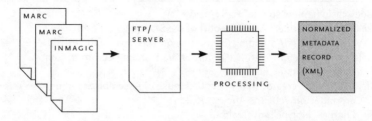

the record processing at this stage includes some data normalization and fine tuning for Solr search functions. These include the addition of date search fields (mentioned earlier) and fields, including a field called "titlesort," that aid in sorting the search-results sets.

Using the resulting records as a source, a Java application extracts the URL for the target documents referred to in the catalogue record (the utility identifies the URL pointing to the copy of the document held by the contributing library rather than by the publishing organization). The utility copies the target document to a processing server. At this point the process determines the text status of the document—whether it contains text or it requires conversion to text through OCR. Should OCR be required, a sub-routine is initiated to run the document through Abbyy FineReader[15] to identify and extract the full text.

Once the full text of the target document has been isolated, it is incorporated into a field in the Dublin Core record, and finally the whole is indexed using Solr (see fig. 9.4). At the end of the process, the copy of the target document used for full-text extraction is deleted.

GALLOP has found that the processing and indexing of content works well on the whole. However, and not unusually, some issues have arisen that need to be addressed in future software upgrades.

Subject to the state of the incoming records and their associated target documents, the process can be somewhat time consuming. Compound PDF documents, and documents that have been locked to prevent access, require separate processing streams that, depending on the volume of documents being processed, can add a significant amount of work for the operator.

FIGURE 9.4
Full-Text and Metadata Indexing Work Flow

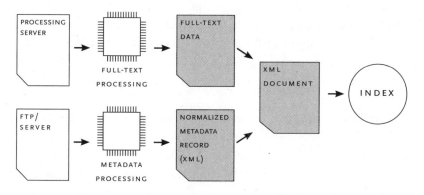

As the size of the indexes has grown,[16] the process of indexing tends to consume significant computer resources, contributing to a degradation of processing turnover. Future developments will focus on creating separate indexes for each contributing jurisdiction. Working on smaller, focused indexes will allow for easier management of resources during the indexing process. Solr supports this approach as it allows searching of a collection of indexes each time that a user makes a request to the application.

GALLOP PORTAL CONTENT

Content contributors to the GALLOP portal include all but two of the provinces and territories.[17] In 2011, APLIC entered into negotiations with the Depository Services Program (DSP) to have Canadian federal government documents added to the GALLOP portal. While not a member of APLIC, the DSP saw the utility of a pan-Canadian government document finding tool and, beginning in 2012, began contributing its government document records to the portal. The DSP now represents the largest contributor. Without its participation, the portal would have a much narrower collection of Canadian federal government documents.

As of 2016, the GALLOP portal contained some 470,000 items. The type of content varies slightly from jurisdiction to jurisdiction, but the common focus of the indexed collections is government monographs and serials. Some jurisdictions have supplied legislative publications such as committee reports, annual reports, speeches, press releases, and reports of Royal Commissions and commissions of inquiry. The number of items contributed to the portal by jurisdictions reflects both the publishing output of those jurisdictions and the varied collection policies of the contributing libraries. Contributions range from over 150,000 records—in the case of the DSP—to a little over 1,600 from New Brunswick.

Notable exceptions to the content of the GALLOP portal include debates and bills. Some jurisdictions did not feel that they had the authority to distribute these documents.

The capacity to provide access to target documents varies as well. The majority of jurisdictions provide full access to target documents, while some jurisdictions, not having their documents available to the public, have chosen to supply the portal with catalogue records only.

The date coverage of material in the portal is considerable; some jurisdictions have supplied content from as early as the 1868 Quebec provincial budget, but the majority of documents in the portal date from the 1990s or later.

SEARCHING THE PORTAL

Using the fields identified by the schema allows granular searching on the GALLOP portal content. The interface was designed with simplicity in mind, with the expectation that the ability to search the full text of documents would compensate for somewhat reduced access to metadata. The design also acknowledged that the interface could only search fields that were common to all records contributed by APLIC members. In that regard, the search interface has a considerably "lighter weight" than that of interfaces used for library catalogues proper.

The search does allow relatively advanced searching techniques such as fuzzy searching.[18] During the requirements and design phase of developing the interface, the consensus among members was to cater to the expectations of users who were experienced with Google searching rather than catalogue searching. In that respect the focus is on keyword searching. That emphasis is moderated by the ranking of search results,

such that records with keywords found in the metadata will be presented before records with the keyword in the full text alone.

FUTURE ISSUES

GALLOP faces some challenges for the future. The creators and supporters of the portal recognized that some compromises would have
to be made in order to achieve the goal of a usable, functional finding
aid for Canadian government documents. Given the available resources,
it was agreed that success would be measured by the realization of a
functioning tool to help the APLIC community and others to search and
find documents, and, to that end, the principle of "best effort" would
be applied where appropriate. This is reflected in some aspects of the
portal that continue to require attention.

Removing duplicate records, for example, has not been the focus of
a concerted effort. It was expected that, because each library would be
supplying material published by its own jurisdiction, the number of
duplicate items would be minimal. That has indeed proven to be the
case, and duplicate records are generally restricted to multi-provincial
reports and publications of cross-jurisdictional bodies.

The translation of metadata was also a compromise. Not every incoming record has a Library of Congress subject heading (LCSH) or a
Canadian subject heading (CSH) that can be used for translation, and
there is no program in place to apply consistently those non-standard
subject headings. The development of a reliable means of mapping
French subject headings to English continues to be explored. The translation of content in general has proven to be an issue requiring continued effort to resolve appropriately. Although the current solution can
accommodate some portion of language requirements, a broader approach is required. This, of course, is not unique to GALLOP, and the
expectation is that, as solutions are developed to meet requirements in
other applications, they can be adopted for GALLOP's needs.

Date-range searching also provides inconsistent results. The treatment of dates in the cataloguing records varies enough from jurisdiction
to jurisdiction that efforts to normalize that data fully have met with dis-
appointing results. Indeed, it was decided that the date representations

in the metadata were inconsistent enough that the ability to sort on that field should be removed until the issue had been resolved.

Compliance with accessibility standards is another area that will require attention. Much of the content found through the GALLOP portal is based on PDF documents, and many of these documents do not comply with existing accessibility standards (e.g., the *Accessibility for Ontarians with Disabilities Act*).[19] While target documents are not the direct responsibility of GALLOP, having the portal point to non-compliant documents is an issue that will require resolution, especially since the portal is operated in Ontario.

CONCLUSION

By increasing the availability of collections in jurisdictions across Canada, GALLOP has demonstrated to stewards of unique collections the important role that they play in maintaining access to the publishing output of government. At the same time, the exposure the portal has provided has given consumers of those collections increased confidence that the material will continue to be available and will be managed appropriately. That confidence can be enhanced through the development of true pan-Canadian preservation initiatives, such as the Canadian Government Information Private LOCKSS Network (see chapter 10).

The GALLOP portal has made an important contribution to maintaining the availability of Canadian government documents. It was developed at a time when the growth of government document publishing to the Web had not been matched by formal efforts to preserve and maintain access to the output of that growth. The successful development of a collaborative model of access to collections is an example of the possibility of achieving goals in a context of scarce resources. Collaboration at the level required to build the portal was relatively new to the APLIC membership, and GALLOP can be seen as much as an achievement in collaboration as a technological success.

Notes

1. Association of Parliamentary Libraries in Canada, "Welcome to The Association of Parliamentary Libraries in Canada (APLIC)."
2. APLIC Working Group on Legislative and Government Documents, minutes of July 2008 meeting. APLIC Portal Repository Committee, "Mandate and Overview of Work," February 2009.
3. See Burton, LeBlanc, and Marshall, *Overview of Legislative Library Repository*; and Mircea, "OZone," 202–11.
4. TSpace is an institutional repository managed by the University of Toronto, https://tspace.library.utoronto.ca/. It uses the DSpace institutional repository software, http://www.dspace.org/.
5. National and State Libraries Australasia, *The Big Bang*.
6. Enosawa, "Government and Legislative Libraries Online Publications Portal."
7. It was recognized that open source did not mean free, by any means. APLIC, though it could contribute staff resources, could not offer capital for the purchase of software licensing.
8. See http://lucene.apache.org/solr/.
9. Knowledge Ontario was an organization affiliated with the Ontario Library Association and funded by grants from the Ontario Ministry of Culture. Its goal was to provide "everyone with equal access to the information and leading-edge digital tools they need to support life-long learning by transforming online discovery, connecting communities and building research and critical thinking skills" (http://knowledgeontario.ca/). The OurOntario Gov. Docs portal (http://govdocs.ourdigitalworld.org/) provides full-text access to the Legislative Library's digital government documents collections.
10. The development of the GALLOP portal owes a great deal to the generosity of OurOntario in sharing its knowledge and, in particular, to Art Rhyno and Walter Lewis, lead developers of that application.
11. The size of the index relative to the unstructured content being indexed is approximately 25 percent for Lucene. Other full-text engines require considerably larger index sizes (Middleton and Baeza-Yates, "A Comparison of Open Source Search Engines," 33).
12. While the majority of contributing libraries use MARC records for cataloguing, some use self-developed cataloguing standards.
13. See https://rvmweb.bibl.ulaval.ca/en/.
14. MarcEdit is an open-source MARC-editing utility. See http://marccdit.reeset.net/.
15. https://www.abbyy.com/finereader/.

16. At the time of writing, the GALLOP portal's index size was approximately 63 gigabytes, representing some 260 gigabytes of text.
17. To date, Prince Edward Island and Nunavut have been unable to contribute content to the portal.
18. Fuzzy searching retrieves records based on variant spellings of a term. The greater the degree of "fuzziness" the more the variant spellings are retrieved. Although these features are available, the popularity of their use remains modest.
19. See the *Accessibility for Ontarians with Disabilities Act*, http://www.aoda.ca.

Bibliography

Accessibility for Ontarians with Disabilities Act (S.O. 2005, c. 11). Accessed April 25, 2016. https://www.ontario.ca/laws/statute/05a11.

Association of Parliamentary Libraries in Canada. "Welcome to The Association of Parliamentary Libraries in Canada (APLIC)." Accessed April 25, 2016. http://www.aplic-abpac.ca/aplic_home.html.

———. APLIC Portal Repository Committee. "Mandate and Overview of Work." February 2009.

———. APLIC Working Group on Legislative and Government Documents. Minutes, July 2008.

Burton, Donna, Helene LeBlanc, and Karen Marshall. *Overview of Legislative Library Repository*. Accessed April 25, 2016. http://www.accessola2.com/superconference2006/sat/1804/ozone.ppt.

Enosawa, Yasuko. "Government and Legislative Libraries Online Publications Portal (GALLOPP)." *Journal of Information Processing and Management* 56, no. 4 (2013): 251–54. Accessed April 25, 2016. https://www.jstage.jst.go.jp/article/johokanri/56/4/56_251/_article.

Knowledge Ontario. Accessed April 25, 2016. http://knowledgeontario.ca/.

Middleton, Christian, and Ricardo Baeza-Yates. "A Comparison of Open Source Search Engines." Web Research Group, October 2007. Accessed April 25, 2016. http://wrg.upf.edu/WRG/dctos/Middleton-Baeza.pdf.

Mircea, Gabriela. "OZone: A Shared Institutional Repository Service." *New Review of Information Networking* 11, no. 2 (2005): 202–11.

National and State Libraries Australasia. *The Big Bang: Creating the New Library Universe, 2007–2009*. Accessed April 25, 2016. http://www.nsla.org.au/sites/www.nsla.org.au/files/publications/NSLA.Discussion-Paper-The.Big_.Bang_200707.pdf.

OurDigitalWorld. Ontario Gov. Docs Portal. Accessed April 24, 2016. http://govdocs.ourdigitalworld.org/.

University of Toronto. "TSpace." Accessed April 25, 2016. https://tspace.library.utoronto.ca/.

10

THE CANADIAN GOVERNMENT INFORMATION DIGITAL PRESERVATION NETWORK

A Collective Response to a National Crisis

Amanda Wakaruk and Steve Marks

The problems of preserving cultural content can only be, and have only ever been, addressed by communal solutions. As Kathleen Fitzpatrick observes,[1] it took libraries centuries to develop standardized practices for preserving print works. Sustainable solutions evolved from best practices following decades of trial and error and the slow creation of symbiotic relationships between publishers, libraries, archives, and readers. Today, working with digital media, we do not have the luxury of centuries to develop best practices for the preservation of works dependent on computer code and technological compatibility.

The last two decades of government information librarianship have taught us that digital government information is much more precarious than its print equivalent has proven to be during the past one hundred years. Much of this precarity can be linked to technological obsolescence, but more problematic are the ways in which digital media are understood (or not), shared (or not), and stored (or not). It was not bit rot or technological obsolescence but rather a lack of infrastructure development, the dismissal of professional judgment, and highly partisan policy decisions that brought us to a government information "crisis" situation in Canada in the first decade of the twenty-first century. And, as noted by Paul Romer, "A crisis is a terrible thing to waste."[2]

Consider this: one has an easier time finding and reading a surveyor's report of Aboriginal lands that was submitted to and published by the Government of Canada in 1897 than finding and reading an academic research paper submitted to the Royal Commission on Aboriginal Peoples (RCAP) and published for the Government of Canada by a private company in 1997. As noted in other chapters of this book, print government documents and publications were distributed to multiple libraries in this country via print depository services programs. Later in the twentieth century, digitization projects relied on the network of libraries to provide missing volumes, and today we enjoy unprecedented access to nineteenth- and early twentieth-century works (i.e., mostly works no longer restricted by Crown copyright) via a digital infrastructure built in partnership with academic libraries. Conversely, research papers submitted to RCAP were only disseminated to libraries via a CD-ROM that ran a proprietary program, which no longer works on modern operating systems. More problematic, however, was the fact that the copyright statement reserved rights to the private publisher of the CD-ROM, and not the Government of Canada. One of the often-cited strengths of digital media is that it is easily copied—unless someone or some policy, law, or practice prevents this from happening.

The RCAP experience is a much-lamented example of obstructed access, both intellectual and physical, that appears to have been finally addressed.[3] However, the underlying issues that created the problem were never addressed. Instead, digital content, both online via the Web and off-line via internal government servers, replaced print content before any digital preservation or access plans had been created.

The half-life of government web content is notoriously short. Furthermore, link-rot studies that include government content have shown a steady increase in the rate of loss.[4] Very little of this type of analysis has been started here in Canada, but preliminary results comparing the availability of Government of Canada database content in 2005 with that in 2015 indicate that much digital content has been lost.[5]

For practitioners in academic libraries it has become increasingly common to field requests for access to government information that "used to be on the website." Sometimes content can be tracked down through dogged determination, which often includes repeated and persistent communication with federal government employees. More often, however, web content that has been removed from early government sites is at serious risk of being lost forever. This transition has occurred with federal governments under the leadership of multiple political parties. For example, transcripts from public consultations and stakeholder submissions associated with the Royal Commission on the Future of Health Care in Canada (also known as the Romanow Commission) were removed from the Health Canada website under Liberal Party rule. After numerous telephone calls and weeks of tracing the fate of these documents, one of the authors was told by a Health Canada employee that a single copy of these "removed" documents remained on a CD-ROM in the federal employee's office-desk drawer. At one point in the ensuing conversation the federal employee asked, "Who would want them?" As an aside, and thanks in part to a discussion on the communal DSP listserv, government information librarians were informed that these and other documents were held by Library and Archives Canada (LAC) but were not yet available to the public via the LAC website. This is one example of many that illustrates the benefits of having a strong community of government information professionals (both within and outside the government) involved in the stewardship of the pillar of democratic governance that is access to government information.

In the print-based publishing world most public consumption of government information included a visit to a depository library's collection of government documents and publications. Even if an author agency stopped producing a serial publication or changed its mandate and stopped publishing altogether, its back catalogue of works would be available through the network of depository libraries. Although the "Lots of copies keep stuff safe" motto of the LOCKSS Program would come much later, the founding principles of the print depository network were the same. The depository system was a network solution to the problems of perpetual access, relying on the work and professional expertise of public and academic librarians employed by depository libraries. In this environment it was common practice to call colleagues at other institutions to track down government publications and, later, to rely on the DSP's email list, InfoDep, and on regular advisory-committee meetings[6] to learn about federal government plans and priorities related to publishing and dissemination. These communication networks supported the government information ecosystem in the print world.

Unfortunately, an equivalent network for digital publishing was not established prior to the massive budget reductions and clawbacks of public information services in the first decade of the twenty-first century.

HISTORY OF THE CANADIAN GOVERNMENT INFORMATION DIGITAL PRESERVATION NETWORK

The late 1990s, with the implementation of the "Common Look and Feel" protocols, was likely the first time that librarians had to deal with disappearing Canadian government web content. However, it was not until the more radical 2008 removals, related to a Charter court case, that the issue of digital preservation was noted as a potential problem at DSP Advisory Committee meetings and via listserv conversations.[7] As no registry of removed content exists, it is impossible to know how many databases (including library catalogues) and PDFs were removed from government websites during this period. In addition, LAC had stopped web harvesting programs in late 2007,[8] and the DSP confirmed that it only collected PDFs from author agency websites, not from databases or "regular" web pages.

With the *Deficit Reduction Action Plan* forcing the closure of many federal libraries, and with no digital preservation plan in place, the launch of *Canada's Action Plan on Open Government* in 2011 was not taken very seriously by practising government information librarians. Web content was still disappearing. From Parks Canada curricula to Immigration Canada ministerial speeches to PDFs formerly available on the defunct Aboriginal Portal of Canada, content was missing, and, once again, there was no record of what had been removed. In retrospect, many suspected that this disappearance was linked to the 2012 announcement made by the president of the Treasury Board Secretariat

(TBS) to deputy ministers, informing them that the government's 1,500 websites would be consolidated into a single site by 2015. Details of this plan were only obtained after a protracted access-to-information request that cost more than $2,000.[9]

As a former chair of the Government Information Interest Group of the Canadian Library Association (CLA), Amanda Wakaruk used this forum at CLA's 2012 annual conference to announce a call for proposals[10] to join a LOCKSS project for government information in Canada. Experience gained through her home institution's membership on various LOCKSS networks, including acting as a node for the U.S. Digital Federal Depository Library Program (also known as the USDocs Private LOCKSS Network),[11] coupled with her work on the International Documents Task Force and the Government Documents Round Table (GODORT) of the American Library Association, provided the group with a first-hand account of how this type of digital preservation network might operate.

The LOCKSS Program is a digital preservation project based at Stanford University. Originally conceived to preserve the output of scholarly journals, it operates a well-established service for that purpose specifically, providing both technical and administrative solutions, including publisher negotiation. However, the LOCKSS software is also used outside of this original mission in order to serve as the technical core for a number of significant digital preservation projects.[12] In these implementations (called private LOCKSS networks, or PLNS) the LOCKSS software manages the geographic replication of the preserved content objects, ensures that they have not become corrupt or tampered with, and provides access to the content should it become inaccessible elsewhere.[13] Given the demonstrated effectiveness of the LOCKSS software in distributed, digital preservation scenarios, and since Wakaruk and others in the conversation had developed a familiarity with the operation of PLNS through projects such as the Council of Prairie and Pacific University Libraries (COPPUL) PLN,[14] initial conversations about a technical solution to the government information crisis coalesced around a proposed solution utilizing a PLN.

The LOCKSS project proposed at the 2012 CLA meeting eventually came to be called the Canadian Government Information Digital

Preservation Network (CGI DPN). Through its established partnerships with various digital initiatives, the University of Alberta Libraries was able to provide the technical infrastructure and initial support for the set-up of the CGI DPN. Building from the organizational structure of the COPPUL LOCKSS network, the collaborative-governance model mirrors that of other Canadian LOCKSS networks, with all member institutions represented on a steering committee and also having an opportunity to serve on a technical advisory committee.

The steering committee, originally representing nine academic libraries located in Quebec, Ontario, Saskatchewan, Alberta, and British Columbia, first met over a conference call in September 2012.[15] Setting up the LOCKSS boxes at member institutions was the first order of business. Umar Qasim, the digital preservation officer at the University of Alberta Libraries, took the lead on this task, working closely with colleagues at Simon Fraser University and Scholars Portal, the latter of which was planning to co-administer the box based at the University of Toronto.

Acquiring content, however, was another matter. Long-standing relationships between DSP manager Gay Lepkey and government information librarians at the University of Alberta and Simon Fraser University resulted in the transfer of the DSP's entire catalogue of PDFS. Comprising more than 100,000 PDFS, collected between 1995 and 2013, it served as the first collection in the nascent network.

As the network boxes were being set up, the community of government information librarians continued to learn about content removal from Government of Canada websites. For example, federal government budget cuts were forcing the closure of many departmental libraries and related services, and there was some discussion about the loss of public access to these resources via the DSP catalogue (similar losses, notably from Human Resources Development Canada and Environment Canada, were well known). Wakaruk brought these concerns to the American Library Association via the Government Documents Round Table at the winter 2013 meeting in Seattle,[16] where she also made a presentation with James Jacobs from Stanford University about the use of LOCKSS networks for the preservation of government information.[17]

The working relationships established by the University of Alberta

Libraries' Digital Initiatives and Collections units with the LOCKSS and Archive-It (Internet Archive), as well as related liaison work, were critical to the founding of the CGI DPN and its subsequent, but unplanned, operation as a "bright" archive (i.e., publicly accessible archive). Originally intended as a "dark" preservation archive, the aggressive removal of government web content as a result of the TBS implementation of guidelines to reduce "redundant, outdated, and trivial" content[18] made it clear to the government information community that the government of the day was not making the stewardship and preservation of government web content a priority.

Thankfully, lines of communication were established between a group of Canadian librarians working with the American Library Associations' Government Documents Round Table, and the Internet Archive, which conducted a pro bono and relatively comprehensive crawl of the entire Government of Canada web domain. As per Internet Archive protocol, the content acquired through this crawl was made immediately available online in an open environment. This collection continues to be used by journalists, researchers, and librarians to access the government information that was formerly available on Government of Canada websites. The project also served as a sample case for using existing Archive-It infrastructure as an ingest mechanism for the CGI DPN.

While the Internet Archive crawl yielded and continues to yield an important collection, it did not fulfill the need of a Canadian solution for stewardship and preservation. For example, this broad crawl failed to capture some content and was also potentially subject to take-down requests under U.S. law. Furthermore, it perpetuated the problem of trusting a single organization to be responsible for what was often a single digital copy of a government-produced work. For these reasons, as well as the need to manage its own collections, the CGI DPN Steering Committee opted to subscribe to the Internet Archive's Archive-It service. This account would allow member institutions to ingest harvested content to Canadian-based LOCKSS boxes, to collect new targeted content on specified timelines, and to run the much-needed quality controls to ensure that all relevant content on the sites was collected. Moreover, the Archive-It account would provide a publicly accessible platform for all content. This opportunity, discussed and approved by the steering committee, shifted the mandate of the CGI DPN from a "dark" preservation network to a "bright" archive and preservation system. Thus, access to content would not be restricted to members following a trigger event and would be available to anyone with access to the Internet.

While all steering committee representatives clearly had the support of their home institutions, the grassroots nature of the CGI DPN complicated the pursuit of basic operational needs. First and foremost, members were reluctant to ask their home institutions for the additional funds required to set up the joint Archive-It account. Although the costs were minimal, at approximately $500 a year (far beneath the costs to process DSP print shipments, which had almost ceased at this point and would stop being shipped at all in 2014), academic library budgets were being drastically reduced across all jurisdictions. Furthermore, the CGI DPN was an informal collective organization, not a registered non-profit, and thus had no way to handle a financial transaction. Thankfully, Gwen Bird, then director of COPPUL, offered the council's administrative assistance with processing payments from CGI DPN members, which was required to set up and maintain an account with Archive-It.

Thanks to the commitment of the CGI DPN members and to COPPUL's administrative support, an Archive-It account was established in February 2013. The first collection, titled "Government of Canada Publications," provides access to PDFs acquired through the DSP. A second collection, titled "Government of Canada Web Content," was established in November 2014 and provides access to web content harvested by the steering committee. On numerous occasions the web content collection has been used to harvest quickly the content of an agency website that has been identified as being at risk of imminent closure. Both collections are available at https://www.archive-it.org/organizations/700.

TECHNOLOGY OF THE CGI DPN

The backbone of the CGI DPN is the LOCKSS software, configured to create a private LOCKSS network, of which each partner member serves as a node and maintains a digital preservation box. These nodes are administered independently at each institution, and the network as a whole is registered as a private LOCKSS network with the LOCKSS project. This affiliation (which is free for LOCKSS network members and requires a small fee for non-members) provides support for the set-up and administration of the box, as well as access to the central infrastructure operated by the LOCKSS team.

As far as getting content into the LOCKSS boxes, Archive-It is used to create a fixed copy of the web content in Internet Archive's web archive. This proceeds in one of two ways, depending upon the collection to which the harvested content belongs. For the Government of Canada Publications collection (i.e., the DSP collection), this is done by processing a list of records provided by the DSP in order to extract seed URLS. Although a seed URL generally represents the starting point for a web crawl, in the case of DSP records the seed URL consists of the location of the document itself, with no further crawling necessary. In the case of the Government of Canada Web Content collection, which consists of more traditional web archives, the seed URLS are determined and entered manually by a member of the CGI DPN. In either case, once the harvest has been completed, the documents can be accessed within the CGI DPN's Archive-It collection. The documents in this Archive-It collection are considered to be the access copies of the network.

The next significant step is the generation of the preservation copies through ingest of the harvested documents into the PLN itself. This is accomplished by means of an Archive-It plug-in for the LOCKSS system.[19] At this point, the content enters the CGI PLN and is considered "preserved" by the network.

The steps taken next vary by institution. Some institutions have opted to continue providing access to the Government of Canada link supplied by the DSP via their local catalogues. Others continue to provide access to the Government of Canada links but also include the link to the Internet Archive in case the original link becomes inaccessible. The final option is to utilize the LOCKSS software's ability to act as a proxy that automatically detects when a target resource has become inaccessible and redirects a user to the locally stored copy. No institutions are using this method currently, owing to the fact that the network's access copies continue to be served by the Internet Archive.

SIGNIFICANCE OF THE CGI DPN

Having a preservation and distribution system that is at arm's length from the government agencies that published the works results in both strengths and weaknesses for the network. Unlike the DSP, the CGI DPN is not restricted by TBS policy to acquire only PDFS produced by a select list of federal agencies.[20] And unlike LAC, the CGI DPN is not restricted to a (potentially politically influenced) priority list for its acquisitions. Instead, the CGI DPN enjoys the freedom of harvesting and providing access to content required by its users, regardless of current political interest or jurisdiction. Indeed, its steering committee has begun adding provincial-level collections to the web content collection.[21]

The downsides of existing at arm's length from author agencies are largely related to communication. For example, in the period between LAC ceasing its web harvesting program in 2007 and providing access to its reinstated program in 2016, the community was informed that a "behind the scenes" harvest was occurring. However, this content was not available to the public. Not wanting to repeat the web-crawling work being completed by LAC, the steering committee repeatedly requested access to what were known as "seed lists" or lists of websites being crawled by LAC. The intent, which was clearly stated, was to crawl content that LAC was not crawling, that is, to work together with LAC to improve the breadth and depth of access to government information in Canada. Despite repeated meetings and promises extending from March 2013 to July 2014, the CGI DPN Steering Committee was never provided with a seed list.

Secondly, on numerous occasions the CGI DPN web crawler has encountered Government of Canada web content that is protected by a robots.txt file and/or a Terms of Use Statement that appears to indicate that harvesting and redistributing the content via the Archive-It account might not be sanctioned by the author agency. Unfortunately, with the closure of the Crown Copyright Licensing office in 2013, the government employees who could have provided across-the-board clarity on this issue no longer exist. Instead, steering committee members (or their designates) have spent considerable time in attempting to clarify acceptable non-commercial terms of use for content made accessible on public websites. Responses vary by department, slowing down and sometimes ceasing efforts to acquire at-risk government information.

Even with these challenges, the establishment of an arm's-length bright archive offers an important public service to consumers of Canadian government information. A service like the CGI DPN, developed during a precarious period of access to government information in Canada, does not happen without broad community support. In addition to the obvious support of the founding members, the network relied on early and generous support from the steering committee of the Government Documents Round Table; members of the International Documents Task Force; LOCKSS champions and personnel at Stanford University; and COPPUL.

Network governance and member contributions were never envisioned as the responsibility of one or two institutional members. Rather, a more sustainable, communal approach was encouraged at the outset and is taking shape. Librarians at the University of Toronto stepped into leadership roles on both the steering and technical committees in 2015, and, at the time of writing, the chair of the steering committee was based at the University of British Columbia. Ideally, these governance committees will be led by librarians from all member institutions in the years to come.

The genesis of the CGI DPN was a collective desire among government information librarians in Canada to address concerns about the increasingly ephemeral nature of government material online. These concerns were the result of ongoing questions about the federal government's commitment to maintaining persistent access to online information resources, brought to a head by the removal of content from and the shuttering of several high-profile government websites, including the Aboriginal Canada Portal. The CGI DPN represents a new approach to fulfilling part of the mandate of government information librarians across Canada. While academic libraries continue to act as cultural memory institutions for government information, the evolving role is much more proactive and, thus, demands a higher level of engagement and leadership from librarians.

Appendix 10.1.

PROPOSAL AND CALL FOR PARTNERS

Canadian Government Information Private LOCKSS Network
Distributed via various listservs on August 22, 2012.

Goal: To preserve and provide perpetual access to digital content originally published by government agencies in Canada.

Statement of Need: Memory institutions have played a vital role in preserving government publications and making them accessible for long-term use. A distributed, tamper-evident preservation infrastructure is required to maintain this stewardship role in a digital environment.

Proposed Solution: Establish a private LOCKSS network (PLN) that includes partners from multiple libraries and jurisdictions. The LOCKSS Program (http://www.lockss.org) is an open-source, library-led digital preservation system that utilizes web harvesting, a distributed storage structure, and an open URL resolver to acquire, preserve the integrity of, and provide access to digital files in perpetuity. The initial collection for preservation will be an e-archive collected by the Depository Services Program of Canada.

Call for Participation: The University of Alberta Libraries seeks partners to develop and maintain a Canadian Government Information Private LOCKSS Network. The initial group of network members will establish a steering committee and governance structure with work beginning in September 2012. Additional partners will be solicited shortly thereafter. See documentation from the COPPUL PLN as a possible template for discussion: http://coppullockssgroup.pbworks.com/w/page/11478105/ FrontPage. The initial network members must be able to fulfill the requirements listed below.

Partner Requirements:

▷ provide the financial and human resource commitment to set up and maintain a LOCKSS node that meets the technical specifications required by the LOCKSS software and the minimum storage requirements as decided on by the partnership (see LOCKSS web site; e.g., static IP address, server with 2 TB of storage, etc.)
▷ agree to participate in the PLN for a minimum of three years
▷ pay the associated LOCKSS fees (free for current LOCKSS Alliance members, to be determined for non-members but tentative fee is around $1500/year); these fees provide technical support, software patches and upgrades, etc.

Deadline for Confirmation of Partnership: contact Amanda Wakaruk, Government Information Librarian at amanda.wakaruk@ualberta.ca before August 31, 2012

▶ *Frequently Asked Questions*
GOVERNANCE

Q: Who can be a member of the CGI PLN?
A: Any institution that meets the partnership requirements as stated in the Call for Partners.
Q: What will the governance structure look like?
A: There will be a Steering Committee, membership to be discussed at the PLN's initial conference call (planned for September). There will be a Technical Committee, made up of systems administrators and/or other technical staff. The membership of both committees will be drawn from member institutions.
Q: How will collection decisions be made?
A: Collection decisions will be made by the Steering Committee with input from the membership at large. The first collection will be the Depository Services Program's e-archive. Many people have already stated an interest in adding provincial materials and,

Amanda Wakaruk and Steve Marks ◁ 287

because of this, we are striving to obtain regional representation in the PLN.

Q: How will members communicate?

A: Because of the geographic distribution of the membership, we anticipate that most communication will be over conference calls and email. This will be one of the first things determined by the Steering Committee.

(This governance structure is similar to that of the COPPUL PLN noted in the Call for Partners.)

TECHNICAL

Q: How much technical work will each member be expected to contribute?

A: Once a LOCKSS network is established, there are basically two types of technical work: preparing content for harvesting and maintaining the LOCKSS node (box) at each member institution. The former is more time intensive and will be largely handled by IT staff at the UofA and the Stanford University LOCKSS Program. The latter is fairly simple and well documented on the LOCKSS web site: http://www.lockss.org/support/. Support will be offered, where needed, to help members with the initial setup and maintenance of the nodes (boxes).

Q: Beyond preservation, what other benefit does a LOCKSS network provide?

A: The LOCKSS content can be integrated with an OpenURL resolver (e.g., SFX, ExLibris, etc.), providing access when the source is unavailable. While we will be watching how this type of access evolves, it is not a requirement of PLN members.

LOCKSS COSTS

Q: Who receives our fees?

A: The LOCKSS Program, based at Stanford University.

Q: What do the fees pay for?

A: Technical support including software upgrades and training. See http://www.lockss.org/join/ for more information.

Q: Are there any other human resource or technical commitments we should know about?

A: Aside from the occasional conference call and other communication for committee members, there are no resource commitments that we are aware of beyond setting up and maintaining a LOCKSS box/node.

OTHER

Q: Who else knows about this?

A: We have been in fairly consistent communication with the LOCKSS Partnership and the DSP about this project since May. Consortia administrators at COPPUL and OCUL are also aware of the project.

Appendix 10.2.

RESOLUTION ON ACCESS TO CANADIAN FEDERAL GOVERNMENT INFORMATION

The resolution was proposed but not passed at the American Library Association's biannual meeting held in Seattle in January 2013. A subsequent letter of support was sent by ALA's office of the president to the Treasury Board of Canada Secretariat with copies to the Canadian Library Association and Library and Archives Canada.

Whereas ALA is a long-standing advocate of open access to government information;

Whereas businesses small and large in the United States rely on information collected and disseminated by the Canadian government;

Whereas ALA member libraries rely on open access to government information published and disseminated by the Government of Canada;

Whereas the Government of the United States and the Government of Canada are major trading partners and signatories of NAFTA, in which the preamble states a commitment to strengthening cooperation between these nations;

Whereas the Government of Canada's budget reductions have resulted in the following changes in access to government information:

▷ cessation of the distribution of print materials via the Depository Services Program (DSP), effectively eliminating the distributed federal depository structure for Canadian government publications and ending this service to 41 libraries in the United States that hold depository status with the DSP,

▷ reductions in programs and services at Library and Archives Canada, including the cessation of international exchange agreements and ILL [interlibrary loan] programs,
▷ closure of Canadian federal libraries in at least ten agencies and departments including Transport Canada, National Round Table on Energy and Environment, and Citizenship and Immigration Canada,
▷ removal of legacy publications from the Statistics Canada web site;

Whereas the Treasury Board of Canada, the body responsible for the Communications Policy that determines how federal government information is collected, published and disseminated by and within the Government of Canada, states that "In the Government of Canada, information is safeguarded as a public trust and managed as a strategic asset";

Whereas the Treasury Board of Canada implemented the Common Look and Feel web protocol that resulted in the removal of web content from Canadian federal government web sites, including the removal of pdfs and access to databases;

Whereas the Treasury Board of Canada has been internally distributing a Web site convergence program that would realize a reduction of Canadian government web domains down to six or fewer without first consulting with external stakeholders; now, therefore, be it

Resolved that ALA calls upon the President of the Treasury Board of Canada to recognize that Government of Canada publications are a strategic asset and critical to current and future research and business; and be it further

Resolved that ALA calls upon the President of the Treasury Board of Canada to honor the spirit and intent of NAFTA by, in part, ensuring that Government of Canada publications, including current web content, are archived and continue to be made available in a no-fee publicaly accessible online environment.

Notes

1. Fitzpatrick, "Preservation," 122.
2. Quoted in Rosenthal, "A Terrible Thing to Waste."
3. In 2015, Anna St. Onge (York University) and Amanda Wakaruk began investigating ways to make RCAP research papers publicly available online. In November 2016, LAC launched the RCAP database, finally providing access to many of the documents that had been largely inaccessible on the CD-ROM for over a decade. http://www.bac-lac.gc.ca/eng/discover/aboriginal-heritage/royal-commission-aboriginal-peoples/Pages/search.aspx.
4. Rhodes, "Breaking Down Link Rot."
5. See Wakaruk, "Government of Canada Historical Database Project," and "Here Today, Where Tomorrow?"
6. Meeting minutes of the DSP Advisory Committee, formerly known as the Library Advisory Committee, are available at http://publications.gc.ca/site/eng/depositoryLibraries/dsp-lac/overview.html.
7. For a rough chronology of the period leading up to 2014, see Wakaruk, "Government of Canada Historical Database Project."
8. LAC launched a new archive, with previously unavailable harvested content, in April 2016. This content can be found on a page that does not reference the cessation of the program or the restricted access to the web content between 2007 and 2016: http://www.bac-lac.gc.ca/eng/discover/archives-web-government/Pages/web-archives.aspx.
9. The request was funded by the British Columbia Freedom of Information and Privacy Association, and the documents are available at http://fipa.bc.ca/library/government%20documents/goc_web_plan_part1.pdf and http://fipa.bc.ca/library/Government%20Documents/GoC_web_plan_Part2.pdf.
10. See appendix 10.1, "Proposal and Call for Partners."
11. LOCKSS, "U.S. Digital Federal Depository Library Program," http://www.lockss.org/community/networks/digital-federal-depository-library-program/.
12. LOCKSS, "Global & Private LOCKSS Networks," https://www.lockss.org/community/networks/.
13. A good non-technical overview of the administration and operation of the LOCKSS stack can be found at http://www.lockss.org/about/how-it-works/.
14. Council of Prairie and Pacific University Libraries, "COPPUL Private LOCKSS Network," http://coppul.ca/pln.
15. The original CGI DPN members (west to east) were University of Victoria, University of British Columbia, University of Calgary, University of Alberta,

University of Saskatchewan, University of Toronto, and McGill University. Dalhousie University, based in Halifax, joined in 2013, making the network a coast-to-coast community.

16. See appendix 10.2, "Proposed Resolution on Access to Canadian Federal Government Information."

17. Most CGI DPN presentations provided by the founding steering committee chair, Amanda Wakaruk, can be found at https://sites.google.com/a/ualberta.ca/wakaruk/presentations and via the CGI DPN website at https://plnwiki.lockss.org/index.php?title=CGI_network.

18. Wakaruk, "Government of Canada Historical Database Project," and "Here Today, Where Tomorrow?"

19. Based on https://github.com/lockss/lockss-plugins/tree/master/src/org/lockss/plugin/archiveit.

20. Paterson, Worby, and Fichter. "Web Harvesting and Reporting Fugitive Government Materials," chapter 11 herein.

21. In addition to provincial materials being excluded from LAC's legal-deposit responsibilities (see http://www.bac-lac.gc.ca/eng/services/legal-deposit/pages/legal-deposit.aspx), it was announced in 2012 that provincial materials would no longer be collected by LAC, and much of the organization's provincial collection was distributed to academic and legislative libraries in the provinces. Reference to this decision can be found in a November 18, 2012, letter from the Bibliographical Society of Canada to Minister Moore (https://web.archive.org/web/20160314093858/http://bsc-sbc.ca/en/moore2.pdf).

Bibliography

Fitzpatrick, Kathleen. "Preservation." In *Planned Obsolescence: Publishing, Technology, and the Future of the Academy*, 121–54. New York: NYU Press, 2011.

Paterson, Susan, Nicholas Worby, and Darlene Fichter. "Web Harvesting and Reporting Fugitive Government Materials: Collaborative Stewardship of At-Risk Documents." In *Government Information in Canada*, edited by Amanda Wakaruk and Sam-chin Li. Edmonton: University of Alberta Press, 2019.

Rhodes, Sarah. "Breaking Down Link Rot: The Chesapeake Project Legal Information Archive's Examination of URL Stability." *Law Library Journal* 102, no. 4 (2010): 581–97. http://scholarship.law.georgetown.edu/digitalpreservation_publications/6/.

Rosenthal, Jack. "A Terrible Thing to Waste." In *New York Times Magazine*, July 31, 2009. http://www.nytimes.com/2009/08/02/magazine/02FOB-onlanguage-t.html.

Wakaruk, Amanda. "Government of Canada Historical Database Project." Dataverse, 2015. https://doi.org/10.7939/DVN/10656.

———. "Here Today, Where Tomorrow? Monitoring and Making Sense of Government of Canada Web Content Changes in a Post-Depository Environment." Canadian Library Association Annual Conference, Ottawa, Ontario, June 4, 2015. http://hdl.handle.net/10402/era.41980.

11

WEB HARVESTING AND REPORTING FUGITIVE GOVERNMENT MATERIALS
Collaborative Stewardship of At-Risk Publications

Susan Paterson, Nicholas Worby, and Darlene Fichter

Libraries and archives are faced with the paradoxical problem of providing access to an explosion of electronic government information while functioning with reduced resources and staff. There are fewer specialists working exclusively with government information in libraries. Mack and Prescod analyzed American job postings and found a sharp decline in listings for academic librarians working specifically with government information between 1997 and 2007, a time that many government entities were transitioning to electronic dissemination models.[1] They also found that the postings for librarian positions involved with government information were far more likely to be blended positions with multiple duties.[2] It is not just academic libraries that have experienced an erosion of resources for government collections in the last two decades. Smugler documents the profound budget and staffing cuts as well as the closure of many federal government libraries.[3] National institutions entrusted with Canada's documentary heritage have also been subject to austere reductions in resources. Library and Archives Canada experienced six consecutive years of budget cuts, from 2009 to 2015.[4] During this time, LAC discontinued essential programs like its interlibrary loan service and ceased collecting provincial government documents.[5] There is still a great need for students, scholars, journalists, and citizens to have long-term access to government information and for it to be preserved, despite the decline in resources allocated toward this important work. The transition to electronic government information has complicated many of the traditional roles of librarians and archivists. The size and scope of the tasks associated with collecting born-digital government information outstrips the resources of most single institutions and requires cross-institutional collaborations to meet the challenges of continued stewardship. This chapter describes two collaborative approaches to digital stewardship of government information. The projects involve academic libraries and different levels of government seeking to address the challenges of managing electronic government information in the face of declining resources.

COLLABORATIVE WEB HARVESTING

Web archiving is an emerging approach to dealing with born-digital government information. In chapter 2, Tom Smyth described Library and Archive Canada's (LAC's) comprehensive crawls of federal government websites. In the United States similar efforts are underway to capture select government-agency sites through the Government Printing Office's Federal Depository Library Program Web Archive,[6] and federal congressional websites through the National Archives and Records Administration and the Library of Congress.[7] While these initiatives are valuable steps toward ensuring long-term access to electronic government information, the volume of government information on the Web makes it impossible for any one institution in any one jurisdiction to web archive on the scale that collecting institutions could previously collect material in the print depository era. Moreover, the above-mentioned initiatives have been predominantly targeted at federal governments, which have large budgets and large pools of stakeholders with a shared interest in protecting born-digital government information.

The resource-intensive nature of web archiving necessitates having a focused scope and constraining efforts to collecting only material within an institution's mandate. Not all governments are equipped to capture all or even some of their electronic output. For example, with the exception of the Bibliothèque et Archives nationales du Québec, no Canadian provincial or territorial library or archive has a comprehensive strategy in place or an established mandate for capturing government websites, at the time of writing this chapter. Similarly, very few municipal archives are engaged in collecting municipal government websites. Consequently, there are many sources of electronic government information in Canada that are not covered under any archival mandate.

A central anxiety that runs through many chapters in this book relates to the way in which librarians and other information professionals are to respond to the unstable and uncertain qualities of electronic government information. A plan of action is less clear for those working in academic or public libraries with no explicit mandate to capture government information on the Web in an era of post–print depository services. However, librarians and archivists working outside of government entities are still tasked with providing instruction and research support for born-digital government material and have a vested interested in doing something to prevent it from slipping through their fingers. Canadian academic libraries are actively web archiving government websites. For example, the University of Toronto, the University of Alberta, and the University of Victoria have archived select federal government and provincial websites. Pending a federal plan to consolidate and remove government websites, Samchin Li of the University of Toronto also worked with the non-profit organization the Internet Archive.[8] Together they organized all of the Internet Archive's captures of Canadian federal government websites from December 2007 to 2013 into a single collection to fill the gap in coverage between the discontinuation of Library and Archives Canada's comprehensive crawls of federal sites until the resumption of the LAC program in the fall of 2013.[9] Quality assurance was performed on the collection and it is now searchable and accessible to the public through the University of Toronto's Archive-It collection.[10]

There are valuable steps being taken by government organizations and academic libraries toward capturing and managing electronic government information, but they are occurring in isolation from each other. Isolated efforts are more vulnerable to the vagaries of funding shortfalls and shifts in an individual institution's policy. Though speaking specifically about data archives and repositories, Shankar and Eschenfelder argue that a critical component of an archive's sustainability is the multi-institutional relationships and networks that surround the archive.[11] Stronger networks of funders, resources, and advocates are needed to perform web archiving and digital stewardship on a greater scale. Collective efforts across stakeholder institutions may be a potential working model for librarians and archivists wanting to develop more sustainable and comprehensive web archives.

▶ *Building a Web Archive*

Web archiving requires a significant investment by collecting institutions. Determining the extent of the material to be captured is critical. Subscription services, like the Internet Archive's Archive-It, have pricing models based on the amount of data captured each year. Open-source tools like Heretrix require local storage and hosting resources. Libraries and archives need to decide on the scope of what they collect and whether they can afford to collect those sites for an extended period of time. Entire government web domains, for example, which have the potential to grow in size with the addition of rich media, may be too costly for a single institution to capture over the long term. Dividing responsibilities, at least from a cost perspective, is more sustainable in the long run.

Web archiving is not a simple "black-box" technology that can be pointed at a series of websites and be expected to effectively capture them with minimal effort. While tools like Archive-It provide excellent training and technical support, the testing, scoping, and executing of production crawls take an investment in time. Web harvesting approaches can take the shape of either "snapshots" of a large number of sites that generally are not crawled deeply and lack quality control, or a "selective" approach that captures a handful of sites deeply, with quality control and patch crawling to improve the completeness of content.[12] Web archiving of government information, because of the interest in getting to the document level, requires a selective approach. The most time-consuming part of web archiving in this manner, given the state of current web archiving tools, is quality assurance. Often quality assurance goes beyond using automated tools and delves into the time-intensive tasks of manually checking captures in browsers, and troubleshooting. In a survey by the University of North Texas, web archiving institutions, by and large, have yet to develop automated quality-assurance tools that fully eliminate the need for manual quality assurance.[13] Medium- to large-scale web archiving, with quality assurance, requires many hours of human labour, which may not be available at a single library or archive. Bearing the above resource requirements in mind, University of Toronto Libraries (UTL) initiated a collaborative web archiving project with the City of Toronto Archives aimed at dividing the burden of web archiving across two institutions. The following case study illustrates the way in which collaborative web archiving projects can work, and some of their immediate challenges.

LOCAL GOVERNMENT AND ACADEMIC LIBRARY PARTNERSHIPS

In spring 2014, Li of UTL approached the City of Toronto's communications and archival staff regarding harvesting the City's websites. University of Toronto had been capturing at-risk government sites at the federal and provincial levels since 2013. The City did not, at that time, have a plan in place for capturing municipal government websites. There was also an impending municipal election in the fall with the potential to cause, like most elections, major changes to the municipal government's web presence. The City of Toronto Archives, with its clear mandate to provide "access to records of enduring value regardless of media or format, that provide evidence of the decisions, policies, and activities of the City of Toronto," and the UTL, with its experience in web harvesting, created an opportunity for a mutually beneficial partnership.[14]

▶ Establishing Terms of Partnership

Meetings with the City of Toronto Archives and City of Toronto communications staff were initially very positive. The Archives, the City of Toronto, and UTL had a shared interest in harvesting the City's municipal government sites. Copyright and licensing issues were fairly uncomplicated because the project complied with the City's existing open government licence.[15] More challenging was coming to an agreement on how to share the burden of web archiving on a semi-annual basis. UTL was reluctant to take on the job alone for a number of reasons. Like most libraries subject to annual budget approvals, it could not guarantee long-term funding for web archiving initiatives. The main City of Toronto site and the separate Toronto City Council site, as well as the municipal open data portal, were fairly data rich and continue to form a significant portion of the University of Toronto's Archive-It data budget. Moreover, the troubleshooting and quality-assurance work necessary to capture effectively the City sites would take time and could potentially overextend the already limited staff members working on web archiving projects at UTL.

Even if the UTL web archiving team had sufficient staffing to take on the full work flow for all City of Toronto sites in perpetuity, doing the work without assistance would also mean a missed opportunity to build web archiving capacity in a local partner institution. Building capacity for web archiving locally helps improve the overall sustainability of the project. For example, if one partner could no longer participate in the project, the other could seek new partners provided that any funding gaps could be resolved.

The resulting arrangement had the University of Toronto team crawling several City of Toronto sites using its subscription to Archive-It and providing training and technical support, while the City of Toronto Archives staff agreed to perform manual quality assurance and create Dublin Core metadata for the captures.

One of the most difficult issues to reconcile with a large collaborative web archiving project is the management of partner expectations and understanding of web archives. The initial expectation of the City of Toronto Archives was that the web crawler would create an exact surrogate of the municipal sites, preserving the same functionality of the live Web. The state of crawler technology makes capturing certain aspects of websites difficult. At the time of the writing of this chapter, there were a series of technical limitations that prevented some of the most prevalent web crawlers from capturing content behind databases, dynamic content without stable URLs, and some streaming media. Developing a common understanding with partners about the limits of web archiving was necessary to ensure that they could still see the value of the project, despite the shortcomings of the crawler.

Training for City of Toronto Archives staff was a significant investment. None of the staff members had any previous involvement with web archiving. Only a few had used the Internet Archive's Wayback Machine. Web archiving has been more quickly adopted by academic libraries and archives compared to other types of memory institutions. For example, in the National Digital Stewardship Alliance's 2014 report on web archiving in the United States, academic institutions made up more than half of the web archiving institutions surveyed.[16] Local governments (below state level in the United States), even in a combined category with other types of institutions, still made up less than 10 percent of total respondents.[17] Although a similar survey does not exist in Canada, Canadian universities are far more likely than government memory institutions to subscribe to a service like Archive-It. Currently there is just one Canadian regional archive listed in Archive-It's list of partners, compared to eleven Canadian universities.[18] Canadian university libraries and archives have built capacity for web archiving and can provide a significant training role for other institutions.

Maintaining commitment to a web archiving project is challenging, particularly for partners involved in some of the less glamorous stages of its work flow. Manual quality assurance, though necessary to ensure the presence of essential documents in the archive, requires a great deal of time in unskilled labour. Although City of Toronto Archives staff members were able to provide this level of support for the project, there may be circumstances in the future in which professional archival staff members are unwilling or unable to provide quality-assurance support due to other more pressing priorities. Until better automated quality-assurance methods have been developed, finding inexpensive methods of dealing with quality assurance is necessary. So far, UTL has enlisted volunteers for quality-assurance support for other web archiving projects. It has held several web archiving workshops during which, in exchange for attending a workshop on web archiving and receiving a tutorial on using Archive-It, students at the University of Toronto's Faculty of Information contributed an hour of quality-assurance work. Other options, such as utilizing paid crowdsourcing platforms like Amazon Mechanical Turk, have been employed for checking the quality of web captures;[19] however, these projects require the financial resources and technological competency that may not be available to individual libraries and archives. Until technology can support scalable quality assurance, the success and sustainability of web archiving initiatives will depend on the efforts of many people. Collaborations across institutions are the most feasible way of supporting web archiving on a useful scale. Ensuring the success of these collaborations depends on stakeholders from all types of institutions taking up some kind of role with flexible methods of participation for partners with varying levels of resources.

FUGITIVE GOVERNMENT MATERIALS

Fugitive government materials are government information materials that could be but are not collected by an official depository program such as those collected by Publishing and Depository Services (PDS) in Canada. In the United States, the U.S. Government Printing Office (G P O) defines a tangible fugitive document as a U.S. government publication that falls within the scope of the Federal Depository Library Program (F D L P) but has not been included in it.[20] Online fugitives result from U.S. federal government agencies' failing to notify the G P O of new online materials and publishing directly onto the Web without notification. When government materials are neither deposited in government repositories nor captured either electronically or physically by libraries or archives, they have a greater chance of disappearing—making them fugitive and ultimately lost. Examples such as the Aboriginal Canada Portal, the National Round Table on the Environment and the Economy, and federal departmental sites that have either been removed from the Web or absorbed into new sites such as the government's Canada.ca portal all illustrate materials removed by the government.

On June 16, 2016, the *Globe and Mail*, the *National Post*, and other news agencies reported on a Canadian Press story dealing with the issue of government information removal. According to the report, the current Trudeau government had requested that Google delete the former Harper government search results from its results index. Specifically the government had requested that Harper's daily posts and his 24 *Seven* video diary, as well as news releases in both official languages, be removed.[21] The Privy Council Office, who made the request, explained that removal of former government content was common. In the government's view, the main purpose of the portal (Canada.ca) was to provide the public with current, accurate, and up-to-date information rather than act as an archive.

> On Nov. 9, the P C O asked Google to clear its index for any page published on the domain pm.gc.ca before Nov. 4, but Google did not offer such a service. In January, requests were made for more deletions year-by-year through Harper's tenure and the government reply says pages no longer show up search results. In all, the P C O asked Google 51 times to remove Harper material from its search results. The office said, however, that Harper's website material was saved in its entirety in the archives.[22]

This example illustrates how easily websites and online documents can be removed.

▶ The Fugitive Situation in the United States

When one researches "fugitive materials" in the Library Information and Sciences Abstracts database, one sees that many of the articles discussing the fugitive issue derive from the United States. Many are written by American government publications librarians from academic university libraries. Academic institutions, legal guardians of government material, are invested in the issue of fugitive materials because their researchers, students, and faculty depend upon government materials for their research.

Why are fugitive materials increasingly becoming an issue? One of the reasons is the move toward online publishing and born-digital publications.

James Jacobs, U.S. government information librarian at Stanford University, who has written extensively on government information in the digital age, points out that "fugitives are a rapidly growing problem as, according to GPO, 97% of all US documents are now born-digital, and most federal agencies are now publishing born-digital documents on their own .gov sites, thus cutting GPO out of the publishing process—and eroding the national bibliography that is the Catalog of Government Publications (CGP)."[23]

The concern of the impermanence of websites and digital documents is repeated throughout the library literature. In his 1998 article, Daniel P. O'Mahony discussed the fears of disappearing government information: "it is highly suspect, however, whether much of this information still will be available for users in 5, 10, 20 or 100 years or more, especially the information that is available today in electronic format only."[24] From 2009, Sproles and Clemons' article explains the continuing fears of federal electronic documents becoming fugitive:

> Fugitive documents, or government-produced information
> which escapes distribution through the Federal Depository
> Library System (FDLP), have always been a major concern.

In our current environment, where the vast majority of
government information is distributed electronic-only, this
problem has only worsened. That, coupled with the ability
to completely destroy electronic documents with the click
of a mouse, has made the task of finding and ensuring
permanent public access to this information even more
daunting.[25]

Jacobs sums up the problem succinctly: "The simple fact is that no one
knows how much born-digital U.S. Federal government information
has been created or where it all is."[26]

Digital publishing has had a direct effect on the increase of publications being produced, resulting in more government documents becoming fugitive. Jacobs states: "One might estimate that there are more
born-digital government information items produced *in a single year*
than all the two to three million non-digital government information
items accumulated in the FDLP *over 200 years.*"[27]

In the print world, locating government reports could be complicated, but one could argue that tracking down an online government report can be even trickier—even impossible. Print indexes such as the
Government of Canada Publications Index or the *Monthly Catalog of U.S.
Government Publications* were available to verify if a report had been
published. If a department wanted a report to be published, safeguards
were established so that there would be a record of the publication's
existence. In an age where people believe that all information is online
and all they need to do is google the title, it can be difficult for them to
comprehend that all material is not on the Web—especially if one is not
even made aware of what is being published.

As Jacobs states, the ease of publishing on the Web has increased
the sheer number of born-digital publications. This increase in pro-
ductivity, combined with the lack of digital publishing standards and
a compliance problem, has contributed to the fugitive problem. As
mentioned previously, there has been a concerted effort in the United
States to crawl, capture, and preserve U.S. federal government information. Examples include the Digital Federal Depository Library Program
(USDocs), which replicates key aspects of the United States Federal

Depository System. The content is held in geographically distributed sites and replicated many times.[28] Other collaborative U.S. preservation initiatives include the Lost Docs Blog, part of James Jacobs's Free Government Information project (http://lostdocs.freegovinfo.info/); CyberCemetery (http://govinfo.library.unt.edu/), a collaborative project between the GPO and the University of North Texas; and the Zotero Everyday Electronic Materials Group, a group established to report documents that are within the scope of the GPO's Cataloging and Indexing Program but have escaped notice.

The task of tracking down government fugitive documents is an enormous undertaking, requiring collaborative efforts across stakeholder groups. In a time when organizational resources are very limited, collaborative projects are a necessity.

▶ The Fugitive Situation in Canada

Government librarians in Canada have taken note of the efforts of their American colleagues to collect, build, and preserve digital government information collections. While the Canadian fugitive environment has some similarities to that of the United States, such as the lack of bibliographic control over electronic documents, there are also differences in publishing government information and in the depository library programs. To comprehend the scope of the Canadian fugitive problem, it is useful to take a step back and review the history and practice of government publishing and the role of depository libraries.

DIGITAL PUBLISHING AND A LACK OF ISBNS

Canadian depository libraries and the Depository Services Program (DSP) had the advantage of decades of experience in fine-tuning the DSP print environment to ensure that well-established procedures were in place so that publications could be discovered, collected, and preserved.[29] Before an item was published, federal departments were required to apply for an International Standard Book Number (ISBN) through Library and Archives Canada (LAC). ISBNs create a unique identity for each publication that is on record and helps in the identifying and depositing with the DSP.

In the digital publishing environment, ISBNS are not always used. Wakaruk succinctly describes the problem with digital publishing: "Electronic publications exacerbated the problem (deposit compliance) because many departments were publishing PDFs without any ISBN or GC (Government of Canada) catalogue numbers. Thus, there was no systematic way for the DSP or LAC to identify everything that was being published in electronic format."[30]

By the time that the DSP had been eliminated as part of the government's Federal Reduction Plan, the bulk of federal publications were being published online by individual departments, often bypassing the DSP. The Publishing and Depository Services Program (PDS) website states that by "November 2013, over 90% of the publications listed in the Weekly Checklist were in downloadable electronic formats."[31] The DSP's policies and procedures ensured that print materials were tracked and the historical record preserved. In the born-digital world, the safeguards that had been established for printed matter are currently lacking.

DSP E-COLLECTION LIMITATIONS

The DSP e-collection is now one of the main portals for federal government documents in Canada and contains approximately 130,000 monograph and serial publications. Once a document has been deposited in the e-collection, it is considered to be safe and will be preserved.[32] The collection is continually being updated, and approximately one thousand titles are added each month.[33] Both the lack of bibliographic control and the sheer volume of titles produced by the federal government make checking for fugitives a difficult task and underlines the importance and benefits of collaborative endeavours.

Libraries are asked to report any missing volumes or titles to the DSP via InfoDep, the DSP's listserv, to ensure that the documents are preserved in the e-collection. The DSP e-collection's policy states that the materials must be in PDF and that the Government of Canada must be the copyright holder. The DSP primarily collects PDF documents and will rarely collect documents in other electronic formats, such as spreadsheets, slide presentations, word-processing documents, databases, websites, digital maps, and data files. Even when some publications are in PDF, they fail to meet the requirements. For example, news releases, single articles, forms, memoranda, and fact sheets are excluded from the e-collection.

TREASURY BOARD OF CANADA SECRETARIAT POLICIES

In order to decipher how fugitive documents occur, it is necessary to look at government policies and procedures for government publishing. It should be noted that the policies have changed since 2013, with the transition to an electronic-only publishing model. The Treasury Board of Canada Secretariat (TBS) has two policies concerning the obligations of federal government departments to make their publications publicly available.

The TBS's *Communications Policy*, section 27, states that "institutions must facilitate public access to their publications—all information materials, regardless of publishing medium, produced for public dissemination or for limited circulation outside of government."[34] Although this policy states "all" information materials, not all need to be widely circulated such as being posted on a website.[35]

Section 6.10, "Monitoring and Reporting of the TBS Procedures for Publishing," explains the roles of heads of departments in ensuring compliance. The issue of compliance among departments is important and necessary in reducing the number of fugitive documents; however, strict enforcement of the policy is needed. Heads of communications are responsible for monitoring compliance with these procedures within their department. Public Services and Procurement Canada, and LAC, are responsible for monitoring the implementation of these procedures in their areas of responsibility and for informing the TBS of any significant or systemic non-compliance issues. The TBS is responsible for working with Public Services and Procurement Canada and LAC to address any significant or systemic non-compliance issues; for monitoring government-wide compliance with these procedures; and for reviewing these procedures and their effectiveness at the five-year mark of implementation.[36]

The second policy is the TBS's *Procedures for Publishing*, established on June 1, 2013, which directs agencies to maintain an index of all departmental publications, electronic or print, and to forward it to the Publishing and Depository Services Directorate. This is a very important directive. It is a starting point for the DSP to ensure that these publications are added to the e-collection. According to this procedure, departmental heads of communications or their designates are responsible for "forwarding electronic copies of the index mentioned twice a year (November and April) to the Publishing and Depository Services Directorate at Public Services and Procurement Canada and the Digital Legal Deposit Unit at Library and Archives Canada."[37] As Wakaruk explains, "the very people who decide what should be published are also responsible for reporting on whether or not they were in compliance with sending those publications to the DSP and/or LAC,"[38] which can be problematic, potentially leading to compliance issues. Departments are also required to provide electronic copies of the publications to PDS.

The *Procedures for Publishing* guidelines also indicate the agencies that are required to forward publications to the PDS. "These procedures apply to all departments listed in schedules I, I.1, and II of the *Financial Administration Act*, unless excluded by specific acts, regulations, or orders in council policy."[39] The *Financial Administration Act* has an extensive list of federal agencies, but not all agencies are included in the schedules listed, which is problematic for ensuring a comprehensive collection. Communication Canada, Indian Oil and Gas Canada, Canadian Mortgage and Housing Corporation, and Export Development Canada are just a few of the agencies excluded from the schedules, and as a result their documents are often not captured.

Quasi–federal government agencies play a significant federal government role; however, they are frequently excluded from the DSP e-collection due to copyright. Library professionals often suggest the addition of documents from quasi-government agencies to the DSP, but unless the Government of Canada is the copyright holder, the documents are rejected. An example of a quasi-federal agency is the Health Council of Canada, which was established by the prime minister and the provincial and territorial premiers to monitor and assess Canada's health system. The Health Council was funded by Health Canada and established as a non-profit organization. Its publications are excluded from the DSP e-collection because the copyright is not held by Government of Canada. When the Health Council was decommissioned in March 2014, its publications would have been lost if Carleton University Library had not successfully arranged to archive the site along with the news releases and other important publications.[40] Without this archiving initiative, separate from the government, all content would have been lost.

Federal departments are supposed to comply and deposit PDF materials with the DSP as per the TSB's *Publishing Procedures*. It is difficult to know how many publications are escaping, without a compliance audit program in place. Departmental compliance has been an ongoing issue. As Monty explains, the DSP, since it was created in 1927, has struggled to ensure that departments deposit materials in the DSP. Since there is no legislation mandating that departments deposit materials, the DSP lacks the authority to mandate compliance.[41]

LIMITATIONS OF WEB ARCHIVING

One of the solutions for ensuring the preservation of government materials is through web harvesting activities, as discussed in chapter 2 and earlier in this chapter. Web harvesting is an important component of a preservation tool kit, and, on the surface, it would be easy to assume that web archiving software captures everything; however, there are limitations. As mentioned, web archiving crawlers have difficulty in capturing databases, some streaming media content, and dynamically generated web pages that rely heavily on user interaction.

▶ Databases

One example of publications that change from one form to another is government directories. Historically, directories were published in print. When they are published online, they are often converted into databases. Government telephone directories were publications that presented a snapshot of the government of the day, including a list of all the agencies. These directories also served as organizational charts showing the departments, branches, committees, and boards and acted as a who's who for a particular government. Without the ability to web archive the directory information stored in a database, this useful government information is not captured for researchers.

▶ Dynamic and Interactive Content

Another example of content that is challenging to capture is the *Atlas of Canada*. Historically the *Atlas* was published in print. In more recent years it was available as a PDF document. For a while, it developed into a curated collection of online maps, some of which could be captured by a web crawler. Most recently the *Atlas* has become an interactive application, a "build-your-own-map" service in which the user combines elements such as geography and other characteristics to generate a map dynamically. Crawling this, even if possible, is not feasible due to disk requirements.

Other dynamic materials include the interactive database Trade Data Online, as well as dynamic geographic content available on Natural Resources Canada's Geogratis.[42]

▶ Multimedia Content

Some other formats can be tricky to harvest such as multimedia content and videos. Fortunately the Government of Canada's *Standard on Web Accessibility* has helped to ensure that most content is made available for web crawlers to archive.

▶ Content Not Accessible Online

Web archiving is an effective practice when the content is online, accessible, and retrievable. Some Canadian federal departmental websites post brief summaries of electronic documents that can be harvested. However, the actual document may not accessible and must be retrieved by request via a web form or by other means such as email, FTP, or on a flash drive. This underlines the importance of collaborating with producers of such government information.

▶ Content Not Discoverable

Web archiving ensures that materials are preserved, but preservation does not automatically make the materials discoverable. As with a print collection, librarians need to curate and describe these digital collections with appropriate metadata so that the materials are accessible and discoverable. The DSP has made a concerted effort to facilitate the findability of federal serial titles by compiling all volumes of a serial title under one record.

Despite a mandate to preserve government information, LAC ceased government website archiving in 2007. After intensive lobbying from the academic community, LAC resumed archiving in 2013, but unfortunately a six-year gap remained.[43] LAC's archive of government websites from 2005 to 2007 and 2013 onward was made publicly accessible in 2016; however, indexing and searching capabilities are still lacking, which is a hindrance to the discoverability of the content.[44]

▶ Content Protected by Web Administrators

Administrators of websites may potentially block web crawlers from some or all areas of their sites. This is often done to protect content or to prevent undue resource demands on a server. A common example of a tool used to block web crawlers is the robots exclusion protocol. Although many web crawlers can circumvent these protocols, tools like Archive-It respect exclusion protocols by default and require manual modification and re-crawling to capture blocked content.[45] In the process, websites and content may have already disappeared from the live Web. More advanced security features may also confuse web archiving crawlers with potential threats and block requests at the server level. In these circumstances, one must contact web administrators directly to have them unblock IP ranges and the web crawler. Even if administrators co-operate, the process of making such requests can take time and has the potential to hinder the prompt archiving of content. Establishing communication with site owners and administrators has traditionally been a significant issue for web archiving initiatives. Response rates for permission requests, for example, are typically 30–50 percent.[46]

This creates an added potential for accidentally blocked crawls to never capture.

CGI DPN TAKES THE LEAD ON CAPTURING FUGITIVE MATERIALS

▶ *Fugitive Documents Working Group*

In view of all the noted limitations of digital publishing and archiving of government information, the steering committee of the Canadian Government Information Digital Preservation Network (CGI DPN) created the Fugitive Document Working Group (FDWG) in July 2014 to assist in designing processes for collecting and reporting fugitive materials. The FDWG was tasked with identifying gaps in the existing CGI DPN federal government archive, investigating the way in which libraries were identifying fugitive materials, and finding out if any national, regional, or local systematic efforts had been established to preserve materials. Policies and preservation activities by government agencies, such as the DSP and LAC, and the Open Government Portal were examined, as well as the scope and limitations of TBS's *Publications Procedures*.

▶ *Survey on Fugitive Canadian Government Information*

A subgroup within the FDWG developed a survey to help understand the current practices around identifying, collecting, cataloguing, and reporting fugitive government information in Canadian public, special, and academic libraries. The survey had four main goals: to determine whether respondents were taking the initiative to collect fugitive materials; to learn about work flows and challenges in dealing with fugitive materials; to help identify potential strategies and actions that the CGI DPN might take to strengthen the collection of fugitive materials; and to help identify priorities for web crawling. The survey was announced nationally via the GOVINFO listserv on September 11, 2014, and remained open for responses until October 1, 2014. In total, there were thirty-one responses to the survey, of which twenty-three emanated from academic libraries. Academic libraries have always actively collected federal government materials. When the print depository program still existed, research libraries had full federal-depository-library status, meaning that they received all of the federal government's publications. The high proportion of responses from the academic sector was not surprising, because these institutions have a vested interest in ensuring that their government information collections are comprehensive, and proper assurances are created to preserve the collections for future researchers.

Six respondents indicated that they collected fugitive government materials frequently, twenty responded that they collected fugitive government material occasionally, and five responded that they had never collected fugitive materials. Of the respondents that collected fugitive materials, six collected materials from the international, federal, provincial, and municipal levels of government. The other twenty respondents indicated that they collected fugitive materials from some combination of these levels of government.

The electronic version of fugitive publications was the preferred format for the majority of the respondents (twenty); however, there was a lack of technological and human resources to support the harvesting of electronic fugitive documents. The survey revealed that respondents who collected fugitive electronic documents did so on an ad hoc basis, using various means; receiving documents via email and downloading them was still the most common means of collection. Five respondents indicated that they used FTP to collect materials, and five others were using web crawling software at their institutions. At the time of the survey, only two institutions (the University of Toronto and the University of Alberta) were systematically crawling government websites.

Many of the institutions that took part in the survey cited the lack of human and technical resources as two large barriers to active participation in comprehensive web harvesting. The two institutions across Canada that are archiving systematically have an undue burden placed on their resources. The model is unsustainable because archiving fugitive documents is an onerous task.

There is also the issue of what to do when fugitive documents are discovered. Once they have been collected, the next step is accessibility. Eleven libraries responded that they printed the documents, catalogued them, and added them to their own library's collection. Twenty-one respondents indicated that they made the fugitive materials available to the public once they had been captured. Five organizations indicated that the materials were restricted to their organization's intranet or to their library cardholders.

From the survey results it is evident that the systematic development of digital collections for fugitive documents has not yet been integrated into an established work flow for most Canadian institutions. For the most part, reporting fugitive documents to the DSP is not taking place as a routine part of collection development work flow. There are many reasons for the gap. People may be unaware of the degree to which government materials are being deleted and lost. The underutilization of the DSP fugitive-reporting mechanism might stem from a belief that the preservation of digital materials lies in the hands of the publisher. There is uncertainty over who should take responsibility for tracking down fugitive documents. As stated earlier, some libraries report that they simply lack the infrastructure to capture and make materials available via a local digital collection or institutional repository. This is not a surprise given that few libraries have a full-time dedicated government librarian. Anecdotally in Canada, if a library is fortunate to have a government information librarian, that person is juggling this work with other liaison or functional duties, as noted at the beginning of the chapter.

The fact that many of the fugitive documents found by respondents are not reported to the DSP is disconcerting. Whatever the reasons for the under-reporting, this is something that might be addressed by raising awareness of the risk of lost content.

The information gleaned through the survey was crucial to uncovering some of the constraints faced by libraries when they tackle fugitive government information, including lack of access to servers for posting electronic publications, and established work flow for cataloguing materials. Any solution to locate and capture fugitive government documents needs to take into account these circumstances. The survey revealed that respondents were acutely aware that government information was at risk and was being lost; this correlated to a strong desire within the community to rectify the way in which libraries can improve the collections and capture these materials.

The FDWG action plan included reviewing the gaps in current government information collections and deciphering whether the gaps were a result of policy, scope, and/or technical limitations. The survey findings were instrumental in informing the FDWG about the current practices in libraries; librarians' concerns and awareness of fugitive documents; and whether there was capacity within the library community to assist in tracking down fugitive publications.

The recommendations in the FDWG's report focused on three key areas: raising awareness of at-risk government information being lost, adopting a collaborative approach to systematically collecting fugitive documents, and including fugitive information in the single point of discovery for government information.

RAISE AWARENESS ABOUT FUGITIVE GOVERNMENT INFORMATION

It is critical to raise awareness within the library community that there are gaps in existing government information collections. It is also important that the strengths and limitations of web crawling are brought to the attention of both colleagues and library directors. The FDWG recommends that CGI DPN work with other partners to help foster greater awareness of the need to collect fugitive materials.

ADOPT A SYSTEMATIC APPROACH TO COLLECTING FUGITIVES

Fugitive government information exists, and there is a need to identify systematically the gaps and to create solutions for preservation and access. Not only will a systematic approach help to minimize duplication of effort, but also it will provide some assurance that the materials of certain departments or agencies have been collected. A systematic approach to fugitive information can only be successful if there is a collaborative effort. No one library or organization has the resources available to pursue this task independently. To ensure wide participation by many partners, fugitive document collection tools need to be simple and effective so that libraries and other interested stakeholders can locate and flag fugitive documents for collection.

ENSURE A SINGLE POINT FOR DISCOVERY OF GOVERNMENT INFORMATION THAT INCLUDES FUGITIVE DOCUMENTS

Current collection processes for fugitive documents are varied. Depending on the library, the material may or may not be catalogued. If it is catalogued, the record may be in a local database of e-publications or in a library catalogue, but currently there is no national standard procedure. Ideally fugitive materials would be included in the CGI DPN web archive. The most straightforward way for this to happen is to report fugitive documents to PDS.

Given the diverse means of acquiring materials (email, FTP, digitizing), appropriate infrastructure needs to be created to ensure that these materials are crawled. The report recommended that the CGI DPN Technical Committee put forward an approach on how to capture and archive both fugitive and non-fugitive materials.

▶ At-Risk Federal Web Content Archive

Based on the FDWG recommendations, the CGI DPN has increased efforts to preserve at-risk federal web content as well as fugitive documents. In the first case, CGI DPN captured content from federal government agencies that were not required by the TBS to provide publications to PDS. A list of "agencies identified in the *Financial Administration Act* with directive to deposit publications" was first compiled after a comparison had been made of the schedules in the *Financial Administration Act* and the directory of agencies on the Government of Canada websites. Three tables were generated from the list to help create the seed list for the archiving of at-risk federal web content. An Archive-It account via the COPPUL consortial licence, with ten CGI DPN libraries equally sharing the annual cost, was set up to harvest the at-risk federal web content in 2014.[47]

Susan Paterson, Nicholas Worby, and Darlene Fichter ◁ 317

In 2015, after reviewing the FDWG report, the CGI DPN Steering Committee developed a collaborative approach to collect fugitive documents systematically. The committee adopted a proposed work flow that was designed by Sam-chin Li, Reference and Government Information Librarian, University of Toronto.[48] Li developed a straightforward system for locating and reporting fugitive documents. Additional software and access to digital repositories were not required, which helped to ensure the participation of libraries as well as project sustainability.

Li conducted the first pilot to test the proposed fugitive document work flow. During the pilot, reference desk assistants at the University of Toronto were trained to look for documents, agency by agency, using advanced Google search queries. Then they checked the documents to see if they were already included in the DSP e-collection. If not, the document information was recorded in a shared spreadsheet. The documents found by the reference desk assistants were checked by Li to confirm that they were fugitive before being forwarded to DSP.

The pilot was successful, and more than six hundred documents were identified. The reference assistants, who were graduate students from the University of Toronto's iSchool, gained valuable experience in working with government documents.

Organizations other than libraries were included in the collaborative efforts to collect fugitives. Li reached out to PDS to see if staff members could periodically check the spreadsheet rather than having librarians vet the results. PDS agreed to do so in December 2015 and has started collecting fugitives to add to its collection. In the winter of 2018, students at the Government Information and Publications class of the iSchool program at the University of Toronto were asked to locate digital fugitive documents as part of their assignment. This part of the assignment was marked by a staff from the PDS. A total of 110 documents were identified, and among them 65 would be added to the DSP e-collection.

It is still early days for this new collaborative effort, but there are already signs of success.[49] While work on fugitive documents is still happening on an ad hoc basis, there are definite signs that the library community is willing to work together to try to close the gaps. With greater promotion and awareness, it is expected that more libraries will volunteer to participate.

CONCLUSION

Born-digital government information presents new opportunities and new roles for librarians. It is difficult to predict the strategies that will be the most effective for preserving government information. The projects outlined in this chapter are still in their infancy and have yet to be challenged further by technological changes or the loss of resources. One thing that has become increasingly clear throughout the experience of both of these projects is that the stewardship of government information in Canada cannot be considered the sole purview of a single institution. There will always be gaps and oversights, just as there are in analog collections; however, collaborative stewardship across institutions and across sectors insulates government information from the budget crises and politics of individual institutions. Moreover, recognition of individual institutions' strengths and realities, as well as the creation of flexible participation models that allow partners to contribute what they can, will improve the overall viability of these projects.

Instead of catalyzing the irrelevancy of librarians and archivists, the move to a born-digital world is an opportunity for those institutions collecting government information to look to each other for help and capacity building. It is an opportunity to re-situate some of the traditional roles of government information professionals in an electronic realm; however, the volume of work necessary in a post-depository-services world requires more stakeholders to take an active role.

Notes

1. Mack and Prescod, "Where Have All the Government Documents Librarians Gone?," 99–111.
2. Mack and Prescod, "Where Have All the Government Documents Librarians Gone?," 103.
3. Smugler, *Facing Change*.
4. Canada, Department of Finance, *Archived Budget Documents*.
5. Ex Libris Association, "Library and Archives Canada Service Decline after 2004."
6. United States, Government Printing Office, "Federal Depository Library Program: Web Archiving."
7. United States, Library of Congress, "Web Archive Collections."
8. Li, "Page Not Found," 10–11.
9. Li, "Page Not Found," 13.
10. University of Toronto Libraries. Canadian Government Information Collection. Archive-It. https://archive-it.org/collections/3608.
11. Shankar and Eschenfelder, "Sustaining Data Archives over Time," 251.
12. Brügger, "Web Archiving," 24.
13. Reyes Ayala, Phillips, and Ko, "Current Quality Assurance Practices in Web Archiving."
14. City of Toronto, "Archives Mandate," http://bit.ly/29D4Yz1.
15. City of Toronto, "Open Government Licence."
16. Bailey et al., "Web archiving in the United States."
17. Bailey et al., "Web archiving in the United States."
18. Archive-It, "Show All Organizations."
19. Brunelle et al. "Not All Mementos Are Created Equal."
20. Baldwin, "Fugitive Documents."
21. The Canadian Press, "Internet History of Harper PMO."
22. The Canadian Press, "Internet History of Harper PMO."
23. Jacobs, "What Makes a 'Fugitive Document' a Fugitive?"
24. O'Mahony, "Here Today, Gone Tomorrow," 112.
25. Sproles and Clemons, "Permanent Access to Electronic Government Information."
26. Jacobs, "Born-Digital U.S. Federal Government Information."
27. Jacobs, "Born-Digital U.S. Federal Government Information."
28. LOCKSS, "Digital Federal Depository Library Program," http://www.lockss.org/community/networks/digital-federal-depository-library-program/.
29. For a comprehensive overview of the Canadian Depository Services Program please refer to chapter 1.
30. Wakaruk, "What the Heck Is Happening Up North?," 16.

31. Government of Canada, "Government of Canada Publications: E-Collection," accessed April 1, 2015, https://web.archive.org/web/20160309191956/ http://publications.gc.ca/site/eng/search/eCollection.html.

32. For a discussion about the scope of preservation activities, see chapters 2 and 10.

33. Government of Canada, "Government of Canada Publications: E-Collection," accessed April 1, 2015, https://web.archive.org/web/20160309191956/ http://publications.gc.ca/site/eng/search/eCollection.html.

34. Government of Canada, "Policy Requirements."

35. For a detailed description of the Treasury Board of Canada Secretariat please refer to chapter 2, "Library and Archives Canada: Official Publications and Select Digital Library Collections, 1923–2017," by Tom J. Smyth.

36. Government of Canada, *Procedures for Publishing*.

37. Government of Canada, *Procedures for Publishing*, section 6.5.2.

38. Wakaruk, "What the Heck Is Happening Up North?," 18–19.

39. Government of Canada, *Procedures for Publishing*.

40. See the disclaimer on the Health Council of Canada Archive website, https://healthcouncilcanada.ca, which states: "Health Council of Canada is no longer operating. This archived Web page remains online for reference, research or recordkeeping purposes by Carleton University Library."

41. Monty, "Canadian Government Information."

42. Li, "On the Hunt for Fugitive Documents."

43. Li, "Page Not Found," 12.

44. As per Tom Smyth's presentation at the Ontario Government Publications round table on March 24, 2017, there are 558 million assets (26.2 terabytes) in LAC's web archive as of the third quarter of 2016–17.

45. Ewing and Rollason-Cass, "Robots Exclusion Protocol."

46. International Internet Preservation Consortium, "Legal Issues."

47. For further details of the Archive-It account please refer to chapter 10.

48. For the work flow, see https://web.archive.org/web/20160804155654/ https://plnwiki.lockss.org/index.php?title=CGI_network.

49. While the DSP was able to acquire more than six hundred of the approximately two thousand items identified from 2015 to 2017, links to some of these works were already broken before the DSP could acquire them.

Bibliography

Archive-It. "Show All Organizations." Accessed May 15, 2016. https://web.archive. org/web/20160801203938/https://archive-it.org/explore?show=Organizations.

Bailey, Jefferson, Abigail Grotke, Kristine Hanna, Cathy Hartman, Edward McCain, Christie Moffat, and Nicholas Taylor. "Web Archiving in the United States:

A 2013 Survey; An NDSA Report." National Digital Stewardship Alliance. Accessed May 15, 2016. https://web.archive.org/save/_embed/http://www. digitalpreservation.gov/documents/NDSA_USWebArchivingSurvey_2013. pdf?loclr=blogsig.

Baldwin, Gil. "Fugitive Documents: On the Loose or on the Run." Presentation by Director, Library Programs Service, GPO American Association of Law Libraries Conference, Seattle, WA, July 15, 2003. *Administrative Notes* 24, no. 10 (August 15, 2003).

Brügger, Niels. "Web Archiving: Between Past, Present, and Future." In *The Handbook of Internet Studies,* edited by Mia Consalvo and Charles Ess, 24–42. Oxford: Blackwell, 2011. https:/doi.org/10.1002/9781444314861.

Brunelle, Justin F., Mat Kelly, Hany Salaheldeen, Michele C. Weigle, and Michael L. Nelson. "Not All Mementos Are Created Equal: Measuring the Impact of Missing Resources." *International Journal on Digital Libraries* 16, nos. 3–4 (2015): 283–301. https://doi.org/10.1007/s00799-015-0150-6.

Canada. *Canada's Action Plan on Open Government, 2014–2016.* Accessed August 2, 2016. https://web.archive.org/web/20160719224034/http://open.canada.ca/ en/content/canadas-action-plan-open-government-2014-16.

———. "Government of Canada Publications: E-Collection." Accessed April 1, 2015. https://web.archive.org/web/20160309191956/http://publications.gc.ca/site/ eng/search/eCollection.html.

———. Open Government Information Portal. Accessed August 2, 2016. https:// web.archive.org/web/20160803010831/http://open.canada.ca/en.

———. "Policy Requirements." In *Communications Policy of the Government of Canada* [Rescinded May 11, 2016], section 27. Accessed August 2, 2016. https:// web.archive.org/web/20160712235216/http://tbs-sct.gc.ca/pol/doc-eng. aspx?id=12316.

———. *Procedures for Publishing.* Accessed August 2, 2016. http://www.tbs-sct. gc.ca/pol/doc-eng.aspx?id=27167.

———. *Standard on Web Accessibility.* Accessed August 2, 2016. https:// web.archive.org/web/20160712234452/http://tbs-sct.gc.ca/pol/doc-eng. aspx?id=23601.

———. Department of Finance. *Archived Budget Documents.* [Ottawa:] Department of Finance, 2016. Accessed May 15, 2016. http://www.budget.gc.ca/pdfarch/ index-eng.html.

———. Treasury Board of Canada Secretariat. *Web Renewal Initiative: Streamlining the Government of Canada's Web Presence.* Accessed August 2, 2016. https://web. archive.org/web/20160713084106/http://tbs-sct.gc.ca/wr-rw/index-eng.asp.

The Canadian Press. "Internet History of Harper PMO Deleted from Google Results at Ottawa's Request." *Globe and Mail,* June 16, 2016. http://www. theglobeandmail.com/news/politics/internet-history-of-harper-pmo-deleted-from-google-results-at-ottawas-request/article30493213/.

City of Toronto. "Archives Mandate." Accessed May 15, 2016. https://web.
    archive.org/web/20160321150121/https://www1.toronto.ca/wps/portal/
    contentonly?vgnextoid=e1dd96ff00d31410VgnVC.
———. "Open Government Licence." Accessed May 15, 2016. https://web.
    archive.org/web/20160730095050/http://www1.toronto.ca/wps/portal/
    contentonly?vgnextoid=4a37e03bb8d1e310VgnVCM10000071d60f89RCRD.
Ewing, Renata, and Sylvia Rollason-Cass. "Robots Exclusion Protocol." Archive-It
    Help. Accessed May 29, 2015. https://webarchive.jira.com/wiki/display/ARIH/
    Robots+Exclusion+Protocol.
Ex Libris Association. "Library and Archives Canada Service Decline after 2004:
    Ex Libris Association Timeline." Accessed May 15, 2016. http://www.exlibris.
    ca/doku.php?id=activities:letters:library_and_archives_canada_servive_decline.
International Internet Preservation Consortium. "Legal Issues." 2012.
    http://www.netpreserve.org/web-archiving/legal-issues.
Jacobs, James A. "Born-Digital U.S. Federal Government Information:
    Preservation and Access." Paper presented at the Leviathan: Libraries and
    Government Information in the Age of Big Data conference, Chicago, March
    17, 2014. https://web.archive.org/web/20150701111619/http://www.crl.edu/
    sites/default/files/d6/attachments/pages/Leviathan%20Jacobs%20Report%20
    CRL%20%C6%92%20(3).pdf.
———. "What Makes a 'Fugitive Document' a Fugitive?" *Free Government
    Information Blog.* December 18, 2014. https://web.archive.org/
    web/20160603064701/http://freegovinfo.info/node/9352.
Li, Sam-chin. "On the Hunt for Fugitive Documents." October 16, 2014.
    http://gsg.uottawa.ca/gov/docs/government-information-day/programme/
    11_li_on-the-hunt-for-fugitive-documents.pdf.
Li, Sam-chin, Nicholas Worby, and Jesse Carliner. "Page Not Found: Web
    Archiving Government Information and Beyond," TALL *Quarterly* 33, no.1
    (Spring 2014): 10–15. https://www.talltoronto.ca
LOCKSS. "Digital Federal Depository Library Program." Accessed August 2,
    2016. https://web.archive.org/web/20160509185125/http://www.lockss.org/
    community/networks/digital-federal-depository-library-program/.
Mack, Thura, and Janette Prescod. "Where Have all the Government
    Documents Librarians Gone? Moving Beyond Collections to Information
    Literacy." *Reference Services Review* 37, no. 1 (2009): 99–111. https://doi.
    org/10.1108/00907320910935020.
Monty, Vivienne. "Canadian Government Information: An Update." *Government
    Publications Review* 20, no. 3: 273–82.
O'Mahony, Daniel P. "Here Today, Gone Tomorrow: What Can Be Done to Assure
    Permanent Public Access to Electronic Government Information?" *Advances in
    Librarianship* 22, 1998: 107–21. https://doi.org/10.1108/S0065-2830(1998)
    0000022009.

Reyes Ayala, Brenda, Mark E. Phillips, and Lauren Ko. "Current Quality Assurance Practices in Web Archiving." 2013. Accessed May 15, 2016. https://web. archive.org/web/20141113023927/http://digital.library.unt.edu/ark:/67531/ metadc333026/m2/1/high_res_d/QA_in_WebArchiving.pdf.

Shankar, Kalpana, and Kristin R. Eschenfelder. "Sustaining Data Archives over Time: Lessons from the Organizational Studies Literature." *New Review of Information Networking* 20, nos. 1–2 (2015): 251. https://doi.org/10.1080/136145 76.2015.1111699.

Smugler, Sherry. *Facing Change: A Perspective on Government Publications Services in Canadian Academic Libraries in the Internet Age.* GODORT Occasional Papers, no. 9 (November 2013). Accessed August 2, 2016. https://web.archive.org/ web/20160127154723/http://wikis.ala.org/godort/images/1/19/OP9-smugler. pdf.

Sproles, Claudine, and Angel Clemons. "Permanent Access to Electronic Government Information: A Study of Federal, State, and Local Documents." *Electronic Journal of Academic and Special Librarianship* 10, no. 2 (July 2009). http://southernlibrarianship.icaap.org/content/v10n02/sproles_c01.html.

United States. Government Printing Office. "Federal Depository Library Program: Web Archiving." Accessed May 15, 2016. http://www.fdlp.gov/377-projects-active/2020-web-archiving-project.

———. Library of Congress. "Web Archive Collections." Accessed May 15, 2016. http://www.loc.gov/webarchiving/collections.html.

Wakaruk, Amanda. "What the Heck Is Happening Up North?" DTTP: *Documents to the People* 42, no. 1 (Spring 2014): 15–20. https://web.archive.org/save/_ embed/http://wikis.ala.org/godort/images/9/9c/DttP_42n1.pdf.

CONTRIBUTORS

GRAEME CAMPBELL, MLIS (University of Western Ontario, 2008), is the Open Government librarian at Queen's University in Kingston, Ontario. His current research interests focus on how Canadian government information is disseminated, accessed, and preserved. Graeme has been a co-moderator of the Ontario Council of University Libraries' Government Information Community and editor-in-chief of *Insideo CULA*, the official publication of the Ontario College and University Library Association.

TALIA CHUNG, MLIS (McGill University, 1994), GrDip CompSci. (Concordia University, 2001), is the associate university librarian of research services at the University of Ottawa Library. She has held many previous roles at the University of Ottawa including director of the Morisset Arts and Science Library, director of the Health Sciences Library, and head of the Geographic, Statistical, and Government Information Centre and Social Sciences Library. Before joining the University of Ottawa, Talia held administrative, systems, and research support roles at Canada's Library of Parliament. Her areas of interest include leadership, human resource management, academic library research support services, data management, and government information.

SANDRA CRAIG, MLIS (University of Toronto, 1986), is the supervisor of metadata services at the Legislative Assembly of Ontario. She has been involved in building and maintain the Legislative Library's digital repository of Ontario government documents since its beginning in 2000. She is the past chair of the Ontario Government Libraries Council and a long-serving member of the council's Working Group on Ontario Government

Publications. Sandra's research interests include access to and preservation of government publications, website archiving, metadata, and taxonomies.

PETER ELLINGER, MLS (University of Toronto, 1995), is the manager of the portfolio management office at the Legislative Assembly of Ontario. He has worked in a variety of roles at the Legislative Library and has also been involved in the broader library community, including terms as president of the Ontario Library Information Technology Association and as a member of the OurOntario Technical Committee. As systems librarian, Peter helped to design and implement numerous data and information applications for the Legislative Assembly. His current interests involve developing and implementing long-term strategy to provide pertinent, reliable, and usable information to users of data and information created by the Legislative Assembly.

DARLENE FICHTER, MLIS (University of Toronto, 1987), works at the Murray Library, University of Saskatchewan. For more than two decades, her professional practice has focused on developing government, data, and geospatial collections. Since the mid-1990s Darlene has been working with colleagues at the University of Saskatchewan to capture and preserve born-digital Saskatchewan documents. She publishes and presents on the subject of new technologies that can be harnessed by libraries to enhance use, access, and discovery.

MICHELLE LAKE, MLIS (University of Western Ontario, 2007), is the government publications librarian and subject librarian for Concordia University's Department of Political Science, School of Community and Public Affairs, and First Peoples Studies, in Montreal, Quebec. Michelle's research interests include Canadian government information, academic library services for Indigenous students, Canadian Indigenous studies collections, and the transition from print to digital in libraries and government.

SAM-CHIN LI, MA (University of Toronto, 1988), MLS (University of Toronto, 1990), is the reference and government information librarian at the University of Toronto. She has worked on many digitization and web archiving projects for government information. She was the coordinator of the first Government Information Day in Ontario (2013) and the co-chair of the Steering Committee of the Canadian Government Information Digital Preservation Network (2015–17). She taught the Government Information and Publications course at the Faculty of Information at the University of Toronto in winter 2018.

STEVE MARKS, MIS (University of Toronto, 2009), is the digital preservation librarian at the University of Toronto, where he is responsible for planning, policy, and work flows to ensure the longevity of the university's digital assets. His research interests include digital forensics, digital preservation at scale, and the preservation of software and new media.

MAUREEN MARTYN, MLIS (McGill University, 1988), has more than twenty years' experience working in the Canadian parliamentary milieu. From her early days as a reference librarian to her current role as chief of Branches and Reference Services, Maureen has been involved in many parliamentary projects, including LEGISinfo and *HillNotes*, the Library's research publications blog. She has held several management positions, including managing multidisciplinary teams at both the Library of Parliament and the House of Commons.

CATHERINE MCGOVERAN, MLIS (Dalhousie University, 2013), is a government information librarian at the University of Ottawa. Her current research interests focus on academic librarianship and Canadian government information dissemination, access, and preservation. Catherine has also been a co-moderator of the Ontario Council of University Libraries' Government Information Community and the American Library Association's International

Documents Task Force, as well as a volunteer with Open Data Ottawa.

MARTHA MURPHY, MLIS (University of Western Ontario, 1987), is the library manager at Ontario Workplace Tribunals Library. She has been an advocate for making government documents accessible through preservation strategies such as digitization initiatives with ministries, agencies, and Ontario Council of University Libraries. She is the past chair of the Ontario Government Libraries Council and a member of the Ontario Government Publications Working Group. Martha is actively involved in the Canadian Association of Law Libraries and is co-chair of the Membership Development Committee.

DANI J. PAHULJE, MLS (University of British Columbia, 1976), was the liaison librarian for government information, political science, and public policy at Libraries and Cultural Resources, University of Calgary. She is now librarian emerata. She worked in the area of government information for over twenty-five years. Her research interests included access to information and government publishing.

SUSAN PATERSON, MLIS (University of Western Ontario, 2002), has been the government information librarian and liaison librarian for French language literature and social work at the University of British Columbia since 2008. She previously worked at the Legislative Library of British Columbia. Susan is interested in digitization and web archiving preservation.

CAROL PERRY, MLIS (University of Western Ontario, 2007), is a research and scholarship librarian at the University of Guelph, coordinating the data management consultation and repository services as well as the university's institutional repository, the Atrium. She is also the acting academic director of the Branch Research Data Centre at the university. Her research interests centre on research data management and data preservation. Carol is currently the regional secretary for Canada with the International Association for Social Science Information Service and Technology.

CARON ROLLINS, MLS (University of Alberta, 1988), is the law and government publications librarian at the University of Victoria, Diana M. Priestly Law Library, where she is responsible for the government publication collections for the University of Victoria Libraries. Her research interests include legal research, legal collections, web archiving, digitization, and last-copy print projects.

GREGORY SALMERS, MLS (University of Western Ontario, 1982), is the director of support services at the Saskatchewan Legislative Library. His current and past interests, publications, and presentations relate to Saskatchewan government publications; the GALLOP portal; digitization of local heritage content such as Saskatchewan military history; current military operations; and combined school public library services.

TOM J. SMYTH, MA (University of Toronto, 2004), MIST (University of Toronto, 2008), PMP (Project Management Institute, 2015), is a senior librarian and manager of the Digital Integration group within the Digital Preservation and Migration Division at Library and Archives Canada. His work involves innovation and managing next-generation digital library and archival programs, projects, and services in digital curation and systems contexts. He has managed official publications and led Library and Archive Canada's Web Archiving Program since 2009.

BRIAN TOBIN, MLS (University of Toronto, 1984), recently retired from the Ontario Legislative Library where he had worked for thirty years. His last position was as manager of content management.

AMANDA WAKARUK, MLIS (University of Alberta, 1999), MES (York University, 2009), is the copyright librarian at the University of Alberta. She has worked as an academic government information librarian for more than fifteen years, served in a range of related professional roles, and co-founded the Canadian Government Information Digital Preservation Network. Amanda's current research interests include the role of Crown copyright in the stewardship of government information.

NICHOLAS WORBY, MI (University of Toronto, 2013), is the government information and statistics librarian as well as the Web Archives Program coordinator at the University of Toronto. In addition to providing research and instruction support for government information, he oversees collection development, production crawls, staff training, and researcher outreach for web archive collections.

INDEX

Aboriginal Affairs and Northern Development Canada Aboriginal portal, 65
academic libraries *see* university libraries
accessibility standards, 215, 216, 220, 272, 311
access to information
  and budget changes, 290–91
  and democracy, xiii, xv, 191
  in library collections, 314–15
  policies, 227
  preservation of, xxvi–xxvii
  under open government, 58–60, 170–71
  web content, 311–13
Access to Information Act, xxvii, 122
access-to-information requests, xiv
acquisitions
  Alberta selection tools, 162–66
  library procedures, 158, 159–60, 162
  and technology advancements, 174
adjournment tabling, 95
Administrative Law in Canada, 139
agencies, 309–10
  see also tribunals
Alberta
  access to information, 162–66
  government information distribution, 16–18, 157–62
  open government concept and plans, 167–71
  parliamentary system, 153
  printing and publishing, 154–57, 167
  public access, 166–67
  publications guideline (Open Government Program), 172–76
Alberta Deposit Library Program (ADLP), 16–18, 158–62, 172, 174, 175

Alberta Electronic Government Documents Archive, 181
Alberta Energy Regulator, 161
Alberta Government Library (AGL), 17, 161, 174–75, 179
Alberta Government Publications, 165
Alberta Innovation and Advanced Education, 161
Alberta Law Collection, 181
Alberta Legislature Library, 17, 159, 176–79, 181
Alberta Public Affairs Bureau, 155, 159, 160, 164–65, 166–67
Alberta Queen's Printer, 17, 19, 155–57, 159, 160, 161, 165–66, 170–71
Alberta Research Council, 165, 167
Alberta Royal Commissions project, 181
American Library Association, 280, 290–91
AMICUS, 56, 57, 122, 125
APLIC (Association of Parliamentary Libraries in Canada), 259–60, 261–63, 269, 272
  see also GALLOP portal
Archer, John H., 6, 14
Archive-It
  accounts, xxvii, 281, 301, 317
  collections, 125, 298
  operations, 283, 312
archives *see* web archives
Archives of Ontario, 212
assessments and surveys
  on digital preparedness, 22
  digitization projects, 249–50
  fugitive materials, 313–15
  Saskatchewan government information, 199–204
Atlas of Canada, 311
Australian government documents, 262

Bhatia, Mohan, 166
Bibliographic Services Centre (Ontario), 219–20
bibliographies
    Alberta government publications, 163
    commissions of inquiry, 121–22
    MacTaggart bibliographies, 219
Bibliothèque et Archives nationales du Québec (BAnQ), 12, 24, 297
bills
    gun control example, 104–11
    in legislative process, 80, 84, 96–100, 101
    see also Orders-in-Council
Bird, Gwen, 282
Blakeney, Allan, 190
blocked content, 284, 312–13
boards, 139
    see also tribunals
branches of government, 95
British Columbia
    deposit and distribution programs, 18–19
    Government Information Day conference, xxvii
Brodie, Nancy, 22
Brooke, Hilda M., 223
budgets
    documents, 229–30
    federal, 47, 52–53, 118
    Klein government, 178

Cabinet business, 97
Cable Public Affairs Channel (CPAC), 125
Canada.ca, 65
Canada Energy Law Service, 140
Canada Gazette, 54, 100–101, 120
Canada's Action Plan on Open Government, 58–59, 278
Canadiana.org, 80, 103, 230
Canadian Association of Research Libraries (CARL), 23
Canadian Electronic Library, 180
Canadian Environmental Assessment Agency, 141

Canadian Government Information Digital Preservation Network (CGI DPN)
    access and operations, xxiii, 23–24, 282–85, 286–89
    fugitive government documents, 313, 317–19
    history, 279–82, 290–91
Canadian Government Publications (Higgins), 232
Canadian Government Publications Portal, 244
Canadian Institute for Historical Microreproductions, 230
Canadian Legal Information Institute (CANLII), 118, 119, 140, 141
Canadian Library Association (CLA), 279
Canadian Parliamentary Historical Resources portal, 80
Canadian Provincial Government Publications (Bhatia), 166
Canadian Public Policy (Des Libris), 121
Canadian Research Index, 180
Canadian Research Knowledge Network, 230
Canadian Wheat Board, 139
CANLII see Canadian Legal Information Institute (CANLII)
CARL (Canadian Association of Research Libraries), 23
Carleton University Library, 310
Caron, Daniel, xix
Catalog of Government Publications (US), 304
catalogue record conversions, 265–68
catalogues
    approaches, xvi, xvii, 14, 17–18, 21, 27–28
    and born-digital documents, 176
    linking and sharing, 23, 262–63
    see also checklists; specific catalogues
CD-ROMS, xvii, 126–27
Centre for Newfoundland Studies, 7–8, 24
CGI DPN see Canadian Government Information Digital Preservation Network (CGI DPN)

checklists
  for commissions of inquiry, 121–22
  in Depository Services Program,
    54–55, 56–58
  see also specific provinces and
    legislative libraries
City of Toronto Archives, 299–302
Civil Resolution Tribunal (British
  Columbia), 139
CLA (Canadian Library Association),
  279
Clemons, Angel, 304
CODOC, xvi
COIS *see* commissions of inquiry (COIS)
collaborations
  APLIC and GALLOP portal, 259–60,
    261–63, 269, 272
  Depository Services Program, 23–24
  fugitive documents discovery,
    318–19
  interests in, xxvii, 223
  Ontario digitization, 235–39, 247–48,
    249–50, 251–52
  web harvesting, 299–302
collections
  brief history, xvi–xix, 48–50
  Canadian Government Publications
    Portal (Internet Archive), 244
  commercial, xxvi, 140, 179–80
  commissions of inquiry, 119–22,
    124–25, 127–29
  and fugitive documents, 313–15,
    316–19
  LAC vs. DSP methodologies, 55–56
  tribunals, 140, 142
  see also Archive-It; CGI DPN; DSP
    e-collection; GALLOP portal;
    specific libraries and provinces
commercial printers, 20, 156–57
commercial publishers, 128, 140,
  179–80
Commission of Inquiry into the Decline
  of Sockeye Salmon in the Fraser
  River, 137–38
Commission of Inquiry into the
  Wrongful Conviction of David
  Milgaard, 126

Commission of Inquiry on the Blood
  System in Canada, 129, 135
Commission on the Future of Health
  Care in Canada (Romanow), 136,
  277
*Commissions of Inquiry and Policy
  Change*, 123
commissions of inquiry (COIS)
  access, 61, 124–29, 142
  creation and information, 118–20
  digitized materials, 181, 239–40
  outputs and checklists, xx, 50, 120–22
  overview, 60, 117
  stewardship and dissemination,
    123–24, 130–38
committees (parliamentary), xiv, 80,
  90–93, 98
Common Look and Feel protocol, xviii,
  278, 291
Communications Policy (Alberta),
  168–70, 174
*Companion to the Rules of the Senate of
  Canada*, 82
*Compendium of House of Commons
  Procedure*, 83
compliance challenges and assessments,
  xxi–xxii, 200–202, 221, 305, 308–10
*The Conduct of Public Inquiries: Law,
  Policy, and Practice*, 119
Constitution Act (1982), 79
COPPUL *see* Council of Prairie and
  Pacific University Libraries
  (COPPUL)
copyright, Crown
  challenges, xxv, 179, 181
  clearance, 173, 235, 236, 237, 239, 240
  policies and practices, 244–45, 276,
    284, 309–10
  see also permissions
Council of Prairie and Pacific University
  Libraries (COPPUL), 279, 282, 285
CPAC (Cable Public Affairs Channel),
  125
crowdsourcing, 302
Crown copyright *see* copyright, Crown
CyberCemetery project, 306

data
  definitions, 222
  standards, 104
databases, 140, 310–11
Debates (Hansard) (federal parliament)
  content, 80, 84, 86, 88, 93–94, 99,
    120
  portal, 95
  searches, 87, 107, 109
Debates (Hansard) (Ontario), 234
decentralization
  in Alberta model, 154, 158–61, 167,
    174, 182
  problems of, xxi, 4
Delayed answers, 86–87
democracy and access, xiii, xv, 191
deposit and distribution programs
  federal, 5–6
  overview, 3–5, 25–26
  provincial and territorial overview,
    6–7
  see also specific provinces and
    territories
Depository Services Program (DSP)
  and CGI DPN, 283
  electronic publications, 23–24
  and GALLOP portal, 269–70
  history, 5, 27–34, 51–53, 56–58
  operations, 277–78, 306–08
  overview, xix
  roles and responsibilities, 53–56, 309
  see also DSP e-collection
Dickison, Meredith, 22
digital content
  losses, xvii–xviii, 278, 280, 281, 284,
    303
  PDFS VS. HTML, 214–15, 216, 220–21
  preservation challenges, 275–77,
    310–13
  scope, 50, 203
Digital Federal Depository Library
  Program (USDOCS), 305–06
digital publications
  and accessibility standards, 220–21
  commissions of inquiry material, 118
  definition, xv
  DSP e-collection, 307–08, 309–10, 318

as fugitive materials, 304–05
digital publishing
  by default (federal government), 52–53
  early experiences with, xvii–xviii, 161
  and fugitive materials, 304–05
  transition from print, 21, 22–26, 47
digitization
  definition and scope, 228
  foldouts and maps, 230–31, 232
  loan agreements, 239
  metadata, 245–47
  procedures documentation, 240, 243
  scanning operations, 233–34
*Digitization of Publications Relating to the
  Parliament of Canada*, 250
digitization projects
  initiatives and experiences, xxv,
    103–04, 122, 222, 228–34, 251–53,
    276
  library surveys, 249–50
  tracking of, 250–51
  see also Ontario Digitization Initiative
    (ODI)
Directive on Open Government, 58–59
*Directive on the Management of
  Communication*, 61, 62
directories, 159, 166–67, 310–11
discoverability, 56, 312
discovery tools, 166–67, 176, 177,
  179–80, 182
dissemination
  of commissions of inquiry outputs,
    118, 123–24, 128, 130–38
  historical overviews, xix, 157–62
  transition to digital, 22–26, 52–53,
    276
  see also deposit and distribution
    programs; Depository Services
    Program (DSP)
dissolution of parliament, 85
documents, defined, xiv
Dolan, Elizabeth, 4, 5, 22
Drake, Judith Anne, 10
DSpace, 215, 261
DSP e-collection, 307–08, 309–10, 318
Dublin Core conversion, 265–68
dynamic content, 311

Early Canadiana Online (ECO), 229, 238
Early Official Publications collection, 229
e-Bookmark (Alberta), 166
ECO (Early Canadiana Online), 229, 238
Economic Action Plan 2013, 47, 52–53
Edmonton Public Library, 163
electronic publications *see* digital publications
electronic publishing *see* digital publishing
Eschenfelder, Kristin R., 298

Federal Depository Library Program (US), 250, 296, 303, 304–05
federal government
    department compliance, 310
    deposit and distribution programs, 5–6
Federal Royal Commissions in Canada (1867–1968) (Henderson), 121
fifteen-day rule, 87
Financial Administration Act, 62, 309, 317
Fitzpatrick, Kathleen, 275
Footz, Val, 177
For Seven Generations CD-ROM, xvii, 126–27
Forsythe, John, 163
Fugitive Documents Working Group, 313–17
fugitive government materials
    action plan and pilot, 316–19
    definition, 302–03
    experiences, 303–10
    library collections, 313–15

GALLOP portal *see* Government and Legislative Libraries Online Publications (GALLOP) portal
Gibson Library Connections, 180
Gnassi, Bruno, 22
Google searches, 303
Gosling Memorial Library, 7–8
Gov. Docs portal, 215, 249
Government and Legislative Libraries Online Publications (GALLOP) portal

content, 125, 141, 215–16, 269–70
features and challenges, xxiii, 263, 270–72
participants, 24, 177, 202, 206
processing work flow, 264–68
Government Documents Round Table, 280, 285, 290–91
government information
    characteristics, xiv, xv–xvi, xxvi
    and decentralization, 154
    as junk mail, 157–58
    librarians of, xvi, 285, 315
    transition to digital, 296
Government Information Day conferences, xxvii, 250
Government of Alberta Publication (GAP) Search, 175–76
Government of Alberta Publications (GAP) Catalogue, 159, 160, 165
Government of Canada *see* federal government
Government of Canada Publications, 125, 141, 282, 283, 305
Government of Canada web archives, 65–66, 80, 122, 125, 127–28, 282, 283
Government orders, 88
government publications
    ambiguities, 202–03, 204
    definitions and scope, xiv, xv, 4, 154, 172–73, 194, 217–18
    re-hosting, 23, 24
Government Publications Relating to Alberta (Forsyth), 163
government publishing, brief history, xvi–xix, xxi, xxii–xxiii
Governor General, 84, 85, 99
GPO (United States Government Printing Office), 296, 303, 306
grey literature, 218
Guidelines for Legal Deposit Legislation (UNESCO), 48–49
A Guide to the Identification and Acquisition of Canadian Provincial Government Publications (Pross), 166
gun control case study, 104–11

Hansard see Debates (Hansard)
Harper government, xix, 303
Health Council, 309–10
Henderson checklist, 121
Heretrix, 298
historical document collections, 229–30
House of Commons
 business, 82–83, 86, 88–89, 96–100
 committees, 92
 records and search tools, 90, 102–03
 search examples, 93–94
 sessional papers, 95
House of Commons Debates, xiv
*House of Commons Procedure and
 Practice*, 82–83
Hubbertz, Andrew, 23
Human Rights Tribunal (Ontario) cases,
 241

Immigration and Refugee Board, 140
indexing solutions, 263–64, 268–69
Index to Federal Royal Commissions, 61,
 121–22, 125
*Indian Residential Schools Settlement
 Agreement*, 128
InfoDep, 33, 278, 307
*InfoSource: Directory of Federal
 Government Databases*, 139
Inquiries Act, 118, 119
interactive content, 311
International Documents Task Force,
 279, 285
International Internet Preservation
 Consortium (IIPC), 63
International Standard Book Numbers
 (ISBNS), 21, 54–55, 173, 219, 220,
 306–07
International Standard Serial Numbers
 (ISSNS), 54, 55, 173, 219, 220
Internet access, 22
Internet Archive, xviii, 232, 239, 246–47,
 250, 281, 297
Internet Archive Canada
 operations, 231, 242, 244
 projects, 230, 232, 233–34, 237, 238,
 240
Internet content sampling, 48

Inwood, Gregory J., 123
Island Information Service (Prince
 Edward Island), 10, 24

Jacobs, James, 280, 304, 305
Jarvi, Edith T., 6, 7, 20
Johns, Carolyn, 123
joint parliamentary committees, 92
Journal of Upper Canada, 233
Journals
 content, 87–88, 90, 94, 95, 99, 120
 searches, 102, 107, 109
Journals of the Legislative Assembly
 (Ontario), 233–34

Kahle, Brewster, 242
King's Printer, 51–52
 see also Queen's Printer offices
Klein government, 179

LAC Act see Library and Archives Canada
 Act (LAC Act)
LAC Electronic Collection, 57, 59
Law Foundation of Ontario, 239–40
Law Library Microform Consortium
 (LLMC), 238
legal deposit
 legislation, 5–6, 20, 48–50
 outreach, 199–203, 204
Legal Deposit (LAC), 53, 309
*Legal Deposit of Publications Regulations
 (LD Regulations)*, 5, 48, 49–50
LEGISinfo, 101, 109
Legislative Assembly (Alberta), 157,
 167–68
legislative committees, xiv, 91, 92
legislative process, 95–101
Lepkey, Gay, 280
LexisNexis Quicklaw, 140
librarians
 government information, xvi, 285, 315
 job postings, 295
 and mailing lists, 158
 roles of, xvi, xvii, xviii, xxv–xxvi,
 276–77, 319
libraries
 and CGI DPN, 285

challenges, xvii, xxiv–xxvii, 295–97

as depositories, xix, 6, 23, 24, 51–52, 158–62, 175, 192–93, 212

exchange agreements, 191

fugitive materials capture, 313–15

outreach, 199–202

practices, 176

surveys of, 22, 249–50

see also specific provincial and university libraries

Library and Archives Canada Act (LAC Act), 48, 49–50, 62, 64

Library Archives Canada (LAC)

collaborations and partnerships, xxvii, 63, 65–66, 284

collection gap, xxvi, 297, 312

collections, 57–58, 60–63, 122, 125, 127, 229

compliance monitoring, 308, 309

mandate, xviii–xix, xx, xxv, 5–6, 53–56, 58–59, 278, 296

Web Archiving Program, 64–65, 80

Library Association of Alberta, 159

Library of Parliament

collaborations and partnerships, 80, 103, 267

as depository, 51

operations, 93, 98, 101

Library Transformation Project (Alberta), 161

Li, Sam-chin, 297, 299, 318

LOCKSS Program

with CGI DPN, 282–83, 286–89

liaison, 280–81, 285

overview, 277, 279

Lost Docs Blog, 306

MacDonald, Christine, 190–91

Mackenzie Valley Pipeline Inquiry, 119, 127, 131

Mack, Thura, 295

MacTaggart Publications of the Government of Ontario, 219, 223

mailing lists, 157–58

Manager's Manual 300, 9

Manitoba deposit and distribution programs, 14–15

maps, 230–31, 232, 311

MARC to Dublin Core conversion, 265–68

Members of Parliament biographical information, 102

Memorial University of Newfoundland, 7

metadata standards, 104, 241, 245–47, 250

microfiche/microfilm, 16, 140, 164, 177, 196, 230

see also Micromedia Limited

MicroLog service, 121, 140, 180

Micromedia Limited, 16, 121, 127, 164, 179–80, 193

Microsoft, 242

Monthly Catalog of U.S. Government Publications, 305

Monty, Vivienne, 310

Moon, Jeff, 22

Moore, Carol, 242

motions in parliament, 87, 93–94, 97

multimedia content, 311

National Centre for Truth and Reconciliation (NCTR), 128–29

National Council of Welfare, 65

National Digital Stewardship Alliance report, 301

National Energy Board, 139, 140, 141

National Inquiry into Missing and Murdered Indigenous Women and Girls, 129

National Library of Canada, 49

National Round Table on the Environment and the Economy, 65

NEOS consortium, 179

New Brunswick deposit and distribution programs, 10–11

Newfoundland and Labrador deposit and distribution programs, 7–8, 24

Nilsen, Kirsti, 22

Northwest Territories deposit and distribution programs, 20–21

Notice Papers, 85, 86, 87, 97, 98

Notices of Motions for the Production of Papers, 88

Nova Scotia deposit and distribution
programs, 8–9
Nunavut deposit and distribution
programs, 21, 25

O'Brien and Bosc (*House of Commons
Procedure and Practice*), 82–83
OCLC Worldcat, 121, 122, 125, 141
OCUL *see* Ontario Council of University
Libraries (OCUL)
OCUL Government Information
Community (OCUL GIC), 241, 242
ODI *see* Ontario Digitization Initiative
(ODI)
*Official Report of Debates (Hansard) of
the Legislative Assembly of Ontario*,
234
OGLC (Ontario Government Libraries
Council), 216–18
OICS *see* Orders-in-Council (OICS)
O'Mahony, Daniel P., 304
Ontario
*Accessibility for Ontarians with
Disabilities Act (AOD Act)*, 215, 216
copyright terms, 245
depository library systems, 13–14,
218–21
Government Information Day
conference, xxvii, 250
Queen's Printer, 245
status of government publications,
211–13, 216, 220–22
Ontario Agricultural College bulletins,
240
Ontario Bills digitization project, 237
Ontario.ca, 215, 216, 220–21
Ontario Council of University Libraries
(OCUL)
digitization projects, 235–36, 238,
239–42
partnerships, 215, 261
round tables, 247–48
see also Scholars Portal
Ontario Department of Agriculture,
240
Ontario Digitization Initiative (ODI),
xxii, 234–40, 241, 253

Ontario Government Libraries Council
(OGLC), 216–18
Ontario Government Publications
round table, 247–48, 249
Ontario Legislative Library
as depository, 13
operations, 212, 213–16, 219–20
projects, 232–34, 260–61
Ontario Ministry of Environment
collection, 237
Ontario Ministry of Government
Services, 245
Ontario Sessional Papers project,
238–39
open data, 171, 175, 222–23
open government
concepts, xxv, 103, 167–68
licence, xxiv–xxv, 175
policies and initiatives, xxiv, 58–60,
168–71, 174
Open Government Partnership, 58
Open Government Portals, xxiv, 18, 142,
161, 175–76, 179
Open Information and Open Data Policy
(Alberta), 170, 174
Open Information Portal, 59–60
openparliament.ca, 103
Order Papers, 80, 85, 86, 87, 97, 98
Orders-in-Council (OICS), 100–101, 118,
120, 142
Ordonnance de Montpellier, 49
ourcommons.ca, 94, 102
OurDigitalWorld (ODW), 215, 248–49

parl.ca, 80, 92–93
parliamentary calendar, 84–85
Parliament of Canada
cycle of business, 84–85
daily business, 85–89
digitized content, 229, 250
gun control example, 104–11
information, 79–80, 92–95, 101–04
rules and procedures, 81–84
see also legislation
Parlvu, 93, 102–03
PCO *see* Privy Council Office

PDS *see* Publishing and Depository Services Directorate (PDS)

Periodical Publishing Record (PPR) (Alberta), 164–65

permissions
to blocked content, 312
open government licence, xxiv–xxv
see also copyright, Crown

PLNS (private LOCKSS networks), 279

political environment
information policies, xiv, xviii–xix
information removal, 303–04

POR *see* Public Opinion Research (POR)

Powers, J.W., 191–92

Prescod, Janette, 295

preservation
digitization as, 180–81, 227–28, 233–34
and print analogs, xxvi, 23
problems with digital, 22, 275–77
responsibility for, xix, 65, 315

Prince Edward Island deposit and distribution programs, 9–10, 24

printing cost management, 51–52, 154–57

printing facilities, 18, 20, 155–56
see also Queen's Printer

print publications
deposit and distribution, 5, 276, 277
retention of, xxvi, 23

private member's business, 85, 88, 93–94

Privy Council database, 120

Privy Council Office (PCO), 61, 122, 125, 128, 303

Procedures for Publishing (TBS), 53, 55, 309

ProFile Index, 179–80

pro forma bills, 84, 97

Projected Order of Business, 86

prorogation of parliament, 85

Pross, A. Paul and Catherine A., 4–5, 6, 9, 16, 18, 154, 194

provinces
commissions of inquiry, 119, 120, 125
deposit programs, 6

and web archiving, 297
see also specific provinces

public
access to government, 166–67, 168–71, 177–78
information interests, xiii–xiv, xv–xvi, 103, 123, 139

publications
definitions, xiv–xv, 48, 55
serial, 215, 261
standardization, 170, 305
see also government publications

Publications Catalogue (Alberta), 164

Publications of the Government of Ontario (MacTaggart), 219, 223

Publications Ontario, 13, 211–12, 216, 218–19, 245

Public Opinion Research Contract Regulations, 62

Public Opinion Research (POR), 50, 61–63

Public Services and Procurement Canada, 308, 309

publishers, definition, 50

Publishing and Depository Services Directorate (PDS), 302, 307, 309, 318

Qasim, Umar, 280

quality assurance
digitization, 234, 237–38
web archiving, 299, 302

Quebec deposit and distribution programs, 11–12, 24

Queen's Printer
Alberta, 17, 155–57, 159, 160, 161, 165–66, 170–71
other provinces, 6, 9, 10, 11–12, 16, 19, 20, 245
websites, 125
see also King's Printer

Question Period, 86, 88

Questions, written, 94

Quicklaw, 140

Records of Federal Royal Commissions (Whalen), 122

Registry of Canadian Government Information Digitization Projects, 251, 252
retention protocols, xiv, 14, 172
RITE Directory, 159, 166–67
robots exclusion protocol, 312
robots.txt file, 284
Routine proceedings, 86
Royal Assent, 99
Royal Commission of Aboriginal Peoples, 126–27, 133–34, 276
Royal Commission on New Reproductive Technologies, 132
Royal Commission on the Status of Women, 130
Royal Commissions, 117, 118–19
    see also commissions of inquiry (COIS)
RSS feeds, 102
Rules of the Senate of Canada, 81–82

sampling from Internet, 48
Saskatchewan
    deposit and distribution programs, 15–16, 24–25
    government publications, 190–91
    legal deposit legislation, 189–90
    Legislative Assembly and Executive Council Act (1982), 195–96
    Legislative Assembly and Executive Council Act (2005), 197–99
Saskatchewan Legislative Assembly, 191–92, 194–95
Saskatchewan Legislative Library
    assessment and outreach, 199–204
    as depository, 15–16
    digital repository system, 204–05
    legislation and operations, 195–99
    mandate and goals, 189–94, 206–07
Saskatchewan Library Association, 193–94
scanning operations, 233–34, 237–38
Scholars Portal, 215, 239, 247, 280
search tools, 270–71, 303
Senate of Canada
    business, 85, 86–88, 96, 97
    committees, 91

rules and procedures documents, 81–82
Twitter account, 103
Senate Procedural Notes, 82
Senate Procedure in Practice, 82
serial publications, 215, 232, 261
Service Alberta, 170, 172
sessional papers, 95, 230–31
    Ontario Sessional Papers project, 238–39
Sessional Papers of Canada by Title, 231–32, 252–53
Shankar, Kalpana, 298
Simon Fraser University, 280
Smugler, Sherry, 295
social media, 103, 203, 214
Solr (software), 263–64, 265, 268–69
Speakers in parliament, 83–84, 99
Speech from the Throne, 84, 229
SPIRES database, 164–65, 167, 177
Sproles, Claudine, 304
staffing for projects, 231, 240, 302, 318
standing committees, 91, 92
Standing Orders of the House of Commons, 82
Stanford University, 164, 279, 285, 288
Statements by members, 88
Statistics Canada Library, 229
Status of House Business, 90, 93–94, 102, 109
stewardship
    in digital era, 47, 118, 139, 296
    principles, xvi
    responsibilities for, xxii–xxiii, 319
surveys *see* assessments and surveys

tagging, 221
TAL (The Alberta Library) service, 177
TBS *see* Treasury Board of Canada Secretariat (TBS)
Toronto city archives project, 299–302
translations, 267, 271–72
Transportation Safety Board (TSB), 141
Treasury Board of Canada Secretariat (TBS)
    directives, 61, 62, 65, 278–79, 281, 284

policies and procedures, xix, 47, 53, 308, 309
tribunals, xx, 117, 139–42
Trudeau government, 303
Truth and Reconciliation Commission (TRC), 119, 128–29
TSpace repository, 261

United States government information, 250, 296, 303, 304–06
United States Government Printing Office (GPO), 296, 303, 306
university libraries, xvii, 22, 295, 297, 301, 304, 313–14
University of Alberta Libraries
  CGI DPN, 280, 286–89
  digitization projects, 230
  preservation projects, 181–82, 314
University of Alberta printing plant, 155
University of British Columbia, 285
University of Calgary, 181
University of Guelph, 238, 240
University of Manitoba, 128
University of North Texas, 299, 306
University of Prince Edward Island Library, 10
University of Saskatchewan, 24–25, 126, 127
University of Toronto, 261
University of Toronto Libraries (UTL)
  in CGI PLN, 285
  projects, 216, 230–31, 232, 238, 241, 298, 299–302, 314, 318
University of Victoria Archives, 127
URLS (uniform resource locators)
  in collections, 173, 283
  stability of, 22, 161, 172
USDOCS, 305–06

van Haaften, Jami, 19
Vaughan, Liwen Qiu, 22
video archives, 125
virtual libraries, 59, 171
votes, 94–95, 98

Wakaruk, Amanda, 139, 279, 280, 307, 309

web archives, bright vs. dark, 281
web archiving
  adoption and support, 301–02
  approaches, 296–99
  harvest of content for, 310–13
  historical overview, 63
  projects, xxiv, xxvii, 58, 65–66, 127–28, 216, 299–302
  proposed resolution on, 290–91
  see also web crawls
Web Archiving Program (LAC), 56, 63, 64–65, 80
webcasting, 102–03
web content
  sampling, 48
  see also digital content
web crawls
  approaches, 298–99
  of Government of Canada information, 281, 283, 284, 311
  limitations, 301, 310, 312–13
  see also web archiving
Weber, Gary, 172
web harvesting, 310–13
Web Renewal Initiative, xviii, 65–66
Websites of Reconciliation project, 128
Website Watcher, 214
Weekly Checklist of Canadian Government Publications, 4, 5, 56–58, 139
Western Canadiana Collection, 163
Whalen, James Murray, 122
Whitmell, Vicki, 212–13, 261
Working Group on Ontario Government Publications, 216
Worldcat see OCLC Worldcat
Written questions (parliamentary), 94
www.parl.gc.ca, 79, 80

York University, 238
Yukon deposit and distribution programs, 19

Zotero Everyday Electronic Materials Group, 306

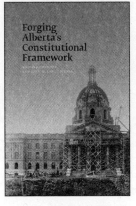